Monty Python's Flying Circus

Just the Words

VOLUME ONE

Other books by Monty Python

A Pocketful of Python, Volume 1
A Pocketful of Python, Volume 2
Monty Python's Big Red Book
The Brand New Monty Python Papperbok
Monty Python and the Holy Grail (Book)
Monty Python's Life of Brian
Monty Python's The Meaning of Life
Monty Python's Flying Circus: Just the Words VOLUME TWO
The Monty Python Songbook

Monty

JUST THE WORDS

Python's

VOLUME ONE

Flying

Written and conceived by
GRAHAM CHAPMAN
JOHN CLEESE
TERRY GILLIAM
ERIC IDLE
TERRY JONES
MICHAEL PALIN

Circus

Methuen

Acknowledgements

Enormous, Mr Equator-like thanks to those who put so much effort into assembling this book: Roger Wilmut, Geoffrey Strachan, Alison Davies, Suzanne Lindop, Roger Saunders.

Published by Methuen 1999

1 3 5 7 9 10 8 6 4 2

First published in Great Britain by Methuen London in 1989
First published in paperback as an omnibus edition (containing *Just the Words: One*
and *Just the Words: Two*) by Mandarin Paperbacks in 1990

This edition published by Methuen Publishing Limited
215 Vauxhall Bridge Road, London SW1V 1EJ

Peribo Pty Ltd, 58 Beaumont Road, Mount Kuring-Gai
NSW 2080, Australia, ACN 002 273 761
(for Australia and New Zealand)

Copyright © Python Productions 1989
Illustrations copyright © Python (Monty) Pictures Ltd 1989

Edited from the original scripts by Roger Wilmut
Editor's introduction copyright © Roger Wilmut 1989

Python Productions has asserted its rights under the Copyright, Designs
and Patents Act, 1988, to be identified as the author of this work

Methuen Publishing Limited Reg. No. 3543167

A CIP catalogue record for this book is available from the British Library

ISBN 0 413 74100 1

Printed and bound in Great Britain by
Cox & Wyman Ltd, Reading, Berkshire

To Ian MacNaughton,
who somehow understood it all,
and everyone else who joined the Circus,
especially Carol Cleveland.

Editor's note

The complete scripts from the four Monty Python series, first shown on BBC television between 1969 and 1974, have been collected in two companion volumes, the first twenty-three episodes in volume one and the second twenty-two in volume two. Transmission details are given in the appendix on p. 320.

Characters' names – often not spoken – are given as in the original camera scripts, with the name of the actual performer added on their first appearance (usually on their first line of dialogue). Small parts taken by walk-ons have not always been identified.

A deliberate decision was made not to include most of the cartoon animations, and in most cases the presence of the cartoon has been simply noted, with occasional reference to the subject matter. The photographs have been taken from videotapes of the series.

Roger Wilmut

Contents

One Whither Canada?

A seashore. Some way out to sea a ragged man is struggling his way to shore. Slowly and with difficulty he makes his way up onto the beach, flops down exhausted and announces:

Man (MICHAEL) It's . . .

Voice Over (JOHN) Monty Python's Flying Circus.

Titles beginning with words 'Monty Python's Flying Circus'. Various bizarre things happen. When the titles end:

Ordinary grey-suited announcer standing by desk. He smiles confidently.

Announcer (GRAHAM) Good evening.

The announcer confidently moves to chair and sits down. There is a squeal as of a pig being sat upon.

Cut to a blackboard with several lines of pigs drawn on it in colour. A man steps into view and with a piece of chalk crosses out one of the pigs.

CAPTION: 'IT'S WOLFGANG AMADEUS MOZART'

Mozart sitting at piano tinkling with the keys. He finishes tinkling.

Mozart (JOHN) Hello again, and welcome to the show. Tonight we continue to look at some famous deaths. Tonight we start with the wonderful death of Genghis Khan, conqueror of India. Take it away Genghis.

Cut to Genghis Khan's tent. Genghis strides about purposefully.

Indian-style background music. Suddenly the music cuts out and Genghis Khan with a squawk throws himself in the air and lands on his back. This happens very suddenly.

Judges hold up cards with points on, in the manner of ice skating judges.

Voice Over (GRAHAM) 9.1, 9.3, 9.7, that's 28.1 for Genghis Khan.

Mozart still at piano.

Mozart Bad luck Genghis. Nice to have you on the show. And now here are the scores.

Scoreboard with Eddie Waring figure standing by it. The scoreboard looks a little like this:

ST STEPHEN	29.9
RICHARD III	29.3
JEAN D'ARC	29.1
MARAT	29.0
A. LINCOLN (U.S of A)	28.2
G. KHAN	28.1
KING EDWARD VII	3.1

Eddie (ERIC) Well there you can see the scores now. St Stephen in the lead there with his stoning, then comes King Richard the Third at

Bosworth Field, a grand death that, then the very lovely Jean d'Arc, then Marat in his bath – best of friends with Charlotte in the showers afterwards – then A. Lincoln of the U.S of A, a grand little chap that, and number six Genghis Khan, and the back marker King Edward the Seventh. Back to you, Wolfgang.

Mozart still at piano.

Mozart   Thank you, Eddie. And now time for this week's request death. *(taking card off piano)* For Mr and Mrs Violet Stebbings of 23 Wolverston Road, Hull, the death of Mr Bruce Foster of Guildford.

Middle-class lounge. Mr Foster sitting in chair.

Foster (GRAHAM)   Strewth! *(he dies)*

Mozart still there. He looks at watch.

Mozart   Oh blimey, how time flies. Sadly we are reaching the end of yet another programme and so it is finale time. We are proud to be bringing to you one of the evergreen bucket kickers. Yes, the wonderful death of the famous English Admiral Nelson.

Cut to a modern office block, as high as possible. After a pause a body flies out of the top window looking as much like Nelson as possible. As it plummets there is a strangled scream.

Nelson   Kiss me Hardy!

The body hits the ground. There is the loud noise of a pig squealing. Cut to polytechnic night school. Teacher looking down out of classroom window. He crosses to a long wall blackboard with line of pigs drawn on near end. He crosses one off, walks along blackboard to other end which has written on it 'evening classes 7–8 p.m.'. He writes 'Italian' below this and turns to camera.

Teacher (TERRY J)   Ah – good evening everyone, and welcome to the second of our Italian language classes, in which we'll be helping you brush up your Italian. Last week we started at the beginning, and we learnt the Italian for a 'spoon'. Now, I wonder how many of you can remember what it was?

Shout of 'Si! Si! Si!' from the class whom we see for the first time to be swarthy Italians.

Teacher   Not all at once . . . sit down Mario. Giuseppe!

Giuseppe (MICHAEL)   Il cucchiaio.

Teacher   Well done Giuseppe, or, as the Italians would say: 'Molto bene, Giuseppe'.

Giuseppe   Grazie signor . . . grazie di tutta la sua gentilezza.

Teacher   Well, now, this week we're going to learn some useful phrases to help us open a conversation with an Italian. Now first of all try telling him where you come from. For example, I would say: 'Sono

Inglese di Gerrard's Cross', I am an Englishman from Gerrard's Cross. Shall we all try that together?

All Sono Inglese di Gerrard's Cross.

Teacher Not too bad, now let's try it with somebody else. Er . . . Mr . . . ?

Mariolini (JOHN) Mariolini.

Teacher Ah, Mr Mariolini, and where are you from?

Mariolini Napoli, signor.

Teacher Ah . . . you're an Italian.

Mariolini Si, si signor!

Teacher Well in that case you would say: 'Sono Italiano di Napoli'.

Mariolini Ah, capisco, mille grazie signor . . .

Francesco (ERIC) Per favore, signor!

Teacher Yes?

Francesco Non conosgeve parliamente, signor devo me parlo sono Italiano di Napoli quando il habitare de Milano.

Teacher I'm sorry . . . I don't understand!

Giuseppe *(pointing to Francesco)* My friend say 'Why must he say . . .'

Hand goes up at back of room and a Lederhosen Teutonic figure stands up.

German (GRAHAM) Bitte mein Herr. Was ist das Wort für Mittelschmerz?

Teacher Ah! Helmut – you want the German classes.

German Oh ja! Danke schön. *(he starts to leave)* Ah das deutsche Klassenzimmer . . . Ach! *(he leaves)*

Giuseppe My friend he say, 'Why must I say I am Italian from Napoli when he lives in Milan?'

Teacher Ah, I . . . well, tell your friend . . . if he lives in Milan he must say 'Sono Italiano di Milano . . .'

Francesco *(agitatedly, leaping to his feet)* Eeeeeee! Milano è tanto meglio di Napoli. Milano è la citta la più bella di tutti . . . nel mondo . . .

Giuseppe He say 'Milan is better than Napoli'.

Teacher Oh, he shouldn't be saying that, we haven't done comparatives yet.

In the background everyone has started talking in agitated Italian. At this point a genuine mandoline-playing Italian secreted amongst the cast strikes up: 'Quando Caliente Del Sol . . .' or similar. The class is out of control by this time. The teacher helplessly tries to control them but eventually gives up and retreats to his desk and sits down. There is a loud pig squeal and he leaps up.

ANIMATION: *The blackboard with the coloured pigs drawn on it, is reproduced on the first few frames of the animation film. A real hand comes into picture and crosses off a third pig. Thereafter action follows the dictates of Señor Gilliam's wonderfully visual mind.*

At the end of this animation we have an advertisement for Whizzo butter.

Voice Over (TERRY G.) *(on animation)* Yes, mothers, new improved Whizzo butter containing 10% more or less is absolutely indistinguishable from a dead crab. Remember, buy Whizzo butter and go to HEAVEN!

Cut to four middle-aged lower-middle-class women (hereinafter referred to as 'Pepperpots') being interviewed.

First Pepperpot (GRAHAM) I can't tell the difference between Whizzo butter and this dead crab.

Interviewer (MICHAEL) Yes, you know, we find that nine out of ten British housewives can't tell the difference between Whizzo butter and a dead crab.

Pepperpots It's true, we can't. No.

Second Pepperpot (JOHN) Here. Here! You're on television, aren't you?

Interviewer *(modestly)* Yes, yes.

Second Pepperpot He does the thing with one of those silly women who can't tell Whizzo butter from a dead crab.

Third Pepperpot (TERRY J) You try that around here, young man, and we'll slit your face.

CAPTION: 'IT'S THE ARTS'

Linkman sitting at desk.

Linkman (MICHAEL) Hello, good evening and welcome to another edition of 'It's the Arts'. We kick off tonight with the cinema.

Cut to second interviewer and Ross.

Second Interviewer (JOHN) Good evening. One of the most prolific of film producers, of this age, or indeed any age, is Sir Edward Ross, back in this country for the first time for five years to open a season of his works at the National Film Theatre, and we are very fortunate to have him with us here in the studio this evening.

Ross (GRAHAM) Good evening.

Second Interviewer Edward . . . you don't mind if I call you Edward?

Ross No, not at all.

Second Interviewer Only it does worry some people . . . I don't know why . . . but they are a little sensitive, so I do take the precaution of asking on these occasions.

Ross No, no, no that's fine.

Second Interviewer So Edward's all right. Splendid. Splendid. Sorry to have brought it up, only eh . . .

Ross No, no, Edward it is.

Second Interviewer Well, thank you very much indeed for being so helpful . . . only it's more than my job's worth to . . . er . . .

Ross Quite, yes.

Second Interviewer Makes it rather difficult to establish a rapport . . . to put the other person at their ease.

Ross Quite.

Second Interviewer Yes, silly little point, but it does seem to matter. Still – less said the better. Um . . . Ted . . . when you first started in . . . you don't mind if I call you Ted?

Ross No, no, no, everyone calls me Ted.

Second Interviewer Well it's shorter, isn't it.

Ross Yes it is.

Second Interviewer Yes, and much less formal.

Ross Yes, Ted, Edward, anything.

Second Interviewer Splendid, splendid. Incidentally, do call me Tom, I don't want you playing around with any of this Thomas nonsense ha ha ha. Now where were we? Oh yes, Eddie-baby, when you first started in the . . .

Ross I'm sorry, but I don't like being called Eddie-baby.

Second Interviewer I'm sorry?

Ross I don't like being called Eddie-baby.

Second Interviewer Did I call you Eddie-baby?

Ross Yes you did. Now get on with it.

Second Interviewer I don't think I did call you Eddie-baby?

Ross You did call me Eddie-baby.

Second Interviewer *(looking off-screen)* Did I call him Eddie-baby?

Voices Yes. No. Yes.

Second Interviewer I didn't *really* call you Eddie-baby did I, sweetie?

Ross Don't call me sweetie!!

Second Interviewer Can I call you sugar plum?

Ross No!

Second Interviewer Pussy cat?

Ross No.

Second Interviewer Angel-drawers?

Ross No you may not!! Now get on with it!

Second Interviewer Frank.

Ross What?

Second Interviewer Can I call you Frank?

Ross Why Frank?

Second Interviewer It's a nice name. Robin Day's got a hedgehog called Frank.

Ross What is going on?

Second Interviewer Frannie, little Frannie, Frannie Knickers . . .

Ross *(getting up)* No, I'm leaving. I'm leaving, I'm off . . .

Second Interviewer Tell us about your latest film, Sir Edward.

Ross *(off-screen)* What?

Second Interviewer Tell us about your latest film, if you'd be so kind, Sir Edward.

Ross *(returning)* None of this 'pussy cat' nonsense?

Second Interviewer Promise. *(pats seat)* Please, Sir Edward.

Ross *(sitting down)* My latest film?

Second Interviewer Yes, Sir Edward.

Ross Well the idea, funnily enough, came from an idea I had when I first joined the industry in 1919. Of course in those days I was only a tea boy.

Second Interviewer Oh, *shut* up.

Cut to linkman, as before.

Linkman Sir Edward . . . Ross. Now, later in the programme we will be bringing you a unique event in the world of modern art. Pablo Picasso will be doing a special painting for us, on this programme, live, on a bicycle. This is the first time that Picasso has painted whilst cycling. But right now it's time to look at a man whose meteoric rise to fame . . .

A pig squeals. Interviewer leaps up, grabs a revolver from his desk drawer and fires off-screen.

CAPTION: 'PIGS 3, NELSON 1'

Third Interviewer and Arthur 'Two Sheds' Jackson. Musical score blow-up behind.

Third Interviewer (ERIC) Last week The Royal Festival Hall saw the first performance of a new symphony by one of the world's leading modern composers, Arthur 'Two Sheds' Jackson. Mr Jackson.

Jackson (TERRY J) Good evening.

Third Interviewer May I just sidetrack you for one moment. Mr Jackson, this, what should I call it, nickname of yours.

Jackson Oh yes.

Third Interviewer 'Two Sheds'. How did you come by it?

Jackson Well I don't use it myself, it's just a few of my friends call me 'Two Sheds'.

Third Interviewer I see, and do you in fact have two sheds?

Jackson No. No, I've only one shed. I've had one for some time, but a few years ago I said I was thinking of getting another one and since then some people have called me 'Two Sheds'.

Third Interviewer In spite of the fact that you have only one.

Jackson Yes.

Third Interviewer I see, and are you thinking of purchasing a second shed?

Jackson No.

Third Interviewer To bring you in line with your epithet.

Jackson No.

Third Interviewer I see, I see. Well let's return to your symphony. Ah, now then, did you write this symphony . . . *in* the shed?

Jackson . . . No.

Third Interviewer Have you written any of your recent works in this shed of yours?

Jackson No it's just a perfectly ordinary garden shed.

A picture of a shed appears on the screen behind them.

Third Interviewer I see. And you're thinking of buying this second shed to write in.

Jackson No, no. Look this shed business, it doesn't really matter at all, the sheds aren't important. It's just a few friends call me 'Two Sheds', and that's all there is to it. I wish you'd ask me about my music. I'm a composer. People always ask me about the sheds, they've got it out of proportion, I'm fed up with the shed, I wish I'd never got it in the first place.

Third Interviewer I expect you're probably thinking of selling one.

Jackson I will sell one.

Third Interviewer Then you'd be Arthur 'No Sheds' Jackson.

Jackson Look forget about the sheds. They don't matter.

Third Interviewer Mr Jackson I think with respect, we ought to talk about your symphony.

Jackson What?

Third Interviewer Apparently your symphony was written for organ and tympani.

Jackson *(catches sight of the picture of the shed behind him)* What's that?

Third Interviewer What's what?

Jackson It's a shed. Get it off.

He points to BP screen shed. The picture of the shed disappears and is replaced by a picture of Jackson. Jackson looks at it carefully.

Jackson Right.

Third Interviewer Now then Mr Jackson . . . your symphony.

CAPTION: 'ARTHUR "TWO SHEDS" JACKSON'

Cut back to studio: the picture of him is replaced by a picture of two sheds, one with a question mark over it.

Third Interviewer I understand that you used to be interested in train spotting.

Jackson What?

Third Interviewer I understand that about thirty years ago you were extremely interested in train spotting.

Jackson What's that got to do with my bloody music?

Enter Second Interviewer from Edward Ross sketch (John).

Second Interviewer Are you having any trouble from him?

Third Interviewer Yes, a little.

Second Interviewer Well we interviewers are more than a match for the likes of you, 'Two Sheds'.

Third Interviewer Yes make yourself scarce 'Two Sheds'. This studio isn't big enough for the three of us.

They push him away and propel him out.

Jackson What are you doing? *(he is pushed out of vision with a crash)*

Second Interviewer Get your own Arts programme you fairy!

Third Interviewer *(to camera)* Arthur 'Two Sheds' Jackson.

Cut to linkman. He is about to speak when:

Third Interviewer *(off-screen)* Never mind, Timmy.

Second Interviewer *(off-screen)* Oh Michael you're such a comfort.

Linkman Arthur 'Two Sheds' . . .

Cut to man in Viking helmet at desk.

Viking (JOHN) . . . Jackson.

Cut back to linkman.

Linkman And now for more news of the momentous artistic event in which Pablo Picasso is doing a specially commissioned painting for us whilst riding a bicycle. Pablo Picasso – the founder of modern art – without doubt the greatest abstract painter ever . . . for the first time painting in motion. But first of all let's have a look at the route he'll be taking.

Cut to Raymond Baxter type standing in front of map. A small cardboard cut-out of Picasso's face is on map and is moved around to illustrate route.

Baxter (MICHAEL) Well Picasso will be starting, David, at Chichester here, he'll then cycle on the A29 to Fontwell, he'll then take the A272 which will bring him on to the A3 just north of Hindhead here. From then on Pablo has a straight run on the A3 until he meets the South Circular at Battersea here. Well, this is a truly remarkable occasion as it is the first time that a modern artist of such stature has taken the A272, and it'll be very interesting to see how he copes with the heavy traffic round Wisborough Green. Vicky.

Cut to Vicky, holding a bicycle.

Vicky (ERIC) Well Picasso will be riding his Viking Super Roadster with the drop handlebars and the dual-thread wheel-rims and with his Wiley-Prat 20-1 synchro-mesh he should experience difficulties on the sort of road surfaces they just don't get abroad. Mitzie.

Cut to linkman at desk with Viking on one side and a knight in armour on the other.

Linkman And now for the latest report on Picasso's progress over to Reg Moss on the Guildford by-pass.

Reg Moss standing with hand mike by fairly busy road.

Reg Moss (ERIC) Well there's no sign of Picasso at the moment, David. But he should be through here at any moment. However I do have

with me Mr Ron Geppo, British Cycling Sprint Champion and this
year's winner of the Derby–Doncaster rally.

Geppo is in full cyclist's kit.

Geppo (GRAHAM)   Well Reg, I think Pablo should be all right provided he
doesn't attempt anything on the monumental scale of some of his
earlier paintings, like Guernica or Mademoiselles d'Avignon or
even his later War and Peace murals for the Temple of Peace
chapel at Vallauris, because with this strong head wind I don't
think even Doug Timpson of Manchester Harriers could paint
anything on that kind of scale.

Reg Moss   Well, thank you Ron. Well, there still seems to be no sign of
Picasso, so I'll hand you back to the studio.

Linkman   Well, we've just heard that Picasso is approaching the Tolworth
roundabout on the A3 so come in Sam Trench at Tolworth.

Cut to Sam Trench at roadside.

Trench (JOHN)   Well something certainly is happening here at Tolworth
roundabout, David. I can now see Picasso, he's cycling down very
hard towards the roundabout, he's about 75–50 yards away and I
can now see his painting . . . it's an abstract . . . I can see some
blue some purple and some little black oval shapes . . . I think I
can see . . .

A Pepperpot comes up and nudges him.

Pepperpot (MICHAEL)   That's not Picasso – that's Kandinsky.

Trench *(excited)*   Good lord, you're right. It's Kandinsky. Wassily
Kandinsky, and who's this here with him? It's Braque. Georges
Braque, the Cubist, painting a bird in flight over a cornfield and
going very fast down the hill towards Kingston and . . . *(cyclists pass
in front of him)* Piet Mondrian – just behind, Piet Mondrian the
Neo-Plasticist, and then a gap, then the main bunch, here they
come, Chagall, Max Ernst, Miro, Dufy, Ben Nicholson, Jackson
Pollock and Bernard Buffet making a break on the outside here,
Brancusi's going with him, so is Géricault, Fernand Léger,
Delaunay, De Kooning, Kokoschka's dropping back here by the
look of it, and so's Paul Klee dropping back a bit and, right at the
back of this group, our very own Kurt Schwitters.

Pepperpot   He's German!

Trench   But as yet absolutely no sign of Pablo Picasso, and so from
Tolworth roundabout back to the studio.

Toulouse-Lautrec pedals past on a child's tricycle.
Cut back to studio.

Linkman   Well I think I can help you there Sam, we're getting reports in
from the AA that Picasso, Picasso has fallen off . . . he's fallen off
his bicycle on the B2127 just outside Ewhurst, trying to get a short

cut through to Dorking via Peaslake and Gomshall. Well, Picasso is reported to be unhurt, but the pig has a slight headache. And on that note we must say goodnight to you. Picasso has failed in his first bid for international cycling fame. So from all of us here at the 'It's the Arts' studio, it's goodnight. *(pig's head appears over edge of desk; linkman gently pushes it back)* Goodnight.

ANIMATION: *Cartoon sequence of animated Victorian photos, at the end of which a large pig descends, fatally, on a portrait of a man.*
Cut to wartime planning room. Two officers are pushing model pigs across the map. A private enters and salutes.

Private Dobson's bought it, sir.

Officer Porker, eh? Swine.

Cut to a suburban house in a rather drab street. Zoom into upstairs window. Serious documentary music. Interior of small room. A bent figure (Michael) huddles over a table, writing. He is surrounded by bits of paper. The camera is situated facing the man as he writes with immense concentration lining his unshaven face.

Voice Over (ERIC) This man is Ernest Scribbler ... writer of jokes. In a few moments, he will have written the funniest joke in the world ... and, as a consequence, he will die ... laughing.

The writer stops writing, pauses to look at what he has written ... a smile slowly spreads across his face, turning very, very slowly to uncontrolled hysterical laughter ... he staggers to his feet and reels across room helpless with mounting mirth and eventually collapses and dies on the floor.

Voice Over It was obvious that this joke was lethal ... no one could read it and live ...

The scribbler's mother (Eric) enters. She sees him dead, she gives a little cry of horror and bends over his body, weeping. Brokenly she notices the piece of paper in his hand and (thinking it is a suicide note – for he has not been doing very well for the last thirteen years) picks it up and reads it between her sobs. Immediately she breaks out into hysterical laughter, leaps three feet into the air, and falls down dead without more ado.
Cut to news type shot of commentator standing in front of the house.

Commentator (TERRY J) *(reverentially)* This morning, shortly after eleven o'clock, comedy struck this little house in Dibley Road. Sudden ... violent ... comedy. Police have sealed off the area, and Scotland Yard's crack inspector is with me now.

Inspector (GRAHAM) I shall enter the house and attempt to remove the joke.

At this point an upstairs window in the house is flung open and a doctor, with stethoscope, rears his head out, hysterical with laughter, and dies hanging over the window sill. The commentator and the inspector look up briefly and sadly, and then continue as if they are used to such sights this morning.

Inspector   I shall be aided by the sound of sombre music, played on gramophone records, and also by the chanting of laments by the men of Q Division . . . *(he indicates a little knot of dour-looking policemen standing nearby)* The atmosphere thus created should protect me in the eventuality of me reading the joke.

He gives a signal. The group of policemen start groaning and chanting biblical laments. The Dead March is heard. The inspector squares his shoulders and bravely starts walking into the house.

Commentator   There goes a brave man. Whether he comes out alive or not, this will surely be remembered as one of the most courageous and gallant acts in police history.

The inspector suddenly appears at the door, helpless with laughter, holding the joke aloft. He collapses and dies.
Cut to stock film of army vans driving along dark roads.

Voice Over   It was not long before the Army became interested in the military potential of the Killer Joke. Under top security, the joke was hurried to a meeting of Allied Commanders at the Ministry of War.

Cut to door at Ham House: Soldier on guard comes to attention as dispatch rider hurries in carrying armoured box. (Notice on door: 'Conference. No Admittance'.) Dispatch rider rushes in. A door opens for him and closes behind him. We hear a mighty roar of laughter . . . series of doomphs as the commanders hit the floor or table. Soldier outside does not move a muscle.
Cut to a pillbox on the Salisbury Plain. Track in to slit to see moustachioed top brass peering anxiously out.

Voice Over   Top brass were impressed. Tests on Salisbury Plain confirmed the joke's devastating effectiveness at a range of up to fifty yards.

Cut to shot looking out of slit in pillbox. Zoom through slit to distance where a solitary figure is standing on the windswept plain. He is a bespectacled, weedy lance-corporal (Terry J) looking cold and miserable. Pan across to fifty yards away where two helmeted soldiers are at their positions beside a blackboard on an easel covered with a cloth.
Cut in to corporal's face – registering complete lack of comprehension as well as stupidity. Man on top of pillbox waves flag. The soldiers reveal the joke to the corporal. He peers at it, thinks about its meaning, sniggers, and dies. Two watching generals are very impressed.

Generals   Fantastic.

Cut to colonel talking to camera.

Colonel (GRAHAM) All through the winter of '43 we had translators working, in joke-proof conditions, to try and produce a German version of the joke. They worked on one word each for greater safety. One of them saw two words of the joke and spent several weeks in hospital. But apart from that things went pretty quickly, and we soon had the joke by January, in a form which our troops couldn't understand but which the Germans could.

Cut to a trench in the Ardennes. Members of the joke brigade are crouched holding pieces of paper with the joke on them.

Voice Over So, on July 8th, 1944, the joke was first told to the enemy in the Ardennes . . .

Commanding NCO. Tell the . . . joke.

Joke Brigade *(together)* Wenn ist das Nunstück git und Slotermeyer? Ja! . . . Beiherhund das Oder die Flipperwaldt gersput!

Pan out of the British trench across war-torn landscape and come to rest where presumably the German trench is. There is a pause and then a knot of Germans rear up in hysterics.

Voice Over It was a fantastic success. Over sixty thousand times as powerful as Britain's great pre-war joke . . .

Stock film of Chamberlain brandishing the 'Peace in our time' bit of paper.

Voice Over . . . and one which Hitler just couldn't match.

Film of Hitler rally. Hitler speaks; subtitles are superimposed.

SUBTITLE: 'MY DOG'S GOT NO NOSE'

A young soldier responds:

SUBTITLE: 'HOW DOES HE SMELL?'

Hitler speaks:

SUBTITLE: 'AWFUL'

Voice Over In action it was deadly.

Cut to a small squad with rifles making their way through forest. Suddenly one of them (a member of joke squad) sees something and gives signal at which they all dive for cover. From the cover of a tree he reads out joke.

Joke Corporal (TERRY J) Wenn ist das Nunstück git und Slotermeyer? Ja! . . . Beiherhund das Oder die Flipperwaldt gersput!

Sniper falls laughing out of tree.

Joke Brigade *(charging)* Wenn ist das Nunstück git und Slotermeyer? Ja! . . . Beiherhund das Oder die Flipperwaldt gersput.

They chant the joke. Germans are put to flight laughing, some dropping to ground.

Voice Over The German casualties were appalling.

Cut to a German hospital and a ward full of casualties still laughing hysterically.
Cut to Nazi interrogation room. An officer from the joke brigade has a light shining in his face. A Gestapo officer is interrogating him; another (clearly labelled 'A Gestapo Officer') stands behind him.

Nazi (JOHN) Vott is the big joke?

Officer (MICHAEL) I can only give you name, rank, and why did the chicken cross the road?

Nazi That's not funny! *(slaps him)* I vant to know the joke.

Officer All right. How do you make a Nazi cross?

Nazi *(momentarily fooled)* I don't know . . . how do you make a Nazi cross?

Officer Tread on his corns. *(does so; the Nazi hops in pain)*

Nazi Gott in Himmel! That's not funny! *(mimes cuffing him while the other Nazi claps his hands to provide the sound effect)* Now if you don't tell me the joke, I shall hit you properly.

Officer I can stand physical pain, you know.

Nazi Ah . . . you're no fun. All right, Otto.

Otto (Graham) starts tickling the officer who starts laughing.

Officer Oh no – anything but that please no, all right I'll tell you.

They stop.

Nazi Quick Otto. The typewriter.

Otto goes to the typewriter and they wait expectantly. The officer produces piece of paper out of his breast pocket and reads.

Officer Wenn ist das Nunstück git und Slotermeyer? Ja! . . . Beiherhund das Oder die Flipperwaldt gersput.

Otto at the typewriter explodes with laughter and dies.

Nazi Ach! Zat iss not funny!

Bursts into laughter and dies. A guard (Terry G) bursts in with machine gun. The British officer leaps on the table.

Officer *(lightning speed)* Wenn ist das Nunstück git und Slotermeyer? Ja! . . . Beiherhund das Oder die Flipperwaldt gersput.

The guard reels back and collapses laughing. British officer makes his escape.
Cut to stock film of German scientists working in laboratories.

Voice Over But at Peenemunde in the Autumn of '44, the Germans were working on a joke of their own.

Cut to interior. A German general (Terry J) seated at an imposing desk. Behind him stands Otto, labelled 'A Different Gestapo Officer'. Bespectacled German scientist/joke writer enters room. He clears his throat and reads from card.

German Joker (ERIC) Die ist ein Kinnerhunder und zwei Mackel über und der bitte schön ist den Wunderhaus sprechensie. 'Nein' sprecht der Herren 'Ist aufern borger mit zveitingen'.

He finishes and looks hopeful.

Otto   We let you know.

He shoots him.

More stock film of German scientists.

Voice Over   But by December their joke was ready, and Hitler gave the order for the German V-Joke to be broadcast in English.

Cut to 1940's wartime radio set with couple anxiously listening to it.

Radio *(crackly German voice)*   Der ver zwei peanuts, valking down der strasse, and von vas . . . assaulted! peanut. Ho-ho-ho-ho.

Radio bursts into 'Deutschland Über Alles'. The couple look at each other and then in blank amazement at the radio.

Cut to modern BBC 2 interview. The commentator in a woodland glade.

Commentator (ERIC)   In 1945 Peace broke out. It was the end of the Joke. Joke warfare was banned at a special session of the Geneva Convention, and in 1950 the last remaining copy of the joke was laid to rest here in the Berkshire countryside, never to be told again.

He walks away revealing a monument on which is written: 'To the unknown Joke'. Camera pulls away slowly through idyllic setting. Patriotic music reaches crescendo.

Cut to football referee who blows whistle. Silence. Blank screen.

CAPTION: 'THE END'

The seashore again, with the 'It's' man lying on the beach. A stick from off-screen prods him. Exhausted, he rises and staggers back into the sea.

CAPTION: ' "WHITHER CANADA?" WAS CONCEIVED WRITTEN AND PERFORMED BY . . . (CREDITS)'

Announcer (GRAHAM)   And here is the final score: Pigs 9 – British Bipeds 4. The Pigs go on to meet Vicki Carr in the final.

Two Sex and violence

A man appears on the top of a sand dune some way away. He looks in direction of camera and runs towards it. He disappears on top of a closer dune and continues towards camera, disappearing again into a dip. This time while he is out of sight, the sound of him running is the sound of someone running along a prison corridor, followed by a big door opening and closing. He appears again only two sand dunes away. Still running towards camera he disappears again from sight. This time there is a loud metallic series of sounds followed by a pig squealing. He appears over the nearest dune and runs up to camera.

It's Man (MICHAEL) It's . . .

Voice Over (JOHN) Monty Python's Flying Circus.

These words are followed by various strange images, possibly connected with the stretching of owls, and proceeding from a bizarre American immigrant's fevered brain. At the end of this expensive therapy:

CAPTION: 'PART 2'

CAPTION: 'SHEEP'

A small set of a gate in the country overlooking a field. A real rustic in smock and floppy hat is leaning on the gate. A city gent on holiday appears behind him. Off-screen baa-ing noises throughout.

City Gent (TERRY J) Good afternoon.

Rustic (GRAHAM) Arternoon.

City Gent Ah, lovely day isn't it?

Rustic Ar, 'tis that.

City Gent Are you here on holiday or . . . ?

Rustic No no, I live here.

City Gent Oh, jolly good too. *(surveys field; he looks puzzled)* I say, those *are* sheep, aren't they?

Rustic Ar.

City Gent Yes, yes of course, I thought so . . . only . . . er why are they up in the trees?

Rustic A fair question and one that in recent weeks has been much on my mind. It is my considered opinion that they're nesting.

City Gent Nesting?

Rustic Ar.

City Gent Like birds?

Rustic Ar. Exactly! Birds is the key to the whole problem. It is my belief that these sheep are labouring under the misapprehension that they're birds. Observe their behaviour. Take for a start the sheeps' tendency to hop about the field on their back legs. *(off-screen baa-ing)* Now witness their attempts to fly from tree to tree. Notice they do not so much fly as plummet. *(sound of sheep plummeting)*

•

Observe for example that ewe in that oak tree. She is clearly trying to teach her lamb to fly. *(baaaaaa . . . thump)* Talk about the blind leading the blind.

City Gent But why do they think they're birds?

Rustic Another fair question. One thing is for sure; a sheep is not a creature of the air. It has enormous difficulty in the comparatively simple act of perching. *(crash)* As you see. As for flight, its body is totally unadapted to the problems of aviation. Trouble is, sheep are very dim. And once they get an idea into their heads there's no shifting it.

City Gent But where did they get the idea from?

Rustic From Harold. He's that sheep over there under the elm. He's that most dangerous of animals – a clever sheep. He's the ring-leader. He has realized that a sheep's life consists of standing around for a few months and then being eaten. And that's a depressing prospect for an ambitious sheep. He's patently hit on the idea of escape.

City Gent But why don't you just get rid of Harold?

Rustic Because of the enormous commercial possibilities should he succeed.

Voice Over (ERIC) And what exactly are the commercial possibilities of ovine aviation?

Two Frenchmen stand in front of a diagram of a sheep adapted for flying. They speak rapidly in French, much of it pseudo.

First Frenchman (JOHN) Bonsoir – ici nous avons les diagrammes modernes d'un mouton anglo-français . . . maintenant . . . baa-aa, baa-aa . . . nous avons, dans la tête, le cabine. Ici, on se trouve le petit capitaine Anglais, Monsieur Trubshawe.

Second Frenchman (MICHAEL) Vive Brian, wherever you are.

First Frenchman D'accord, d'accord. Maintenant, je vous présente mon collègue, le pouf célèbre, Jean-Brian Zatapathique.

Transfers his moustache to Second Frenchman.

Second Frenchman Maintenant, le mouton . . . le landing . . . les wheels, bon.

Opens diagram to show wheels on sheep's legs.

First Frenchman Bon, les wheels, ici.

Second Frenchman C'est formidable, n'est ce pas . . . *(unintelligibly indicates motor at rear of sheep)*

First Frenchman Les voyageurs . . . les bagages . . . ils sont . . . ici!

Triumphantly opens the rest of the diagram to reveal the whole brilliant arrangement. They run round flapping their arms and baa-ing.
Cut to pepperpots in supermarket with off-screen interviewer.

First Pepperpot (GRAHAM) Oh yes, we get a lot of French people round here.

Second Pepperpot (TERRY J)   Ooh Yes.

Third Pepperpot (MICHAEL)   All over yes.

Interviewer   And how do you get on with these French people?

First Pepperpot   Oh very well.

Fourth Pepperpot (JOHN)   So do I.

Third Pepperpot   Me too.

First Pepperpot   Oh yes I like them. I mean, they think well don't they? I mean, be fair – Pascal.

Second Pepperpot   Blaise Pascal.

Third Pepperpot   Jean-Paul Sartre.

First Pepperpot   Yes, Voltaire.

Second Pepperpot   Ooh! – René Descartes.

> *René Descartes is sitting thinking. Bubbles come from his head with 'thinks'. Suddenly he looks happy. In thought bubble appears 'I THINK THEREFORE I AM'. A large hand comes into picture with a pin and pricks the thought bubble. It deflates and disappears. After a second, René disappears too.*
>
> *Studio: Smart looking and confident announcer sitting at desk.*

Announcer (ERIC)   And now for something completely different. A man with three buttocks.

> *Interviewer and Arthur Frampton, in interview studio.*

Interviewer (JOHN)   Good evening. I have with me, Mr Arthur Frampton, who has . . . Mr Frampton, I understand that you . . . er . . . as it were . . . have er . . . well, let me put it another way . . . I believe, Mr Frampton that whereas most people have . . . er . . . two . . . two . . . you . . . you.

Frampton (TERRY J)   I'm sorry.

Interviewer   Ah! Yes, yes I see . . . Um. Are you quite comfortable?

Frampton   Yes fine, thank you.

Interviewer *(takes a quick glance at Frampton's bottom)*   Er, Mr Frampton . . . vis-à-vis . . . your . . . rump.

Frampton   I beg your pardon?

Interviewer   Er, your rump.

Frampton   What?

Interviewer   Your posterior . . . derrière . . . sit upon.

Frampton   What's that?

Interviewer *(whispers)*   . . . Buttocks.

Frampton   Oh, me bum!

Interviewer   Sh! . . . Well Mr Frampton I understand Mr Frampton, you have a . . . 50% bonus in the . . . in the region of what you said.

Frampton   I got three cheeks.

Interviewer   Yes, yes. Splendid, splendid. Well . . . we were wondering Mr Frampton if you . . . could . . . see your way clear . . .

Frampton *(seeing a camera moving round behind him)* Here? What's that camera doing?

Interviewer Er, nothing, nothing at all, sir. We were wondering if you could see your way clear . . . to giving us . . . a quick . . . a quick . . . visual . . . Mr Frampton, will you take your trousers down?

Frampton What? *(slapping away a hand from off-screen)* 'Ere, get off. I'm not taking me trousers off on television. Who do you think I am?

Interviewer Please take them down.

Frampton No.

Interviewer Just a little bit.

Frampton No.

Interviewer Now er, ahem . . . *(firmly)* Now look here Mr Frampton . . . it's perfectly easy for somebody just to come along here to the BBC, simply claiming . . . that they have a bit to spare in the botty department . . . but the point is Mr Frampton . . . our viewers need proof.

Frampton I've been on Persian Radio . . . Get off! Arthur Figgis knows I've got three buttocks.

Interviewer How?

Frampton We go cycling together.

> *Cut to shot of two men riding tandem. The one behind (Graham) looks down, looks up and exclaims 'strewth'.*
>
> *Announcer's desk: confident announcer again.*

Announcer And now for something completely different. A man with three buttocks.

> *Interview studio again.*

Interviewer Good evening, I have with me Mr Arthur Frampton, who . . . Mr Frampton – I understand that you, as it were – well let me put it another way . . . I believe Mr Frampton that whereas most people . . . didn't we do this just now?

Frampton Er . . . yes.

Interviewer Well why didn't you *say* so?

Frampton I thought it was the continental version.

> *Announcer's desk: confident announcer.*

Announcer And now for something completely the same – a man with three buttocks. *(phone on desk rings – he answers it)* Hullo? . . . Oh, did we. *(puts phone down; to camera)* And now for something completely different. A man with three noses.

Off-Screen Voice (JOHN) He's not here yet!

Announcer Two noses?

> *Stock shot of audience of Women's Institute type, applauding. A man flourishing a handkerchief blows his nose. Then he puts his handkerchief inside his shirt and blows again. Stock shot women applauding again.*

Compère (MICHAEL) Ladies and gentlemen isn't she just great eh, wasn't she just great. Ha, ha, ha, and she can run as fast as she can sing, ha, ha, ha. And I'm telling you – 'cos I know. No, only kidding. Ha, ha, ha. Seriously now, ladies and gentlemen, we have for you one of the most unique acts in the world today. He's ... well I'll say no more, just let you see for yourselves ... ladies and gentlemen, my very great privilege to introduce Arthur Ewing, and his musical mice.

Cut to Ewing.

Ewing (TERRY J) Thank you, thank you, thank you, thank you. Ladies and gentlemen. I have in this box twenty-three white mice. Mice which have been painstakingly trained over the past few years, to squeak at a selected pitch. *(he raises a mouse by its tail)* This is E sharp ... and this one is G. You get the general idea. Now these mice are so arranged upon this rack, that when played in the correct order they will squeak 'The Bells of St Mary's'. Ladies and gentlemen, I give you on the mouse organ 'The Bells of St Mary's'. Thank you.

He produces two mallets. He starts striking the mice while singing quietly 'The Bells of St Mary's'. Each downward stroke of the mallet brings a terrible squashing sound and the expiring squeak. It is quite clear that he is slaughtering the mice. The musical effect is poor. After the first few notes people are shouting 'Stop it, stop him someone, Oh my God'. He cheerfully takes a bow. He is hauled off by the floor manager.
Cut to man holding up cards saying 'Marriage Counsellor'. The counsellor sits behind a desk. He puts down the card and says:

Counsellor (ERIC) Next!

A little man enters, with a beautiful blond buxom wench, in the full bloom of her young womanhood (Carol Cleveland).

Man (MICHAEL) Are you the marriage guidance counsellor?

Counsellor Yes. Good morning.

Man Good morning, sir.

Counsellor *(stares at the wife, fascinated)* And good morning to you madam. *(pause, he shrugs himself out of it, says to man ...)* Name?

Man Mr and Mrs Arthur Pewtey, Pewtey.

Counsellor *(writes without looking down; he is staring at the wife)* And what is the name of your ravishing wife? *(holds up hand)* Wait. Don't tell me – it's something to do with moonlight – it goes with her eyes – it's soft and gentle, warm and yielding, deeply lyrical and yet tender and frightened like a tiny white rabbit.

Man It's Deirdre.

Counsellor Deirdre. What a beautiful name. What a beautiful, beautiful name. *(leans across and lightly brushes his hand across the wife's cheek)* And what seems to be the trouble with your marriage Mr Pewtey?

Man Well, it all started about five years ago when we started going on holiday to Brighton together. Deirdre, that's my wife, has always been a jolly good companion to me and I never particularly anticipated any marital strife – indeed the very idea of consulting a professional marital adviser has always been of the greatest repugnance to me, although far be it from me to impugn the nature of your trade or profession.

The counsellor and wife are not listening, fascinated by each other.

Counsellor *(realizing Pewtey has stopped)*   Do go on.

Man   Well, as I say, we've always been good friends, sharing the interests, the gardening and so on, the model aeroplanes, the sixpenny bottle for the holiday money, and indeed twice a month settling down in the evenings doing the accounts, something which, er, Deirdre, Deirdre that's my wife, er, particularly looked forward to on account of her feet. *(the counsellor has his face fantastically close to the wife's, as close as they could get without kissing)* I should probably have said at the outset that I'm noted for having something of a sense of humour, although I have kept myself very much to myself over the last two years notwithstanding, as it were, and it's only as comparatively recently as recently that I began to realize – well, er, perhaps realize is not the correct word, er, imagine, imagine, that I was not the only thing in her life.

Counsellor *(who is practically in a clinch with her)*   You suspected your wife?

Man   Well yes – at first, frankly, yes. *(the counsellor points the wife to a screen; she goes behind it)* Her behaviour did seem at the time to me, who after all was there to see, to be a little odd.

Counsellor   Odd?

Man   Yes well, I mean to a certain extent yes. I'm not by nature a suspicious person – far from it – though in fact I have something of a reputation as an after-dinner speaker, if you take my meaning . . .

A piece of his wife's clothing comes over the top of the screen.

Counsellor   Yes I certainly do.

The wife's bra and panties come over the screen.

Man   Anyway in the area where I'm known people in fact know me extremely well . . .

Counsellor *(taking his jacket off)*   Oh yes. Would you hold this.

Man   Certainly. Yes. *(helps him off with it; the counsellor continues to undress)* Anyway, as I said, I decided to face up to the facts and stop beating about the bush or I'd never look myself in the bathroom mirror again.

Counsellor *(down to his shorts)*   Er, look would you mind running along for ten minutes? Make it half an hour.

Man   No, no, right-ho, fine. Yes I'll wait outside shall I? . . . *(the counsellor* *has already gone behind screen)* Yes, well that's p'raps the best thing. Yes. You've certainly put my mind at rest on one or two points, there.

Exits through door. He is stopped by a deep rich southern American voice.

Southerner (JOHN) Now wait there stranger. A man can run and run for year after year until he realizes that what he's running from . . . is hisself.

Man Gosh.

Southerner A man's got to do what a man's got to do, and there ain't no sense in runnin'. Now you gotta turn, and you gotta fight, and you gotta hold your head up high.

Man Yes!

Southerner Now you go back in there my son and be a man. Walk tall. *(he exits)*

Man Yes, I will. I will. I've been pushed around long enough. This is it. This is your moment Arthur Pewtey – this is it Arthur Pewtey. At last you're a man! *(opens door determinedly)* All right, Deirdre, come out of there.

Counsellor Go away.

Man Right. Right.

He is hit on the head with a chicken by a man in a suit of armour.

Voice Over (JOHN) and CAPTION: 'SO MUCH FOR PATHOS'

Film Leader:

9 . . . 8 . . . 7 . . . 6 . . . 31 . . . 6 . . . Jimmy Greaves . . . 6 . . . 3 . . . 2 . . . 1 . . . And Interviewer:

Queen Victoria Film: the texture of the film reproduces as accurately as possible an animated Victorian photograph. Queen Victoria (Terry J) and Gladstone (Graham) are walking on the lawn in front of Osborne.

Voice Over (JOHN) These historic pictures of Queen Victoria, taken in 1880 at Osborne show the Queen with Gladstone. This unique film provides a rare glimpse into the private world of a woman who ruled half the earth. The commentary, recorded on the earliest wax cylinders, is spoken by Alfred Lord Tennyson, the Poet Laureate. *(Michael continues with jolly American accent)* Well hello, it's the wacky Queen again! *(the Queen repeatedly nudges Gladstone in the ribs and chucks him under the chin)* And who's the other fella? It's Willie Gladstone! And when these two way-out wacky characters get together there's fun a-plenty. *(they come up to a gardener with a hosepipe)* And, uh-oh! There's a hosepipe! This means trouble for somebody! *(the Queen takes the hose and kicks the gardener; he falls over)* Uh-oh, Charlie Gardener's fallen for that old trick. The Queen has put him in a *heap* of trouble! *(the Queen turns the hose on Gladstone)* Uh-oh that's one in the eye for Willie! *(the Queen hands Gladstone the hose)* Here, you have a go! *(she goes back to the tap and* *turns off the water)* Well, doggone it, where's the water? *(Gladstone examines the end of the hose; the water flow returns, spraying him)* Uh-oh, there it is, all over his face! *(she lifts her skirts and runs as he chases her across the lawn; next we see the Queen painting a fence; Gladstone approaches from the other side)* Well, hello, what's Britain's wacky Queen up to now? Well, she's certainly not *sitting* on the fence. She's *painting* it. Surely nothing can go wrong here? Uh-oh, here's the PM coming back for more. *(Gladstone walks into line with the end of the fence; the Queen daubs paint on him)* And he certainly gets it! *(he takes the bucket from her and empties it over her head; she kicks him; he falls through the fence)* Well, that's one way to get the housework done!

Cut to the Queen and Gladstone having tea on the lawn. She pushes a custard pie into his face. As he retaliates the picture freezes; the camera pulls back to reveal that it is a photo on the mantelpiece of a working-class sitting room.

Cut to sitting room straight out of D. H. Lawrence. Mum, wiping her hands on her apron is ushering in a young man in a suit. They are a Northern couple.

Mum (TERRY J) Oh dad ... look who's come to see us ... it's our Ken.

Dad (GRAHAM) *(without looking up)* Aye, and about bloody time if you ask me.

Ken (ERIC) Aren't you pleased to see me, father?

Mum *(squeezing his arm reassuringly)* Of course he's pleased to see you, Ken, he ...

Dad All right, woman, all right I've got a tongue in my head – I'll do t'talkin'. *(looks at Ken distastefully)* Aye ... I like yer fancy suit. Is that what they're wearing up in Yorkshire now?

Ken It's just an ordinary suit, father ... it's all I've got apart from the overalls.

Dad turns away with an expression of scornful disgust.

Mum How are you liking it down the mine, Ken?

Ken Oh it's not too bad, mum ... we're using some new tungsten carbide drills for the preliminary coal-face scouring operations.

Mum Oh that sounds nice, dear ...

Dad Tungsten carbide drills! What the bloody hell's tungsten carbide drills?

Ken It's something they use in coal-mining, father.

Dad *(mimicking)* 'It's something they use in coal-mining, father'. You're all bloody fancy talk since you left London.

Ken Oh not that again.

Mum *(to Ken)* He's had a hard day dear ... his new play opens at the National Theatre tomorrow.

Ken Oh that's good.

Dad Good! *good?* What do you know about it? What do you know about getting up at five o'clock in t'morning to fly to Paris . . . back at the Old Vic for drinks at twelve, sweating the day through press interviews, television interviews and getting back here at ten to wrestle with the problem of a homosexual nymphomaniac drug-addict involved in the ritual murder of a well known Scottish footballer. That's a full working day, lad, and don't you forget it!

Mum Oh, don't shout at the boy, father.

Dad Aye, 'ampstead wasn't good enough for you, was it? . . . you had to go poncing off to Barnsley, you and yer coal-mining friends. *(spits)*

Ken Coal-mining is a wonderful thing father, but it's something you'll never understand. Just look at you!

Mum Oh Ken! Be careful! You know what he's like after a few novels.

Dad Oh come on lad! Come on, out wi' it! What's wrong wi' me? . . . yer *tit!*

Ken I'll tell you what's wrong with you. Your head's addled with novels and poems, you come home every evening reeling of Château La Tour . . .

Mum Oh don't, don't.

Ken And look what you've done to mother! She's worn out with meeting film stars, attending premières and giving gala luncheons . . .

Dad There's nowt wrong wi' gala luncheons, lad! I've had more gala luncheons than you've had hot dinners!

Mum Oh please!

Dad Aaaaaaagh! *(clutches hands and sinks to knees)*

Mum Oh no!

Ken What is it?

Mum Oh, it's his writer's cramp!

Ken You never told me about this . . .

Mum No, we didn't like to, Kenny.

Dad I'm all right! I'm all right, woman. Just get him out of here.

Mum Oh Ken! You'd better go . . .

Ken All right. I'm going.

Dad After all we've done for him . . .

Ken *(at the door)* One day you'll realize there's more to life than culture . . . There's dirt, and smoke, and good honest sweat!

Dad Get out! Get out! Get OUT! You . . . LABOURER!

Ken goes. Shocked silence. Dad goes to table and takes the cover off the typewriter.

Dad Hey, you know, mother, I think there's a play there, . . . get t'agent on t'phone.

Mum Aye I think you're right, Frank, it could express, it could express a vital theme of our age . . .

Dad Aye.

In the room beneath a man is standing on a chair, banging on the ceiling with a broom.

Man (MICHAEL) Oh shut up! *(bang bang)* Shut up! *(they stop talking upstairs)* Oh, that's better. *(he climbs down and addresses camera)* And now for something completely different . . . a man with three buttocks . . .

Mum and Dad *(from upstairs)* We've done that!

The man looks up slightly disconcerted.

Man Oh all right. All right! A man with nine legs.

Voice Off (JOHN) He ran away.

Man Oh . . . Bloody Hell! Er . . . a Scotsman on a horse!

Cut to film of a Scotsman (John) riding up on a horse. He looks around, puzzled.
Cut to stock film of Women's Institute audience applauding.
Cut to the man with two noses (Graham); he puts a handkerchief to his elbow and we hear the sound of a nose being blown.
Cut to Women's Institute audience applauding.
Cut to cartoon of a flying sheep.

Voice Over (MICHAEL) Harold! Come back, Harold! Harold! Come back, Harold! Oh, blast!

The sheep is shot down by a cannon.
Cut to film of an audience of Indian ladies not applauding.

CAPTION: 'THE EPILOGUE, A QUESTION OF BELIEF'

Interview studio: interviewer in the middle. There is a monsignor in full clerical garb with skull-cap, and opposite him a tweed-suited, old Don figure.

Interviewer (JOHN) Good evening, and welcome once again to the Epilogue. On the programme this evening we have Monsignor Edward Gay, visiting Pastoral Emissary of the Somerset Theological College and author of a number of books about belief, the most recent of which is the best seller 'My God'. And opposite him we have Dr Tom Jack: humanist, broadcaster, lecturer and author of the book 'Hello Sailor'. Tonight, instead of discussing the existence or non-existence of God, they have decided to fight for it. The existence, or non-existence, to be determined by two falls, two submissions, or a knockout. All right boys, let's get to it. Your master of ceremonies for this evening – Mr Arthur Waring.

The participants move into a wrestling ring.

MC (ERIC) Good evening ladies and gentlemen and welcome to a three-round contest of the Epilogue. Introducing on my right in the blue corner, appearing for Jehovah – the ever popular Monsignor Eddie Gay. *(there are boos from the crowd)* And on my left in the red corner – author of the books 'The Problems of

Kierkegaard' and 'Hello Sailor' and visiting Professor of Modern
Theological Philosophy at the University of East Anglia – from
Wigan – Dr Tom Jack! *(cheers; gong goes for the start)*

CAPTION: 'ROUND I'

They are real wrestlers. They throw each other about.

Interviewer *(commentating)* Now Dr Jack's got a flying mare there. A
flying mare there, and this is going to be a full body slam. A full
body slam, and he's laying it in there, and he's standing back. Well
... there we are leaving the Epilogue for the moment, we'll be
bringing you the result of this discussion later on in the
programme.

Interviewer Oh my God! *(pulls out a revolver and shoots something
off-screen)*

ANIMATION: *We see a cowboy just having been shot. This leads into
cartoon film, which includes a carnivorous pram and music from Rodin's
statue 'The Kiss'. Then a protest march appears carrying banners. Close
in on banners which read: End Discrimination: Mice Is Nice; Ho Ho Ho
Traps Must Go; Hands Off Mice: Repeal Anti-Mouse Laws Now;
Kidderminster Young Methodists Resent Oppression: A Fair Deal For
Mice Men.*

CAPTION: 'THE WORLD AROUND US'

*Photo of newspaper headlines: Pop Stars In Mouse Scandal; Peer Faces
Rodent Charges. A man in mouse skin running into police station with
bag over head.*

CAPTION: 'THE MOUSE PROBLEM'

*Cut to a policeman leading a man in mouse costume into a police station.
Photo of headline: Mouse Clubs On Increase.
Cut to: photos of neon signs of clubs: Eek Eek Club; The Little White
Rodent Room; Caerphilly A Go-Go.
Cut to studio: ordinary grey-suited linkman.*

Linkman (MICHAEL) Yes. The Mouse Problem. This week 'The World
Around Us' looks at the growing social phenomenon of Mice and
Men. What makes a man want to be a mouse.

*Interviewer, Harold Voice, sitting facing a confessor. The confessor is
badly lit and is turned away from camera.*

Man (JOHN) *(very slowly and painfully)* Well it's not a question of *wanting*
to be a mouse ... it just sort of happens to you. All of a sudden
you realize ... that's what you want to be.

Interviewer (TERRY J) And when did you first notice these ... shall we
say ... tendencies?

Man Well ... I was about seventeen and some mates and me went to a
party, and, er ... we had quite a lot to drink ... and then some of

the fellows there . . . started handing . . . cheese around . . . and well just out of curiosity I tried a bit . . . and well that was that.

Interviewer And what else did these fellows do?

Man Well some of them started dressing up as mice a bit . . . and then when they'd got the costumes on they started . . . squeaking.

Interviewer Yes. And was that all?

Man That was all.

Interviewer And what was your reaction to this?

Man Well I was shocked. But, er . . . gradually I came to feel that I was more at ease . . . with other mice.

Cut to linkman.

Linkman A typical case, whom we shall refer to as Mr A, although his real name is this:

Voice Over (JOHN) and CAPTION: ARTHUR JACKSON
32A MILTON AVENUE,
HOUNSLOW, MIDDLESEX.

Linkman What is it that attracts someone like Mr A to this way of life? I have with me a consultant psychiatrist.

The camera pulls back to reveal the psychiatrist who places in front of himself a notice saying 'The Amazing Kargol And Janet'.

Kargol (GRAHAM) Well, we've just heard a typical case history. I myself have over seven hundred similar histories, all fully documented. Would you care to choose one?

Janet (Carol), dressed in showgirl's outfit, enters and offers linkman the case histories fanned out like cards, with one more prominent than the others; he picks it out.

Kargol (*without looking*) Mr Arthur Aldridge of Leamington.

Linkman Well, that's amazing, amazing. Thank you, Janet. (*chord; Janet postures and exits*) Kargol, speaking as a psychiatrist as opposed to a conjuror . . .

Kargol (*disappointed*) Oh . . .

Linkman . . . what makes certain men want to be mice?

Kargol Well, we psychiatrists have found that over 8% of the population will always be mice. I mean, after all, there's something of the mouse in all of us. I mean, how many of us can honestly say that at one time or another he hasn't felt sexually attracted to mice. (*linkman looks puzzled*) I know I have. I mean, most normal adolescents go through a stage of squeaking two or three times a day. Some youngsters on the other hand, are attracted to it by its very illegality. It's like murder – make a thing illegal and it acquires a mystique. (*linkman looks increasingly embarrassed*) Look at arson – I mean, how many of us can honestly say that at one time or another he hasn't set fire to some great public building. I know I have. (*phone on desk rings; the linkman picks it up but does not answer* *it)* The only way to bring the crime figures down is to reduce the number of offences – get it out in the open – I know I have.

Linkman *(replacing phone)* The Amazing Kargol And Janet. What a lot of people don't realize is that a mouse, once accepted, can fulfil a very useful role in society. Indeed there are examples throughout history of famous men now known to have been mice.

Cut to Julius Caesar (Graham) on beach. He shouts 'Veni Vidi, Vici'. Then he adds a furtive squeak. Napoleon (Terry J) pulls slice of cheese out of jacket and bites into it.
Cut to linkman.

Linkman And, of course, Hillaire Belloc. But what is the attitude . . .

Cut to man in a Viking helmet.

Viking (ERIC) . . . of the man in the street towards . . .
Linkman . . . this growing social problem?

Vox pops films.

Window Cleaner (ERIC) Clamp down on them.
Off-screen Voice How?
Window Cleaner I'd strangle them.
Stockbroker (JOHN) Well speaking as a member of the Stock Exchange I would suck their brains out with a straw, sell the widows and orphans and go into South American Zinc.
Man (TERRY J) Yeh I'd, er, stuff sparrows down their throats, er, until the beaks stuck out through the, er, stomach walls.
Accountant (GRAHAM) Oh well I'm a chartered accountant, and consequently too boring to be of interest.
Vicar (JOHN) I feel that these poor unfortunate people should be free to live the lives of their own choice.
Porter (TERRY J) I'd split their nostrils open with a boat hook, I think.
Man (GRAHAM) Well I mean, they can't help it, can they? But, er, there's nothing you can do about it. So er, I'd kill 'em.

Cut to linkman.

Linkman Clearly the British public's view is a hostile one.
Voice Over and CAPTION: 'HOSTILE'
Linkman But perhaps this is because so little is generally known of these mice men. We have some film now taken of one of the notorious weekend mouse parties, where these disgusting little perverts meet.

Cut to exterior house (night). The blinds are drawn so that only shadows of enormous mice can be seen, holding slices of cheese and squeaking.

Linkman's Voice Mr A tells us what actually goes on at these mouse parties.

Cut to Mr A.

Mr A (JOHN) Well first of all you get shown to your own private hole in the skirting board . . . then you put the mouse skin on . . . then you

> scurry into the main room, and perhaps take a run in the wheel.

Linkman   The remainder of this film was taken secretly at one of these mouse parties by a BBC cameraman posing as a vole. As usual we apologize for the poor quality of the film.

Very poor quality film, shadowy shapes, the odd mouse glimpsed.

Mr A's Voice   Well, er, then you steal some cheese, Brie or Camembert, or Cheddar or Gouda, if you're on the harder stuff. You might go and see one of the blue cheese films . . . there's a big clock in the middle of the room, and about 12.50 you climb up it and then . . . eventually, it strikes one . . . and you all run down.

Cut to a large matron with apron and carving knife.

Linkman's Voice   And what's that?

Mr A's Voice   That's the farmer's wife.

Cut to the linkman at desk.

Linkman   Perhaps we need to know more of these mice men before we can really judge them. Perhaps not. Anyway, our thirty minutes are up.

Sound of baa-ing. The linkman looks up in air, looks startled, pulls a gun from under the desk and fires in the air. The body of a sheep falls to the floor.

Linkman   Goodnight.

CAPTION: 'SEX AND VIOLENCE' WAS CONCEIVED, WRITTEN AND PERFORMED BY: . . . (CREDITS)'

Voice Over (JOHN)   And here is the result of the Epilogue: God exists by two falls to a submission.

Three How to recognise different types of trees from quite a long way away

Opening as usual – man running through a forest towards camera with clothes tattered; arrives at camera, and says:

Man (MICHAEL) It's . . .

Voice Over (JOHN) Monty Python's Flying Circus.

ANIMATION: *Titles sequence as usual. And pretty flowers blooming. This finishes, and a magic lantern slide (done graphically) clicks into vision.*

Voice Over (JOHN) and CAPTIONS:

'EPISODE 12B'
'HOW TO RECOGNIZE DIFFERENT TYPES OF TREES FROM QUITE A LONG WAY AWAY'
'NO. 1'
'THE LARCH'

Photo of a larch tree.

Voice Over The larch. The larch.

Courtroom: a judge sitting at higher level and a prisoner in the dock.

Judge (TERRY J) Mr Larch, you heard the case for the prosecution. Is there anything you wish to say before I pass sentence?

Prisoner (ERIC) Well . . . I'd just like to say, m'lud, I've got a family . . . a wife and six kids . . . and I hope very much you don't have to take away my freedom . . . because . . . well, because m'lud freedom is a state much prized within the realm of civilized society. *(slips into Olivier impression)* It is a bond wherewith the savage man may charm the outward hatchments of his soul, and soothe the troubled breast into a magnitude of quiet. It is most precious as a blessed balm, the saviour of princes, the harbinger of happiness, yea, the very stuff and pith of all we hold most dear. What frees the prisoner in his lonely cell, chained within the bondage of rude walls, far from the owl of Thebes? What fires and stirs the woodcock in his springe or wakes the drowsy apricot betides? What goddess doth the storm toss'd mariner offer her most tempestuous prayers to? Freedom! Freedom! Freedom!

Judge It's only a bloody parking offence.

The counsel strides into court.

Counsel (JOHN) I'm sorry I'm late m'lud I couldn't find a kosher car park. Er . . . don't bother to recap m'lud, I'll pick it up as we go along. Call Mrs Fiona Lewis.

A pepperpot walks into the court and gets up into the witness box.

Clerk of the Court Call Mrs Fiona Lewis.

Pepperpot (GRAHAM) *(taking bible)* I swear to tell the truth, the whole truth and nothing but the truth, so *anyway*, I said to her, I said, they can't afford that on what he earns, I mean for a start the feathers get up your nose, I ask you, four and six a pound, and him with a wooden leg, I don't know how she puts up with it after all the trouble she's had with her you-know-what, anyway it *was* a white wedding much to everyone's surprise, of course they bought everything on the hire purchase, I think they ought to send them back where they came from, I mean you've got to be cruel to be kind so Mrs Harris said, so she said, she said, she said, the dead crab she said, she said. Well, her sister's gone to Rhodesia what with her womb and all, and her youngest, her youngest as thin as a filing cabinet, and the goldfish, the goldfish they've got whooping cough they keep spitting water all over their Bratbys, well, they *do* don't they, I mean you *can't*, can you, I mean they're not even married or anything, they're not even *divorced*, and he's in the KGB if you ask me, he says he's a tree surgeon but I don't like the sound of his liver, all that squeaking and banging every night till the small hours, his mother's been much better since she had her head off, yes she has, I said, don't you talk to me about bladders, I said . . .

During all this counsel has been trying to ask questions. Eventually he gives up and Mrs Lewis is pushed out of court still talking.

Judge Mr Bartlett, I fail to see the relevance of your last witness.

Counsel My next witness will explain that if m'ludship will allow. I call the late Arthur Aldridge.

Clerk of the Court The late Arthur Aldridge.

Judge The *late* Arthur Aldridge?

Counsel Yes m'lud.

A coffin is brought into the court and laid across the witness box.

Judge Mr Bartlett, do you think there is any relevance in questioning the deceased?

Counsel I beg your pardon m'lud.

Judge Well, I mean, your witness *is* dead.

Counsel Yes, m'lud. Er, well er, virtually, m'lud.

Judge He's not completely dead?

Counsel No he's not completely dead m'lud. No. But he's not at all well.

Judge But if he's not dead, what's he doing in a coffin?

Counsel Oh, it's purely a precaution m'lud – if I may continue? Mr Aldridge, you were a . . . you *are* a stockbroker of 10 Savundra Close, Wimbledon. *(from the coffin comes a bang)* Mr Aldridge . . .

Judge What was that knock?

Counsel It means 'yes' m'lud. One knock for 'yes', and two knocks for 'no'. If I may continue? Mr Aldridge, would it be fair to say that you are not at all well? *(from the coffin comes a bang)* In fact Mr

Aldridge, not to put too fine a point on it, would you be prepared to say that you are, as it were, what is generally known as, in a manner of speaking, 'dead'? *(silence; counsel listens)* Mr Aldridge I put it to you that you are dead. *(silence)* Ah ha!

Judge Where is all this leading us?

Counsel That will become apparent in one moment m'lud. *(walking over to coffin)* Mr Aldridge are you considering the question or are you just dead? *(silence)* I think I'd better take a look m'lud. *(he opens the coffin and looks inside for some time; then he closes the coffin)* No further questions m'lud.

Judge What do you mean, no further questions? You can't just dump a dead body in my court and say 'no further questions'. I demand an explanation.

Counsel There are no easy answers in this case m'lud.

Judge I think you haven't got the slightest idea what this case is about.

Counsel M'lud the strange, damnable, almost diabolic threads of this extraordinary tangled web of intrigue will shortly m'lud reveal a plot so fiendish, so infernal, so heinous . . .

Judge Mr Bartlett, your client has already pleaded guilty to the parking offence.

Counsel Parking offence, schmarking offence, m'lud. We must leave no stone unturned. Call Cardinal Richelieu.

Judge Oh, you're just trying to string this case out. Cardinal Richelieu?

Counsel A character witness m'lud.

Fanfare of trumpets. Cardinal Richelieu enters witness box in beautiful robes.

Cardinal (MICHAEL.) 'Allo everyone, it's wonderful to be 'ere y'know, I just love your country. London is so beautiful at this time of year.

Counsel Er, you are Cardinal Armand du Plessis de Richelieu, First Minister of Louis XIII?

Cardinal Oui.

Counsel Cardinal, would it be fair to say that you not only built up the centralized monarchy in France but also perpetuated the religious schism in Europe?

Cardinal *(modestly)* That's what they say.

Counsel Did you persecute the Huguenots?

Cardinal Oui.

Counsel And did you take even sterner measures against the great Catholic nobles who made common cause with foreign foes in defence of their feudal independence?

Cardinal I sure did that thing.

Counsel Cardinal. Are you acquainted with the defendant, Harold Larch?

Cardinal Since I was so high *(indicating)*.

Counsel Speaking as a Cardinal of the Roman Catholic Church, as First Minister of Louis XIII, and as one of the architects of the modern world already – would you say that Harold Larch was a man of good character?

Cardinal Listen. Harry is a very wonderful human being.

Counsel M'lud. In view of the impeccable nature of this character witness may I plead for clemency.

Judge Oh but it's only thirty shillings.

Enter Inspector Dim.

Dim (GRAHAM) Not so fast!

Prisoner Why not?

Dim (*momentarily thrown*) None of your smart answers . . . you think you're so clever. Well, I'm Dim.

CAPTION: 'DIM OF THE YARD'

Omnes (*in unison*) Dim! Consternation! Uproar!

Dim Yes, and I've a few questions I'd like to ask Cardinal so-called Richelieu.

Cardinal Bonjour Monsieur Dim.

Dim So-called Cardinal, I put it to you that you died in December 1642.

Cardinal That is correct.

Dim Ah ha! He fell for my little trap.

Court applauds and the Cardinal looks dismayed.

Cardinal Curse you Inspector Dim. You are too clever for us naughty people.

Dim And furthermore I suggest that you are none other than Ron Higgins, professional Cardinal Richelieu impersonator.

Cardinal It's a fair cop.

Counsel My life you're clever Dim. He'd certainly taken me in.

Dim It's all in a day's work.

Judge With a brilliant mind like yours, Dim, you could be something other than a policeman.

Dim Yes.

Judge What?

Piano starts playing introduction.

Dim (*singing*) If I were not in the CID
Something else I'd like to be
If I were not in the CID
A window cleaner, me!
With a rub-a-dub-dub and a scrub-a-dub-dub
And a rub-a-dub all day long
With a rub-a-dub-dub and a scrub-a-dub-dub
I'd sing this merry song!
He mimes window cleaning movements and the rest of the court

enthusiastically mimes and sings the chorus again with him. When the chorus verse ends the counsel enthusiastically takes over but this time the court all sit and watch him as though he has gone completely mad.

Counsel If I were not before the bar
Something else I'd like to be
If I were not a barr-is-ter
An engine driver me!
With a chuffchuffchuff etc.

He makes engine miming movements. As before. After a few seconds he sees that the rest of the court are staring at him in amazement and he loses momentum rapidly, almost as rapidly as he loses confidence and dignity. At last he subsides. Our knight in armour walks up to the counsel and hits him with the traditional raw chicken.

Voice Over (JOHN) and CAPTION: 'NO. 1'
'THE LARCH'
Photo of larch tree.

Voice Over The larch. The larch.

Voice Over and CAPTION: 'AND NOW . . . NO. 1 . . . THE LARCH . . . AND NOW . . .'

Superman film: shot from below of Superman (Michael) striding along against the sky.

Commentator (JOHN) (*American accent*) This man is no ordinary man. This is Mr F. G. Superman. To all appearances no different from any other law-abiding citizen.

Pull back to reveal he is in a modern street full of Supermen walking along shopping, waiting at bus queues etc. F. G. Superman gets onto a bus. The bus is full of Supermen, most of them with shopping baskets on their knees. F. G. Superman finds a seat . . . during the commentary the camera slowly tracks in on his face.

Commentator But Mr F. G. Superman has a secret identity . . . when trouble strikes at any time . . . at any place . . . he is ready to become . . . Bicycle Repair Man!

The camera is by now in very tight close-up. A country lane. A Superman rides into shot on a bicycle, whistling innocently. Suddenly he veers off to one side and crashes down into a ditch.
Cut to a launderette. Pan along a row of Supermen, one or two of whom are poring over magazines such as: 'The Adventures of an Insurance Broker', 'Income Tax Comics' and 'The Grocer'. Suddenly the door flies open and a youngish Superboy bursts in dramatically.

Superboy (*dramatically*) Hey, there's a bicycle broken! Up the road. (*he points dramatically*)

General consternation.

Bicycle Repair Man (MICHAEL) (*voice over*) Mmmmmm. Thinks – this sounds like a job for Bicycle Repair Man . . . but how to change without revealing my secret identity?

Close-up F. G. Superman. He narrows his eyes.

First Superman (JOHN) *(heavily)* If only Bicycle Repair Man were here!

F. G. Superman *(heavily)* Yes. Wait! I think I know where I can find him – look over *there*!

F. G. Superman points out of window; they turn and look obediently.
F. G. Superman whips overalls out of case and puts them on.

CAPTION: 'FLASH!'

Fantastically speeded-up for this. His overalls have 'Bicycle Repair Man' written across the chest. He completes the transformation with a pair of little round specs and a bag of tools. He makes for the door and all the Supermen turn and raise their hands in amazement.

Supermen Bicycle Repair Man! But . . . how?!

Cut to three Supermen digging the road up. One suddenly looks up.

First Superman Oh look – is it a Stockbroker?

Second Superman (GRAHAM) Is it a Quantity Surveyor?

Third Superman (TERRY J) Is it a Church Warden?

All No! It's BICYCLE REPAIR MAN!

Country road. Superman is standing over the mangled bits looking at it and scratching his head. Bicycle Repair Man speeds up to him. Superman stands back in surprise, with arms raised.

Superman (TERRY J) My! BICYCLE REPAIR MAN! Thank goodness you've come! *(he points stiltedly)* Look!

Bicycle Repair Man pushes him to one side and kneels beside the broken bicycle. Speeded up: he mends the bike with spanners etc. Graphics.

CAPTIONS:
'CLINK!'
'SCREW!'
'BEND!'
'INFLATE!'
'ALTER SADDLE!'

A little group of Supermen has gathered to watch him work. As he does so they point in amazement.

Second Superman Why! He's mending it with his own hands.

First Superman See! How he uses a spanner to tighten that nut!

Cut to see Bicycle Repair Man presenting the Superman with a glittering drop-handlebarred bike.

Superman *(taking bike)* Oh . . . Oh! Bicycle Repair Man! How can I ever repay you!

Bicycle Repair Man Oh, you don't need to guv, it's all right, it's all in a day's work for . . . Bicycle Repair Man! *(he shuffles away)*

Supermen Our hero! *(shot of Bicycle Repair Man shuffling, speeded up, into sunset)*

Commentator (JOHN) Yes! Wherever bicycles are broken, or menaced by International Communism, Bicycle Repair Man is ready!

Cut to commentator in garden with earphones on, and in front of microphone, which is on a garden table.

Commentator Ready to smash the communists, wipe them up, and shove them off the face of the earth ... *(his voice rises hysterically)* Mash that dirty red scum, kick 'em in the teeth where it hurts. *(commentator rises from his canvas chair, and flails about wildly, waving script, kicking over table, knocking down sunshade)* Kill! Kill! Kill! The filthy bastard commies, I hate 'em! I hate 'em! Aaargh! Aaargh!

Wife *(off-screen)* Norman! Tea's ready.

He immediately looks frightened, and goes docile.

Commentator *(calmly)* Coming dear!

He gathers up his script, picks up chair, and walks out of frame. Pause, then the man in the suit of armour crosses frame after him.

ANIMATION: *Five seconds of Gilliam animation. To gentle children's programme music, we see bunnies jumping up and down.*
Cut to children's storyteller in studio.

Storyteller (ERIC) *(sitting with large children's book, at desk)* Hello, Children, hello. Here is this morning's story. Are you ready? Then we'll begin. *(opens book; reads)* 'One day Ricky the magic Pixie went to visit Daisy Bumble in her tumbledown cottage. He found her in the bedroom. Roughly he grabbed her heavy shoulders pulling her down on to the bed and ripping off her ...' *(reads silently, turns over page quickly, smiles)* 'Old Nick the Sea Captain was a rough tough jolly sort of fellow. He loved the life of the sea and he loved to hang out down by the pier where the men dressed as ladies ...' *(reads on silently; a stick enters vision and pokes him; he starts and turns over)* 'Rumpletweezer ran the Dinky Tinky shop in the foot of the magic oak tree by the wobbly dum dum bush in the shade of the magic glade down in Dingly Dell. Here he sold contraceptives and ... discipline? ... naked? ... (without looking up, reads a bit; then, incredulously to himself)* With a melon!?

ANIMATION: *A hippo squashes the bunnies ... and other things happen. Cut to a seaside beach. By a notice, 'Donkey Rides', run two men carrying a donkey. The compère addresses the camera.*

Compère (MICHAEL) Hello again, now here's a little sketch by two boys from London town. They've been writing for three years and they've called this little number – here it is, it's called – Restaurant sketch.

Film clip of Women's Institute applauding. A couple are seated at a table in a restaurant.

Lady (CAROL) It's nice here, isn't it?

Man (GRAHAM) Oh, very good restaurant, three stars you know.

Lady Really?

Man Mmm . . .

Waiter (TERRY J) Good evening, sir! Good evening, madam! And may I say what a pleasure it is to see you here again, sir!

Man Oh thank you. Well there you are dear. Have a look there, anything you like. The boeuf en croute is fantastic.

Waiter Oh if I may suggest, sir . . . the pheasant à la reine, the sauce is one of the chef's most famous creations.

Man Em . . . that sounds good. Anyway just have a look . . . take your time. Oh, er by the way – got a bit of a dirty fork, could you . . . er . . . get me another one?

Waiter I beg your pardon.

Man Oh it's nothing . . . er, I've got a fork a little bit dirty. Could you get me another one? Thank you.

Waiter Oh . . . sir, I do apologize.

Man Oh, no need to apologize, it doesn't worry me.

Waiter Oh no, no, no, I do apologize. I will fetch the head waiter immediatement.

Man Oh, there's no need to do that!

Waiter Oh, no no . . . I'm sure the head waiter, he will want to apologize to you himself. I will fetch him at once.

Lady Well, you certainly get good service here.

Man They really look after you . . . yes.

Head Waiter (MICHAEL) Excuse me monsieur and madame. *(examines the fork)* It's filthy, Gaston . . . find out who washed this up, and give them their cards immediately.

Man Oh, no, no.

Head Waiter Better still, we can't afford to take any chances, sack the entire washing-up staff.

Man No, look I don't want to make any trouble.

Head Waiter Oh, no please, no trouble. It's quite right that you should point these kind of things out. Gaston, tell the manager what has happened immediately! *(waiter runs off)*

Man Oh, no I don't want to cause any fuss.

Head Waiter Please, it's no fuss. I quite simply wish to ensure that nothing interferes with your complete enjoyment of the meal.

Man Oh I'm sure it won't, it was only a dirty fork.

Head Waiter I know. And I'm sorry, bitterly sorry, but I know that . . . no apologies I can make can alter the fact that in our restaurant you have been given a dirty, filthy, smelly piece of cutlery . . .

Man It wasn't smelly.

Head Waiter It was smelly, and obscene and disgusting and I hate it, I hate it . . . nasty, grubby, dirty, mingy, scrubby little fork. Oh . . . oh . . . oh . . . *(runs off in a passion as the manager comes to the table)*

Manager (ERIC) Good evening, sir, good evening, madam. I am the manager. I've only just heard . . . may I sit down?

Man Yes, of course.

Manager I want to apologize, humbly, deeply, and sincerely about the fork.

Man Oh please, it's only a tiny bit . . . I couldn't see it.

Manager Ah you're good kind fine people, for saying that, but *I* can see it . . . to me it's like a mountain, a vast bowl of pus.

Man It's not as bad as that.

Manager It gets me *here.* I can't give you any excuses for it – there *are* no excuses. I've been meaning to spend more time in the restaurant recently, but I haven't been too well . . . *(emotionally)* things aren't going very well back there. The poor cook's son has been put away again, and poor old Mrs Dalrymple who does the washing up can hardly move her poor fingers, and then there's Gilberto's war wound – but they're good people, and they're kind people, and together we were beginning to get over this dark patch . . . there was light at the end of the tunnel . . . now this . . . now this . . .

Man Can I get you some water?

Manager *(in tears)* It's the end of the road!!

The cook comes in; he is very big and carries a meat cleaver.

Cook (JOHN) *(shouting)* You bastards! You vicious, heartless bastards! Look what you've done to him! He's worked his fingers to the bone to make this place what it is, and you come in with your petty feeble quibbling and you grind him into the dirt, this fine, honourable man, whose boots you are not worthy to kiss. Oh . . . it makes me mad . . . mad! *(slams cleaver into the table)*

The head waiter comes in and tries to restrain him.

Head Waiter Easy, Mungo, easy . . . Mungo . . . *(clutches his head in agony)* the war wound! . . . the wound . . . the wound . . .

Manager This is the end! The end! Aaargh!! *(stabs himself with the fork)*

Cook They've destroyed him! He's dead!! They killed him!!! *(goes completely mad)*

Head Waiter *(trying to restrain him)* Mungo . . . never kill a customer. *(in pain)* Oh . . . the wound! The wound! *(he and the cook fight furiously and fall over the table)*

CAPTION: 'AND NOW THE PUNCH-LINE'

Man Lucky we didn't say anything about the dirty knife . . .

Boos of disgust from off-screen. Cut back to seaside.

Compère Well, there we are then, that was the restaurant sketch, a nice little number ... a bit vicious in parts, but a lot of fun ... but how about that punch-line, eh? ... Oh you know what I mean – oh ... oh ... really.

The man from the sketch borrows the knight's chicken and hits commentator with it.

A cartoon advertising 'Interesting Lives' leads to film of milkman (Michael) delivering milk to a suburban house. As he puts the milk down, the front door opens and a seductively dressed young lady (Carol) beckons him inside. Glancing round furtively he follows her into the house and up the stairs. She leads him to the bedroom door, opens it, and ushers him inside, closing the door behind him. Inside, he is bewildered to see several elderly milkmen, who have obviously been there for a very long time.

Cut to a BBC News studio, where the newsreader is just putting the phone down. At his desk is an old-fashioned microphone with 'BBC' on it. He is in evening dress, and speaks in beautifully modulated tones.

Newsreader (JOHN) Good evening, here is the 6 o'clock News read by Michael Queen. It's been a quiet day over most of the country as people went back to work after the warmest July weekend for nearly a year. The only high spot of the weekend was the meeting between officials of the NEDC and the ODCN in Bradford today.

At this point, axes split open the studio door behind him. Through the hole, men with stockings over their heads leap in firing guns in all directions. The newsreader continues, unperturbed. Cut to marauders pushing the newsreader, still at his desk down a passage in the BBC. They rush him out of the TV Centre and onto the back of a lorry.

Newsreader *(continuing)* In Geneva, officials of the Central Clearing Banks met with Herr Voleschtadt of Poland to discuss non-returnable loans on a twelve-year trust basis for the construction of a new zinc-treating works in the Omsk area of Krakow, near the Bulestan border. The Board of Trade has ratified a Trade Agreement with the Soviet Union for the sale of 600 low gear electric sewing machines. The President of the Board of Trade said he hoped this would mark a new area of expansion in world trade and a new spirit of co-operation between East and West. There has been a substantial drop in Gold Reserves during the last twelve months. This follows a statement by the Treasury to the effect that the balance of imports situation had not changed dramatically over the same period. *(cut to lorry hurtling through London with newsreader still reading news on the back (facing backwards); cut to lorry hurtling through country lane and flashing past camera)* Still no news of the National Savings book lost by Mr Charles Griffiths of Porthcawl during a field expedition to the

Nature Reserves of Swansea last July. Mr Griffiths' wife said that
her husband was refusing to talk to the Press until the Savings
Certificate had been found. *(cut to gang hoisting him on to the back of
an open lorry, still in desk etc.)* In Cornwall the death has been
announced today of the former Minister without Portfolio, General
Sir Hugh Marksby-Smith. Sir Hugh was vice-president of the
Rotarian movement. *(a long shot of a jetty; we see the gangsters pushing
the newsreader still on his desk along the jetty; they reach the end and
push him over into the sea)* In the match between Glamorgan and
Yorkshire, the Yorkshire bowler Nicholson took eight wickets for
three runs. Glamorgan were all out for the thirty-six and therefore
won the match by an innings and seven runs. Weather for
tomorrow will be cloudy with occasional outbreaks of rain. And
that is the end of the néws.

FX splash. Gurgle gurgle.

Voice Over (JOHN) and CAPTIONS

> 'AND NOW'
> 'NO. 1'
> 'THE LARCH'
> *Picture of larch tree.*

Voice Over The larch.

Voice Over and CAPTIONS:

> 'AND NOW'
> 'NO. 3'
> 'THE LARCH'
> 'AND NOW . . .'
> *Picture of chestnut tree.*

Voice Over The horse chestnut.

> *Film clip of cheering crowd. Then to interviewer bending down to speak to
> children in playground.*

Interviewer (JOHN) Eric . . . do you think you could recognize a larch
tree?

Eric (ERIC) *(after much deliberation)* Don't know.

> *Roars of delighted pre-recorded laughter from unseen audience.*

Interviewer What's your name?

Michael (MICHAEL) Michael.

> *Laughter.*

Interviewer Michael, do you think you know what a larch tree looks like?

Michael *(bursting into tears)* I want to go home.

> *Shrieks from unseen audience.*

Terry (TERRY J) Bottom!

> *More shrieks.*

Interviewer Are there any other trees that any of you think you could recognize from quite a long way away?

Terry I ... want ... to see a sketch of Eric's please ...

Interviewer What?

Terry I want to see a sketch of Eric's. Nudge Nudge.

Interviewer A sketch?

Terry Eric's written ...

Eric I written a sketch.

Michael Nudge nudge, Eric's written ...

Eric Nudge nudge ... nudge ... nudge.

> *Two men in a pub.*

Norman (ERIC) Is your wife a ... goer ... eh? Know what I mean? Know what I mean? Nudge nudge. Nudge nudge. Know what I mean? Say no more ... know what I mean?

Him (TERRY J) I beg your pardon?

Norman Your wife ... does she, er, does she 'go' – eh? eh? eh? Know what I mean, know what I mean? Nudge nudge. Say no more.

Him She sometimes goes, yes.

Norman I bet she does. I bet she does. I bet she does. Know what I mean? Nudge nudge.

Him I'm sorry, I don't quite follow you.

Norman Follow me! *Follow* me! I like that. That's good. A nod's as good as a wink to a blind bat, eh? *(elbow gesture; rubs it)*

Him Are you trying to sell something?

Norman Selling, selling. Very good. *Very* good. *(hand tilting quickly)* Oh, wicked. Wicked. You're wicked. Eh? Know what I mean? Know what I mean? Nudge nudge. Know what I mean? Nudge nudge. Nudge nudge. *(leaning over to him, making eye gesture; speaks slowly)* Say ... no ... more. *(leans back as if having imparted a great secret)*

Him But ...

Norman *(stops him with finger which he lays alongside nose; gives slight tap)* Your wife is she, eh ... is she a sport? Eh?

Him She *likes* sport, yes.

Norman I bet she does. I bet she does.

Him She's very fond of cricket, as a matter of fact.

Norman *(leans across, looking away)* Who isn't, eh? Know what I mean? Likes games, likes games. Knew she would. Knew she would! Knew she would! She's been around, eh? Been around?

Him She's travelled. She's from Purley.

Norman Oh ... oh. Say no more, say no more. Say no more – *Purley*, say no more. Purley, eh. Know what I mean, know what I mean? Say no more.

Him *(about to speak; can't think of anything to say)*

Norman *(leers, grinning)* Your wife interested in er ... *(waggles head, leans* *across)* photographs, eh? Know what I mean? Photographs, 'he asked him knowingly'.

Him Photography.

Norman Yes. Nudge nudge. Snap snap. Grin, grin, wink, wink, say no more.

Him Holiday snaps?

Norman Could be, could be taken on holiday. Could be yes – swimming costumes. Know what I mean? Candid photography. Know what I mean, nudge nudge.

Him No, no we don't have a camera.

Norman Oh. Still *(slaps hands lightly twice)* Woah! Eh? Wo-oah! Eh?

Him Look, are you insinuating something?

Norman Oh ... no ... no ... Yes.

Him Well?

Norman Well. I mean. Er, I mean. You're a man of the world, aren't you ... I mean, er, you've er ... you've been there haven't you ... I mean you've been around ... eh?

Him What do you mean?

Norman Well I mean like you've er ... you've done it ... I mean like, you know ... you've ... er ... you've slept ... with a lady.

Him Yes.

Norman What's it like?

Enormous artificial laugh on sound track. Closing film, starting with referee blowing whistle and then into 'It's' man running away from camera.

ROLLER CAPTION: ' "HOW TO RECOGNIZE DIFFERENT TYPES OF TREES FROM QUITE A LONG WAY AWAY" WAS CONCEIVED, WRITTEN AND PERFORMED BY ... (CREDITS)'

Voice Over The larch.

Four Owl-stretching time

> *A cliff. Suddenly the 'It's' man is thrown over it, landing on the shale beach beneath. Painfully he crawls towards the camera and announces:*

Man (MICHAEL) It's . . .

Voice Over (JOHN) and CAPTION: 'MONTY PYTHON'S FLYING CIRCUS'

> CAPTION: 'EPISODE ARTHUR'
> CAPTION: 'PART 7'
> CAPTION: 'TEETH'

> *Singer in spangly jacket sitting on high stool with guitar.*

Singer (ERIC) *(singing to the tune of Jerusalem)* And did those teeth in ancient time . . .

> CAPTION: 'LIVE FROM THE CARDIFF ROOMS, LIBYA'

Singer . . . walk upon England's mountains green. *(he stops playing)* Good evening and welcome ladies and gentlemen. At this time we'd like to up the tempo a little, change the mood. We've got a number requested by Pip, Pauline, Nigel, Tarquin, and old Spotty – Tarquin's mother – a little number specially written for the pubescence of ex-King Zog of Albania, and it's entitled 'Art Gallery'. Hope you like it.

> *Interior of art gallery. Two figures enter. They are both middle-aged working mothers. Each holds the hand of an unseen infant who is beneath the range of the camera.*

Janet (JOHN) 'Allo, Marge!

Marge (GRAHAM) Oh hello, Janet, how are you love?

Janet Fancy seeing you! How's little Ralph?

Marge Oh, don't ask me! He's been nothing but trouble all morning. Stop it Ralph! *(she slaps at unseen infant)* Stop it!

Janet Same as my Kevin.

Marge Really?

Janet Nothing but trouble . . . leave it alone! He's just been in the Florentine Room and smeared tomato ketchup all over Raphael's Baby Jesus. *(shouting off sharply)* Put that Baroque masterpiece down!

Marge Well, we've just come from the Courtauld and Ralph smashed every exhibit but one in the Danish Contemporary Sculpture Exhibition.

Janet Just like my Kevin. Show him an exhibition of early eighteenth-century Dresden Pottery and he goes berserk. No, I said no, and I meant no! *(smacks unseen infant again)* This morning we were viewing the early Flemish Masters of the Renaissance and Mannerist Schools, when he gets out his black aerosol and squirts Vermeer's Lady At A Window!

Marge Still, it's not as bad as spitting, is it?

Janet *(firmly)* No, well Kevin knows *(slaps the infant)* that if he spits at a painting I'll never take him to an exhibition again.

Marge Ralph used to spit – he could hit a Van Gogh at thirty yards. But he knows now it's wrong – don't you Ralph? *(she looks down)* Ralph! Stop it! Stop it! Stop chewing that Turner! You are . . . *(she disappears from shot)* You are a naughty, naughty, vicious little boy. *(smack; she comes back into shot holding a copy of Turner's Fighting Temeraire in a lovely gilt frame but all tattered)* Oh, look at that! The Fighting Temeraire – ruined! What shall I do?

Janet *(taking control)* Now don't do a thing with it love, just put it in the bin over there.

Marge Really?

Janet Yes take my word for it, Marge. Kevin's eaten most of the early nineteenth-century British landscape artists, and I've learnt not to worry. As a matter of fact, I feel a bit peckish myself. *(she breaks a bit off the Turner)* Yes . . .

Marge also tastes a bit.

Marge I never used to like Turner.

Janet *(swallowing)* No . . . I don't know much about art, but I know what I like.

Cut to a book-lined study. At a desk in front of the shelves sits an art critic with a mouthful of Utrillo.

SUPERIMPOSED CAPTION: 'AN ART CRITIC'

Critic (MICHAEL) *(taking out stringy bits as he speaks)* Mmmm . . . *(munches)* Well I think Utrillo's brushwork is fantastic . . . *(stifles burp)* But he doesn't always agree with me . . . *(belches)* Not after a Rubens, anyway . . . all those cherries . . . ooohh . . . *(suddenly looks down)* Urgh! I've got Vermeer all down my shirt . . .

Wife (KATYA) *(bringing in a water jug and glass on a tray and laying it on his desk)* Watteau, dear?

Critic What a terrible joke.

Wife But it's my only line.

Critic *(rising vehemently)* All right! All right! But you didn't *have* to say it! You could have kept quiet for a change!

Wife cries.

Critic Oh, that's typical. Talk talk talk. Natter natter natter!

Cut back to singer.

Singer *(singing)* Bring me my arrows of desire . . . Bring me my spear oh clouds unfold . . . Bring me my chariot of fire.

A sexy girl (Katya Wyeth) enters and starts fondling him.

CAPTION: 'IT'S A MAN'S LIFE IN THE CARDIFF ROOMS, LIBYA'

Cut to colonel: army recruitment posters on wall behind him.

Colonel (GRAHAM) Right, cut to me. As Officer Commanding the Regular Army's Advertising Division, I object, in the strongest possible terms, to this obvious reference to our own slogan 'It's a dog's life . . . *(correcting himself rapidly)* a man's life in the modern army' and I warn this programme that any recurrence of this sloppy long-haired civilian plagiarism will be dealt with most severely. Right, now on the command 'cut', the camera will cut to camera two, all right, director . . . *(cut to a man sitting at desk)* Wait for it! *(cut back to colonel)* Camera cut. *(cut to man; he has a Viking helmet on)*

Man (TERRY G) This is my only line. *(catcalls)* *(defensively)* Well, it's my only line.

Cut to a gentleman (Terry J) in striped blazer, boater and cricket flannels walking down to beach clutching towel and bathing trunks. He puts his towel on a breakwater next to another towel and starts to change. He suddenly looks up and we see everyone on the beach has turned to watch him – not with any disapproval – just a blank English stare. He grabs his towel off the breakwater and starts to take his trousers off under that. Girl in a bikini has been sitting on other side of the breakwater, stands up looking for her towel. She sees that the man is using it and she whisks it off him leaving him clutching his half-down trousers. Shot of everyone staring at him again. He pulls them up and makes for a beach hut . . . embarrassed. He goes into beach hut. Inside he is about to take his trousers off, when he becomes aware of a pair of feet which come up to the back of the beach hut – there is a 6-inch gap along bottom – and stop as if someone were peering through the crack. The man looks slightly outraged and pulls his trousers up, goes outside and edges cautiously round to the back of the beach hut. There he finds a man (Michael) bending close to the side of the beach hut with his hand to his face. Terry kicks him hard in the seat of the pants. The man turns in obvious surprise, to reveal he was merely trying to light his cigarette out of the wind. The changing gentleman backs away with embarrassed apologies. We cut to the front of the beach hut to see gentleman backing round at the same time as a large matronly woman marches into the hut . . . the man follows her in. He is promptly thrown out on his ear. In desperation he looks around. On the promenade he suddenly sees an ice-cream van. He walks up to it, looks around, then nips behind to start changing. At the same time a policeman (Graham) strolls up to the ice-cream van and tells it to move on. The van drives off, exposing the gentleman clutching his trousers round his ankles. Close-up policeman's reaction. The man hurriedly pulls trousers up as policeman approaches him pulling out note book. Still covered in confusion he runs away from the policeman. In long shot we see him approach the commissionaire of the Royale Palace De Luxe Hotel. He whispers to the commissionaire, indicates by mime that

*he wants to take his trousers off. The commissionaire reacts to the gesture.
The man nods. The commissionaire starts to take his trousers off. Man
backs away once more in confusion – he has been misunderstood. Back on
the beach again. He hides behind a pile of deckchairs. At that moment a
beach party of jolly trippers arrive and each takes one. The deckchair pile
rapidly disappears leaving the gentleman once again exposed. He dashes
behind the deckchair attendant's hut which is next to him. Enter two
workmen who dismantle it. Desperate by now he goes onto the pier. He
goes into the amusement arcade, looking around furtively. Nips behind a
'what the butler saw' machine. Woman comes and puts penny in and
starts to look, beckons over husband; he comes, looks in the machine, sees
the man changing his trousers. They chase him off. Still pursued he nips
into door. Finds himself in blackness. Relieved – at last he has found
somewhere to change. He relaxes and starts to take his trousers off.
Suddenly hears music and applause . . . curtains swishes back to reveal he
is on stage of the pier pavilion. The audience applauds. Resigned to his
fate, he breaks into striptease routine.*

Voice Over and CAPTION: 'IT'S A MAN'S LIFE TAKING YOUR CLOTHES
OFF IN PUBLIC'

Cut to colonel.

Colonel Quiet. Quiet. Now wait a minute. I have already warned this
programme about infringing the Army copyright of our slogan 'It's
a pig's life . . . *man's* life in the modern army'. And I'm warning
you if it happens again, I shall come down on this programme like
a ton of bricks . . . right. Carry on sergeant major.

A gym. Four men waiting there, with an ex-RSM type.

RSM (JOHN) Sir! Good evening class.

All Good evening.

RSM Where's all the others then?

All They're not here.

RSM I can see that. What's the matter with them?

All Don't know.

First Man (GRAHAM) Perhaps they've got flu.

RSM Flu . . . flu? They've eaten too much fresh fruit. *(does terrible twitch
or tic)* Right. Now, self-defence. Tonight I shall be carrying on
from where I got to last week, when I was showing you how to
defend yourself against anyone who attacks you armed with a piece
of fresh fruit.

All *(disappointed)* Oh.

Second Man (MICHAEL) You promised you wouldn't do fruit this week.

RSM What do you mean?

Third Man (TERRY J) We've done fruit for the last nine weeks.

RSM What's wrong with fruit? You think you know it all, eh?

Second Man But couldn't we do something else, for a change?

Fourth Man (ERIC)   Like someone who attacks you with a pointed stick?

RSM *(scornfully)*   Pointed sticks! Ho ho ho. We want to learn how to defend ourselves against pointed sticks, do we? Getting all high and mighty, eh? Fresh fruit not good enough for you, eh? Oh well, well, well, I'll tell you something my lad. When you're walking home tonight and some homicidal maniac comes after you with a bunch of loganberries, don't come crying to me. Right . . . the passion fruit. When your assailant lunges at you with a passion fruit, thus . . . *(demonstrates)*

All   We've done the passion fruit.

RSM   What?

First Man   We've done the passion fruit.

Second Man   We've done oranges, apples, grapefruits.

Third Man   Whole and segments.

Second Man   Pomegranates, greengages.

First Man   Grapes, passion fruits.

Second Man   Lemons.

Third Man   Plums.

First Man   Yes, and mangoes in syrup.

RSM   How about cherries?

All   We done them.

RSM   Red *and* black?

All   Yes.

RSM   All right then . . . bananas!

All   Oh.

RSM   We haven't done them have we?

All   No.

RSM   Right! Bananas! How to defend yourself against a man armed with a banana. *(to first man)* Here, you, take this. *(throws him a banana)* Now it's quite simple to defend yourself against the banana fiend. First of all, you force him to drop the banana, next, you eat the banana, thus disarming him. You have now rendered him helpless.

Second Man   Supposing he's got a bunch.

RSM   Shut up!

Fourth Man   Supposing he's got a pointed stick.

RSM   Shut up. Right. Now, you, Mr Apricot.

First Man   Harrison.

RSM   Harrison, Mr Harrison. Come at me with that banana then. Come on attack me with it. As hard as you like. Come on. *(Harrison moves towards him rather half-heartedly)* No no no. Put something into it for God's sake. Hold it, like that. Scream. Now come on, come on . . . attack me, come on, come on *(Harrison runs towards him shouting; RSM draws a revolver and fires it, right in Harrison's face; Harrison dies immediately, falling to the ground; RSM puts gun away and walks to banana)* Now . . . I eat the banana.

He does so; the rest of the class gather round Mr Harrison's body.

All You shot him. He's dead . . . dead. He's completely dead. You've shot him.

RSM *(finishing the banana)* I have now eaten the banana. The deceased Mr Apricot is now disarmed.

Second Man You shot him. You shot him dead.

RSM Well he was attacking me with a banana.

Third Man Well, you told him to.

RSM Look, I'm only doing me job. I have to show you how to defend yourself against fresh fruit.

Fourth Man And pointed sticks.

RSM Shut up!

Second Man Supposing someone came at you with a banana and you haven't got a gun?

RSM Run for it.

Third Man You could stand and scream for help.

RSM You try that with a pineapple down your windpipe.

Third Man A pineapple?

RSM *(jumping with fear)* Where? Where?

Third Man Nowhere. I was just saying pineapple.

RSM Oh blimey. I thought my number was on that one.

Third Man *(amazed)* What, on the pineapple?

RSM *(jumping)* Where? Where?

Third Man No I was just repeating it.

RSM Oh. Oh! Right. That's the banana then. Next . . . the raspberry. *(pulling one out of pocket)* Harmless looking thing, isn't it. Now you, Mr Tinned Peach . . .

Third Man Thompson.

RSM Mr Thompson, come at me with that raspberry then. Come on, be as vicious as you like with it.

Third Man No.

RSM Why not?

Third Man You'll shoot me.

RSM I won't.

Third Man You shot Mr Harrison.

RSM That was self-defence. Come on. I promise I won't shoot you.

Fourth Man You promised you'd tell us about pointed sticks.

RSM Shut up. Now. Brandish that . . . brandish that raspberry. Come on, be as vicious as you like with it. Come on.

Third Man No. Throw the gun away.

RSM I haven't got a gun.

Third Man Oh yes, you have.

RSM I haven't.

Third Man You have. You shot Mr Harrison with it.

RSM Oh . . . *that* gun.

Third Man Throw it away.

RSM All right. *(throws it away)* How to defend yourself against a
raspberry, without a gun.

Third Man You were going to shoot me!

RSM I wasn't.

Third Man You were.

RSM Wasn't. Come on, come on you worm . . . you miserable little man.
Come at me then . . . come on, do your worst, you worm. *(third
man runs at him; the RSM steps back and pulls a lever; a sixteen-ton
weight falls upon the man)* If anyone ever attacks you with a
raspberry, simply pull the lever . . . and a sixteen-ton weight will
drop on his head. I learnt that in Malaya.

Second Man Suppose you haven't got a sixteen-ton weight.

RSM Well that's planning, isn't it. Forethought.

Second Man How many sixteen-ton weights are there?

RSM Look . . . look, smarty pants, the sixteen-ton weight is just one way,
just one way of dealing with the raspberry killer. There are millions
of others.

Second Man Like what?

RSM Shoot him.

Second Man Well, supposing you haven't got a gun or a sixteen-ton
weight.

RSM All right clever dick, all right clever dick. You two, come at me with
raspberries, there you are, a whole basket each. Come on, come at
me with them, then.

Second Man No gun?

RSM No.

Second Man No sixteen-ton weight?

RSM No.

Fourth Man No pointed stick?

RSM Shut up.

Second Man No rocks up in the ceiling?

RSM No.

Second Man You won't kill us.

RSM I won't kill you.

Second Man Promise.

RSM I promise I won't kill you. Now are you going to attack me?

Second and Fourth Men All right.

RSM Right, now don't rush me this time. I'm going to turn me back. So
you can stalk me . . . right? Come up as quietly as you can, right
close up behind me, then, in with the raspberries, right? Start
moving *(they start to creep up on him)* Now . . . the first thing to do
when you're being stalked by an ugly mob with raspberries, is to
. . . release the tiger. *(he presses button and a tiger flashes past him in
direction of second and fourth men; cries are heard from them as well as*

roaring) The great advantage of the tiger in unarmed combat is that it not only eats the raspberry-laden foe, but also the raspberries. The tiger, however, does not relish the peach. The peach assailant should be attacked with a crocodile. *(he turns to look at the scene)* Right . . . I know you're there – lurking under the floorboards with your damsons and your prunes . . . now, the rest of you – I know you're hiding behind the wall bars with your quinces. Well I'm ready for you. I've wired myself up to two hundred tons of gelignite and if any of you so much as tries anything we'll all go up together. I've warned you . . . I warned you, right! That's it.
Big explosion.

ANIMATION: *Ends with cut-out animation of sedan chair; matching shot links into next film.*
Cut to deserted beach. Sedan chair arrives at deserted beach. Flunkey opens the door. Gentleman gets out in his eighteenth-century finery. The flunkeys help him to change into a lace-trimmed striped bathing costume. He then gets back into the sedan chair and they all trot off into the sea. Cut to singer in bed with woman. Singer reclining with guitar, strumming.

Singer And did those feet in ancient times, walk upon England's mountains green . . . we'd like to alter the mood a little, we'd like to bring you something for mum and dad, Annie, and Roger, Mazarin and Louis and all at Versailles, it's a little number called 'England's Mountains Green'. Hope you like it. And did those feet in ancient time . . .
Cut to a man standing in the countryside.

Man (JOHN) *(rustic accent)* Yes, you know it's a man's life in England's Mountain Green.
The colonel enters briskly.

Colonel (GRAHAM) Right I heard that, I heard that, I'm going to stop this sketch now, and if there's any more of this, I'm going to stop the whole programme. I thought it was supposed to be about teeth anyway. Why don't you do something about teeth – go on. *(walks off)*

Man What about my rustic monologue? . . . I'm not sleeping with that producer again.
Cut to film of various sporting activities, wild west stage coach etc.

Voice Over (JOHN) *(with big music, excited)* Excitement, drama, action, violence, fresh fruit. Passion. Thrills. Spills. Romance. Adventure, all the things you can read about in a book.
Cut to bookshop. A bookseller is standing behind the counter. Arthur enters the shot and goes up to the counter. The bookseller jumps and looks around furtively.

Bookseller (JOHN) Er . . . oh!

Arthur (ERIC) Good morning, I'd like to buy a book please.

Bookseller Oh, well I'm afraid we don't have any. *(trying to hide them)*

Arthur I'm sorry?

Bookseller We don't have any books. We're fresh out of them. Good morning.

Arthur Well what are all these?

Bookseller All what? Oh! All these, ah ah ha ha. You're referring to these . . . books.

Arthur Yes.

Bookseller They're um . . . they're all sold. Good morning.

Arthur What *all* of them?

Bookseller Every single man Jack of them. Not a single one of them in an unsold state. Good morning.

Arthur Who to?

Bookseller What?

Arthur Who are they sold to?

Bookseller Oh . . . various . . . good Lord is that the time? Oh my goodness I must close for lunch.

Arthur It's only half past ten.

Bookseller Ah yes, well I feel rather peckish . . . very peckish actually, I don't expect I'll open again today. I think I'll have a really good feed. I say! Look at that lovely bookshop just across the road there, they've got a much better selection than we've got, probably at ridiculously low prices . . . just across the road there. *(he has the door open)* Good morning.

Arthur But I was told to come here.

Bookseller *(bundling him back in)* Well. Well, I see. Er . . . *(very carefully)* I hear the gooseberries are doing well this year . . . and so are the mangoes. *(winks)*

Arthur I'm sorry?

Bookseller Er . . . oh . . . I was just saying . . . thinking of the weather . . . I hear the gooseberries are doing well this year . . . and so are the mangoes.

Arthur Mine aren't.

Bookseller *(nodding keenly with anticipation)* Go on . . .

Arthur What?

Bookseller Go on – mine aren't . . . but . . .

Arthur What?

Bookseller Aren't you going to say something about 'mine aren't but the Big Cheese gets his at low tide tonight'?

Arthur No.

Bookseller Oh, ah, good morning. *(starts to bundle him out then stops)* Wait. Who sent you?

Arthur The little old lady in the sweet shop.

Bookseller She didn't have a duelling scar just here . . . and a hook?

Arthur No.

Bookseller Of course not, I was thinking of somebody else. Good morning.

Arthur Wait a minute, there's something going on here.

Bookseller *(spinning round)* What, where? You didn't see anything did you?

Arthur No, but I think there's something going on here.

Bookseller No no, well there's nothing going on here at all *(shouts off)* and he didn't see anything. Good morning.

Arthur *(coming back into shop)* There *is* something going on.

Bookseller Look there is nothing going on. Please believe me, there is abso . . . *(a hand comes into view behind Arthur's back; bookseller frantically waves at it to disappear; it does so)* . . . lutely nothing going on. Is there anything going on?

A man appears, fleetingly: he is Van der Berg (Dick Vosburgh).

Van der Berg No there's nothing going on. *(disappears)*

Bookseller See there's nothing going on.

Arthur Who was that?

Bookseller That was my aunt, look what was this book you wanted then? Quickly! Quickly!

Arthur Oh, well, I'd like to buy a copy of an 'Illustrated History of False Teeth'.

Bookseller My God you've got guts.

Arthur What?

Bookseller *(pulling gun)* Just how much do you know?

Arthur What about?

Bookseller Are you from the British Dental Association?

Arthur No I'm a tobacconist.

Bookseller Get away from that door.

Arthur I'll just go over the other . . .

Bookseller Stay where you are. You'd never leave this bookshop alive.

Arthur Why not?

Bookseller You know too much, my dental friend.

Arthur I don't know anything.

Bookseller Come clean. You're a dentist aren't you.

Arthur No, I'm a tobacconist.

Bookseller A tobacconist who just happens to be buying a book on . . . teeth?

Arthur Yes.

Bookseller Ha ha ha ha . . .

Lafarge enters room with gun. He is swarthy, French, dressed all in black and menacing.

Lafarge (MICHAEL) Drop that gun, Stapleton.

Bookseller Lafarge! *(he drops the gun)*

Arthur There is something going on.

Bookseller No there isn't.

Lafarge OK Stapleton, this is it. Where's Mahoney hidden the fillings?

Bookseller What fillings?

Lafarge You know which fillings, Stapleton. Upper right two and four, lower right three and two lower left one. Come on. *(he threatens with the gun)* Remember what happened to Nigel.

Arthur What happened to Nigel?

Bookseller Orthodontic Jake gave him a gelignite mouth wash.

Arthur I knew there was something going on.

Bookseller Well there isn't.

Lafarge Come on Stapleton. The fillings!

Bookseller They're at 22 Wimpole Street.

Lafarge Don't play games with me! *(pokes bookseller in eye with the gun)*

Bookseller Oh, oh, 22a Wimpole Street.

Lafarge That's better.

Bookseller But you'll need an appointment.

Lafarge OK *(shouting out of shop)* Brian! Make with the appointment baby. No gas.

> *Van der Berg appears with machine gun and a nurse (Katya), he is basically dressed as a dentist. But with many rings, chains, wristlets, cravats, buckled shoes and an ear-ring.*

Van der Berg Not so fast Lafarge!

Lafarge Van der Berg!

Van der Berg Yes. Now drop the roscoe.

Arthur There *is* something going on.

Bookseller No there isn't.

Van der Berg Get the guns.

> *The nurse runs forward, picks up the gun and puts it on steel surgeon's tray and covers it with a white cloth, returning it to Van der Berg.*

Arthur Who's that?

Bookseller That's Van der Berg. He's on our side.

Van der Berg All right, get up against the wall Lafarge, and you too Stapleton.

Bookseller Me?

Van der Berg Yes, you!

Bookseller You dirty double-crossing rat.

Arthur *(going with bookseller)* What's happened?

Bookseller He's two-timed me.

Arthur Bad luck.

Van der Berg All right . . . where are the fillings? Answer me, where are they?

Arthur This is quite exciting.

Brian enters carrying a bazooka. Brian is dressed in operating-theatre clothes, gown, cap and mask, with rubber gloves and white wellingtons.

Brian (TERRY J) Not so fast.

All Brian!

Arthur Ooh, what's that?

The Others It's a bazooka.

Brian All right. Get against the wall Van der Berg . . . and you nurse. And the first one to try anything moves to a practice six feet underground . . . this is an anti-tank gun . . . and it's loaded . . . and you've just got five seconds to tell me . . . whatever happened to Baby Jane?

All What?

Brian Oh . . . I'm sorry . . . my mind was wandering . . . I've had a terrible day . . . I really have . . . you've got five seconds to tell me . . . I've forgotten. I've forgotten.

Bookseller The five seconds haven't started yet have they?

Van der Berg Only we don't know the question.

Arthur Was it about Vogler?

Brian No, no . . . no . . . you've got five seconds to tell me . . .

Van der Berg About Nigel?

Brian No.

Lafarge Bronski?

Brian No. No.

Arthur The fillings!

Brian Oh yes, the fillings, of course. How stupid of me. Right, you've got five seconds . . . *(clears throat)* Where are the fillings? Five, four, three, two, one, zero! *(there is a long pause, Brian has forgotten to fire the bazooka but he can't put his finger on what has gone wrong)* Zero! *(looks at gun)* Oh! I've forgotten to fire it. Sorry. Silly day. Very well. *(quite rapidly)* Five, four, three, two, one.

A panel slides back and the Big Cheese appears in sight seated in a dentist's chair. The Big Cheese is in dentist's gear, wears evil magnifying-type glasses and strokes a rabbit lying on his lap.)

Big Cheese (GRAHAM) Drop the bazooka Brian.

All The Big Cheese!

Brian drops the bazooka.

Big Cheese I'm glad you could all come to my little . . . party. And Flopsy's glad too, aren't you, Flopsy? *(he holds rabbit up as it does not reply)* Aren't you Flopsy? *(no reply again so he pulls a big revolver out and fires at rabbit from point-blank range)* That'll teach you to play hard to get. There, poor Flopsy's dead. And never called me mother. And soon . . . you will all be dead, dead, dead, dead. *(the crowd start to hiss him)* And because I'm so evil you'll all die the slow way . . . under the drill.

Arthur It's one o'clock.

Big Cheese So it is. Lunch break, everyone back here at two.

They all happily relax and walk off. Arthur surreptitiously goes to telephone and, making sure nobody is looking, calls.

Arthur Hallo ... give me the British Dental Association ... and fast.

Cut to Arthur dressed normally as dentist leaning over patient in chair. He looks up to camera.

Arthur You see, I knew there was something going on. Of course, the Big Cheese made two mistakes. First of all he didn't recognize me: Lemming, Arthur Lemming, Special Investigator, British Dental Association, and second ... *(to patient)* spit ... by the time I got back from lunch I had every dental surgeon in SW1 waiting for them all in the broom cupboard. Funny isn't it, how naughty dentists always make that one fatal mistake. Bye for now ... keep your teeth clean.

Cut to photo of Arthur Lemming.

SUPERIMPOSED CAPTION: 'LEMMING OF THE BDA'

Over this we hear a song which Graham knows the tune of.

Song *(Voice over pre-recorded)* Lemming, Lemming ... Lemming of the BDA ... Lemming, Lemming ... Lemming of the BD ... Lemming of the BD ... BD, BDA.

Voice Over (ERIC) and CAPTION: 'IT'S A MAN'S LIFE IN THE BRITISH DENTAL ASSOCIATION'

Colonel *(knocking the photo aside)* Right! No, I warned you, no, I warned you about the slogan, right. That's the end. Stop the programme! Stop it.

Cut to referee blowing whistle.

The 'It's' man, lying on beach, is poked with a stick from off-screen. He gets up and limps away.

CAPTION: '"OWL-STRETCHING TIME" WAS CONCEIVED, WRITTEN AND PERFORMED BY ... (CREDITS)'

End titles finish as the 'It's' man reaches the top of the cliff and disappears. As soon as he has disappeared we hear:

Voice Over (GRAHAM) Ah! Got you my lad. Still acting eh? Over you go! *'It's' man reappears hurled back over cliff.*

Five Man's crisis of identity in the latter half of the twentieth century

A river. The 'It's' man rows towards the camera and announces:

Man (MICHAEL) It's . . .

Voice Over (JOHN) and CAPTION: MONTY PYTHON'S FLYING CIRCUS
> *Title animation.*

> SUPERIMPOSED CAPTION: 'SUBURBAN LOUNGE NEAR ESHER'
> *Elderly couple, Mr A and Mrs B are staring through french windows at a cat that is sitting in the middle of their lawn motionless and facing away from them. A car is heard drawing up.*

Mr A (MICHAEL) Oh good, that'll be the vet, dear.

Mrs B (TERRY J) I'd better go and let him in.
> *Mrs B goes out and comes back into the room with the vet.*

Mrs B *(stage whisper)* It's the vet, dear.

Mr A Oh very glad indeed you could come round, sir.

Vet (GRAHAM) Not at all. Now what seems to be the problem? You can tell me – I'm a vet, you know.

Mrs B See! Tell him, dear.

Mr A Well . . .

Mrs B It's our cat. He doesn't do anything. He just sits out there on the lawn.

Vet Is he . . . dead?

Mr A Oh, no!

Vet *(to camera, dramatically)* Thank God for that. For one ghastly moment I thought I was . . . too late. If only more people would call in the nick of time.

Mrs B He just sits there, all day and every day.

Mr A And at night.

Mrs B Sh! Almost motionless. We have to take his food out to him.

Mr A And his milk.

Mrs B Sh! He doesn't do anything. He just sits there.

Vet Are you at your wits' end?

Mrs B Definitely, yes.

Vet Hm. I see. Well I think I may be able to help you. You see . . . *(he goes over to armchair, puts on spectacles, sits, crosses legs and puts finger tips together) . . .* your cat is suffering from what we vets haven't found a word for. His condition is typified by total physical inertia, absence of interest in its ambience – what we vets call environment – failure to respond to the conventional external stimuli – a ball of string, a nice juicy mouse, a bird. To be blunt, your cat is in a rut. It's the old stockbroker syndrome, the suburban fin de siècle ennui, angst, weltschmertz, call it what you will.

Mrs B Moping.

Vet In a way, in a way ... hum ... moping, I must remember that. Now, what's to be done? Tell me sir, have you confused your cat recently?

Mr A Well we ...

Mrs B Sh! No.

Vet Yes ... well I think I can definitely say that your cat badly needs to be confused.

Mrs B What?

Mr A Sh! What?

Vet Confused. To shake it out of its state of complacency. I'm afraid I'm not personally qualified to confuse cats, but I can recommend an extremely good service. Here is their card.

Mrs B *(reading card)* Oooh. 'Confuse-a-Cat Limited'.

Mr A 'Confuse-a-Cat Limited'.

Mrs B Oh.

Cut to large van arriving. On one side of van is a large sign reading 'Confuse-a-Cat Limited: Europe's leading cat-confusing service. By appointment to ...' and a crest. Several people get out of the van, dressed in white coats, with peaked caps and insignia. One of them has a sergeant's stripes.

Sergeant (MICHAEL) Squad! Eyes front! Stand at ease. Cat confusers ... shun!

From a following car a general alights.

General (JOHN) Well men, we've got a pretty difficult cat to confuse today so let's get straight on with it. Jolly good. Thank you sergeant.

Sergeant Confusers attend to the van and fetch out ... wait for it ... fetch out the funny things. *(the men unload the van)* Move, move, move. One, two, one, two, get those funny things off.

The workmen are completing the erection of a proscenium with curtains in front of the still immobile cat. A and B watch with awe. The arrangements are completed. All stand ready.

Sergeant Stage ready for confusing, sir!

General Very good. Carry on, sergeant.

Sergeant Left turn, double march!

General Right men, confuse the ... cat!

Drum roll and cymbals. The curtains draw back and an amazing show takes place, using various tricks: locked camera, fast motion, jerky motion, jump cuts, some pixilated motion etc. Long John Silver walks to front of stage.

Long John Silver My lords, ladies and Gedderbong.

*Long John Silver disappears. A pause. Two boxers appear. They circle
each other. On one's head a bowler hat appears, vanishes. On the other's
a stove-pipe hat appears. On the first's head a fez. The stove-pipe hat
becomes a stetson. The fez becomes a cardinal's hat. The stetson becomes a
wimple. Then the cardinal's hat and the wimple vanish. One of the
boxers becomes Napoleon and the other boxer is astonished. Napoleon
punches the boxer with the hand inside his jacket. The boxer falls,
stunned. Horizontally he shoots off stage. Shot of cat, watching
unimpressed. Napoleon does one-legged pixilated dance across stage and
off, immediately reappearing on other side of stage doing same dance in
same direction. He reaches the other side, but is halted by a traffic
policeman. The policeman beckons onto the stage a man in a penguin skin
on a pogostick. The penguin gets half way across and then turns into a
dustbin. Napoleon hops off stage. Policeman goes to dustbin, opens it and
Napoleon gets out. Shot of cat, still unmoved. A nude man with a towel
round his waist gets out of the dustbin. Napoleon points at ground. A
chair appears where he points. The nude man gets on to the chair, jumps
in the air and vanishes. Then Napoleon points to ground by him and a
small cannon appears. Napoleon fires cannon and the policeman
disappears. The man with the towel round his waist gets out of the
dustbin and is chased off stage by the penguin on the pogostick. A sedan
chair is carried on stage by two chefs. The man with the towel gets out
and the penguin appears from the dustbin and chases him off. Napoleon
points to sedan chair and it changes into dustbin. Man in towel runs
back on to stage and jumps in dustbin. He looks out and the penguin
appears from the other dustbin and hits him on the head with a raw
chicken. Shot of cat still unimpressed. Napoleon, the man with the towel
round his waist, the policeman, a boxer, and a chef suddenly appear
standing in a line, and take a bow. They immediately change positions
and take another bow. The penguin appears at the end of the line with a
puff of smoke. Each one in turn jumps in the air and vanishes. Shot of
passive cat.
Cut to Mr A and Mrs B watching with the general.*

General I hope to God it works. Anyway, we shall know any minute now.

*After a pause, the cat gets up and walks into the house. Mr A and Mrs B
are overcome with joy.*

Mrs B I can't believe it.

Mr A Neither can I. It's just like the old days.

Mrs B Then he's cured. Oh thank you, general.

Mr A What can we ever do to repay you?

General No need to, sir. It's all in a day's work for Confuse-a-Cat.

*Picture freezes and over still of general's face are superimposed the words
'Confuse-a-Cat Limited'. Dramatic music. The words start to roll, like
ordinary credits but read:*

CONFUSE-A-CAT LIMITED
INCORPORATING
AMAZE-A-VOLE LTD
STUN-A-STOAT LTD
PUZZLE-A-PUMA LTD
STARTLE-A-THOMPSON'S GAZELLE LTD
BEWILDEREBEEST INC
DISTRACT-A-BEE

ANIMATION: *People's heads appear in frame due to Mr Gilliam's animation on film.*
Film animation leads us into customs hall.

Officer (JOHN) Have you read this, sir? *(holds up notice)*

Man (MICHAEL) No! Oh, yes, yes – yes.

Officer Anything to declare?

Man Yes . . . no! No! No! No! Nothing to declare, no, nothing in my suitcase no . . .

Officer No watches, cameras, radio sets?

Man Oh yes . . . four watches . . . no, no, no. No. One . . . one watch . . . No, no. Not even one watch. No, no watches at all. No, no watches at all. No precision watches, no.

Officer Which country have you been visiting, sir?

Man Switzerland . . . er . . . no . . . no . . . not Switzerland . . . er . . . not Switzerland, it began with S but it wasn't Switzerland . . . oh what could it be? Terribly bad memory for names. What's the name of that country where they don't make watches at all?

Officer Spain?

Man Spain! That's it. Spain, yes, mm.

Officer The label says 'Zurich', sir.

Man Yes well . . . it *was* Spain then.

Officer Zurich's in Switzerland, sir.

Man Switzerland, yes mm . . . mm . . . yes.

Officer Switzerland – where they make the watches.

Man Oh, nice shed you've got here.

Officer Have you, er, got any Swiss currency, sir?

Man No . . . just the watches . . . er just my watch, er, my watch on the currency . . . I've kept a watch of the currency, and I've watched it and I haven't got any.

Officer That come out a bit glib didn't it? *(an alarm clock goes off inside his case; the man thumps it, unsuccessfully)* Have you got an alarm clock in there, sir?

Man No, no, heavens no, no . . . just vests. *(he thumps the case and the alarm stops)*

Officer Sounded a bit like an alarm going off.

Man Well it can't have been . . . it must be a vest, er, going off.

Officer Going off.

> *Clocks start ticking and chiming in the case. The man desperately thumps the case.*

Man All right, I confess, I'm a smuggler ... This whole case is crammed full of Swiss watches and clocks. I've been purposely trying to deceive Her Majesty's Customs and Excise. I've been a bloody fool.

Officer I don't believe you, sir.

Man It's true. I'm, er, guilty of smuggling.

Officer Don't give me that, sir ... you couldn't smuggle a piece of greaseproof paper let alone a case full of watches.

Man What do you mean! I've smuggled watches before, you know! I've smuggled bombs, cameras, microfilms, aircraft components, you name it – I've smuggled it.

Officer Now come along please, you're wasting our time ... move along please.

Man Look! *(he opens his case to reveal it stuffed full of watches and clocks)* Look – look at this.

Officer Look, for all I know, sir, you could've bought these in London before you ever went to Switzerland.

Man What? I wouldn't buy two thousand clocks.

Officer People do, now close your case move along please come on. Don't waste our time, we're out to catch the real smugglers. Come on.

Man *(shouting)* I am a real smuggler. I'm a smuggler! Don't you understand, I'm a smuggler, a lawbreaker ... a smuggler. *(he is removed struggling)*

> *A vicar is next.*

Vicar (ERIC) Poor fellow. I think he needs help.

Officer Right, cut the wisecracks, vicar. Get to the search room, and strip.

> *Cut to chairman of discussion group.*

Chairman (TERRY J) Well to discuss the implications of that sketch and to consider the moral problems raised by the law-enforcement methods involved we have a duck, a cat and a lizard. Now first of all I'd like to put this question to you please, lizard. How effective do you consider the legal weapons employed by legal customs officers, nowadays? *(shot of lizard; silence)* Well while you're thinking about that, I'd like to bring the duck in here, and ask her, if possible, to clarify the whole question of currency restrictions, and customs regulations in the world today. *(shot of duck; silence)* Perhaps the cat would rather answer that? *(shot of cat; silence)* No? Lizard? *(shot of lizard again and then back)* No. Well, er, let's ask the man in the street what he thinks.

Cut to film: vox pops.

French Au Pair (CAROL) I am not a man you silly billy.

Man on Roof (TERRY J) I'm not in the street you fairy.

Man in Street (JOHN) Well, er, speaking *as* a man in the street . . . *(a car runs him over)* Wagh!

Man (MICHAEL) What was the question again?

Voice Over (JOHN) Just how relevant are contemporary customs regulations and currency restrictions in a modern expanding industrial economy? *(no answer)* Oh never mind.

Pepperpot (ERIC) Well I think customs men should be armed, so they can kill people carrying more than two hundred cigarettes.

Man (JOHN) *(getting up from a deckchair and screaming with indignation and rage: he has a knotted handkerchief on his head and his trousers are rolled up to the knees)* Well I, I think that, er, nobody who has gone abroad should be allowed back in the country. I mean, er, blimey, blimey if they're not keen enough to stay here when they're 'ere, why should we allow them back, er, at the tax-payers' expense? I mean, be fair, I mean, I don't eat squirrels do I? I mean well perhaps I do one or two but there's no law against that, is there? It's a free country. *(enter a knight in armour)* I mean if I want to eat a squirrel now and again, that's me own business, innit? I mean, I'm no racialist. I, oh, oh . . .

The knight is carrying a raw chicken. The man apprehensively covers his head and the knight slams him in the stomach with the chicken.

Woman (CAROL) I think it's silly to ask a lizard what it thinks, anyway.

Chairman *(off)* Why?

Woman I mean they should have asked Margaret Drabble.

Young Man (ERIC) *(very reasonably)* Well I think, er, customs people are quite necessary, and I think they're doing quite a good job really. Check.

We now see that he is playing chess with another young man. They are in an ordinary flat. There is a tremendous battering, banging, hammering and clattering at the door.

Young Man Door's open.

Policeman (GRAHAM) Oh. Yes. *(he enters)* All right. All right, all right, all right. My name's Police Constable Henry Thatcher, and this is a raid. I have reason to believe that there are certain substances on the premises.

Young Man Well what sort of substances, officer?

Policeman Er . . . certain substances.

Young Man Well, what sort of certain substances?

Policeman Er, certain substances of an illicit nature.

Young Man Er, could you be more specific?

Policeman I beg your pardon?

Young Man Could you be 'clearer'.

Policeman Oh, oh . . . yes, er . . . certain substances on the premises. To be removed for clinical tests.

Young Man Have you got anything particular in mind?

Policeman Well what have you got?

Young Man Nothing, officer.

Policeman You are Sandy Camp the actor?

Young Man Yes.

Policeman I must warn you, sir, that outside I have police dog Josephine, who is not only armed, and trained to sniff out certain substances, but is also a junkie.

Young Man What are you after . . . ?

Policeman (*pulling a brown paper package from out of his pocket, very badly and obviously*) Oo! Oh, oh, oh, oh, oh, oh, oh, oh, oh, oh! Here is a brown paper bag I have found on the premises. I must confiscate this, sir, and take it with me for clinical examination.

Young Man Wait a minute. You just got that out of your pocket.

Policeman What?

Young Man (*takes it*) Well what's in it anyway? (*opens it*) Sandwiches.

Policeman Sandwiches? Blimey. Whatever did I give the wife?

> *Cut to viewer's letter in handwriting, read in voice over.*

Voice Over (CAROL) Dear BBC, East Grinstead, Friday. I feel I really must write and protest about that sketch. My husband, in common with a lot of people of his age, is fifty. For how long are we to put up with these things. Yours sincerely, E. B. Debenham (Mrs).

> *Cut to another letter.*

Voice Over (JOHN) Dear Freddy Grisewood, Bagshot, Surrey. As a prolific letter-writer, I feel I must protest about the previous letter. I am nearly sixty and am quite mad, but I do enjoy listening to the BBC Home Service. If this continues to go on unabated . . . Dunkirk . . . dark days of the war . . . backs to the wall . . . Alvar Liddell . . . Berlin air lift . . . moral upheaval of Profumo case . . . young hippies roaming the streets, raping, looting and killing. Yours etc., Brigadier Arthur Gormanstrop (Mrs).

> *Cut to vox pops film.*

Pepperpot (ERIC) Well I think they should attack things, like that – with satire. I mean Ned Sherrin. Fair's fair. I think people should be able to make up their own minds for me.

Woman Journalist (TERRY J) Well I think they should attack the fuddy-duddy attitudes of the lower middle classes which permit the establishment to survive and keep the mores of the whole country back where they were in the nineteenth century and the ghastly days of the pre-sexual revolution.

> *A boxer (Eric) runs up and knocks her out.*

Scotsman (MICHAEL) Well that's, er, very interesting, because, er, I am, in fact, made entirely of wood.

Stockbroker (JOHN) Well I think they should attack the lower classes, er, first with bombs, and rockets destroying their homes, and then when they run helpless into the streets, er, mowing them down with machine guns. Er, and then of course releasing the vultures. I know these views aren't popular, but I have never courted popularity.

A boy scout on his knees. Next to him is a scout master, seen only from the knees down.

Boy (MICHAEL) I think there should be more race prejudice.

He is nudged.

Voice Less.

Boy Less race prejudice.

Cut to news studio with a large screen behind newsreader.

Newsreader (ERIC) *(as if it's the fourth item)* . . . and several butchers' aprons. In Fulham this morning a jeweller's shop was broken into and jewellery to the value of £2,000 stolen. Police have issued this picture of a man they wish to interview. *(on the screen behind, him, there appears an identical picture of him, sitting at his newsreader desk)* The man is in his late twenties wearing a grey suit, a white shirt and a floral tie. *(on the screen behind, police come in and remove the newsreader)* Will anyone who sees this man or can give any information about his whereabouts contact their nearest police station. *(he is handed a piece of paper)* Ah! Oh. We've just heard that police have detained the man they wished to interview in connection with the jewel robbery. Ah, but after questioning police have ruled him out of their enquiries and released him. *(the other newsreader appears back on the screen and sits down)* Sport. *(he is handed another piece of paper)* Ah, they say, however, that acting on his information they now wish to interview a newsreader in the central London area. Ah, police are concentrating their enquiries on the British Broadcasting Corp . . . *(a policeman comes in, and removes newsreader in the foreground)* Excuse me a minute . . .

The newsreader on the screen behind continues.

Other Newsreader We understand a man is now helping police with their enquiries. And that is the end of the news. *(he clips a piece of jewellery on to his ear)* And now, 'Match of the Day'.

'Match of the Day' music. We see a couple. They are standing at the foot of a largish bed. She is in bra and pants. He is in Y-fronts. They kiss ecstatically. After a few seconds there is the sound of a car drawing up. The crunch of footsteps on gravel and the sound of a door opening. The newsreader comes into shot.

Newsreader Ah, I, I'm terribly sorry it's not in fact 'Match of the Day' – it is in fact edited highlights of tonight's romantic movie. Er. Sorry. *(he goes out of shot; the two clinch again; after a second he pops back into shot)* Ooh, I'm sorry, on BBC2 Joan Bakewell will be talking to Michael Dean about what makes exciting television. *(pops out of shot, then pops in again)* Ah, sorry about all that. And now back to the movie. *(he goes)*

The couple continue to neck.

She (CAROL) *(smoking)* Oh, oh, oh Bevis, should we?

Bevis (TERRY J) Oh Dora. Why not?

She Be gentle with me.

Cut to film montage: collapsing factory chimney in reverse motion; pan up tall soaring poplars in the wind; waves crashing; fish in shallow water; fountains; exploding fireworks; volcano erupting with lava; rocket taking off; express train going into a tunnel; dam bursting; battleship broadside; lion leaping through flaming hoop; Richard Nixon smiling; milking a cow; planes refuelling in mid-air; Women's Institute applauding; tossing the caber; plane falling in flames; tree crashing to the ground; the lead shot tower collapsing (normal motion).

Cut back to the girl in bed.

She Oh Bevis, are you going to *do* anything or are you just going to show me films all evening?

We see Bevis, with small projector.

Bevis Just one more, dear.

She Oh.

He starts it. A two-minute extravaganza constructed by Mr Terry Gilliam of America you know.

Cut to an interview room.

Interviewer (JOHN) You know I really enjoy interviewing applicants for this management training course. *(knock at door)* Come in. *(Stig enters)* Ah. Come and sit down.

Stig (GRAHAM) Thank you. *(he sits)*

Interviewer *(stares at him and starts writing)* Would you mind just standing up again for one moment. *(stands up)* Take a seat.

Stig I'm sorry.

Interviewer Take a seat. *(Stig does so)* Ah! *(writes again)* Good morning.

Stig Good morning.

Interviewer Good morning.

Stig Good morning.

Interviewer *(writes)* Tell me why did you say 'good morning' when you know perfectly well that it's afternoon?

Stig Well, well, you said 'good morning'. Ha, ha.

Interviewer *(shakes head)* Good afternoon.

Stig Ah, good afternoon.

Interviewer Oh dear. *(writes again)* Good evening.

Stig . . . Goodbye?

Interviewer Ha, ha. No. *(rings small hand-bell)* . . . Aren't you going to ask me why I rang the bell? *(rings bell again)*

Stig Er why did you ring the bell?

Interviewer Why do you *think* I rang the bell? *(shouts)* Five, four, three, two, one, zero!

Stig Well, I, I . . .

Interviewer Too late! *(singing)* Goodnight, ding-ding-ding-ding-ding. Goodnight. Ding-ding-ding-ding-ding-ding-ding.

Stig Um. Oh this is, is the interview for the management training course is it?

Interviewer *(rings bell)* Yes. Yes it is. Goodnight. Ding, ding, ding, ding, ding, ding, ding, ding.

Stig Oh. Oh dear, I don't think I'm doing very well.

Interviewer Why do you say that?

Stig Well I don't know.

Interviewer Do you say it because you didn't know?

Stig Well. I, I, I, I don't know.

Interviewer Five, four, three, two, one, zero! Right! *(makes face and strange noise)*

Stig I'm sorry, I'm confused.

Interviewer Well why do you think I did that then?

Stig Well I don't know.

Interviewer Aren't you curious?

Stig Well yes.

Interviewer Well, why didn't you ask me?

Stig Well . . . I . . . er . . .

Interviewer Name?

Stig What?

Interviewer Your name man, your name!

Stig Um, er David.

Interviewer David. Sure?

Stig Oh yes.

Interviewer *(writing)* David Shaw.

Stig No, no Thomas.

Interviewer Thomas Shaw?

Stig No, no, David Thomas.

Interviewer *(long look, rings bell)* Goodnight. Ding-ding-ding-ding-ding-ding-ding-ding. Goodnight. Ding-ding-ding-ding-ding-ding-ding-ding-ding.

Stig Oh dear we're back to that again. I don't know what to do when you do that.

Interviewer Well do something. Goodnight. Ding-ding-ding-ding-ding, five, four, three, two, one ... *(Stig pulls face and makes noise)* Good!

Stig Good?

Interviewer Very good – do it again. *(Stig pulls face and makes noise)* Very good indeed, quite outstanding. *(interviewer goes to door)* Ah right. *(calls through door)* Ready now. *(four people come in and line up by desk)* Right, once more. *(rings bell)* Goodnight, ding-ding-ding-ding-ding-ding.

Stig very cautiously pulls face and makes noise. Interviewer rings bell again. Suddenly the four men all hold up points cards like diving or skating judges.

Stig What's going on? What's going on?

Interviewer You've got very good marks.

Stig *(hysterically)* Well I don't care, I want to know what's going on! I think you're deliberately trying to humiliate people, and I'm going straight out of here and I'm going to tell the police exactly what you do to people and I'm going to make bloody sure that you never do it again. There, what do you think of that? What do you think of that?

The judges give him very high marks.

Interviewer *Very* good marks.

Stig Oh, oh well, do I get the job?

Interviewer Er, well, I'm afraid not. I'm afraid all the vacancies were filled several weeks ago.

They fall about laughing.

Cut to man sitting at desk.

Man (MICHAEL) Well that was all good fun, and we all had a jolly good laugh, but I would like to assure you that you'd never be treated like that if you had an interview here at the Careers Advisory Board. Perhaps I should introduce myself. I am the Head of the Careers Advisory Board. I wanted to be a doctor, but there we are, I'm Head of the Careers Advisory Board. *(emotionally)* Or a sculptor, something artistic, or an engineer, with all those dams, but there we are, it's no use crying over spilt milk, the facts are there and that's that. I'm the Head of this lousy Board. *(he weeps, then recovers)* Never mind, now I wonder if you've ever considered what a very profitable line of work *this* man is in.

Cut to front door of a flat. Man walks up to the door and rings bell. He is dressed smartly.

Man (ERIC) Burglar! *(longish pause while he waits, he rings again)* Burglar! *(woman appears at other side of door)*

Woman (JOHN) Yes?

Man Burglar, madam.

Woman What do you want?

Man I want to come in and steal a few things, madam.

Woman Are you an encyclopaedia salesman?

Man No madam, I'm a burglar, I burgle people.

Woman I think you're an encyclopaedia salesman.

Man Oh I'm not, open the door, let me in please.

Woman If I let you in you'll sell me encyclopaedias.

Man I won't, madam. I just want to come in and ransack the flat. Honestly.

Woman Promise. No encyclopaedias?

Man None at all.

Woman All right. *(she opens door)* You'd better come in then.

Man enters through door.

Man Mind you I don't know whether you've really considered the advantages of owning a really fine set of modern encyclopaedias ... *(he pockets valuable)* You know, they can really do you wonders.

Cut back to man at desk.

Man That man was a successful encyclopaedia salesman. But not all encyclopaedia salesmen are successful. Here is an unsuccessful encyclopaedia salesman.

Cut to a very tall building; a body flies out of a high window and plummets.

Cut back to man at desk.

Man Now here are *two* unsuccessful encyclopaedia salesmen.

Cut to a different tall building; two bodies fly out of a high window.

Cut back to man at desk.

Man I think there's a lesson there for all of us.

CAPTION: ' "MAN'S CRISIS OF IDENTITY IN THE LATTER HALF OF THE 20TH CENTURY" WAS CONCEIVED, WRITTEN AND PERFORMED BY ... (CREDITS)'

Six

In the foreground we see a telephone. In the very distant background we see the 'It's' man. The telephone starts to ring. The 'It's' man runs towards the camera and the telephone (speeded up). He arrives at the telephone, picks up the receiver and is about to speak into the mouthpiece when he remembers the camera. He puts his hand over the mouthpiece and says to camera:

It's Man It's . . .

He returns to the receiver.
Animated opening titles.

CAPTION: 'NEXT WEEK'
CAPTION: 'HOW TO FLING AN OTTER'
CAPTION: 'THIS WEEK'
CAPTION: 'THE BBC ENTRY FOR THE ZINC STOAT OF BUDAPEST (CURRENT AFFAIRS)'
CAPTION: 'THESE CAPTIONS COST 12/6D. EACH'

Cut to presenter in studio.

SUPERIMPOSED CAPTION: 'ARTHUR FIGGIS'

Lose caption. Pause.

CAPTION: 'THE SAME, A FEW SECONDS LATER'
SUPERIMPOSED CAPTION: 'THAT'S £4.7.6. SO FAR ON CAPTIONS ALONE'
SUPERIMPOSED CAPTION: 'NOT INCLUDING THAT ONE'

Man (MICHAEL) *(rushing in)* I thought you did that so well Mr Figgis, could I have your autograph?

Figgis (GRAHAM) You certainly can.

Presenter signs autograph. Part of his signature gets away (animation) and eventually leads us into the title: 'It's the Arts'. Classical music plays.

Figgis (GRAHAM) Beethoven, Mozart, Chopin, Liszt, Brahms, Panties . . . I'm sorry . . . Schumann, Schubert, Mendelssohn and Bach. Names that will live for ever. But there is one composer whose name is never included with the greats. Why is it the world never remembered the name of Johann Gambolputty de von Ausfern-schplenden-schlitter-crasscrenbon-fried-digger-dingle-dangle-dongle-dungle-burstein-von-knacker-thrasher-apple-banger-horowitz-ticolensic-grander-knotty-spelltinkle-grandlich-grumblemeyer-spelterwasser-kurstlich-himbleeisen-bahnwagen-gutenabend-bitte-ein-nürnburger-bratwustle-gerspurten-mitz-weimache-luber-hundsfut-gumberaber-shönendancker-kalbsfleisch-mittler-aucher von Hautkopft of Ulm. To do justice to this man,

thought by many to be the greatest name in German Baroque
music, we present a profile of Johann Gambolputty de von
Ausfern-schplenden-schlitter-crasscrenbon-fried-digger-dingle-
dangle-dongle-dungle-burstein-von-knacker-thrasher-apple-
banger-horowitz-ticolensic-grander-knotty-spelltinkle-grandlich-
grumblemeyer-spelterwasser-kurstlich-himbleeisen-bahnwagen-
gutenabend-bitte-ein-nürnburger-bratwustle-gerspurten-mitz-
weimache-luber-hundsfut-gumberaber-shönendanker-kalbsfleisch-
mittler-aucher von Hautkopft of Ulm. We start with an interview
with his only surviving relative Karl Gambolputty de von Ausfern
. . . *(fades out)*

*Cut to old man sitting blanketed, in wheel-chair, as he speaks, intercut
with shot of interviewer nodding and looking interested.*

Karl (TERRY J)   Oh ja. When I first met Johann Gambolputty de von
Ausfern-schplenden-schlitter-crasscrenbon-fried-digger-dingle-
dangle-dongle-dungle-burstein-von-knacker-thrasher-apple-
banger-horowitz-ticolensic-grander-knotty-spelltinkle-grandlich-
grumblemeyer-spelterwasser-kurstlich-himbleeisen-bahnwagen-
gutenabend-bitte-ein-nürnburger-bratwustle-gerspurten-mitz-
weimache-luber-hundsfut-gumberaber-shönendanker-kalbsfleisch-
mittler-aucher von Hautkopft of Ulm, he was with his wife, Sarah
Gambolputty de von . . .

Interviewer (JOHN) *(as he speaks intercut with shots of Karl nodding and
trying to look interested)*   Yes, if I may just cut in on you there, Herr
Gambolputty de von Ausfern-schplenden-schlitter-crasscrenbon-
fried-digger-dingle-dangle-dongle-dungle-burstein-von-knacker-
thrasher-apple-banger-horowitz-ticolensic-grander-knotty-
spelltinkle-grandlich-grumblemeyer-spelterwasser-kurstlich-
himbleeisen-bahnwagen-gutenabend-bitte-ein-nürnburger-
bratwustle-gerspurten-mitz-weimache-luber-hundsfut-gumberaber-
shönendanker-kalbsfleisch-mittler-aucher von Hautkopft of Ulm,
and ask you – just quickly – if there's any particular thing that you
remember about Johann Gambolputty de von Ausfern-schplenden-
schlitter-crasscrenbon-fried-digger-dingle-dangle-dongle-dungle-
burstein-von-knacker-thrasher-apple-banger-horowitz-ticolensic-
grander-knotty-spelltinkle-grandlich-grumblemeyer-spelterwasser-
kurstlich-himbleeisen-bahnwagen-gutenabend-bitte-ein-
nürnburger-bratwustle-gerspurten-mitz-weimache-luber-hundsfut-
gumberaber-shönendanker-kalbsfleisch-mittler-aucher von Hautkopft of Ulm?

*No response. He shakes the old man, then gets up and listens to his
heart. Realizing with exasperation that his interviewee has died, he starts
digging a grave. Cut back to presenter.*

Figgis   A tribute to Johann Gambolputty . . .

Cut to Viking.

Viking (JOHN) ... de von Ausfern-schplenden-schlitter ...

Cut to weedy man in pullover with National Health specs.

Man (MICHAEL) ... crasscrenbon-fried-digger-dingle-dangle-dongle ...

Cut to knight in armour.

Knight in Armour ... dungle-burstein-von-knacker-thrasher ...

Cut to a succession of animated characters.

Mona Lisa ... apple-banger-horowitz-ticolensic ...

Lon Chancy ... grander-knotty-spelltinkle ...

Policeman ... grandlich ...

Pig ... grumblemeyer ...

Policeman ... spelterwasser ...

Boar ... kurstlich-himbleeisen ...

Botticelli Lover ... bahnwagen-gutenabend ...

Medieval Couple ... bitte-ein-nürnburger ...

Family Group ... bratwurstle ...

Doctor ... gerspurten ...

Bishop & Saint ... mitz-weimache-luber-hundsfut ...

Two Dancers ... gumberaber-schönendanker ...

Three Naked Ladies ... kalbsfleisch ...

Cricket Team ... mittler-aucher ...

Policemen ... von Hautkopf ...

Figgis ... of Ulm.

> ANIMATION: *leading to: A garret room with a bare table. Around it are grouped four desperate-looking robbers. The boss has a rolled-up map. One of the gang, the fifth, is looking out of the window.*

Boss (MICHAEL) All clear?

Fifth (JOHN) All clear, boss.

Boss *(unfolding big map across table; talking carefully)* Right ... this is the plan then. At 10.45 ... you, Reg, collect me and Ken in the van, and take us round to the British Jewellery Centre in the High Street. We will arrive outside the British Jewellery Centre at 10.50 a of m. I shall then get out of the car, you Reg, take it and park it back here in Denver Street, right? At 10.51, I shall enter the British Jewellery Centre, where you, Vic, disguised as a customer, will meet me and hand me £5.18.3d. At 10.52, I shall approach the counter and purchase a watch costing £5.18.3d. I shall then give the watch to you, Vic. You'll go straight to Norman's Garage in East Street. You lads continue back up here at 10.56 and we rendezvous in the back room at the Cow and Sickle, at 11.15. All right, any questions?

Larry (TERRY J) We don't seem to be doing anything illegal.

Boss What do you mean?

Larry Well . . . we're paying for the watch.

Boss *(patiently)* Yes . . .

Larry *(hesitating)* Well . . . why are we *paying* for the watch?

Boss *(heavily)* They wouldn't give it to us if we didn't *pay* for it, would they . . . eh?

Larry Look! I don't like this outfit.

Boss Why not?

Larry *(at last feeling free to say what's on his mind)* Well, we never break the bloody law.

> *General consternation.*

Boss What d'you mean?

Larry Well, look at that bank job last week.

Boss What was wrong with that?

Larry Well having to go in there with a mask on and ask for £15 out of my deposit account; that's what was wrong with it.

Boss Listen! What are you trying to say, Larry?

Larry Couldn't we just *steal* the watch, boss!

Boss Oh, you dumb cluck! We spent weeks organizing this job. Reg rented a room across the road and filmed the people going in and out every day. Vic spent three weeks looking at watch catalogues . . . until he knew the price of each one backwards, and now I'm not going to risk the whole raid just for the sake of breaking the law.

Larry Urr . . . couldn't we park on a double yellow line?

Boss No!

Larry Couldn't we get a dog to foul the foot . . .

Boss No!

Reg (ERIC) *(suddenly going pale)* 'Ere, boss!

Boss What's the matter with you?

Reg I just thought . . . I left the car on a meter . . . and it's . . .

Boss Overdue?

Reg Yes, boss.

Boss How much?

Reg *(quaking)* I dunno, boss . . . maybe two . . . maybe five minutes . . .

Boss Five minutes overdue. You fool! You fool! All right . . . we've no time to lose. Ken – shave all your hair off, get your passport and meet me at this address in Rio de Janeiro Tuesday night. Vic – go to East Africa, have plastic surgery and meet me there. Reg – go to Canada and work your way south to Nicaragua by July. Larry – you stay here as front man. Give us fifteen minutes then blow the building up. All right, make it fast.

Larry I can't blow the building up.

Boss Why not?

Larry It's illegal.

Boss Oh bloody hell. Well we'd better give ourselves up then.
Reg We can't, boss.
Boss Why not?
Reg We haven't done anything illegal.

Cut to film. Exterior of bank. Three bandits rush out with swag etc. One of them stops to talk to camera raising mask off head.

Bandit (MICHAEL) No I think being illegal makes it more exciting.
Second Bandit (ERIC) Yes, I agree. I mean, if you're going to go straight you might as well be a vicar or something.

Cut to vicar, wheeling quickly round to reveal he has had his hand in the restoration-fund box.

Vicar (TERRY J) What?

Cut to chartered accountant.

Chartered Accountant (JOHN) I agree. If there were fewer robbers there wouldn't be so many of them, numerically speaking.

Cut to pepperpot.

Pepperpot (MICHAEL) I think sexual ecstasy is over-rated.

Cut to Scotsman.

Scotsman (MICHAEL) Well, how very interesting, because I'm now made entirely of tin.

Cut to Police Inspector Praline.

Praline (JOHN) After a few more of these remarks, I shall be appearing in a sketch, so stay tuned.

Cut to policeman.

Policeman (GRAHAM) It's the uniform that puts them off, that and my bad breath.

Cut to judge in full long wig and robes and a QC also wearing wig and robes.

Judge *(matter of factly)* We like dressing up, yes . . .

Cut to Inspector Praline.

Praline Hello again. I am at present still on film, but in a few seconds I shall be appearing in the studio. Thank you.

Cut to studio. A door opens. Inspector Praline looks round door.

Inspector Praline *(to camera)* Hello. *(he walks in followed by Superintendent Parrot and goes to desk)* Mr Milton? You are sole proprietor and owner of the Whizzo Chocolate Company?
Milton (TERRY J) I am.
Praline Superintendent Parrot and I are from the hygiene squad. We want to have a word with you about your box of chocolates entitled The Whizzo Quality Assortment.
Milton Ah, yes.

Praline *(producing box of chocolates)* If I may begin at the beginning. First there is the cherry fondue. This is extremely nasty, but we can't prosecute you for that.

Milton Agreed.

Praline Next we have number four, 'crunchy frog'.

Milton Ah, yes.

Praline Am I right in thinking there's a real frog in here?

Milton Yes. A little one.

Praline What sort of frog?

Milton A dead frog.

Praline Is it cooked?

Milton No.

Praline What, a raw frog?

Superintendent Parrot looks increasingly queasy.

Milton We use only the finest baby frogs, dew picked and flown from Iraq, cleansed in finest quality spring water, lightly killed, and then sealed in a succulent Swiss quintuple smooth treble cream milk chocolate envelope and lovingly frosted with glucose.

Praline That's as maybe, it's still a frog.

Milton What else?

Praline Well don't you even take the bones out?

Milton If we took the bones out it wouldn't be crunchy would it?

Praline Superintendent Parrot ate one of those.

Parrot (GRAHAM) Excuse me a moment. *(exits hurriedly)*

Milton It says 'crunchy frog' quite clearly.

Praline Well, the superintendent thought it was an almond whirl. People won't expect there to be a frog in there. They're bound to think it's some form of mock frog.

Milton *(insulted)* Mock frog? We use no artificial preservatives or additives of any kind!

Praline Nevertheless, I must warn you that in future you should delete the words 'crunchy frog', and replace them with the legend 'crunchy raw unboned real dead frog', if you want to avoid prosecution.

Milton What about our sales?

Praline I'm not interested in your sales, I have to protect the general public. Now how about this one. *(superintendent enters)* It was number five, wasn't it? *(superintendent nods)* Number five, ram's bladder cup. *(exit superintendent)* What kind of confection is this?

Milton We use choicest juicy chunks of fresh Cornish ram's bladder, emptied, steamed, flavoured with sesame seeds whipped into a fondue and garnished with lark's vomit.

Praline Lark's vomit?

Milton Correct.

Praline Well it don't say nothing about that here.

Milton Oh yes it does, on the bottom of the box, after monosodium glutamate.

Praline *(looking)* Well I hardly think this is good enough. I think it would be more appropriate if the box bore a large red label warning lark's vomit.

Milton Our sales would plummet.

Praline Well why don't you move into more conventional areas of confectionery, like praline or lime cream; a very popular flavour I'm led to understand. *(superintendent enters)* I mean look at this one, 'cockroach cluster', *(superintendent exits)* 'anthrax ripple'. What's this one, 'spring surprise'?

Milton Ah – now, that's our speciality – covered with darkest creamy chocolate. When you pop it in your mouth steel bolts spring out and plunge straight through both cheeks.

Praline Well where's the pleasure in that? If people place a nice chocky in their mouth, they don't want their cheeks pierced. In any case this is an inadequate description of the sweetmeat. I shall have to ask you to accompany me to the station.

Milton *(getting up from desk and being led away)* It's a fair cop.

Praline Stop talking to the camera.

Milton I'm sorry.

Superintendent Parrot enters the room as Inspector Praline and Milton leave, and addresses the camera.

Parrot If only the general public would take more care when buying its sweeties, it would reduce the number of man-hours lost to the nation and they would spend less time having their stomachs pumped and sitting around in public lavatories.

Announcer (JOHN) The BBC would like to apologize for the extremely poor quality of the next announcement, only he's not at all well.

Parrot We present 'The Dull Life of a City Stockbroker'.

Cut to a nice suburban street. Inside the house a stockbroker (Michael) is finishing his breakfast. His attractive wife looks on. He picks up his hat, rises, kisses her goodbye, and leaves. As he does so, she takes off her wrap and two men dressed only in briefs (Graham and Terry J) step out of the kitchen cupboard. In the front garden the stockbroker bids his neighbour (Graham) good morning; as he moves off a large African native throws an assegai, killing the neighbour. The stockbroker, not noticing this, moves on. A high street: he walks into a newsagents. Behind the counter a naked young lady gives him his newspaper. Taking his change without apparently noticing her he leaves. A bus queue: the stockbroker is at the head of it; there are four people behind him. As they wait, the Frankenstein monster comes up behind them and works his way along the queue, killing each member as he goes. He has just reached the stockbroker – who has not seen him – when the bus arrives and the stockbroker gets on. On the bus: all the other passengers are uniformed soldiers. The bus drives along a road past explosions and gunfire. A hand grenade comes through the window and lands on the seat next to the stockbroker. The soldiers leave the bus rapidly; the stockbroker calmly leaves the bus and walks down the street, in which the soldiers are engaging in a pitched battle. The stockbroker hails a taxi; it stops. No driver is visible. The stockbroker gets in and it drives off. In the stockbroker's office: a secretary is dead across her typewriter with a knife in her back; at the back of the office a pair of legs swing gently from the ceiling; a couple are snogging at his desk. Unconcerned, the stockbroker sits down. Furtively he looks round, then takes from the desk drawer a comic-book entitled 'Thrills and Adventure'. We see the frames of the comic strip. A Superman-type character and a girl are shrinking from an explosion. She is saying 'My God, he's just exploded with enough force to destroy his kleenex'. In the next frame, the Superman character is saying 'If only I had a kleenex to lend him – or even a linen handkerchief – but these trousers . . . !! No back pocket!' In the frame beneath, he flies from side to side attempting to escape; finally he breaks through, bringing the two frames above down on himself. Cut to a picture of a safety curtain. An animated man comes in front of it and says:

Man Coming right up – the theatre sketch – so don't move!

The front stalls of a theatre. It is a first night – a lot of people in dinner jackets etc. About three rows back there is a spare seat. A general rustle of programmes, chocolates and theatrical murmurs. Suddenly a Sioux Indian enters, clad only in loin cloth, wearing war paint and with a single strip of hair in the middle of his head and feather. He carries a bow and a quiver of arrows. He settles into the empty seat. The man next to him shifts uneasily and looks straight ahead. The Indian looks his neighbour up and down a couple of times.

Indian (ERIC) *(always speaking with full gestures)* Me heap want see play. Me want play start heap soon.

Man next to him nods.

Man (GRAHAM) Yes well. I think it . . . begins in a minute.

Indian Me heap big fan Cicely Courtneidge.

Man *(highly embarrassed)* Yes . . . she's very good.

Indian She *fine* actress . . . she make interpretation heap subtle . . . she heap good diction and timing . . . she make part really live for Indian brave.

Man Yes . . . yes . . . she's marvellous . . .

Indian My father – Chief Running Stag – leader of mighty Redfoot tribe – him heap keen on Michael Denison and Dulcie Gray.

Man *(unwillingly drawn in)* Do you go to the theatre a lot?

Indian When moon high over prairie . . . when wolf howl over mountain, when mighty wind roar through Yellow Valley, we go Leatherhead

Rep – block booking, upper circle – whole tribe get in on 3/6d each.

Man That's very good.

Indian Stage manager, Stan Wilson, heap good friend Redfoot tribe. After show we go pow-wow speakum with director, Sandy Camp, in snug bar of Bell and Compasses. Him mighty fine director. Him heap famous.

Man Oh – I don't know him myself.

Indian Him say Leatherhead Rep like do play with Redfoot tribe.

Man Oh that's good . . .

Indian We do 'Dial M for Murder'. Chief Running Elk – him kill buffalo with bare hands, run thousand paces when the sun is high – him play Chief Inspector Hardy – heap good fine actor.

Man You do a lot of acting do you?

Indian Yes. Redfoot tribe live by acting and hunting.

Man You don't fight any more?

Indian Yes! Redfoot make war! When Chief Yellow Snake was leader, and Mighty Eagle was in land of forefather, we fight Pawnee at Oxbow Crossing. When Pawnee steal our rehearsal copies of 'Reluctant Debutante' we kill fifty Pawnee – houses heap full every night. Heap good publicity.

The lights start to dim. Auditorium chatter subsides.

Man *(visibly relieved)* I think he's about to start now, thank God for that.

They both look towards stage. The overture starts.

Indian *(leaning across)* Paleface like eat chocolate? *(proffers box)*

Man No, thank you very much.

Indian *(helping himself)* Hmmm – crunchy frog – heap good.

Cut to stage, house manager walks out in front of tabs. He is a very nice young man.

House Manager (MICHAEL) Ladies and gentlemen. Before the play starts, I would like to apologize to you all, but unfortunately Miss Cicely Courtneidge is unable to appear, owing to . . .

He is suddenly struck in the chest by first one arrow and then another. He crumbles to the ground revealing half a dozen in his back. The air is filled with war-whoops and drum beats and screams. Cut to a working-class kitchen.

Mum (TERRY J) *(reading newspaper)* D'you read that, Edgar?

Dad (IAN DAVIDSON) What's that dear?

Mum There's been another Indian massacre at Dorking Civic Theatre.

Dad About time too dear . . .

Mum 'Those who were left alive at the end got their money back'.

Dad That's what live theatre needs – a few more massacres . . .

Mum 'The police are anxious to speak to anyone who saw the crime, ladies with large breasts, or just anyone who likes policemen.'

Suddenly a policeman walks in between the couple and the camera.

Policeman (JOHN) *(to camera)* Yes! Policemen make wonderful friends. So if you are over six feet tall and would like a friend, a pen friend, in the police force, here is the address to write to: 'Mrs Ena Frog, 8 Masonic Apron Street, Cowdenbeath'. Remember – policemen make wonderful friends. So write today and take advantage of our free officer. Thank you. And now for the next sketch.

The policeman removes his helmet, shakes it, proffers it to mum at the table. She takes out a small folded bit of paper, opens and reads.

Mum A Scotsman on a horse.

Policeman For Mrs Emma Hamilton of Nelson, a Scotsman on a horse.

A Scotsman (John) rides up to the camera and looks around puzzled. In long-shot we see him riding off. At a wee Scottish kirk another Scotsman (Michael) is waiting at the head of the aisle to be married. Intercut between first Scotsman galloping through the countryside and the wedding procession coming up the aisle. The wedding takes place; just as it finishes the first Scotsman rides up to the kirk and rushes in. The assembled congregation look at him in alarm as he surveys them; then he picks up Michael and carries him off. Cut to film of Women's Institute audience applauding.

ANIMATION, *which leads us to the 'Twentieth Century Vole' trademark. Cut to film producer's office. Six writers sitting round a table with one very impressive chair empty at the head of the table. They wait reverently. Suddenly the door of the room flies open and Larry Saltzberg, the film producer, walks in. The writers leap to their feet.*

Larry (GRAHAM) Good morning boys.

Writers Good morning Mr Saltzberg.

They run to help him into his chair.

Larry *(sitting)* Sit down! Sit down! Sit down! Sit down! Now, boys, I want you to know that I think you are the best six writers in movies today. *(the writers are overcome)* I want you to know that I've had an idea for the next movie I'm going to produce and I want you boys to write it.

The writers run and kiss him.

Writers Thank you. Thank you.

Larry Oh sit down! Sit down! Sit down! There'll be plenty of time for that later on. Now boys, here's my idea . . .

Third Writer (ERIC) It's great!

Larry You like it huh? *(he looks round the table)*

Writers *(catching on fast)* Yeah, yeah, great! Really great. Fantastic. *(first writer is the only one not having an orgasm about the idea)*

Larry *(to first writer)* Do *you* like it?

First Writer (MICHAEL) *(thrown)* Yeah! Er . . . yeah.

Larry *(still to first writer)* What do you like *best* about it?

First Writer Oh well you haven't told us . . . what it is yet . . .

Larry WHAT!?

First Writer *(pointing at second writer)* I like what he likes.

Larry What do you like?

Second Writer (TERRY J) *(pointing at third writer)* I like what he likes.

Third Writer *(pointing at fourth writer)* I like what he likes.

Fourth Writer (JOHN) I like what he likes *(pointing at fifth writer)*

Fifth Writer (TERRY G) I just crazy about what he likes *(pointing at sixth writer)*

Larry What do you like?

Sixth Writer (IAN DAVIDSON) I . . . I . . . I . . . agree with them.

Larry Good! Now we're getting somewhere. Now, here's the start of the movie . . . I see snow! *(writers applaud)* White snow!

Fourth Writer Think of the colours!

Larry And in the snow, I see . . . a tree!

Writers *(applauding)* Yes! Yes!

Larry Wait, wait I haven't finished yet.

Third Writer There's *more*?

Larry And by this tree, gentlemen, I see . . . a dog!

Writers Olé!

Larry And gentlemen, this dog goes up to the tree, and he piddles on it.

Writers Hallelujah!

Sixth Writer Have we got a movie!

Fifth Writer He tells it the way it is!

Fourth Writer It's where it's at!

Third Writer This is something else!

Second Writer It's out of sight!

First Writer *(finding Larry staring at him)* I like it, I like it.

Larry *(suspicious)* Oh yeah?

First Writer Yeah, yeah, I *promise* I like it!

Fifth Writer Sir, I don't know how to say this but I got to be perfectly frank. I really and truly believe this story of yours is the greatest story in motion-picture history.

Larry Get out!

Fifth Writer What?

Larry If there's one thing I can't stand, it's a yes-man! Get out! *(fifth writer leaves very fast, the others go very quiet)* I'll see you never work again. *(to sixth writer)* What do you think?

Sixth Writer Well . . . I . . .

Larry Just because I have an idea it doesn't mean it's great. It could be lousy.

Sixth Writer It could?

Larry Yeah! What d'ya think?

Sixth Writer It's lousy.

Larry There you are, you see, he spoke his mind. He said my idea was lousy. It just so happens my idea isn't lousy so get out you goddam pinko subversive, get out! *(sixth writer exits)* You . . . *(looking straight at John)*

Fourth Writer Well . . . I think it's an excellent idea.

Larry Are you a yes-man?

Fourth Writer No, no, no, I mean there may be things against it.

Larry You think it's lousy, huh?

Fourth Writer No, no, I mean it takes time.

Larry *(really threatening)* Are you being indecisive?

Fourth Writer Yo. Nes. Perhaps. *(runs out)*

Larry I hope you three gentlemen aren't going to be indecisive! *(they try to hide under the table)* What the hell are you doing under that table?

First Writer We dropped our pencils.

Larry Pencil droppers, eh?

Writers No, no, no, no, no!

Larry Right. Now I want your opinion of my idea . . . *(pointing at first writer)* You . . .

First Writer *(quaking)* Oh . . .

> *First writer looks around and then faints.*

Larry Has he had a heart attack?

Second and Third Writers Er . . .

Larry If there's one thing I can't stand, it's people who have heart attacks.

First Writer *(recovering immediately)* I feel fine now.

Larry Well, what do you think?

Writers Oh! Eh! You didn't ask me you asked him. He didn't ask me, he asked him. No, him.

Larry I've changed my mind. I'm asking you, the one in the middle.

Second Writer The one in the middle?

Larry Yes, the one in the middle. *(the phone rings)* Hello, yes, yes, yes, yes, yes, yes, Dimitri . . . *(all jockey for position desperately trying to put the others in the middle and finish sitting on one chair)* What the hell are you doing?

Second Writer I'm thinking.

Larry Get back in those seats immediately. *(back to phone)* Yes . . . *(second writer is grabbed by the others and held in the middle chair; Larry finishes with the phone)* Right you. The one in the middle, what do you think?

Second Writer *(panic)* Er . . . er . . .

Larry Come on!

Second Writer Splunge.

Larry Did he say splunge?

First and Third Writers Yes.

Larry What does splunge mean?

Second Writer It means . . . it's a great-idea-but-possibly-not-and-I'm-not-being-indecisive!

Larry Good. Right . . . *(to third writer)* What do you think?

Third Writer Er. Splunge?

Larry OK . . .

First Writer Yeah. Splunge for me too.

Larry So all three of you think splunge, huh?

Writers Yes!

Larry Well now we're getting somewhere. No, wait. A new angle! In the snow, instead of the tree, I see Rock Hudson, and instead of the dog I see Doris Day and, gentlemen, Doris Day goes up to Rock Hudson and she kisses him. A love story. Intercourse Italian style. David Hemmings as a hippy Gestapo officer. Frontal nudity. A family picture. A comedy. And then when Doris Day's kissed Rock Hudson she says something funny like . . . *(looks at third writer)*

Third Writer Er . . . Good evening.

Larry Doris Day's a comedienne, not a newsreader. Get out! *(third writer runs)* She says something funny like *(looks at second writer)*

Second Writer Splunge?

Larry That's the stupidest idea I ever heard. Get out! *(second writer leaves)* Doris Dog kisses Rock Tree and she says *(looks at first writer)*

First Writer Er . . . er . . . er . . . I can't take it anymore. *(runs out)*

Larry I like that! I like that, I can't take it any more, and then Rock Hudson says 'I'm a very rich film producer and I need a lobotomy' and then Doris Dog says 'I think you're very handsome and I'm going to take all my clothes off' and then Doris Dog turns into a yak and goes to the bathroom on David Lemming. No, wait, wait! *(picks up phone)* Hello, *(cut to 'It's' man film with Larry continuing voice over)* hello, hello, who are you? You're an out-of-work writer? Well, you're fired. Roll the credits. *(here the credits do start to roll with Larry's voice continuing over)* Produced by Irving C. Saltzberg Jnr. of Irving C. Saltzberg Productions Ltd. and Saltzberg Art Films, Oil, Real Estate, Banking and Prostitution Inc.

The credits read:

PRODUCED BY IRVING C. SALTZBERG JNR.
AND IRVING C. SALTZBERG PRODUCTIONS LTD. AND
SALTZBERG ART FILMS, OIL, REAL ESTATE, BANKING AND
PROSTITUTION INC. CO-PRODUCTION
FROM AN ORIGINAL IDEA BY IRVING C. SALTZBERG JNR.
WRITTEN BY IRVING C. SALTZBERG AND IRVING C. SALTZBERG
ADDITIONAL MATERIAL BY IRVING C. SALTZBERG AND

GRAHAM C. CHAPMANBERG   JOHN C. CLEESEBERG
TERRY C. JONESBERG   MICHAEL C. PALINBERG
TERRY C. GILLIAMBERG   ERIC C. IDLEBERG
ALSO APPEARING WAS IAN C. DAVIDSONBERG
CREDITS BY IRVING C. SALTZBERG

The technical credits continue in the same style.

Seven You're no fun any more

A long hilly scar of land; on either side trees. The track comes straight down from the horizon to camera in valley. At the top of the hill we hear running and heavy breathing. The 'It's' man appears. He runs down the valley to camera but fails to say his line:

Voices Off *(prompting)* It's ... no ... no ... it's ... it's ... it's ...

Man *(finally)* It's ...

By the miracle of money we swing into a fantastically expensive opening animation sequence, produced by one of America's very own drop-outs. In the country. Interviewer, with microphone. Behind him a man sits on a wall, with clip-board, binoculars and spotting gear.

Interviewer (JOHN) Good evening. Tonight we're going to take a hard tough abrasive look at camel spotting. Hello.

Spotter (ERIC) Hello Peter.

Interviewer Now tell me, what exactly are you doing?

Spotter Er well, I'm camel spotting. I'm spotting to see if there are any camels that I can spot, and put them down in my camel spotting book.

Interviewer Good. And how many camels have you spotted so far?

Spotter Oh, well so far Peter, up to the present moment, I've spotted nearly, ooh, nearly one.

Interviewer Nearly one?

Spotter Er, call it none.

Interviewer Fine. And er how long have you been here?

Spotter Three years.

Interviewer So, in, er, three years you've spotted no camels?

Spotter Yes in only three years. Er, I tell a lie, four, be fair, five. I've been camel spotting for just the seven years. Before that of course I was a Yeti spotter.

Interviewer A Yeti spotter, that must have been extremely interesting.

Spotter Oh, it was extremely interesting, very, very – quite ... it was dull; dull, dull dull, oh God it was dull. Sitting in the Waterloo waiting room. Course once you've seen one Yeti you've seen them all.

Interviewer And have you seen them all?

Spotter Well I've seen one. Well a little one ... a picture of a ... I've heard about them.

Interviewer Well, now tell me, what do you do when you spot a camel?

Spotter Er, I take its number.

Interviewer Camels don't have numbers.

Spotter Ah, well you've got to know where to look. Er, they're on the side of the engine above the piston box.

Interviewer What?

Spotter Ah – of course you've got to make sure it's not a dromedary. 'Cos if it's a dromedary it goes in the dromedary book.

Interviewer Well how do you tell if it's a dromedary?

Spotter Ah well, a dromedary has *one* hump and a camel has a refreshment car, buffet, and ticket collector.

Interviewer Mr Sopwith, aren't you in fact a train spotter?

Spotter What?

Interviewer Don't you in fact spot trains?

Spotter Oh, you're no fun anymore.

ANIMATION: *Then a girl in bed. Count Dracula (Graham) enters. The girl reveals her neck. The vampire goes to kiss her but his fangs fall out.*

Girl (DONNA) Oh, you're no fun anymore.

A man at the yardarm being lashed.

Lasher (TERRY J) . . . thirty-nine . . . forty. All right, cut him down, Mr Fuller.

Lashee (ERIC) Oh you're no fun anymore.

Back to camel spotter.

Spotter Now if anybody else pinches my phrase I'll throw them under a camel.

Interviewer *(giggling)* If you can spot one.

Spotter gives him a dirty look. Knight in armour appears beside him. He hits interviewer with chicken.

Cut to small board meeting. An accountant stands up and reads . . .

Accountant (MICHAEL) Lady chairman, sir, shareholders, ladies and gentlemen. I have great pleasure in announcing that owing to a cut-back on surplus expenditure of twelve million Canadian dollars, plus a refund of seven and a half million Deutschmarks from the Swiss branch, and in addition adding the debenture preference stock of the three and three quarter million to the directors' reserve currency account of seven and a half million, plus an upward expenditure margin of eleven and a half thousand lire, due to a rise in capital investment of ten million pounds, this firm last year made a complete profit of a shilling.

Chairman (GRAHAM) A shilling Wilkins?

Accountant Er, roughly, yes sir.

Chairman Wilkins, I am the chairman of a multi-million pound corporation and you are a very new chartered accountant. Isn't it possible there may have been some mistake?

Accountant Well that's very kind of you sir, but I don't think I'm ready to be chairman yet.

Board Member (JOHN) Wilkins, Wilkins. This shilling, is it net or gross?

Accountant It's British sir.

Chairman Yes, has tax been paid on it?

Accountant Yes, this is after tax. Owing to the rigorous bite of the income tax five pence of a further sixpence was swallowed up in tax.

Board Member Five pence of a *further* sixpence?

Accountant *(eagerly)* Yes sir.

Chairman Five pence of a further *sixpence*?

Accountant That's right sir.

Chairman Then where is the other penny?

Accountant ... Er.

Board Member That makes you a penny short Wilkins. Where is it?

Accountant ... Erm.

Chairman Wilkins?

Accountant *(in tears)* I embezzled it sir.

Chairman What all of it?

Accountant Yes all of it.

Board Member You naughty person.

Accountant It's my first. Please be gentle with me.

Chairman I'm afraid it's my unpleasant duty to inform you that you're fired.

Accountant Oh please, please.

Chairman No, out!

Accountant *(crying)* Oh ... *(he leaves)*

Chairman Yes, there's no place for sentiment in big business.

> *He goes over to a wall plaque 'There is no place for sentiment in Big Business'. He turns it over. On the back it says 'He's right you know'.*

Bishop (TERRY J) *(to chairman)* Oh you're no fun anymore.

> *Camel man comes running in shouting.*

Spotter I heard that. Who said that?

All *(pointing at the bishop)* He did! He did!

Bishop No I didn't.

All Ooh!

Spotter Right!

> *Shot of the bishop bound and gagged and tied across a railway line.*

Voice Over (ERIC) Here is the address to complain to ...

> CAPTION: 'MR ALBERT SPIM, 1,000,008 LONDON ROAD, OXFORD'
> *But he reads:*

Voice Over The Royal Frog Trampling Institute, 16 Rayners Lane, London, W.C. Fields. I'll just repeat that ...

> CAPTION: 'FLIGHT LT. & PREBENDARY ETHEL MORRIS, THE DIMPLES, THAXTED, NR BUENOS AIRES'
> *He reads over it:*

Voice Over Tristram and Isolde Phillips, 7.30 Covent Garden Saturday

(near Sunday) and afterwards at the Inigo Jones Fish Emporium.
Cut to Jewish figure.

Jewish Figure (MICHAEL) And they want to put the Licence fee up?
Cut to a photo of a man with pipe.

Voice Over *(continues)* And now here is a reminder about leaving your radio on during the night. Leave your radio on during the night.
Cut to redcoat.

Redcoat (MICHAEL) A little joke, a little jest. Nothing to worry about ladies and gentlemen. Now we've got some science fiction for you, some sci-fi, something to send the shivers up your spine, send the creepy crawlies down your lager and limes. All the lads have contributed to it, it's a little number entitled, Science Fiction Sketch . . .
Zoom through the galaxy to the solar system.

American Voice (JOHN) *(very resonant)* The Universe consists of a billion, billion galaxies . . . 77,000,000,000 miles across, and every galaxy is made up of a billion, zillion stars and around these stars circle a billion planets, and of all of these planets the greenest and the pleasantest is the planet Earth, in the system of Sol, in the Galaxy known as the Milky Way . . . And it was to this world that creatures of an alien planet came . . . to conquer and destroy the very heart of civilization . . .
Mix into close-up of railway station sign: 'New Pudsey'. Pull out to mid-shot of a couple walking towards camera. They are middle-aged. He (Graham) wears a cricket blazer and grey flannels and a carrier bag. She (Eric) wears a fussy print dress.

American Voice *(gently)* It was a day like any other and Mr and Mrs Samuel Brainsample were a perfectly ordinary couple, leading perfectly ordinary lives – the sort of people to whom nothing extraordinary ever happened, and not the kind of people to be the centre of one of the most astounding incidents in the history of mankind . . . So let's forget about them and follow instead the destiny of this man . . . *(camera pans off them; they both look disappointed; camera picks up instead a smart little business man, in bowler, briefcase and pinstripes)* . . . Harold Potter, gardener, and tax official, first victim of Creatures from another Planet.
Weird electronic music. Sinister atmosphere. Follow him out of station. Cut-away to flying saucer, over city skyline. Back to Potter as he walks up suburban road. Back to flying saucer. It bleeps as if it has seen its prey and changes direction. Cut back to Potter just about to open his front gate. Shot from over the other side of the road. Cut to flying saucer sending down ray. Potter freezes . . . shivers and turns into a Scotsman with kilt, and red beard. His hand jerks out in front of him and he spins

round and scuttles up road in fast motion, to the accompaniment of bagpipe music. Cut to close-up of newspaper with banner headline: 'Man turns into a Scotsman'.

Newsvendor's Voice Read all abaht it! Read all abaht it! Man turns into Scotsman!

Mix through to Potter's front gate. His wife is being interviewed by obvious plainclothes man.

Inspector (TERRY J) Mrs Potter – you knew Harold Potter quite well I believe?

Wife (ERIC) Oh yes quite well.

Inspector Yes.

Wife He was my husband.

Inspector Yes. And, er, he never showed any inclination towards being a Scotsman before this happened?

Wife *(shocked)* No, no, not at all. He was not that sort of person . . .

Inspector He didn't wear a kilt or play the bagpipes?

Wife No, no.

Inspector He never got drunk at night or bought home black puddings?

Wife No, no. Not at all.

Inspector He didn't have an inadequate brain capacity?

Wife No, no, not at all.

Inspector I see. So by your account Harold Potter was a perfectly ordinary Englishman without any tendency towards being a Scotsman whatsoever?

Wife Absolutely, yes. *(suddenly remembering)* Mind you he did always watch Dr Finlay on television.

Inspector Ah-hah! . . . Well that's it, you see. That's how it starts.

Wife I beg your pardon?

Inspector Well you see Scottishness starts with little things like that, and works up. You see, people don't just turn into a Scotsman for no reason at all . . . *(goes rigid: with Scots accent:)* No further questions!

The words are hardly out of his mouth when he turns into a Scotsman and spins round and disappears up road in fast motion. Pan with him. Cut to bus queue: man in city suit and bowler hat suddenly changes into a Scotsman with beard, twizzles round and speeds out of shot. Cut to street: policeman pointing way for woman with a pram. Suddenly he changes into a Scotsman and scuffles out of shot. She looks aghast for a moment and then she too changes into a Scotsman and hurtles off after him. The baby suddenly develops a beard and the pram follows her. Single shot of black jazz musician in cellar blowing a blue sax solo. He changes and whizzes off. Squad of soldiers being drilled. Suddenly they all change into bearded Scotsmen and race off in unison. Pan with them past sign: 'Welsh Guard'.

Quick animated shot of flying saucer disappearing over city skyline.

> *Cut to big close-up of passionate kiss. It goes on for some moments. Foggy lens ... romantic music. Keep on big close-up as they talk. She is none too intelligent.*

She (DONNA) Charles ...

Charles (GRAHAM) Darling ...

She Charles ...

Charles Darling, darling ...

She Charles ... there's something I've got to tell you ...

Charles What is it darling?

She It's daddy ... he's turned into a Scotsman ...

Charles What! Mr Llewellyn?

She Yes, Charles. Help me, please help me.

Charles But what can I do?

She Surely, Charles, you're the Chief Scientist at the Anthropological Research Institute, at Butley Down – an expert in what makes people change from one nationality to another.

Charles So I am! *(pull out to reveal they are in a laboratory; he is in a white coat, she is in something absurdly sexy)* This is right up my street!

She Oh good.

Charles Now first of all, why would anyone turn into a Scotsman?

She *(tentatively)* Em, for business reasons?

Charles No, no! Only because he has no control over his own destiny! Look I'll show you ...

> *He presses a button on a control board and a laboratory TV screen lights up with the words 'only because they have no control over their own destinies'.*

She I see.

Charles Yes! So this means that some person or persons unknown is turning all these people into Scotsmen ...

She Oh, what kind of heartless fiend could *do* that to a man?

Charles I don't know ... I don't know ... all I know is that these people are streaming north of the border at the rate of thousands every hour. If we don't act fast, Scotland will be choked with Scotsmen ...

She Ooh! ...

> *Zoom in on her face.*
> *Cut to as many bearded Scotsmen as possible, hurtling through wood in fast motion. Follow them, ending up with skyline shot as per 'Seventh Seal'. They all still have the arm outstretched in front of them and as always they are accompanied by bagpipe music. Shot of border with large notice: 'Scotland Welcomes You'.*

American Voice Soon Scotland was full of Scotsmen. The over-crowding was pitiful.

They all dash across border and then stop abruptly once they're over.
They stand around looking lost.

American Voice Three men to a caber.

Cut to three Scotsmen tossing one caber. Cut to Scots wife in bed with
bearded husband. Pull back to reveal five other Scotsmen in the bed.
Short but brilliant piece of animation from T. Gilliam to show
England emptying of people and Scotland filling up, ending with a till
sound and a till sign coming up out of England reading: 'Empty'. Track
into England. Film of a deserted street. Wind, a dog sniffing, newspaper
blowing along street. Close-up sign on shop door: 'Gone to lunch
Scotland'. Close-up another sign on a shop door: 'McClosed'. Shop sign:
'McWoolworths & Co'.

American Voice For the few who remained, life was increasingly
difficult.

Man suddenly folds up newspaper and runs round corner. Re-emerges
driving bus. Drives it halfway to stop and then leaps out with bus still
moving. Runs to stop, and puts out hand. Bus stops. He leaps on, rings
bell, runs round to front and drives the bus off again. As bus drives out
of frame we just see a couple of Scotsmen flashing past camera with arms
outstretched. Pan slowly round empty football stadium. Eventually we
pick up a solitary spectator, halfway up and halfway along in stand
opposite where the players come out. He suddenly leaps to his feet
cheering. Cut to players' tunnel and one player emerging and a referee
with ball. They kick off. Player goes straight down field and scores.
Spectator disapppointed.
A quick shot of flying saucer again.
Studio: the laboratory again. Charles is looking through microscope, when
the door flies open and she bursts in.

She Charles! Thank goodness I've found you! It's mummy!

Charles Hello mummy.

She No, no, mummy's turned into a Scotsman . . .

Charles Oh how horrible . . . Will they stop at nothing?

She I don't know – do you think they will?

Charles I meant that rhetorically.

She What does rhetorically mean?

Charles It means, I didn't expect an answer.

She Oh I see. Oh, you're so clever, Charles.

Charles Did mummy say anything as she changed?

She *(with an air of tremendous revelation)* Yes! She did, now you come to
mention it!

A long pause as he waits expectantly.

Charles Well, what was it?

She Oh, she said . . . 'Them!' *(thrilling chord of jangling music and quick
zoom into her face)* Is there someone at the door?

Charles No . . . It's just the incidental music for this scene.

She Oh I see . . .

Charles 'Them' . . . Wait a minute!

She A *whole* minute?

Charles No, I meant that metaphorically . . . 'Them' . . . 'Them' . . . She
was obviously referring to the people who turned her into a
Scotsman. If only we knew who 'They' were . . . And why 'They'
were doing it . . . Who *are* 'Them'?

> *Crashing chord . . . cut to a small still of a Scottish crofter's cottage on a
> lonely moor. Slow zoom in on the cottage.*

American Voice Then suddenly a clue turned up in Scotland. Mr Angus
Podgorny, owner of a Dunbar menswear shop, received an order
for 48,000,000 kilts from the planet Skyron in the Galaxy of
Andromeda.

> *Mix to interior of highland menswear shop. An elderly Scottish couple are
> poring over a letter which they have on the counter. Oil lamps etc.*

Mrs Podgorny (TERRY J) Angus how are y'going to get 48,000,000 kilts
into the van?

Angus (MICHAEL) I'll have t'do it in two goes.

Mrs Podgorny D'you not ken that the Galaxy of Andromeda is two
million, two hundred thousand light years away?

Angus Is that so?

Mrs Podgorny Aye . . . and you've never been further than
Berwick-on-Tweed . . .

Angus Aye . . . but think o' the money dear . . . £18.10.od a kilt . . .
that's . . . *(calculates with abacus)* £900,000,000 – and that's without
sporrans!

Mrs Podgorny Aye . . . I think you ought not to go, Angus.

Angus *(with visionary look in his eyes)* Aye . . . we'd be able to afford
writing paper with our names on it . . . We'd be able to buy that
extension to the toilet . . .

Mrs Podgorny Aye . . . but he hasn't signed the order yet, has he?

Angus Who?

Mrs Podgorny Ach . . . the man from Andromeda.

Angus Och . . . well . . . he wasna really a man, d'you ken . . .

> *Creepy music starts to edge in.*

Mrs Podgorny *(narrowing eyes)* Not really a man?

Angus *(sweating as the music rises)* He was as strange a thing as ever I saw,
or ever I hope to see, God willing. He was a strange unearthly
creature – a quivering, glistening mass . . .

Mrs Podgorny Angus Podgorny, what *do* y'mean?

Angus He wasna so much a man as . . . a blancmange!

> *Jarring chord.*

Police station: a police sergeant is talking over the counter to a girl dressed in a short frilly tennis dress. She holds a racquet and tennis balls.

Sergeant (JOHN) A blancmange, eh?

Girl (ERIC) Yes, that's right. I was just having a game of doubles with Sandra and Jocasta, Alec and David . . .

Sergeant Hang on!

Girl What?

Sergeant There's five.

Girl What?

Sergeant Five people . . . how do you play doubles with *five* people?

Girl Ah, well . . . we were . . .

Sergeant Sounds a bit funny if you ask me . . . playing doubles with five people . . .

Girl Well we often play like that . . . Jocasta plays on the side receiving service . . .

Sergeant Oh yes?

Girl Yes. It helps to speed the game up and make it a lot faster, and it means Jocasta isn't left out.

Sergeant Look, are you asking me to believe that the five of you was playing doubles, when on the very next court there was a blancmange playing by itself?

Girl That's right, yes.

Sergeant Well answer me this then – why didn't Jocasta play the blancmange at singles, while you and Sandra and Alec and David had a proper game of doubles with four people?

Girl Because Jocasta always plays with *us*. She's a friend of *ours*.

Sergeant Call that friendship? Messing up a perfectly good game of doubles?

Girl It's not messing it up, officer, we like to play with five.

Sergeant Look it's *your* affair if you want to play with five people . . . but don't go calling it doubles. Look at Wimbledon, right? If Fred Stolle and Tony Roche played Charlie Pasarell and Cliff Drysdale and Peaches Bartcowitz . . . they *wouldn't* go calling it doubles.

Girl But what about the blancmange?

Sergeant That could play Ann Haydon-Jones and her husband Pip.

Cut back to Podgorny's shop. He and his wife are frozen in the positions in which we left them. They pick up the conversation as if nothing had happened.

Mrs Podgorny Oh, a blancmange gave you an order for 48,000,000 kilts?

Angus Aye!

Mrs Podgorny And you *believed* it?

Angus Aye, I did.

Mrs Podgorny Och, you're a stupid man, Angus Podgorny.

Angus (*getting a little angry*) Oh look woman, how many kilts did we sell last year? Nine and a half, that's all. So when I get an order for 48,000,000, I believe it – you *bet* I believe it!

Mrs Podgorny Even if it's from a blancmange?

Angus Och, woman, if a blancmange is prepared to come 2,200,000 light years to purchase a kilt, they must be fairly keen on kilts. So cease yer prattling woman and get sewing. This could be the biggest breakthrough in kilts since the Provost of Edinburgh sat on a spike. Mary, we'll be rich! We'll be rich!

Mrs Podgorny Oh, but Angus . . . he hasna given you an earnest of his good faith!

Angus Ah mebbe not but he has gi' me this . . . *(brings out piece of folded paper from sporran)*

Mrs Podgorny What is it now?

Angus An entry form for the British Open Tennis Championships at Wimbledon Toon . . . signed and seconded.

Mrs Podgorny Och, but Angus, ye ken full well that Scots folk dinna know how to play the tennis to save their lives.

Angus Aye, but I must go though dear, I dinna want to seem ungrateful.

Mrs Podgorny Ach! Angus, I wilna let you make a fool o'yoursel'.

Angus But I must.

Mrs Podgorny Och, no you'll not . . .

Close-up on Angus.

Angus Oh, Mary . . . *(suddenly we hear a strange creaking and a slurping noise; a look of horror comes into his eyes)* Oh, oh, Mary! Look out! Look out!

Big close-up of Mrs Podgorny's eyes starting out from head.

Mrs Podgorny Urrgh. It's the blancmange.

Blur focus.
Cut to a desk for police spokesman. A peaked-capped policeman sits there, reading 'The Rise and Fall of the Roman Empire' by Googie Withers. He lowers book and talks chattily to camera.

Policeman (GRAHAM) Oh, now this is where Mr Podgorny could have saved his wife's life. If he'd gone to the police and told them that he'd been approached by unearthly beings from the Galaxy of Andromeda, we'd have sent a man round to investigate. As it was he did a deal with a blancmange, and the blancmange ate his wife. So if *you're* going out, or going on holiday, or anything strange happens involving other galaxies, just nip round to your local police station, and tell the sergeant on duty – or his wife – of your suspicions. And the same goes for dogs. So I'm sorry to have interrupted your exciting science fiction story . . . but, then, crime's our business you know. So carry on viewing, and my thanks to the BBC for allowing me to have this little chat with you. Goodnight. God bless, look after yourselves.

He is hit on the head by knight in suit of armour with raw chicken.
Cut to CID office: a plainclothes detective is sitting in his office. Podgorny is sobbing.

Detective (ERIC) *(softly and understandingly)* Do sit down, Mr Podgorny ... I ... I ... think what's happened is ... terribly ... terribly ... funny ... tragic. But you must understand that we have to catch the creature that ate your wife, and if you could help us answer a few questions, we may be able to help save a few lives. I know this is the way your wife would have wanted it.

He is sitting on the desk next to Podgorny. Podgorny with superhuman control makes a great effort to stop sobbing.

Angus Aye ... I'll ... do ... my best, sergeant.

Detective *(slapping Podgorny)* Detective inspector!

Angus Er, detective inspector.

Detective *(getting up and talking sharply and fast)* Now then. The facts are these. You received an order for 48,000,000 kilts from a blancmange from the planet Skyron in the Galaxy of Andromeda ... you'd just shown your wife an entry form for Wimbledon, which you'd filled in ... when you turned round and saw her legs disappearing into a blancmange. Is that correct?

Angus Yes, sir.

Detective Are you mad?

Angus No, sir.

Detective Well that's a relief. 'Cos if you were, your story would be less plausible. *(detective brings out photograph of blancmange)* Now then, do you recognize this?

Angus *(with a squeak of fear)* Oh yes. That's the one that ate my Mary!

Detective Good. His name's Riley ... Jack Riley ... He's that most rare of criminals ... a blancmange impersonator and cannibal.

Angus But what about the 48,000,000 kilts and the Galaxy of Andromeda?

Detective I'm afraid that's just one of his stories. You must understand that a blancmange impersonator and cannibal has to use some pretty clever stories to allay suspicion.

Angus Then you mean ...

Detective Yes.

Angus But ...

Detective How?

Angus Yes.

Detective Well ...

Angus Not?

Detective I'm afraid so.

Angus Why?

Detective Who knows?

Angus D'you think?

Detective Could be.

Angus But...

Detective I know.

Angus She was...

Detective Yes.

> *Suddenly we hear a strange noise. Angus looks frightened. Detective narrows his eyes and walks over to the door.*

Detective Good lord what's that? *(he opens the door and we get a close-up of his staring eyes)* Ah, Riley! Come to give yourself up have you, Riley? *(with sudden fear)* Eh Riley? Riley! Riley! It's not Riley!

> *Eating noises. He is dragged out of camera shot. Refocus on Angus ... he averts his eyes as we hear the detective inspector off-screen.*

Detective *(off-screen)* It's an extra-terrestial being! Agggh!

> *Jarring chord: Angus shuts his eyes.*
> *Cut back to laboratory: she is sitting suggestively on a stool. He is pacing up and down looking intense.*

Charles So, everyone in England is being turned into Scotsmen, right?

She Yes.

Charles Now, which is the *worst* tennis-playing nation in the world?

She Er ... Australia.

Charles No. Try again.

She Australia?

Charles *(testily)* No ... try again but say a different place.

She Oh, I thought you meant I'd said it badly.

Charles No, course you didn't say it badly. Now hurry.

She Er, Czechoslovakia.

Charles No! Scotland!

She Of course.

Charles Now ... now these blancmanges, apart from the one that killed Mrs Podgorny, have all appeared in which London suburb?

She Finchley?

Charles No. *Wimbledon* ... Now do you begin to see the pattern? With *what* sport is *Wimbledon* commonly associated?

> *She is thinking really hard.*

Norman Hackforth (TERRY J) *(off-screen)* For viewers at home, the answer is coming up on your screens. Those of you who wish to play it the hard way, stand upside down with your head in a bucket of piranha fish. Here is the question once again.

Charles With what *sport* is *Wimbledon* commonly associated?

SUPERIMPOSED CAPTION: 'TENNIS'

She Cricket.

Charles No.

She Pelote?

Charles No. Wimbledon is most commonly associated with *tennis*.

She Of course! Now I see!

Charles Yes, it all falls into place!

She The blancmanges are really Australians trying to get the rights of the pelote rules from the Czech publishers!

Charles *(heavily)* No . . . not quite . . . but, er, just look in here.

He indicates microscope. As she eagerly bends to look into it he picks up a sock filled with sand and without looking strikes her casually over the head with it. She collapses out of sight under desk. He continues to think out loud.

Charles Yes. So these blancmanges, blancmange-shaped creatures come from the planet Skyron in the Galaxy of Andromeda. They order 48,000,000 kilts from a Scottish menswear shop . . . turn the population of England into Scotsmen (well known as the worst tennis-playing nation on Earth) thus leaving England empty *during Wimbledon fortnight*! Empty during Wimbledon fortnight . . . what's more the papers are full of reports of blancmanges appearing on tennis courts up and down the country – *practising*. This can only mean one thing!

Flash up caption quickly:

Voice Over and CAPTION: 'THEY MEAN TO WIN WIMBLEDON'

Charles They mean to *win Wimbledon*.

Jarring chord.

Cut to commentator in his box.

Commentator (ERIC) Well, here at Wimbledon, it's been a most extraordinary week's tennis. The blancmanges have swept the board, winning match after match. Here are just a few of the results: Billie-Jean King eaten in straight sets, Laver smothered whole after winning the first set, and Pancho Gonzales, serving as well as I've never seen him, with some superb volleys and decisive return volleys off the back hand, was sucked through the net at match point and swallowed whole in just under two minutes. And so, here on the final day, there seems to be no players left to challenge the blancmanges. And this could be their undoing, Dan: as the rules of Wimbledon state quite clearly that there must be at least *one* human being concerned in the final. *(we see a three-foot-high blancmange being shepherded onto a tennis court by a Scotsman)* Well the blancmange is coming out onto the pitch now, and *(suddenly excited)* there is a human with it! It's Angus Podgorny! The plucky little Scottish tailor . . . upon whom everything depends. And so it's Podgorny versus blancmange in this first ever Intergalactic Wimbledon!

> *Cut to the centre court at Wimbledon or, if we can't get it, number one will do. Blancmange and Podgorny on opposite sides of net. Another blancmange sitting in umpire's chair. Blancmange serves . . . a real sizzling ace. Podgorny, who in any case is quivering with fear, doesn't see it.*

Commentator's Voice   And it's blancmange to serve and it's a good one.

Blancmange Umpire   Blurb blurble blurb.

Voice Over   Fifteen-love.

> *Blancmange serves again, and again Podgorny misses hopelessly and pathetically. Collage of speeded-up versions of blancmange serving and Podgorny missing. Cut to scoreboard:*

> BLANCMANGE: 40
> PODGORNY: 0

> *Cut back to the court. Podgorny is serving and each time he fails to hit the ball altogether.*

Commentator's Voice   And Podgorny fails to even hit the ball . . . but this is no surprise as he hasn't hit the ball once throughout this match. So it's 72 match points to the blancmange now . . . Podgorny prepares to serve again.

> *Podgorny fails to serve and we see the scoreboard:*

> BLANCMANGE: 6 6 5 40
> PODGORNY: 0 0

Commentator's Voice   This is indeed a grim day for the human race, Dan.

> *Just as Podgorny is about to serve we see Mr and Mrs Brainsample jump onto the court brandishing forks and spoons and with napkins tucked into their necks.*

Commentator's Voice   But what's this? Two spectators have rushed onto the pitch with spoons and forks . . . what are they going to do?

> *Cut to laboratory.*

Charles   They mean to eat the blancmange.

> *The girl pulls herself up from where she was slumped by microscope. He knocks her out again with a sand-filled sock.*
> *Cut back to Wimbledon. Mr and Mrs Brainsample chasing blancmange and eating it.*

Commentator's Voice   And they're eating the blancmange . . . Yes! The blancmange is leaving the court . . . it's abandoning the game! This is fantastic!

> *Cut to Mr and Mrs Brainsample covered in bits of blancmange and licking their fingers.*

American Voice   Yes it was Mr and Mrs Samuel Brainsample, who, after only a brief and misleading appearance in the early part of the film, returned to save the Earth . . . but *why?*

Mr Brainsample (GRAHAM) Oh, well you see we love blancmanges. My wife makes them.

American Voice She makes blancmanages *that* size?

Mr Brainsample Oh, yes. You see we're from the planet Skyron in the Galaxy of Andromeda, and they're all that size there. We tried to tell you at the beginning of the film but you just panned off us.

Cut back to Podgorny on court still trying to serve; at last he makes contact and runs backward and forward to receive his own services.

American Voice So the world was saved! And Angus Podgorny became the first Scotsman to win Wimbledon . . . fifteen years later.

ROLLER CAPTION: 'YOU'RE NO FUN ANYMORE' . . . (CREDITS)

Eight Full frontal nudity

We see the 'It's' man sitting in the countryside in a garden lounger chair. A sexy young lady in a bikini hands him a glass of wine and gently helps him up and walks him to the camera. Looking very pleased with himself he sips the wine as she caresses him. Then she hands him a smoking round anarchist's type bomb (with 'Bomb' written on it). He realizes what it is only as he says:

Man (MICHAEL) It's . . .

Voice Over (JOHN) Monty Python's Flying Circus.

> *Cartoon credits.*
>
> SUPERIMPOSED CAPTION: 'EPISODE I2B: FULL FRONTAL NUDITY'
>
> *Cut to vox pops.*

Pepperpot (MICHAEL) Speaking as a public opinion poll, I've had enough of the permissive society.

Man In Dirty Raincoat (TERRY J) I haven't had enough of the permissive society.

> CAPTION: 'IN THIS PERFORMANCE THE PART OF DAVID HEMMINGS WILL BE PLAYED BY A PIECE OF WOOD'
>
> *Cut to policeman.*

Policeman (GRAHAM) I would not appear in a frontal nude scene unless it was valid.

> *Stock film of the army. Tanks rolling, troops moving forward etc. Stirring military music.*

Voice Over (JOHN) In 1943, a group of British Army Officers working deep behind enemy lines, carried out one of the most dangerous and heroic raids in the history of warfare. But that's as maybe. And now . . .

> SUPERIMPOSED CAPTION: 'AND NOW . . . UNOCCUPIED BRITAIN 1970'
>
> *Cut to colonel's office. Colonel is seated at desk.*

Colonel (GRAHAM) Come in, what do you want?

> *Private Watkins enters and salutes.*

Watkins (ERIC) I'd like to leave the army please, sir.

Colonel Good heavens man, why?

Watkins It's dangerous.

Colonel What?

Watkins There are people with guns out there, sir.

Colonel What?

Watkins Real guns, sir. Not toy ones, sir. Proper ones, sir. They've all got 'em. All of 'em, sir. And some of 'em have got tanks.

Colonel Watkins, they *are* on our side.

Watkins And grenades, sir. And machine guns, sir. So I'd like to leave, sir, before I get killed, please.

Colonel Watkins, you've only been in the army a day.

Watkins I know sir but people get killed, properly dead, sir, no barley cross fingers, sir. A bloke was telling me, if you're in the army and there's a war you have to go and fight.

Colonel That's true.

Watkins Well I mean, blimey, I mean if it was a big war somebody could be hurt.

Colonel Watkins why did you *join* the army?

Watkins For the water-skiing and for the travel, sir. And *not* for the killing, sir. I asked them to put it on my form, sir no killing.

Colonel Watkins are you a pacifist?

Watkins No sir, I'm not a pacifist, sir. I'm a coward.

Colonel That's a very silly line. Sit down.

Watkins Yes sir. Silly, sir. *(sits in corner)*

Colonel Awfully bad.

Knock at the door, sergeant enters, and salutes.

Sergeant (JOHN) Two civilian gentlemen to see you . . . sir!

Colonel Show them in please, sergeant.

Sergeant Mr Dino Vercotti and Mr Luigi Vercotti.

The Vercotti brothers enter. They wear Mafia suits and dark glasses.

Dino (TERRY J) Good morning, colonel.

Colonel Good morning gentlemen. Now what can I do for you.

Luigi (MICHAEL) *(looking round office casually)* You've . . . you've got a nice army base here, colonel.

Colonel Yes.

Luigi We wouldn't want anything to happen to it.

Colonel What?

Dino No, what my brother means is it would be a shame if . . . *(he knocks something off mantel)*

Colonel Oh.

Dino Oh sorry, colonel.

Colonel Well don't worry about that. But please do sit down.

Luigi No, we prefer to stand, thank you, colonel.

Colonel All right. All right. But what do you want?

Dino What do we want, ha ha ha.

Luigi Ha ha ha, very good, colonel.

Dino The colonel's a joker, Luigi.

Luigi Explain it to the colonel, Dino.

Dino How many tanks you got, colonel?

Colonel About five hundred altogether.

Luigi Five hundred! Hey!

Dino You ought to be careful, colonel.

Colonel We are careful, extremely careful.

Dino 'Cos things *break*, don't they?

Colonel Break?

Luigi Well everything breaks, don't it colonel. *(he breaks something on desk)* Oh dear.

Dino Oh see my brother's clumsy colonel, and when he gets unhappy he breaks things. Like say, he don't feel the army's playing fair by him, he may start breaking things, colonel.

Colonel What is all this about?

Luigi How many men you got here, colonel?

Colonel Oh, er . . . seven thousand infantry, six hundred artillery, and er, two divisions of paratroops.

Luigi Paratroops, Dino.

Dino Be a shame if someone was to set fire to *them*.

Colonel Set *fire* to them?

Luigi Fires happen, colonel.

Dino Things burn.

Colonel Look, what is all this about?

Dino My brother and I have got a little proposition for you colonel.

Luigi Could save you a lot of bother.

Dino I mean you're doing all right here aren't you, colonel.

Luigi Well suppose some of your tanks was to get broken and troops started getting lost, er, fights started breaking out during general inspection, like.

Dino It wouldn't be good for business would it, colonel?

Colonel Are you threatening me?

Dino Oh, no, no, no.

Luigi Whatever made you think that, colonel?

Dino The colonel doesn't think we're nice people, Luigi.

Luigi We're your buddies, colonel.

Dino We want to look after you.

Colonel Look after me?

Luigi We can guarantee you that not a single armoured division will get done over for fifteen bob a week.

Colonel No, no, no.

Luigi Twelve and six.

Colonel No, no, no.

Luigi Eight and six . . . five bob . . .

Colonel No, no this is silly.

Dino What's silly?

Colonel No, the whole premise is silly and it's very badly written. I'm the senior officer here and I haven't had a funny line yet. So I'm stopping it.

Dino You can't do that!

Colonel I've done it. The sketch is over.

Watkins I want to leave the army please sir, it's dangerous.

Colonel Look, I stopped *your* sketch five minutes ago. So get out of shot.
Right director! Close up. Zoom in on me. *(camera zooms in)* That's
better.

Luigi *(off screen)* It's only 'cos you couldn't think of a punch line.

Colonel Not true, not true. It's time for the cartoon. Cue telecine, ten,
nine, eight . . .

> *Cut to telecine countdown.*

Dino *(off screen)* The general public's not going to understand this, are
they?

Colonel *(off-screen)* Shut up you eyeties!

> *Cartoon rubbish entitled 'Full Frontal Nudity': Written, created and
> conceived off the back of a lorry by a demented American.*
> *Cut to two naked men.*

Man (GRAHAM) Full frontal nudity – never. What do you think, Barbara?

Barbara (TERRY J) Oh, no no, no . . . unless it was artistically valid, of
course.

> *Cut to stockbroker.*

Stockbroker (MICHAEL) Full frontal nudity? Yes I'd do it, if it was valid.
Or if the money was valid, and if it were a small part.

> *Cut to art critic examining a nude painting.*
> CAPTION: 'AN ART CRITIC'
> *He sees the camera and starts guiltily.*

Art Critic (MICHAEL) Good evening. I'd like to talk to you tonight about
the place of the nude in my bed . . . um . . . in the history of my
bed . . . of art, of *art*, I'm sorry. The place of the nude in the
history of tart . . . call-girl . . . I'm sorry. I'll start again . . . Bum
. . . oh what a giveaway. The place of the nude in art. *(a seductively
dressed girl enters slinkily)* Oh hello there father, er confessor,
professor, your honour, your grace . . .

Girl (KATYA) *(cutely)* I'm not your Grace, I'm your Elsie.

Art Critic What a terrible joke!

Girl *(crying)* But it's my only line!

> *Cut to an idyllic countryside. Birds sing etc. as the camera starts a lyrical
> pan across the fields.*

Voice Over (TERRY G.) and SUPERIMPOSED CAPTION: 'BUT THERE LET US
LEAVE THE ART CRITIC TO STRANGLE HIS WIFE AND MOVE ON TO
PASTURES NEW'

> *After about ten seconds of mood setting the camera suddenly comes across
> the art critic strangling his wife in middle foreground. As the camera
> passes him he hums nervously and tries to look as though he isn't
> strangling anybody. The camera doesn't stop panning, and just as it goes*

off him we see him start strangling again. The pan carries on and catches up with a bridegroom carrying his bride across a field and finally arriving in a high street where, breathless and panting, he carries her through traffic and into a large department store. Finally cut to the furniture department of the store. The bridegroom and bride enter, he puts her down and addresses one of the assistants.

Groom (TERRY J) We want to buy a bed, please.

Lambert (GRAHAM) Oh, certainly, I'll, I'll get someone to attend to you. *(calling off)* Mr Verity!

Verity (ERIC) Can I help you sir?

Groom Er yes. We'd like to buy a bed ... a double bed ... about fifty pounds?

Verity Oh no, I am afraid not sir. Our cheapest bed is eight hundred pounds, sir.

Groom Eight hundred pounds!

Lambert Oh, er, perhaps I should have explained. Mr Verity does tend to exaggerate, so every figure he gives you will be ten times too high. Otherwise he's perfectly all right, perfectly ha, ha, ha.

Groom Oh I see, I see. *(to Verity)* So your cheapest bed is eighty pounds?

Verity Eight hundred pounds, yes sir.

Groom And how wide is it?

Verity Er, the width is, er, sixty feet wide.

Groom Oh ... *(laughing politely he mutters to wife)* six foot wide, eh. And the length?

Verity The length is ... er ... *(calls off)* Lambert! What is the length of the Comfydown Majorette?

Lambert Er, two foot long.

Groom Two foot long?

Verity Ah yes, you have to, ah, remember of course, to multiply everything Mr Lambert says by three. Er, it's nothing he can help, you understand. Apart from that he's perfectly all right.

Groom I see, I'm sorry.

Verity But it does mean that when he says a bed is two foot wide it is, in fact, sixty feet wide.

Groom Oh, yes I see ...

Verity And that's not counting the mattress.

Groom Oh, how much is that?

Verity Er, Lambert will be able to help you there. *(calls)* Lambert! Will you show these twenty good people the, er, dog kennel please?

Lambert Mm? Certainly.

Groom Dog kennel? No, no, no, mattresses, mattresses.

Verity Oh no, no you have to say dog kennel to Mr Lambert because if you say mattress he puts a bag over his head. I should have explained. Apart from that he's really all right.

> *They go to Lambert.*

Groom Ah, hum, er we'd like to see the dog kennels please.

Lambert Dog kennels?

Groom Yes, we want to see the dog kennels.

Lambert Ah yes, well that's the pets department. Second floor.

Groom Oh, no, no, we want to see the *dog kennels*.

Lambert Yes, pets department second floor.

Groom No, no, no, we don't really want to see dog kennels only your colleague said we ought to . . .

Lambert Oh dear, what's he been telling you now?

Groom Well he said we should say dog kennels to you, instead of mattress.

> *Lambert puts bag over head.*

Groom *(looking round)* Oh dear, hello?

Verity Did you say mattress?

Groom Well, a little yes.

Verity I did *ask* you not to say mattress didn't I. Now I've got to stand in the tea chest. *(he gets in the chest and sings)* 'And did those feet in ancient times, walk upon England's mountains green . . .'

> *The manager enters.*

Manager (JOHN) Did somebody say mattress to Mr Lambert!

> *Manager and Verity continue to sing. Lambert takes bag off head, manager exits after pointing a warning finger at bride and groom.*

Verity *(getting out of chest)* He should be all right now but don't, you know . . . just *don't. (exits)*

Groom Oh, no, no, no, er we'd like to see, see the dog kennels, please.

Lambert Yes, second floor.

Groom No, no look these *(pointing)* dog kennels here, see?

Lambert Mattresses?

Groom Oh *(jumps)* . . . yes.

Lambert Well, if you meant mattress, why didn't you *say* a mattress. I mean it's very confusing for me, if you go and say dog kennels, when you mean mattress. Why not just say mattress?

Groom Well, I mean you put a bag over your head last time I said mattress.

> *Bag goes on. Groom looks around guiltily. Verity walks in. Verity heaves a sigh, jumps in box. Manager comes in and joins him, they sing 'And did those feet . . .'. Another assistant comes in.*

Assistant (MICHAEL) Did somebody say mattress to Mr Lambert?

Verity Twice.

Assistant Hey, everybody, somebody said mattress to Mr Lambert, twice!

> *Assistant, groom and bride join in the therapy.*

Verity It's not working. We need more.

Cut to crowd in St Peter's Square singing 'Jerusalem'.
Cut to department store. Lambert takes the bag off his head and looks at groom and bride.

Lambert Now, er, can I help you?

Bride (CAROL) We want a mattress.

Lambert immediately puts bag back on head.

All Oh. What did you say that for? What did you say that for?

Bride *(weeping)* Well, it's my only line.

All Well, you didn't have to say it.

They all hop off. She howls. Cut to vox pops.

African Native (TERRY J) Full frontal nudity – not in this part of Esher.

Chartered Accountant (JOHN) I would only perform a scene in which there was total frontal nudity.

Cut to colonel.

Colonel Now, I've noticed a tendency for this programme to get rather silly. Now I do my best to keep things moving along, but I'm not having things getting silly. Those last two sketches I did got very silly indeed, and that last one about the bed was even sillier. Now, nobody likes a good laugh more than I do . . . except perhaps my wife and some of her friends . . . oh yes and Captain Johnston. Come to think of it most people like a good laugh more than I do. But that's beside the point. Now, let's have a good clean healthy outdoor sketch. Get some air into your lungs. Ten, nine, eight and all that.

Cut to two hermits on a hillside.

Colonel Ah yes, that's better. Now let's hope this doesn't get silly.

First Hermit (MICHAEL) Hello, are you a hermit by any chance?

Second Hermit (ERIC) Yes that's right. Are you a hermit?

First Hermit Yes, I certainly am.

Second Hermit Well I never. What are you getting away from?

First Hermit Oh you know, the usual – people, chat, gossip, you know.

Second Hermit Oh I certainly do – it was the same with me. I mean there comes a time when you realize there's no good frittering your life away in idleness and trivial chit-chat. Where's your cave?

First Hermit Oh, up the goat track, first on the left.

Second Hermit Oh they're very nice up there aren't they?

First Hermit Yes they are, I've got a beauty.

Second Hermit A bit draughty though, aren't they?

First Hermit No, we've had ours insulated.

Second Hermit Oh yes.

First Hermit Yes, I used birds' nests, moss and oak leaves round the outside.

Second Hermit Oh, sounds marvellous.

First Hermit Oh it's a treat, it really is, 'cos otherwise those stone caves
   can be so grim.
Second Hermit Yes they really can be, can't they? They really can.
First Hermit Oh yes.

   Third hermit passes by.

Third Hermit (GRAHAM) Morning Frank.
Second Hermit Morning Norman. Talking of moss, er you know Mr
   Robinson?
First Hermit With the, er, green loin cloth?
Second Hermit Er no, that's Mr Seagrave. Mr Robinson's the hermit
   who lodges with Mr Seagrave.
First Hermit Oh I see, yes.
Second Hermit Yes well he's put me onto wattles.
First Hermit Really?
Second Hermit Yes. Swears by them. Yes.

   Fourth hermit passes by.

Fourth Hermit (JOHN) Morning Frank.
Second Hermit Morning Lionel. Well he says that moss tends to fall off
   the cave walls during cold weather. You know you might get a
   really bad spell and half the moss drops off the cave wall, leaving
   you cold.
First Hermit Oh well, Mr Robinson's cave's never been exactly nirvana
   has it?
Second Hermit Well, quite, that's what I mean. Anyway, Mr Rogers,
   he's the, er, hermit . . .
First Hermit . . . on the end.
Second Hermit . . . up at the top, yes. Well he tried wattles and he came
   out in a rash.
First Hermit Really?
Second Hermit Yes, and there's me with half a wall wattled, I mean
   what'll I do?
First Hermit Well why don't you try birds' nests like I've done? Or else,
   dead bracken.
Fifth Hermit (TERRY J) *(calling from a distance)* Frank!
Second Hermit Yes Han.
Fifth Hermit Can I borrow your goat?
Second Hermit Er, yes that'll be all right. Oh leave me a pint for
   breakfast will you? . . . *(to first hermit)* You see, you know that is the
   trouble with living half way up a cliff – you feel so cut off. You
   know it takes me two hours every morning to get out onto the
   moors, collect my berries, chastise myself, and two hours back in
   the evening.
First Hermit Still there's one thing about being a hermit, at least you
   meet people.

Second Hermit Oh yes, I wouldn't go back to public relations.

First Hermit Oh well, bye for now Frank, must toddle.

Colonel *(coming on)* Right, you two hermits, stop that sketch. I think it's silly.

Second Hermit What?

Colonel It's silly.

Second Hermit What do you mean, you can't stop it – it's on film.

Colonel That doesn't make any difference to the viewer at home, does it? Come on, get out. Out. Come on out, all of you. Get off, go on, all of you. Go on, move, move. Go on, get out. Come on, get out, move, move.

He shoos them and the film crew off the hillside.

ANIMATION: *including dancing Botticelli Venus, which links to pet shop: Mr Praline walks into the shop carrying a dead parrot in a cage. He walks to counter where shopkeeper tries to hide below cash register.*

Praline (JOHN) Hello, I wish to register a complaint ... Hello? Miss?

Shopkeeper (MICHAEL) What do you mean, miss?

Praline Oh, I'm sorry, I have a cold. I wish to make a complaint.

Shopkeeper Sorry, we're closing for lunch.

Praline Never mind that my lad, I wish to complain about this parrot what I purchased not half an hour ago from this very boutique.

Shopkeeper Oh yes, the Norwegian Blue. What's wrong with it?

Praline I'll tell you what's wrong with it. It's dead, that's what's wrong with it.

Shopkeeper No, no it's resting, look!

Praline Look my lad, I know a dead parrot when I see one and I'm looking at one right now.

Shopkeeper No, no sir, it's not dead. It's resting.

Praline Resting?

Shopkeeper Yeah, remarkable bird the Norwegian Blue, beautiful plumage, innit?

Praline The plumage don't enter into it – it's stone dead.

Shopkeeper No, no – it's just resting.

Praline All right then, if it's resting I'll wake it up. *(shouts into cage)* Hello Polly! I've got a nice cuttlefish for you when you wake up, Polly Parrot!

Shopkeeper *(jogging cage)* There it moved.

Praline No he didn't. That was you pushing the cage.

Shopkeeper I did not.

Praline Yes, you did. *(takes parrot out of cage, shouts)* Hello Polly, Polly *(bangs it against counter)* Polly Parrot, wake up. Polly. *(throws it in the air and lets it fall to the floor)* Now that's what I call a dead parrot.

Shopkeeper No, no it's stunned.

Praline Look my lad, I've had just about enough of this. That parrot is definitely deceased. And when I bought it not half an hour ago, you assured me that its lack of movement was due to it being tired and shagged out after a long squawk.

Shopkeeper It's probably pining for the fiords.

Praline Pining for the fiords, what kind of talk is that? Look, why did it fall flat on its back the moment I got it home?

Shopkeeper The Norwegian Blue prefers kipping on its back. Beautiful bird, lovely plumage.

Praline Look, I took the liberty of examining that parrot, and I discovered that the only reason that it had been sitting on its perch in the first place was that it had been nailed there.

Shopkeeper Well of course it was nailed there. Otherwise it would muscle up to those bars and voom.

Praline Look matey *(picks up parrot)* this parrot wouldn't voom if I put four thousand volts through it. It's bleeding demised.

Shopkeeper It's not, it's pining.

Praline It's not pining, it's passed on. This parrot is no more. It has ceased to be. It's expired and gone to meet its maker. This is a late parrot. It's a stiff. Bereft of life, it rests in peace. If you hadn't nailed it to the perch, it would be pushing up the daisies. It's rung down the curtain and joined the choir invisible. This is an ex-parrot.

Shopkeeper Well, I'd better replace it then.

Praline *(to camera)* If you want to get anything done in this country you've got to complain till you're blue in the mouth.

Shopkeeper Sorry guv, we're right out of parrots.

Praline I see. I see. I get the picture.

Shopkeeper I've got a slug.

Praline Does it talk?

Shopkeeper Not really, no.

Praline Well, it's scarcely a replacement, then is it?

Shopkeeper Listen, I'll tell you what, *(handing over a card)* tell you what, if you go to my brother's pet shop in Bolton he'll replace your parrot for you.

Praline Bolton eh?

Shopkeeper Yeah.

Praline All right.

He leaves, holding the parrot.

CAPTION: 'A SIMILAR PET SHOP IN BOLTON, LANCS'

Close-up of sign on door reading: 'Similar Pet Shops Ltd'. Pull back from sign to see same pet shop. Shopkeeper now has moustache. Praline walks into shop. He looks around with interest, noticing the empty parrot cage still on the floor.

Praline Er, excuse me. This is Bolton, is it?

Shopkeeper No, no it's, er, Ipswich.

Praline *(to camera)* That's Inter-City Rail for you. *(leaves)*

> *Man in porter's outfit standing at complaints desk for railways. Praline approaches.*

Praline I wish to make a complaint.

Porter (TERRY J) I don't have to do this, you know.

Praline I beg your pardon?

Porter I'm a qualified brain surgeon. I only do this because I like being my own boss.

Praline Er, excuse me, this is irrelevant, isn't it?

Porter Oh yeah, it's not easy to pad these out to thirty minutes.

Praline Well I wish to make a complaint. I got on the Bolton train and found myself deposited here in Ipswich.

Porter No, this is Bolton.

Praline *(to camera)* The pet shop owner's brother was lying.

Porter Well you can't blame British Rail for that.

Praline If this is Bolton, I shall return to the pet shop.

> CAPTION: 'A LITTLE LATER LTD'
>
> *Praline walks into the shop again.*

Praline I understand that this *is* Bolton.

Shopkeeper Yes.

Praline Well, you told me it was Ipswich.

Shopkeeper It was a pun.

Praline A pun?

Shopkeeper No, no, not a pun, no. What's the other thing which reads the same backwards as forwards?

Praline A palindrome?

Shopkeeper Yes, yes.

Praline It's not a palindrome. The palindrome of Bolton would be Notlob. It don't work.

Shopkeeper Look, what do you want?

Praline No I'm sorry, I'm not prepared to pursue my line of enquiry any further as I think this is getting too silly.

Colonel *(coming in)* Quite agree. Quite agree. Silly. Silly . . . silly. Right get on with it. Get on with it.

> *Cut to announcer eating a yoghurt.*

Announcer (ERIC) *(seeing camera)* Oh . . . er . . . oh . . . um! Oh! . . . er . . . *(shuffles papers)* I'm sorry . . . and now frontal nudity.

> *Cut to tracking or hand-held shot down street, keeping up with extremely shabby man in long overcoat. His back is to camera. He passes two pepperpots and a girl. As he passes each one he opens his coat wide. They react with shocked horror. He does this three times, after the third time*

he turns to camera and opens his coat wide. He has a big sign hanging round his neck, covering his chest. It says 'boo'.
Cut back to announcer eating yoghurt. The colonel comes in and nudges him.

Announcer Oh, oh I'm sorry. I thought the film was longer. *(shuffling papers)* Ah. Now Notlob, er, Bolton.

Cut to grannies film, which opens with a pan across Bolton. Voice of reporter.

Voice Over (ERIC) This is a frightened city. Over these houses, over these streets hangs a pall of fear. Fear of a new kind of violence which is terrorizing the city. Yes, gangs of old ladies attacking defenceless fit young men.

Film of old ladies beating up two young men; then several grannies walking aggressively along street, pushing passers-by aside.

First Young Man (MICHAEL) Well they come up to you, like, and push you – shove you off the pavement, like. There's usually four or five of them.

Second Young Man (TERRY J) Yeah, this used to be a nice neighbourhood before the old ladies started moving in. Nowadays some of us daren't even go down to the shops.

Third Young Man (JOHN) Well Mr Johnson's son Kevin, he don't go out any more. He comes back from wrestling and locks himself in his room.

Film of grannies harrassing an attractive girl.

Voice Over What are they in it for, these old hoodlums, these layabouts in lace?

First Granny *(voice over)* Well it's something to do isn't it?

Second Granny *(voice over)* It's good fun.

Third Granny *(voice over)* It's like you know, well, innit, eh?

Voice Over Favourite targets for the old ladies are telephone kiosks.

Film of grannies carrying off a telephone kiosk; then painting slogans on a wall.

Policeman (GRAHAM) *(coming up to them)* Well come on, come on, off with you. Clear out, come on get out of it. *(they clear off; he turns to camera)* We have a lot of trouble with these oldies. Pension day's the worst – they go mad. As soon as they get their hands on their money they blow it all on milk, bread, tea, tin of meat for the cat.

Cut to cinema.

Cinema Manager (TERRY J) Yes, well of course they come here for the two o'clock matinee, all the old bags out in there, especially if it's something like 'The Sound of Music'. We get seats ripped up, hearing aids broken, all that sort of thing.

A policeman hustles two grannies out of the cinema.
Cut to reporter walking along street.

Reporter The whole problem of these senile delinquents lies in their complete rejection of the values of contemporary society. They've seen their children grow up and become accountants, stockbrokers and even sociologists, and they begin to wonder if it is all really ... *(disappears downwards rapidly)* arggh!

Shot of two grannies replacing manhole cover.
Cut to young couple.

Young Man (GRAHAM) Oh well we sometimes feel we're to blame in some way for what our gran's become. I mean she used to be happy here until she, she started on the crochet.

Reporter *(off-screen)* Crochet?

Young Man Yeah. Now she can't do without it. Twenty balls of wool a day, sometimes. If she can't get the wool she gets violent. What can we do about it?

Film of grannies on motorbikes roaring down streets and through a shop. One has 'Hell's Grannies' on her jacket.

Voice Over But this is not just an old ladies' town. There are other equally dangerous gangs – such as the baby snatchers.

Film of five men in baby outfits carrying off a young man from outside a shop. Cut to distraught wife.

Wife (RITA DAVIES) I just left my husband out here while I went in to do some shopping and I came back and he was gone. He was only forty-seven.

Voice Over And on the road too, vicious gangs of keep-left signs.

Film: two keep-left signs attack a vicar.

Colonel *(coming up and stopping them)* Right, right, stop it. This film's got silly. Started off with a nice little idea about grannies attacking young men, but now it's got silly. This man's hair is too long for a vicar too. These signs are pretty badly made. Right, now for a complete change of mood.

Cut to man in dirty raincoat.

Man In Dirty Raincoat (TERRY J) I've heard of unisex but I've never had it.

Cut to 'It's' man still holding smoking bomb.

Voice Over (JOHN) David Hemmings appeared by permission of the National Forestry Commission.

SUPERIMPOSED ROLLER CAPTION: ' "FULL FRONTAL NUDITY" WAS CONCEIVED, WRITTEN AND PERFORMED BY ... (CREDITS)'

The 'It's' man realizes that he has a bomb and runs off still carrying it. As the credits end it explodes.

Nine The ant, an introduction

A forest. From an explosion in the far distance the 'It's' man runs very rapidly up to camera and announces:

It's Man It's . . .

Opening animated titles.

CAPTION: 'PART 2'

CAPTION: 'THE LLAMA'

A Spanish guitarist (Eric) and a dancer (Terry J) in traditional Spanish costume.

SUPERIMPOSED CAPTION: 'LIVE FROM GOLDERS GREEN'

Man enters and walks up to a life-size photo of a llama. He delivers the following lecture in Spanish, with help from the guitarist and dancer, and superimposed subtitles.

Man (JOHN) *(but in Spanish with subtitles in English)* The llama is a quadruped which lives in big rivers like the Amazon. It has two ears, a heart, a forehead, and a beak for eating honey. But it is provided with fins for swimming.

Guitarist & Dancer Llamas are larger than frogs.

Man Llamas are dangerous, so if you see one where people are swimming, you shout:

Guitarist & Dancer Look out, there are llamas!

Graham, dressed in a Spanish frock, enters on a moped; he blows up a paper bag and bursts it. They bow. Cut to exterior Ada's Snack Bar (a small café). Hand-held camera moves round the back to where an announcer is seated at desk with an old-fashioned BBC microphone.

Announcer And now for something completely different – a man with a tape recorder up his nose.

We see Michael, in evening dress, on a small stage, with potted plants, etc. He ostentatiously inserts a finger up one nostril. We hear the Marseillaise. He removes the finger; the music stops. He inserts the finger up the other nostril: we hear rewinding noises. Once again he inserts a finger up the first nostril: again we hear the Marseillaise. He bows. Stock film of Women's Institute applauding. He inserts a finger up his nostril again, and we hear:

Voice Over (MICHAEL) And now to something completely different. The office of Sir George Head, OBE.

Large study with maps and photographs on the wall and a large desk at which sits Sir George Head.

Sir (JOHN) Next please.

Bob walks into the room and up to the desk.

Sir *(looking up)* One at a time please.

Bob (ERIC) There is only me, sir.

Sir *(putting a hand over one eye)* So there is. Take a . . .

Bob Seat?

Sir Seat! Take a seat. So! *(looking four feet to Bob's right)* You want to join my mountaineering expedition do you? *(keeps looking off)*

Bob *(rather uncertain)* Me, sir?

Sir Yes.

Bob Yes, I'd very much like to, sir.

Sir Jolly good, jolly good. *(ticking sheet and then looking right at Bob)* And how about you?

Bob There is only me, sir.

Sir *(putting hand over eye and looking both at Bob and to Bob's right)* Well bang goes his application then. *(he tears up form)* Now let me fill you in. I'm leading this expedition and we're going to climb both peaks of Mount Kilimanjaro.

Bob I thought there was only one peak, sir.

Sir *(getting up, putting one hand over one eye again and going to large map of Africa on wall and peering at it at point-blank range)* Well, that'll save a bit of time. Well done. Now the object of this expedition is to see if we can find any traces of last year's expedition.

Bob Last year's expedition?

Sir Yes, my brother was leading that, they were going to build a bridge between the two peaks. *(looks at map with one hand over eye)* My idea I'm afraid. Now, I ought to tell you that I have practically everyone I need for this expedition . . . so what special qualifications do you have?

Bob Well, sir . . .

Sir Yes, you first.

Bob There is only me, sir.

Sir *(to Bob's right)* I wasn't talking to you. *(to Bob)* Carry on.

Bob Well I'm a fully qualified mountaineer.

Sir Mountaineer? Mountaineer *(looks it up in the dictionary)* where the devil are they, mound, mount . . . mountain . . . a mountaineer: 'two men skilled in climbing mountains'. Jolly good, well you're in. Congratulations, both of you. Well, er, what are your names?

Bob Arthur Wilson.

Sir Arthur Wilson, right well look, I'll call you *(to Bob)* Arthur Wilson one, and *you (to Bob's right)* Arthur Wilson two, just to avoid confusion.

Bob Are you actually leading this expedition sir?

Sir Yes, we are leading this expedition to Africa.

Bob *(tartly)* And what routes will you both be taking?

Sir Good questions . . . shall I? Well we'll be leaving on January 22nd and taking the following routes. *(goes over to large map, clearly labelled*

Surrey) The A23s through Purleys down on the main roads near
Purbrights avoiding Leatherheads and then taking the A231s
entering Rottingdeans from the North. From Rottingdeans we go
through Africa to Nairobis. We take the South road out of
Nairobis for about twelve miles and then ask.

Bob Does anyone speak Swahili, sir?

Sir Oh, yes I think most of them do down there.

Bob Does anyone in *our* party speak Swahili sir?

Sir Oh, well Matron's got a smattering.

Bob *(sarcastically)* Apart from the two Matrons . . .

Sir Good God, I'd forgotten about her.

Bob Apart from them, who else is coming on the expedition, sir?

Sir Well we've got the Arthur Brown twins, two botanists called Machin,
the William Johnston brothers . . .

Bob Two of them?

Sir No four of them, a pair of identical twins . . . and a couple of the Ken
Spinoza quads – the other two pulled out. And of course you two.

Bob And none of these are mountaineers?

Sir Well you two are, and we've got a brace of guides called Jimmy
Blenkinsop . . . because Kilimanjaro is a pretty tricky climb you
know, most of it's up until you reach the very very top, and then it
tends to slope away rather sharply. But Jimmy's put his heads
together and worked out a way up. *(opens door)* Jimmy? *(James
Blenkinsop enters; he wears climbing gear)* I don't believe you've met.
Jimmy Blenkinsop – Arthur Wilson, Arthur Wilson – Jimmy
Blenkinsop . . . Arthur Wilson two – James Blenkinsop one, James
Blenkinsop one – Arthur Wilson two. Carry on Jimmies.

Jimmy (GRAHAM) *(to Bob, reassuringly)* Don't worry about the er . . . *(puts
hand over eye)* We'll get him up somehow.

*Jimmy proceeds to walk round the room clambering over every single piece
of available furniture. He doesn't stop talking. Causing a complete
wreckage, he clambers over the desk, onto a bookcase and round the room
knocking furniture over, meanwhile he is saying:*

Now the approach to Kilimanjaro is quite simply over the foothills,
and then we go on after that to . . . ohh . . . to set a base camp,
somewhere in the region of the bottom of the glacier when . . .

*Jimmy staggers out headlong through the door. There are loud crashing
noises.*

Sir He'll be leading the first assault.

Bob Well I'm afraid I shan't be coming on your expedition sir, as I've
absolutely no confidence in anyone involved in it.

He gets up and walks out slamming the door.

Sir Oh dear. *(pause)* Well how about you?

Bob *(still sitting in chair at other angle of desk)* Well I'm game, sir.

Cut back to two sirs, double image, split screen.

Sir So are we.

Cut to two announcers (Johns) at desks. They put telephones down, turn to camera, and announce:

Announcers (JOHNS) And now for something completely different – a man with a tape recorder up his brother's nose.

Cut to Michael on small stage as before, this time also with Graham. Michael puts a finger up Graham's nostril: we hear the Marseillaise. He removes it: the music stops. He puts a finger up Graham's other nostril, and we hear rewinding noises.

Voice Over (JOHN) and CAPTION: 'AND NOW IN STEREO . . .'

Michael simultaneously puts a finger up his own nostril and a finger (on the other hand) up Graham's; we hear two recordings of the Marseillaise together (out of sync).

An animated sequence then leads us to a gents suburban hairdressing salon. A customer comes in. The barber is standing in a white coat washing his hands at a basin.

Customer (TERRY J) Morning.

Barber (MICHAEL) *(flinching slightly)* Ah . . . good morning sir, good morning. I'll be with you in a minute.

Customer sits in barber's chair. Barber carries on washing. He seems to be over-thoroughly washing and rewashing his hands and lower arms. Barber turns and smiles humourlessly at customer. At last he has finished washing. He dries his hands thoroughly, turns and comes over to the customer. There are very obvious blood stains on his coat and his lapel is torn off. One stain could be the mark of a bloodstained hand which has slipped down the length of it. He picks up a sheet and shakes it out. Sound of iron and heavy objects falling on the floor. He throws it around the customer. As he knots the sheet at the back he seems about to pull it tight and strangle the customer. His face sweats, a wild look in his eyes. Then with a supreme effort he controls himself. Customer smiles reassuringly at him.

Barber How . . . how would you like it, sir?

Customer Just short back and sides please.

Barber How do you do that?

Customer Well it's just . . . ordinary short back and sides . . .

Barber It's not a . . . razor cut? *(suddenly)* Razor, razor, cut, cut, blood, spurt, artery, murder . . . *(controlling himself)* Oh thank God, thank God. *(sigh of relief)* It's just a scissors . . .

Customer Yes . . . *(laughs, thinking the barber must be having a little joke)*

Barber You wouldn't rather just have it combed, would you sir?

Customer I beg your pardon?

Barber You wouldn't rather forget all about it?

Customer No, no, no, I want it cut.

> *At the word cut barber winces.*

Barber Cut, cut, cut, blood, spurt, artery, murder, Hitchcock, Psycho . . .
right sir . . . well . . . *(swallows hard)* I'll just get everything ready. In
the meanwhile perhaps you could fill in one of these.

> *He hands him a bit of paper; the barber goes to a cupboard and opens it.*

Customer All right, fine, yes.

> *On the inside of the door there is a large medical chart headed: 'Main
> Arteries'. His shaking hand traces the arteries and he looks occasionally
> back at the customer.*

Customer Excuse me, er . . .

Barber What?

Customer Where it says: 'next of kin' shall I put 'mother'?

Barber Yes, yes . . . yes.

Customer Right there we are. *(hands form to barber)*

Barber Thank you.

> *He gets scissors and comb ready and comes up behind the customer and
> spreads his arms out, opening and shutting scissors as barbers do before
> cutting.*

Barber Right!

> *He can't bring himself to start cutting; after one or two attempts he goes
> to the cupboard again, gets a whisky bottle out and takes a hard swig. He
> comes up behind the customer again.*

Barber Ha, ha, ha . . . there, I've finished.

Customer What?

Barber I've finished cutting . . . cutting . . . cutting your hair. It's all
done.

Customer You haven't started cutting it!

Barber I have! I did it very quickly . . . your honour . . . *sir* . . . sir . . .

Customer *(getting rather testy)* Look here old fellow, I know when a
chap's cut my hair and when he hasn't. So will you please stop
fooling around and get on with it.

> *The barber bends down to the floor and drags out a tape recorder which
> he places behind the barber's chair, talking as he does so.*

Barber Yes, yes, I will, I'm going to cut your hair, sir. I'm going to start
cutting your hair, sir, start cutting now!

> *He switches on tape recorder and then he himself cowers down against the
> wall as far from the chair as he can get, trembling.*

Tape Recorder Nice day, sir.

Customer Yes, flowers could do with a drop of rain though, eh?

Tape Recorder *(snip, snip)* Did you see the match last night, sir?

Customer Yes. Good game. I thought.

Tape Recorder *(snip, snip, snip; sound of electric razor starting up)* I thought Hurst played well sir.

Customer *(straining to hear)* I beg your pardon?

Tape Recorder *(razor stops)* I thought Hurst played well.

Customer Oh yes . . . yes . . . he was the only one who did though.

Tape Recorder Can you put your head down a little, sir.

Customer Sorry, sorry. *(his head is bowed)*

Tape Recorder I prefer to watch Palace nowadays. *(electric razor starts up again)* Oh! Sorry! Was that your ear?

Customer No no . . . I didn't feel a thing.

The customer rises out from his seat, taking the sheet off himself and looking in the mirror and delving into pocket. He turns round for the first time and sees the cowering barber.

Customer Look, what's going on?

Tape Recorder Yes, it's a nice spot, isn't it.

Customer Look, I came here for a haircut!

Barber *(pathetically)* It looks very nice sir.

Customer *(angrily)* It's exactly the same as when I first came in.

Tape Recorder Right, that's the lot then.

Barber All right . . . I confess I haven't cut your hair . . . I hate cutting hair. I have this terrible un-un-uncontrollable fear whenever I see hair. When I was a kid I used to hate the sight of hair being cut. My mother said I was a fool. She said the only cure for it was to become a barber. So I spent five ghastly years at the Hairdressers' Training Centre at Totnes. Can you imagine what it's like cutting the *same head* for *five* years? I didn't want to be a barber anyway. I wanted to be a lumberjack. Leaping from tree to tree as they float down the mighty rivers of British Columbia . . . *(he is gradually straightening up with a visionary gleam in his eyes)* The giant redwood, the larch, the fir, the mighty scots pine. *(he tears off his barber's jacket, to reveal tartan shirt and lumberjack trousers underneath; as he speaks the lights dim behind him and a choir of Mounties is heard faintly in the distance)* The smell of fresh-cut timber! The crash of mighty trees! *(moves to stand in front of back-drop of Canadian mountains and forests)* With my best girlie by my side . . . *(a frail adoring blonde, the heroine of many a mountains film, or perhaps the rebel maid, rushes to his side and looks adoringly into his eyes)* We'd sing . . . sing . . . sing.

The choir is loud by now and music as well.

Barber *(singing)* I'm a lumberjack and I'm OK,
I sleep all night and I work all day.

Lights come up to his left to reveal a choir of Mounties.

Mounties Choir He's a lumberjack and he's OK,
He sleeps all night and he works all day.

Barber I cut down trees, I eat my lunch,
I go to the lavatory.
On Wednesday I go shopping,
And have buttered scones for tea.

Mounties Choir He cuts down trees, he eats his lunch,
He goes to the lavatory.
On Wednesday he goes shopping,
And has buttered scones for tea.
He's a lumberjack and he's OK,
He sleeps all night and he works all day.

Barber I cut down trees, I skip and jump,
I like to press wild flowers.
I put on women's clothing
And hang around in bars.

Mounties Choir He cuts down trees, he skips and jumps,
He likes to press wild flowers.
He puts on women's clothing
And hangs around in bars . . . ?

During this last verse the choir has started to look uncomfortable but they brighten up as they go into the chorus.

Mounties Choir He's a lumberjack and he's OK,
He sleeps all night and he works all day.

Barber I cut down trees, I wear high heels,
Suspenders and a bra.
I wish I'd been a girlie,
Just like my dear Mama.

Mounties Choir *(starting lustily as usual but tailing off as they get to the third line)*
He cuts down trees, he wears high heels,
(spoken rather than sung) Suspenders . . . and a bra? . . .

They all mumble. Music runs down. The girl looks horrified and bursts into tears. The choir start throwing rotten fruit at him.

Girl (CONNIE BOOTH) Oh Bevis! And I thought you were so rugged.

Cut to a hand-written letter.

Voice Over (JOHN) Dear Sir, I wish to complain in the strongest possible terms about the song which you have just broadcast, about the lumberjack who wears women's clothes. Many of my best friends are lumberjacks and only a few of them are transvestites. Yours faithfully, Brigadier Sir Charles Arthur Strong (Mrs). PS I have never kissed the editor of the Radio Times.

Cut to a pepperpot.

Pepperpot (GRAHAM) Well I object to all this sex on the television. I mean I keep falling off.

Shot of a battered trophy.

SUPERIMPOSED CAPTION: 'THAT JOKE WAS BRITAIN'S ENTRY FOR THIS YEAR'S RUBBER MAC OF ZURICH AWARD'

ROLL CAPTION: 'IT CAME LAST'

Cut back to Canadian backdrop. In front, a man with a knotted handkerchief on his head, a woolly pullover, and braces.

SUPERIMPOSED CAPTION: 'PROF. R. J. GUMBY'

Gumby (GRAHAM) Well I think TV's killed real entertainment. In the old days we used to make our own fun. At Christmas parties I used to strike myself on the head repeatedly with blunt instruments while crooning. *(sings)* 'Only make believe, I love you, *(hits himself on head with bricks)* Only make believe that you love me, *(hits himself)* Others find peace of mind . . .'

Cut to a swish nightclub. Compère enters.

Compère (ERIC) Good evening, ladies and gentlemen, and welcome to the refreshment room here at Bletchley. *(applause)* My name is Kenny Lust and I'm your compere for tonight. You know, once in a while it is my pleasure, and my privilege, to welcome here at the refreshment room, some of the truly great international artists of our time. *(applause)* And tonight we have one such artist. *(grovelling)* Ladies and gentlemen, someone whom I've always personally admired, perhaps more deeply, more strongly, more abjectly than ever before. *(applause)* A man, well more than a man, a god *(applause)*, a great god, whose personality is so totally and utterly wonderful my feeble words of welcome sound wretchedly and pathetically inadequate. *(by now on his knees)* Someone whose boots I would gladly lick clean until holes wore through my tongue, a man who is so totally and utterly wonderful, that I would rather be sealed in a pit of my own filth, than dare tread on the same stage with him. Ladies and gentlemen the incomparably superior human being, Harry Fink.

Voice Off He can't come!

Compère Never mind, it's not all it's cracked up to be. Ladies and gentlemen, we give you Ken Buddha and his inflatable knees.

Cut to Ken (Terry J) in evening dress; his knees go 'bang'.

Compère Ken Buddha, a smile, two bangs and a religion. Now ladies and gentlemen, for your further entertainment, Brian Islam and Brucie.

Two animated men dance to jug band music. When they finish we cut to the barber and customer.

Barber So anyway, I became a barber.

Customer *(sympathetically)* Poor chap.

Barber Yes, pity really, I always preferred the outdoor life. Hunting, shooting, fishing. Getting out there with a gun, slaughtering a few of God's creatures – that was the life. Charging about the moorland, blasting their heads off.

Cut to a large country house. A number of sportin' gentlemen dressed in huntin' tweed and carrying shotguns come out, casually firing the guns at random. They climb into a land-rover and drive off. Cut to huntin' country. A line of beaters moves towards the camera; as they do so several young couples leap up out of the undergrowth and run away. Shots of hunters stalking their prey and shooting. One of them breaks his gun into two pieces. Another fires into the air. An egg lands on his head. Cut to two duellists (with pistols) and a referee standing between them. They fire; the referee falls dead. A huntin' gentleman fires into the air, falls over backwards; a young couple get up from close behind him and run away. Another huntin' gentleman is arguing defensively with a pilot who has just landed by parachute. A hunter fires into some bushes; a Red Indian pops up and runs away in alarm. They all return to the house, legs and arms variously in plaster or bandaged. Two of them carry a pole between them from which is slung a very small bird. The picture of the outside of the house freezes and we pull back to reveal that it is a photo on a stand, by which stands the knight in armour, expectantly flexing his raw chicken. The floor manager comes up to him.

Floor Manager I'm sorry, we don't need you this week.

Knight looks dejected, droops and slinks off, still holding chicken. He walks past a hen house from wherein we hear a voice.

Voice (JOHN) And now for something completely different.

Cut to a sitting room. Low sexy lighting – ha ha – soft sexy music. On the sofa are Victor and Iris just beginning to make passes at each other.

Victor (GRAHAM) Would you mind terribly if I hold your hand?

Iris (CAROL) Oh no, no, not at all.

Victor Oh Iris, you're so very beautiful.

Iris Oh, do you really mean that?

Victor I do, I do, I do. I think ... I'm beginning to fall in love with you.

Iris Oh Victor.

Victor It's silly isn't it?

Iris No, no, not at all dear sweet Victor.

Victor No I didn't mean that. Only just us being so close together for so many months in the soft-toy department and yet never daring to ...

Iris Oh, oh Victor.

Victor Oh Iris. *(they move closer to kiss; just before their lips meet the doorbell goes)* Who can that be?

Iris Oh, well you try and get rid of them.

Victor Yes I will, I will.

Victor opens the front door. Arthur Name is standing outside the door.

Arthur (ERIC) Hello!

Victor Hello.

Arthur Remember me?

Victor No I'm . . .

Arthur In the pub. The tall thin one with the moustache, remember? About three years ago?

Victor No, I don't I'm afraid.

Arthur Oh, blimey, it's dark in here, *(switches light on)* that's better. Only you said we must have a drink together sometime, so I thought I'd take you up on it as the film society meeting was cancelled this evening.

Victor Look, to be frank, it is a little awkward this evening.

Arthur *(stepping in; to Iris)* Hello, I'm Arthur. Arthur Name. Name by name but not by nature. I always say that, don't I Vicky boy?

Victor Really . . .

Arthur *(to Victor)* Is that your wife?

Victor Er, no, actually.

Arthur Oh, I get the picture. Eh? Well don't worry about me Vicky boy, I know all about one-night stands.

Victor I *beg* your pardon?

Arthur Mind if I change the record? *(takes the record off)*

Victor Look, look, we put that on.

Arthur Here's a good one, I heard it in a pub. What's brown, what's brown and sounds like a bell?

Victor I beg your pardon?

Arthur What's brown and sounds like a bell? Dung! Ha, ha, ha, that's a good one. I like that one, I won't keep you long. *(the gramophone plays the 'Washington Post March' very loud)* That's better, now don't worry about me. I'll wait here till you've finished.

The doorbell goes again.

Victor Who the hell . . .

Arthur I'll get it. It'll be friends of mine. I took the liberty of inviting them along.

Victor Look, we were hoping to have a quiet evening on our own.

Arthur Oh, they won't mind. They're very broad-minded. Hello!

He opens the door; Mr and Mrs Equator walk in and go straight up to Victor.

Mr Equator (JOHN) Good evening. My name is Equator, Brian Equator. Like round the middle of the Earth, only with an L. *(wheezing laugh)* This is my wife Audrey, she smells a bit but she has a heart of gold.

Audrey (TERRY J) Hello, ha ha ha ha ha ha ha ha ha ha . . .

Victor There must have been some kind of misunderstanding, because this is not the . . .

Mr Equator Who's that then?

Victor What?

Mr Equator Who's the bird?

Victor I'm ...

Mr Equator You got a nice pair there haven't you love. *(puts hand on Iris's boobs and gives a wet kiss; Iris screams)* Shut up you silly bitch, it was only a bit of fun.

Victor Now look here ...

Mr Equator Big gin please.

Arthur I'll get it.

Victor *(going after Arthur)* Look, leave those drinks alone.

Audrey And three tins of beans for me please.

Mr Equator I told you to lay off the beans, you whore!

Audrey I only want three cans.

Mr Equator Button your lip you rat-bag. *(laughs uproariously)*

Audrey *(joins in)* Ha, ha, ha, ha ...

Mr Equator It was rather witty, wasn't it? Where's my gin?

> *The doorbell goes.*

Victor Who the hell's that?

Mr Equator Oh, I took the liberty of inviting an old friend along, as his wife has just passed away, and he's somewhat distraught poor chap. I hope you don't mind.

Arthur *(opening door)* Come on in.

> *In walks Mr Freight in underpants, sequins, eye make-up, white wellies and necklace.*

Mr Freight (TERRY G) Oh? My God, what a simply ghastly place.

Mr Equator Not too good is it? A pint of crème de menthe for my friend. Well how are you, you great poof? *(sits down)* Bit lumpy ... ah, no wonder, I was sitting on the cat. *(throws it into fire)*

Iris Aaaagh! Boo hoo hooo.

Mr Freight I've asked along a simply gorgeous little man I picked up outside the Odeon.

Mr Equator Is he sexy?

> *In walks Mr Cook with a goat. Freight kisses him.*

Mr Cook (MICHAEL) I had to bring the goat, he's not well. I only hope he don't go on the carpet.

Mr Equator *(to Iris)* Come on then love, drop 'em.

Iris Aaaaaaagh! *(runs out)*

Mr Equator Blimey, she don't go much do she.

> *He sits in chair which collapses.*

Mrs Equator Ha, ha, ha, ha, ha, ha, oooooh! I've wet 'em.

Mr Cook The goat's just done a bundle.

> *All the singers run on, dressed as Welsh miners. All talk at once.*

Victor Look, get out all of you. Go on. Get out! Get out!

Mr Equator I beg your pardon?

Victor I'm turning you all out. I'm not having my house filled with filthy perverts, now look, I'm giving you just half a minute then I'm going to call the police, so get out.

Mr Equator I don't much like the tone of your voice. *(shoots him)* Right let's have a ding dong . . .

All *(singing)* Ding dong merrily on high, in Heaven the bells are ringing etc. . . .

Cut to 'It's' man.

Spanish Voices *(in Spanish)* Look out, there are llamas!

'It's' man runs away into forest.

ROLLER CAPTION: 'THE ANT, AN INTRODUCTION, WAS CONCEIVED, WRITTEN AND PERFORMED BY . . . (CREDITS)'

Ten

Boring old 'It's' man hanging on a meat-hook.

It's Man (MICHAEL) It's . . .

Animated titles as per usual.

Lingerie shop set. Assistant standing waiting behind counter. At the side the robber also stands waiting. They hum to themselves and waste time, looking at wristwatches, this takes about fifteen seconds.

Cut to a letter on BBC stationery. The camera pulls back to show a grotty little man reading the letter and sitting at a breakfast table in a small kitchen. His wife is busying herself in wifelike activities.

Man (MICHAEL) Ooh. Ooh.

Wife (TERRY J) Oh, what is it dear?

Man It's from the BBC. They want to know if I want to be in a sketch on telly.

Wife Oooh. That's nice.

Man What? It's acting innit?

Wife Yes.

Man Well I'm a plumber. I can't act.

Wife Oh, you never know till you try. Look at Mrs Brando's son next door. He was mending the fridge when they came and asked him to be the Wild One. What do they want you to do?

Man Well, they just want me to stand at a counter, and when the sketch starts I go out.

Wife Oh, that sounds nice. It's what they call a walk-on.

Man Walk-on? That's a walk-off, that's what this is.

Cut to lingerie shop; assistant and robber still hanging around waiting. A few seconds of this. Floor manager walks on.

Robber (JOHN) *(quietly)* Well, where is he, George?

Floor Manager I don't know, he should have been here hours ago.

Robber He bloody should have been.

Cut to grotty kitchen (still very small).

Wife Well what else does it say?

Man It just says 'We would like you to be in a sketch. You are standing at a counter. When the sketch starts you go off. Yours faithfully, Lord Hill.'

Wife Oh well, you'd better be off then.

Man Yeah, well, what about the cat?

Wife Oh I'll look after the cat. Goodness me, Mrs Newman's eldest never worried about the cat when he went off to do 'The Sweet Bird of Youth'.

Man All right then, all right. Bye. Bye dear.

Wife   Bye bye, and mind you don't get seduced.

Man leaves, wife stands for a moment, then . . .

Wife   Oh, it'll make a change from plumbing. Dad! Frank's got a television part.

She turns on the TV set. On the TV comes the picture of the assistant and the robber and floor manager waiting in the lingerie shop. After a second or two a man is brought in and introduced to floor manager, who positions him and cues him. The man walks out.

Wife   You missed him.

Cut to shop; the robber walks in and points gun at the assistant.

Robber (JOHN)   Good morning, I am a bank robber. Er, please don't panic, just hand over all your money.

Assistant (ERIC) *(politely)*   This is a lingerie shop, sir.

Robber   Fine, fine, fine. *(slightly nonplussed)* Adopt, adapt and improve. Motto of the round table. Well, um . . . what have you got?

Assistant *(still politely)*   Er, we've got corsets, stockings, suspender belts, tights, bras, slips, petticoats, knickers, socks and garters, sir.

Robber   Fine, fine, fine, fine. No large piles of money in safes?

Assistant   No, sir.

Robber   No deposit accounts?

Assistant   No sir.

Robber   No piles of cash in easy to carry bags?

Assistant   None at all sir.

Robber   No luncheon vouchers?

Assistant   No, sir.

Robber   Fine, fine. Well, um . . . adopt, adapt and improve. Just a pair of knickers then please.

Cut to effeminate announcer sitting at continuity desk. Any resemblance to Mel Oxley should be accidental. His name is David Unction.

Unction (GRAHAM)   Well that was a bit of fun wasn't it? Ha, ha, ha. And a special good evening to *you*. Not just an ordinary good evening like you get from all the other announcers, but a special good evening from *me (holds up card saying 'David Unction')* to *you*. Well, what have we got next? This *is* fun isn't it? Look, I'm sorry if I'm interrupting anything that any of you may be doing at home, but I want you to think of me as an old queen. *Friend*, ha, ha, ha. Well, let's see what we've got next. In a few moments 'It's a Tree' and in the chair as usual is Arthur Tree, and starring in the show will be a host of star guests as his star guests. And then at 9.30 we've got another rollocking half hour of laughter-packed squalor with 'Yes it's the Sewage Farm Attendants'. And this week Dan falls into a vat of human dung with hilarious consequences. Ha, ha, ha. But now it's the glittering world of show business with Arthur Tree . . .

Music.

CAPTION: 'IT'S A TREE'

Stock film. Quick cuts. Plane arriving at night. Showbiz lights. Film premières. Audience applauding. Cut to studio: a tree sitting in a middle chair in David Frost type interview set. Zoom in on tree which has a mouth which moves.

Tree (ERIC) Hello. Hello people, and welcome to 'It's a Tree'. We have some really exciting guests for you this evening. A fabulous spruce, back from a tour of Holland, three gum trees making their first appearance in this country, scots pine and the conifers, and Elm Tree Bole – there you go, can't be bad – an exciting new American plank, a rainforest and a bucket of sawdust giving their views on teenage violence, and an unusual guest for this programme, a piece of laminated plastic.

Shot of a piece of laminated plastic with mouth.

Plastic Hi there!

Tree But first, will you please, please welcome – a block of wood.

Shot of large block four feet cube, with a mouth, on the chair next to Tree.

Shot of a forest with the sound of applause over.

Tree Well Block, nice to have you on the show again.

Block (JOHN'S VOICE) Well, er, thanks Tree. I've got to pay the rent.

They both laugh. Shot of forest laughing.

Tree Ha, ha, ha, ha, super. Well, what have you been doing, Block?

Block Well I've just been starring in several major multi-million dollar international films, and, during breaks on the set, I've been designing a Cathedral, doing wonderful unpublicized work for charity, er, finishing my history of the world, of course, pulling the birds, er, photographing royalty on the loo, averting World War Three – can't be bad – and, er, learning to read.

Tree The full Renaissance bit, really . . . super, super. Well I've got to stop you there Block I'm afraid, because we've got someone who's been doing cabaret in the New Forest. From America, will you welcome please a Chippendale writing desk.

ANIMATION: *a Chippendale desk.*

Chip Thank you Mr Tree. And I'd like to do a few impersonations of some of my favourite Englishmen. First off. Long John Sliver. *(suitable animation)* Augh, Jim boy. Augh. And now Edward Heath. Hello sailor. Now a short scene from a play by Harold Splinter. *(a huge hammer smashes it)*

Animated compere:

Compère Wasn't that just great, ladies and gentlemen, wait a minute,

we've got something else I just know you're going to love. *(fanfares)*
Yes sir, coming right up – the Vocational Guidance Counsellor
Sketch. *(more fanfares)*

Animation film into Vocational Guidance Counsellor sketch.

Voices singing Vocational guidance counsellor . . . vocational guidance
counsellor . . . vocational guidance counsellor . . . etc.

*Office set. Man sitting at desk. Mr Anchovy is standing waiting. The
counsellor looks at his watch then starts the sketch.*

Counsellor (JOHN) Ah Mr Anchovy. Do sit down.

Anchovy (MICHAEL) Thank you. Take the weight off the feet, eh?

Counsellor Yes, yes.

Anchovy Lovely weather for the time of year, I must say.

Counsellor Enough of this gay banter. And now Mr Anchovy, you asked
us to advise you which job in life you were best suited for.

Anchovy That is correct, yes.

Counsellor Well I now have the results here of the interviews and the
aptitude tests that you took last week, and from them we've built
up a pretty clear picture of the sort of person that you are. And I
think I can say, without fear of contradiction, that the ideal job for
you is chartered accountancy.

Anchovy But I *am* a chartered accountant.

Counsellor Jolly good. Well back to the office with you then.

Anchovy No! No! No! You don't understand. I've been a chartered
accountant for the last twenty years. I want a new job. Something
exciting that will let me *live*.

Counsellor Well chartered accountancy is rather exciting isn't it?

Anchovy Exciting? No it's *not*. It's dull. Dull. *Dull.* My God it's dull, it's
so desperately dull and tedious and stuffy and boring and
des-per-ate-ly DULL.

Counsellor Well, er, yes Mr Anchovy, but you see your report here says
that you are an extremely dull person. You see, our experts
describe you as an appallingly dull fellow, unimaginative, timid,
lacking in initiative, spineless, easily dominated, no sense of
humour, tedious company and irrepressibly drab and awful. And
whereas in most professions these would be considerable
drawbacks, in chartered accountancy they are a positive boon.

Anchovy But don't you see, I came here to find a new job, a new life, a
new *meaning* to my existence. Can't you help me?

Counsellor Well, do you have any idea of what you want to do?

Anchovy Yes, yes I have.

Counsellor What?

Anchovy *(boldly)* Lion taming.

Counsellor Well yes. Yes. Of course, it's a bit of a jump isn't it? I mean,
er, chartered accountancy to lion taming in one go. You don't think

it might be better if you worked your way *towards* lion taming, say, via banking . . .

Anchovy No, no, no, no. No. I don't want to wait. At nine o'clock tomorrow I want to be in there, taming.

Counsellor Fine, fine. But do you, do you have any qualifications?

Anchovy Yes, I've got a hat.

Counsellor A hat?

Anchovy Yes, a hat. A lion taming hat. A hat with 'lion tamer' on it. I got it at Harrods. And it lights up saying 'lion tamer' in great big neon letters, so that you can tame them after dark when they're less stroppy.

Counsellor I see, I see.

Anchovy And you can switch it off during the day time, and claim reasonable wear and tear as allowable professional expenses under paragraph 335C . . .

Counsellor Yes, yes, yes, I do follow, Mr Anchovy, but you see the snag is . . . if I now call Mr Chipperfield and say to him, 'look here, I've got a forty-five-year-old chartered accountant with me who wants to become a lion tamer', his first question is not going to be 'does he have his own hat?' He's going to ask what sort of experience you've had with lions.

Anchovy Well I . . . I've seen them at the zoo.

Counsellor Good, good, good.

Anchovy Little brown furry things with short stumpy legs and great long noses. I don't know what all the fuss is about, I could tame one of those. They look pretty tame to start with.

Counsellor And these, er, these lions . . . how high are they?

Anchovy *(indicating a height of one foot)* Well they're about so high, you know. They don't frighten me at all.

Counsellor Really. And do these lions eat ants?

Anchovy Yes, that's right.

Counsellor Er, well, Mr Anchovy . . . I'm afraid what you've got hold of there is an anteater.

Anchovy A what?

Counsellor An anteater. Not a lion. You see a lion is a huge savage beast, about five feet high, ten feet long, weighing about four hundred pounds, running forty miles per hour, with masses of sharp pointed teeth and nasty long razor-sharp claws that can rip your belly open before you can say 'Eric Robinson', and they look like this.

The counsellor produces large picture of a lion and shows to Mr Anchovy who screams and passes out.

Counsellor Time enough I think for a piece of wood.

CAPTION: 'THE LARCH'

Picture of a tree.

Voice Over (TERRY J) The larch.

Cut back to office: Mr Anchovy sits up with a start.

Counsellor Now, shall I call Mr Chipperfield?

Anchovy Er, no, no, no. I think your idea of making the transition to lion taming via easy stages, say via insurance . . .

Counsellor Or banking.

Anchovy Or banking, yes, yes, banking that's a man's life, isn't it? Banking, travel, excitement, adventure, thrills, decisions affecting people's lives.

Counsellor Jolly good, well, er, shall I put you in touch with a bank?

Anchovy Yes.

Counsellor Fine.

Anchovy Er . . . no, no, no. Look, er, it's a big decision, I'd like a couple of weeks to think about it . . . er . . . you know, don't want to jump into it too quickly. Maybe three weeks. I could let you know definitely then, I just don't want to make this definite decision. I'm er . . . *(continues muttering nervously to himself)*

Counsellor *(turning to camera)* Well this is just one of the all too many cases on our books of chartered accountancy. The only way that we can fight this terrible debilitating social disease, is by informing the general public of its consequences, by showing young people that it's just not worth it. So, so please . . . give generously . . . to this address: The League for Fighting Chartered Accountancy, 55 Lincoln House, Basil Street, London, SW3.

CAPTION: *gives address.*

Cut back to David Unction reading 'Physique' magazine. He puts it into a brown paper bag.

Unction Oh, well that was fun wasn't it?

Cut to helmeted Viking.

Viking (TERRY J) No it wasn't, you fairy.

Cut back to Unction.

Unction *(sarcastically)* Oh, hello sailor.

Cut to Viking.

Viking Here, you wouldn't have got on one of our voyages – they were all dead butch.

Cut to Unction.

Unction *(camply)* Oh that's not what I've heard.

Cut to the sea. Pan to show Ron Obvious running along beach.

Voice Over (ERIC) There is an epic quality about the sea which has throughout history stirred the hearts and minds of Englishmen of all nations. Sir Francis Drake, Captain Webb, Nelson of Trafalgar and Scott of the Antarctic – all rose to the challenge of the mighty ocean. And today another Englishman may add his name to the golden roll of history: Mr Ron Obvious of Neaps End. For today, Ron Obvious hopes to be the first man to jump the Channel.

Ron runs up to group of cheering supporters. An interviewer addresses him.

Interviewer (JOHN) Ron, now let's just get this quite clear – you're intending to jump across the English Channel?

Ron (TERRY J) Oh yes, that is correct, yes.

Interviewer And, er, just how far is that?

Ron Oh, well it's twenty-six miles from here to Calais.

Interviewer Er, that's to the beach at Calais?

Ron Well, no, no, provided I get a good lift off and maybe a gust of breeze over the French coast, I shall be jumping into the centre of Calais itself.

Brief shot of group of Frenchmen with banner: 'Fin de Cross-Channel jump'.

Interviewer Ron are you using any special techniques to jump this great distance?

Ron Oh no, no. I shall be using an ordinary two-footed jump, er, straight up in the air and across the Channel.

Interviewer I see. Er, Ron, what is the furthest distance that you've jumped, er, so far?

Ron Er, oh, eleven foot six inches at Motspur Park on July 22nd. Er, but I have done nearly twelve feet unofficially.

Ron breaks off to make training-type movements.

Interviewer I see. Er, Ron, Ron, Ron, aren't you worried Ron, aren't you worried jumping twenty-six miles across the sea?

Ron Oh, well no, no, no, no. It is in fact easier to jump over sea than over dry land.

Interviewer Well how is that?

Ron Er, well my manager explained it to me. You see if you're five miles out over the English Channel, with nothing but sea underneath you, er, there is a very great impetus to say in the air.

Interviewer I see. Well, er, thank you very much Ron and the very best of luck.

Ron Thank you. Thank you.

Interviewer *(to camera)* The man behind Ron's cross-Channel jump is his manager Mr Luigi Vercotti. *(turns to speak to Vercotti, who has a Mafia suit and dark glasses)* Mr Vercotti, er Mr Vercotti . . . Mr Vercotti . . .

Mr Vercotti (MICHAEL) What? *(mumbles protestations of innocence)* I don't know what you're talking about.

Interviewer Er, no, we're from the BBC, Mr Vercotti.

Mr Vercotti Who?

Interviewer The BBC.

Mr Vercotti Oh, oh. I see. I thought, I thought you were the er . . . I like the police a lot, I've got a lot of time for them.

Interviewer Mr, er, Mr Vercotti, what is your chief task as Ron's manager?

Mr Vercotti Well my main task is, er, to fix a sponsor for the big jump.

Interviewer And who is the sponsor?

Mr Vercotti The Chippenham Brick Company. Ah, they, er, pay all the bills, er, in return for which Ron will be carrying half a hundredweight of their bricks.

We see a passport officer, checking Ron's passport.

Interviewer I see. Well, er, it looks as if Ron is ready now. He's got the bricks. He's had his passport checked and he's all set to go. And he's off on the first ever cross-Channel jump. *(Ron runs down the beach and jumps; he lands about four feet into the water)* Will Ron be trying the cross-Channel jump again soon?

Mr Vercotti No. No. I'm taking him off the jumps. Er, because I've got something lined up for Ron next week that I think is very much more up his street.

Interviewer Er, what's that?

Mr Vercotti Er, Ron is going to eat Chichester Cathedral.

Chichester Cathedral. Ron walks up to it, cleaning his teeth.

Interviewer Well, there he goes, Ron Obvious of Neaps End, in an attempt which could make him the first man ever to eat an entire Anglican Cathedral.

Ron takes a hefty bite at a buttress, screams and clutches his mouth. Cut to countryside: a map, and a banner saying 'Tunnelling to Java'. Interviewer and Vercotti walk up to map.

Mr Vercotti Well, er, I think, David, this is something which Ron and myself are really keen on. Ron is going to tunnel from Godalming here to Java here. *(indicates inaccurately on map)*

Interviewer Java.

Mr Vercotti Yeah, er, I, I personally think this is going to make Ron a household name overnight.

Interviewer And how far has he got?

Mr Vercotti Er, well, he's quite far now, Dave, well on the way. Well on the way, yeah.

Interviewer Well where is he exactly?

Mr Vercotti Yeah.

Interviewer Where?

Mr Vercotti Oh, er, well, er, you know, it's difficult to say exactly. He's er, you know, in the area of er, Ron, how far have you got?

Ron *(emerging from hole)* Oh about two foot six Mr Vercotti.

Mr Vercotti Yeah well keep digging lad, keep digging.

Ron Mr Vercotti, are you sure there isn't a spade?

Cut to interviewer and Vercotti by a railway track.

Interviewer Er, Mr Vercotti, what do you say to people who accuse you of exploiting Ron for your own purposes?

Mr Vercotti Well, it's totally untrue, David. Ever since I left Sicily I've been trying to do the best for Ron. I know what Ron wants to do, I believe in him and I'm just trying to create the opportunities for Ron to do the kind of things he wants to do.

Interviewer And what's he going to do today?

Mr Vercotti He's going to split a railway carriage with his nose. *(screams, off)*

Cut to a hillside; Vercotti, interviewer, and in the background a banner: 'Running to Mercury'.

Mr Vercotti The only difficult bit for Ron is getting out of the Earth's atmosphere. Er, once he's in orbit he'll be able to run straight to Mercury.

A heavily bandaged Ron leaps off starting platform: freeze frame. Scream. Cut to a tombstone: 'Ron Obvious 1941–1969 – very talented'. Pull back to show Vercotti.

Mr Vercotti I am now extremely hopeful that Ron will break the world record for remaining underground. He's a wonderful boy this, he's got this really enormous talent, this really huge talent.

Over last shot of graveyard and wind whistling, we hear two ladies' voices.

First Lady Oh that was a bit sad, wasn't it?

Second Lady Shh. It's satire.

First Lady No it isn't. This is zany madcap humour.

Second Lady Oh is it?

Cut to a pet shop.

SUPERIMPOSED CAPTION: 'A PET SHOP SOMEWHERE NEAR MELTON MOWBRAY'

Man enters shop and approaches shopkeeper at counter.

Man (JOHN) Good morning. I'd like to buy a cat.

Shopkeeper (MICHAEL) Certainly sir. I've got a lovely terrier. *(indicates a box on the counter)*

Man *(glancing in box)* No, I want a cat really.

Shopkeeper *(taking box off counter and then putting it back on counter as if it is a different box)* Oh yeah, how about that?

Man *(looking in box)* No, that's the terrier.

Shopkeeper Well, it's as near as dammit.

Man Well what do you mean? I want a cat.

Shopkeeper Listen, tell you what. I'll file its legs down a bit, take its snout out, stick a few wires through its cheeks. There you are, a lovely pussy cat.

Man It's not a proper cat.

Shopkeeper What do you mean?

Man Well it wouldn't miaow.

Shopkeeper Well it would howl a bit.

Man No, no, no, no. Er, have you got a parrot?

Shopkeeper No, I'm afraid not actually guv, we're fresh out of parrots. I'll tell you what though ... I'll lop its back legs off, make good, strip the fur, stick a couple of wings on and staple on a beak of your own choice. *(taking small box and rattling it)* No problem. Lovely parrot.

Man And how long would that take?

Shopkeeper Oh, let me see ... er, stripping the fur off, no legs ... *(calling)* Harry ... can you do a parrot job on this terrier straight away?

Harry (GRAHAM) *(off-screen)* No, I'm still putting a tuck in the Airedale, and then I got the frogs to let out.

Shopkeeper Friday?

Man No I need it for tomorrow. It's a present.

Shopkeeper Oh dear, it's a long job. You see parrot conversion ... Tell you what though, for free, terriers make lovely fish. I mean I could do that for you straight away. Legs off, fins on, stick a little pipe through the back of its neck so it can breathe, bit of gold paint, make good ...

Man You'd need a very big tank.

Shopkeeper It's a great conversation piece.

Man Yes, all right, all right ... but, er, only if I can watch.

Vox pops.

Pearson (JOHN) Oh, I thought that was a bit predictable.

Man (ERIC) It's been done before.

Roman Centurion (TERRY J) Yeah, we did it for Caesar's Christmas Show.

Caesar (GRAHAM) No you didn't, you did Jack and the Beanstalk.

Cut to interview room in town hall: a tweedy colonel type chairman; next to him a vicar and a lady with a pince-nez. The chairman is holding up the picture of Caesar. As the camera pulls out he rather obviously throws it away.

Vicar (TERRY J) Here what was that picture?

Chairman (GRAHAM) Ssh! Next! *(a gorilla enters)* Good morning – Mr Fhipps?

Gorilla (ERIC) That's right, yes.

Chairman Er, do take a seat.

Gorilla Right sir. *(sits)*

Chairman Now could you tell us roughly why you want to become a
    librarian?

Gorilla Er, well, I've had a certain amount of experience running a
    library at school.

Chairman Yes, yes. What sort of experience?

Gorilla Er, well for a time I ran the Upper Science Library.

Chairman Yes, yes. Now Mr Phipps, you do realize that the post of
    librarian carries with it certain very important responsibilities. I
    mean, there's the selection of books, the record library, and the art
    gallery. Now it seems to me that your greatest disadvantage is your
    lack of professional experience . . . coupled with the fact that, um,
    being a gorilla, you would tend to frighten people.

Vicar *(aside)* Isn't he a gorilla?

Chairman Yes he is.

Vicar Well why didn't it say on his form that he's a gorilla?

Chairman Well, you see applicants are not required to fill in their
    species.

Vicar What was that picture?

Chairman Sh! . . . Mr Phipps, what is your attitude toward censorship in
    a public library?

Gorilla How do you mean, sir?

Vicar Well I mean for instance, would you for instance stock 'Last Exit to
    Brooklyn' . . . or . . . 'Groupie'?

Gorilla Yes, I think so.

Vicar Good.

Chairman Yes, well, that seems to me to be very sensible Mr Phipps. I
    can't pretend that this library hasn't had its difficulties . . . Mr
    Robertson, your predecessor, an excellent librarian, savaged three
    people last week and had to be destroyed.

Gorilla I'm sorry sir.

Chairman Oh, no, don't be sorry. You see, I don't believe that libraries
    should be drab places where people sit in silence, and that's been
    the main reason for our policy of employing wild animals as
    librarians.

Vicar And also, they're much more permissive. Pumas keep Hank Janson
    on open shelves . . .

Chairman Yes. Yes. Yes. *(a maniacal look in his eyes)* Yes, yes Mr Phipps.
    I love seeing the customers when they come in to complain about
    some book being damaged, and ask to see the chief librarian and
    then . . . you should see their faces when the proud beast leaps
    from his tiny office, snatches the book from their hands and sinks
    his fangs into their soft er . . . *(collects himself)* Mr Phipps . . .
    Kong! You can be our next librarian – you're proud majestic and
    fierce enough . . . will you do it?

Gorilla I . . . don't think I can sir.

Vicar Why not?

Gorilla I, I'm not really a gorilla . . .

Vicar Eh?

Gorilla I'm a librarian in a skin . . .

Chairman Why this deception?

Gorilla Well, they said it was the best way to get the job.

Chairman Get out, Mr Librarian Phipps, seeing as you're not a gorilla, but only dressed up as one, trying to deceive us in order to further your career . . . *(gorilla leaves)* Next. *(a dog comes in)* Ah. Mr Pattinson . . . Sit!

> *Cut to angry letters.*

Voice Over (ERIC) *(reads)* Dear Mirror View, I would like to be paid five guineas for saying something stupid about a television show. Yours sincerely, Mrs Sybil Agro.

Voice Over (JOHN) Dear David Jacobs, East Grinstead, Friday. Why should I have to pay sixty-four guineas each year for my television licence when I can buy one for six. Yours sincerely, Captain R. H. Pretty. PS Support Rhodesia, cut motor taxes, save the Argylls, running-in please pass.

Voice Over (GRAHAM) Dear Old Codgers, some friends of mine and I have formed a consortium, and working with sophisticated drilling equipment, we have discovered extensive nickel deposits off Western Scotland. The Cincinnatti Mining Company.

Voices Over Good for you, ma'am.

Voice Over (MICHAEL) Dear Old Codgers, I am President of the United States of America, Yours truly, R. M. Nixon.

Voices Over Phew! Bet that's a job and a half, ma'am.

Voice Over (TERRY J) Dear Sir, I am over three thousand years old and would like to see any scene with two people in bed.

Voices Over Bet that's a link ma'am.

> *Cut to bedroom of a middle-aged, middle-class wealthy couple. It is dark. They are both lying fast asleep on their backs. The husband is a colonel type with a moustache to boot. She has her hair in curlers and face cream on. Someone climbs in through the window and pads across to the wife. He is a dapper little Frenchman in a beret and a continental nylon mac, carrying a french loaf. He kisses her on the forehead. She wakes.*

Maurice (ERIC) Vera . . . Vera . . . darling! Wake up my little lemon. Come to my arms.

Vera (TERRY J) Maurice! What are you doing here?

Maurice I could not keep away from you. I must have you all the time.

Vera Oh this is most inconvenient.

Maurice Don't talk to me about convenience, love consumes my naughty mind, I'm delirious with desire.

He kisses her hand repeatedly. The husband suddenly wakes up with a start and sits up bolt upright and looks straight ahead.

Husband (MICHAEL) What's that, Vera?

Vera Oh nothing, dear. Just a trick of the light.

Husband Righto! *(he goes straight to sleep again)*

Vera Phew! That was close.

Maurice Now then my little banana, my little fruit salad, I can wait for you no longer. You must be mine utterly . . .

Vera Oh, Maurice!

Suddenly beside them appears a young public-school man in a check suit with a pipe.

Roger (JOHN) Vera! How dare you!

Vera Roger!

Roger What's the meaning of this?

Vera Oh I can explain everything, my darling!

Roger Who is this?

Vera This is Maurice Zatapathique . . . Roger Thompson . . . Roger Thompson . . . Maurice Zatapathique.

Maurice How do you do.

Roger How do you do . . . *(kneeling)* How could you do this to me, Vera . . . after all we've been through? Dammit, I love you.

Maurice Vera! Don't you understand, it's *me* that loves you.

The husband wakes up again.

Husband What's happening, Vera?

Vera Oh, nothing dear. Just a twig brushing against the window.

Husband Righto. *(he goes back to sleep)*

Roger Come to me Vera!

Vera Oh . . . not now, Roger.

Maurice Vera, my little hedgehog! Don't turn me away!

Vera Oh it cannot be, Maurice.

Enter Biggles. He wears flying boots, jacket and helmet as for First World War. He wears a notice round his neck: 'Biggles'.

Biggles (GRAHAM) Hands off, you filthy bally froggie! *(kneels by the bed)*

Vera Oh Ken, Ken Biggles!

Biggles Yes, Algy's here as well.

Vera Algy Braithwaite?

Into the light comes Algy. Tears streaming down his face. He wears a notice round his neck which reads: 'Algy's here as well'.

Algy (IAN) That's right . . . Vera . . . *(he chokes back the tears)* Oh God you know we both still bally love you.

Vera Oh Biggles! Algy. Oh, but how wonderful!

She starts to cry. Husband wakes up again.

Husband What's happening, Vera?

Vera Oh, er, nothing dear. It's just the toilet filling up.

Husband Righto. *(he goes fast asleep again)*

> *By this stage all the men have pulled up chairs in a circle around Vera's side of the bed. They are all chatting amongst themselves. Biggles is holding her hand. Maurice has produced a bottle of vin ordinaire. At this moment, four Mexican musicians appear on the husband's side of the bed. The leader of the band nudges the husband, who wakes.*

Mexican (reading from a scruffy bit of paper) Scusey . . . you tell me where is . . . Mrs Vera Jackson . . . please.

Husband Yes . . . right and right again.

Mexican Muchas gracias . . .

Husband Righto.

> *He immediately goes back to sleep again. The Mexicans all troop round the bed and enter the group. The leader conducts them and they start up a little conga . . . once they've started he turns and comes over to Vera with a naughty glint in his eye. They play a guitar, a trumpet and maracas.*

Mexican Oh Vera . . . you remember Acapulco in the Springtime . . .

Vera Oh. The Herman Rodrigues Four!

> *Suddenly the husband wakes up.*

Husband Vera! *(there is immediate silence)* I distinctly heard a Mexican rhythm combo.

Vera Oh no, dear . . . it was just the electric blanket switching off.

Husband Hm. Well I'm going for a tinkle.

> *He gets out of bed and disappears into the gloom.*

Vera Oh no you can't do that. Here, we haven't finished the sketch yet!

Algy Dash it all, there's only another bally page.

Roger I say. There's no one to react to.

Maurice Don't talk to the camera.

Roger Oh sorry.

> *Enter a huge man dressed as an Aztec god (viz: Christopher Plummer in 'Royal Hunt of the Sun'). He stretches arms open wide and is about to speak when owing to lack of money he is cut short by Vera.*

Vera Here it's no good *you* coming in . . . He's gone and left the sketch.

Biggles Yes, he went for a tinkle.

> *Cut to close-up of husband and a dolly bird with a lavatory chain hanging between them. She is about to pull the chain when he stops her.*

Husband Sh! I think my wife is beginning to suspect something . . .

> *Cut to animation of various strange and wonderful creatures saying to the effect:*

Hartebeeste I thought that ending was a bit predictable.

Crocodile *(eating it)* Yes indeed there was a certain lack of originality.

Ostrich *(eating the crocodile)* Anyway it's not necessarily a good thing just to be different.

A Lady *(emerging from hatch in ostrich)* No, quite, there is equal humour in the conventional.

Pig *(eating ostrich)* But on the other hand, is it what the public wants? I mean with the new permissiveness, not to mention the balance of payments. It's an undeniable fact that . . .

Coelocanth *(eating the pig)* I agree with that completely.

Rodent That's it . . . let's get out of this show before it's too late . . .
('The End' descends on it) Too late!

Two men detach the 'It's' man from his meat-hook and carry him off.

CREDITS

Eleven

Film: The Amazing World of The 'It's' Man
Animated titles.

CAPTION: 'EPISODE TWO'S'

CAPTION: 'THE ROYAL PHILHARMONIC ORCHESTRA GOES TO THE BATHROOM'

Cut to bathroom door, outside. Man knocks on door.

Man (MICHAEL) Have you finished in there yet?

From inside comes a burst of the Tchaikovsky piano concerto. He tuts.
Cut to letter and voice over.

Voice Over (JOHN) Dear Sir, I object strongly to the obvious lavatorial turn this show has already taken. Why do we never hear about the good things in Britain, like Mary Bignall's wonderful jump in 1964? Yours etc., Ken Voyeur.

Stock film of Mary Bignall's winning jump at the Rome Olympics.
Letter and voice over.

Voice Over (ERIC) Dear Sir, I object strongly to the obvious athletic turn this show has now taken. Why can't we hear more about the human body? There is nothing embarrassing or nasty about the human body except for the intestines and bits of the bottom.

Letter and voice over.

Voice Over (MICHAEL) Dear Sir, I object strongly to the letters on your programme. They are clearly not written by the general public and are merely included for a cheap laugh. Yours sincerely etc., William Knickers.

Stock film of the whole of an orchestra finishing an orchestral item. When they finish playing we hear the sound of flushing.

ANIMATION: *a beautiful and not zany introduction, perhaps with photos of famous historical characters, finishing with the words: 'The World of History'. Cut to man at desk.*

CAPTION: 'PROFESSOR R. J. CANNING'

Canning (GRAHAM) 1348. The Black Death, typhus, cholera, consumption, bubonic plague.

Cut to five undertakers sitting on a coffin in a country road.

First Undertaker (ERIC) Ah, those were the days . . .

Back to Canning at his desk.

Canning Now I'm . . . I'm . . . Now I'm not prepared to go on with this, unless these interruptions cease. All right? Right. The devastating effect of these, em . . .

Cut to film of hearses racing. Crashing out of shot. Sign: 'Accident Black Spot', and the undertakers picnicking.

Canning *(he is packing up his papers and putting on his mac as he walks away from desk, camera pans with him)* No, don't follow me and ... *(camera zooms in)* And don't zoom in on me, no I'm off, I'm off. That's it. That's all. I'm off.

He walks out of shot. Empty frame. A short pause. An undertaker comes into frame.

Second Undertaker (TERRY J) *(to camera)* Are you nervy, irritable, depressed, tired of life. *(winks)* Keep it up.

CAPTION: 'MEANWHILE INSIDE'

Cut to drawing room of large English country house. Sitting around are various standard Agatha Christie type characters, Colonel Pickering, Lady Amanda Velloper, Kirt, Anona Winn. They drink tea, read etc. Outside there is thunder. Inspector Tiger enters the room.

Inspector Tiger (JOHN) This house is surrounded. I'm afraid I must not ask anyone to leave the room. No, I must ask nobody ... no, I must ask everybody to ... I must not ask anyone to leave the room. No one must be asked by me to leave the room. No, no one must ask the room to leave. I ... I ... ask the room shall by someone be left. Not. Ask nobody the room somebody leave shall I. Shall I leave the room? Everyone must leave the room ... as it is ... with them in it. Phew. Understand?

Colonel Pickering (GRAHAM) You don't want anybody to leave the room.

Inspector Tiger *(clicking fingers to indicate Colonel Pickering has hit the nail on the head)* Now, alduce me to introlow myslef. I'm sorry. Alself me to myduce introlow. Introme to-lose mylow alself. Alme to you introself mylowduce. Excuse me a moment. *(bangs himself on the side of the head)* Allow me to introduce myself. I'm afraid I must ask that no one leave the room. Allow me to introduce myself. I'm Inspector Tiger.

All Tiger?

Inspector Tiger *(jumping)* Where? Where? What? Ah. Me Tiger. You Jane. Grrr. Beg your pardon, allow me to introduce myself I'm afraid I must ask that no one leave the room.

Lady Velloper (CAROL) Why not?

Inspector Tiger Elementary. Since the body was found in this room, and no one has left it. Therefore ... the murderer must be somebody in this room.

Colonel Pickering What body?

Inspector Tiger Somebody. In this room. Must the murderer be. The murderer of the body is somebody in this room, which nobody must leave ... leave the body in the room not to be left by anybody. Nobody leaves anybody or the body with somebody.

Everybody who is anybody shall leave the body in the room body. Take the tablets Tiger. Anybody *(as he searches for the tablets)* with a body but not the body is nobody. Nobody leaves the body in the ... *(he takes the tablet)* Albody me introbody albodyduce.

At this moment a surgeon enters with two nurses and starts to operate on his head with sawing noises.

CAPTION: 'THE SAME DRAWING ROOM. ONE LOBOTOMY LATER'

The surgeon is packing up. Inspector Tiger's head is bandaged.

Surgeon Now for Sir Gerald.

Inspector That's better, now I'm Inspector Tiger and I must ask that nobody leave the room. *(he gives thumbs up to the surgeon who is at door)* Now someone has committed a murder here, and that murderer is someone in this room. The question is ... who?

Colonel Pickering Look, there hasn't been a murder.

Inspector Tiger No murder.

All No.

Inspector Tiger Oh. I don't like it. It's too simple, too clear cut. I'd better wait. *(he sits on sofa)* No, too simple, too clear cut.

The lights go out. There is a scream followed by a shot. The light goes up. Inspector Tiger is dead. He has a bullet hole in his forehead, an arrow through his neck and there is a bottle marked poison on his lap.

Colonel Pickering By jove, he was right.

Chief Superintendent Lookout enters, with constable.

Lookout (ERIC) This house is surrounded. I must ask that no one leave the room. I'm Chief Superintendent Lookout.

Lady Velloper Look out?

Lookout *(jumping)* What, where, oh, me, Lookout. Lookout of the Yard.

Lady Velloper Why, what would we see?

Lookout I'm sorry?

Lady Velloper What would we see if we look out of the yard?

Lookout ... I'm afraid I don't follow that at all. Ah ha. The body. So the murderer must be somebody in this room. Unless he had very long arms. Say thirty or forty feet. I think we can discount that one. Ha, ha, ha, *(he starts really laughing)* Lookout of the Yard. Very good. Right. Now, we'll reconstruct the crime. I'll sit down here. Constable, you turn off the lights. *(lights go out, we hear Lookout's voice)* Good. Now then, there was a scream *(scream)* then just before the lights went up there was a shot.

There is a shot. The lights go up and Chief Superintendent Lookout is sitting dead, bullet hole, arrow and all. In walks Assistant Chief Constable Theresamanbehindyer.

ACCT (TERRY J) All right ... all right, the house is surrounded and nobody leave the room and all the rest of it. Allow me to introduce myself. I'm Assistant Chief Constable Theresamanbehindyer.

All Theresamanbehindyer?

ACCT Ah, you're not going to catch me with an old one like that. Right let's reconstruct the crime. Constable you be Inspector Tiger.

Constable (MICHAEL) Right, sir. Nobody leave the room ask shall – somebody I leave nobody in the room body shall, take the tablets Tigerbody. Alself me to my duce introlow left body in the roomself.

ACCT Very good. Just sit down there. Right now we'll pretend the lights have gone out. Constable, you scream. *(constable screams)* Somebody shoots you *(pulls gun and shoots constable through head)* and the door opens . . .

The door flies open. Enter policeman.

Fire Nobody move! I'm Chief Constable Fire.

All Fire! Where?

He jumps. Immediately cut to undertaker as before.

Second Undertaker (TERRY J) We're interrupting this sketch but we'll be bringing you back the moment anything interesting happens. Meanwhile here are some friends of mine.

Film of four undertakers carrying a coffin. They surreptitiously tip the body out of the coffin and go skipping lightly up the road. Letter and voice over.

Voice Over (GRAHAM) Dear Sir, I'm sorry this letter is late, it should have come at the beginning of the programme. Yours, Ivor Bigbottie, (age two).

Two chairs in interview set. Smart interviewer and footballer (who is not over bright) in blazer.

Interviewer (ERIC) From the plastic arts we turn to football. Last night in the Stadium of Light, Jarrow, we witnessed the resuscitation of a great footballing tradition, when Jarrow United came of age, in a European sense, with an almost Proustian display of modern existentialist football. Virtually annihilating by midfield moral argument the now surely obsolescent catennachio defensive philosophy of Signor Alberto Fanfrino. Bologna indeed were a side intellectually out argued by a Jarrow team thrusting and bursting with aggressive Kantian positivism and outstanding in this fine Jarrow team was my man of the match, the arch-thinker, free scheming, scarcely ever to be curbed, midfield cognoscento, Jimmy Buzzard.

Buzzard (JOHN) Good evening Brian.

Interviewer Jimmy, at least one ageing football commentator was gladdened last night by the sight of an English footballer breaking free of the limpid tentacles of packed Mediterranean defence.

Buzzard Good evening Brian.

Interviewer Were you surprised at the way the Italian ceded midfield dominance so early on in the game?

Buzzard Well Brian . . . I'm opening a boutique.

Interviewer This is of course symptomatic of a new breed of footballer as it is indeed symptomatic of your whole genre of player, is it not?

Buzzard Good evening Brian. ·

Interviewer What I'm getting at, Jimmy, is you seem to have discovered a new concept with a mode in which you dissected the Italian defence, last night.

Buzzard *(pauses for thought)* I hit the ball first time and there it was in the back of the net. *(smiles and looks round)*

Interviewer Do you think Jarrow will adopt a more defensive posture for the first leg of the next tie in Turkey?

Buzzard *(confidently)* I hit the ball first time and there it was in the back of the net.

Interviewer Yes, yes – but have you any plans for dealing with the free-scoring Turkish forwards?

Buzzard Well Brian . . . I'm opening a boutique.

Cut to undertaker.

Second Undertaker And now let's take a look at the state of play in the detective sketch.

Cut to drawing room. There is an enormous pile of dead policemen on and around the sofa.

Constable Alself me to introlow mybody . . .

Inspector shoots him in the head.

CAPTION: 'CONSTABLES 13 SUPERINTENDENTS 9'

Cut to four undertakers carrying a coffin up a hill. One of them falters and drops. The others lower the coffin to the ground, take out a fresh undertaker, put the fallen one in the coffin, and proceed.

Cut to animated sequence, leading to big glittering flashing lights saying 'Interesting People'. A compère sits at desk, with guest chairs beside it.

Compère (MICHAEL) Hello, good evening, and welcome to yet another edition of 'Interesting People'. And my first interesting person tonight is the highly interesting Mr Howard Stools from Kendal in Westmorland.

He puts a matchbox on desk in front of him. He presses a button on the desk and we hear applause. Releases button; applause stops abruptly. He opens the box a little and speaks into it.

Compère Good evening Mr Stools.

Voice *(from inside box)* Hello, David.

Compère Mr Stools, what makes you particularly interesting?

Voice Well, I'm only half an inch long.

Compère Well that's *extremely* interesting, thank you for coming along on the show tonight Mr Stools.

Mr Stools I thought you'd think that was interesting David, in fact . . .

Compère *(shuts matchbox; applause)* Mr Alan Stools from Kendal in Westmorland . . . half an inch long. *(applause)* Our next guest tonight has come all the way from Egypt, he's just flown into London today, he's Mr Ali Bayan, he's with us in the studio tonight and he's stark raving mad.

Applause. Cut to Ali Bayan (Terry J) who looks at camera in a very mad way. Applause.

Compère Mr Ali Bayan, stark raving mad. Now it's time for our music spot and we turn the spotlight tonight on the Rachel Toovey Bicycle Choir, *(applause)* with their fantastic arrangement of 'Men of Harlech' for bicycle bells only.

Cut to six men in oilskins and sou'westers. They sing 'Men of Harlech', and at the end of each line mournfully ring bells. Applause at end.

Compère The Rachel Toovey Bicycle Choir. Really interesting. Remember, if you're interesting and want to appear on this programme, write your name and address and your telephone number and send it to this address: *(reads caption)* The BBC, c/o E. F. Lutt, 18 Rupee Buildings, West 12. *(applause)* Thank you, thank you. Now here's an interesting person. Apart from being a full-time stapling machine, he can also give a cat influenza.

Cut to a smartly dressed man (John) who coughs copiously into a cat basket. We hear a miaow and a feline sneeze. Cut back to compère.

Compère Well, you can't get much more interesting than that, or *can* you? With me now is Mr Thomas Walters of West Hartlepool who is totally invisible. Good evening, Mr Walters. *(turns to empty chair)*

Walters (ERIC) *(off-screen)* Over here, Hughie.

Compère turns to find a boringly dressed man sitting by him.

Compère Mr Walters, are you sure you're invisible?

Walters Oh yes, most certainly.

Compère Well, Mr Walters, what's it like being invisible?

Walters *(slowly and boringly)* Well, for a start, at the office where I work I can be sitting at my desk all day and the others totally ignore me. At home, even though we are in the same room, my wife does not speak to me for hours, people pass me by in the street without a glance in my direction, and I can walk into a room without . . .

Compère Well, whilst we've got interesting people, we met Mr Oliver Cavendish who . . .

Walters *(droning on)* . . . Even now you yourself, you do hardly notice me . . .

Compère Mr Oliver Cavendish of Leicester, who claims to be able to recite the entire Bible in one second, whilst being struck on the head with a large axe. Ha, ha, wow. We've since discovered that he was a fraud, yes a fraud, he did not in fact recite the entire Bible he merely recited the first two words, 'In the . . .' before his death.

Cut to film montage of sporting clips.

Compère *(voice over)* Now it's time for 'Interesting Sport', and this week it's all-in cricket, live from the Municipal Baths, Croydon.

Boxing ring; two fully kitted out cricketers, who as the bell goes, approach each other and start hitting each other with cricket bats. Applause.

Compère With me now is Mr Ken Dove, twice voted the most interesting man in Dorking. Ken, I believe you're interested in shouting.

Dove (JOHN) *(shouting)* Yes, I'm interested in shouting all right, by jove you certainly hit the nail on the head with that particular observation of yours then.

Compère What does your wife think of this?

Wife *(voice off, full-blooded)* I agree with him.

Dove Shut up!

Walters . . . At parties for instance people never come up to me, I just sit there and everybody totally . . .

Man holding cat enters.

Compère That is Tiddles, I believe?

Man (GRAHAM) Yes, this is, this is Tiddles.

Compère Yes, and what does she do?

Man She flies across the studio and lands in a bucket of water.

Compère By herself?

Man No, I fling her.

Compère Well that's extremely interesting. Ladies and gentlemen – Mr Don Savage and Tiddles.

Man whirls the cat round and round. He lets go of the cat, it flies across studio. A hollow splash and a miaow. Quick shot of a real cat sitting in a bucket.

Dove *(shouting)* I'm more interesting than a wet pussycat.

Walters . . . for hour after hour . . . *(we see only his empty chair)*

Compère Yes, great, well now for the first time on television 'Interesting People' brings you a man who claims he can send bricks to sleep by hypnosis. Mr Keith Maniac from Guatemala.

Maniac is sitting by compère. He wears a top hat and an opera cloak.

Maniac (TERRY J) Good evening.

Compère Keith, you claim you can send bricks to sleep.

Maniac Yes, that is correct, I can . . .

Compère Entirely by hypnosis.

Maniac Yes . . . I use no artificial means, whatsoever. *(leans and picks* *matchbox off desk to light pipe, opens it and strikes match)*

Voice *(from matchbox)* Aaagh!

Dove You've injured Mr Stools!

Maniac *(picks up other box and lights pipe)* I simply stare at the brick and it goes to sleep.

Compère Well, we have a brick here, Keith. *(indicates brick on desk)* Perhaps you can send it to sleep for us . . .

Maniac Oh . . . Ah, well, I am afraid that is already asleep.

Compère How do you know?

Maniac Well, it's not moving . . .

Compère Oh, I see – have we got a moving brick? Yes, we've got a moving brick, Keith, it's coming over now.

    We see a man in a white coat preparing to throw brick. He throws it gently. It lands on the desk in front of Keith. Keith stares at it as it falls.

Maniac There we are, fast asleep.

Compère Very good, very good indeed.

Maniac All done with the eyes.

Compère Yes, Mr Keith Maniac from Guatemala.

Dove *(distressed – to matchbox)* Mr Stools – speak to me, Howard.

    Quick cut back to all-in cricket.

Compère Mr Keith Maniac of Guatemala . . . and now four tired undertakers.

    Cut to film of four undertakers struggling up a hill carrying a coffin. One staggers and drops. The others lower the coffin, pick him up, and place him inside. Raising the coffin again they stagger off up the hill. Another undertaker collapses; the remaining two place him in the coffin.
    Exhaustedly they pick up the coffin, but have only gone two or three paces when one of them collapses. The remaining one drags him into the coffin, pushing him in with some difficulty, and forces the lid shut. He debates with himself for a moment on how to pick up the coffin, then disgustedly throws away his hat and climbs into the coffin, shutting the lid behind him. The coffin moves off by itself.

Voice Over (ERIC) We interrupt this very quickly to take you back to the Jimmy Buzzard interview, where we understand something exciting's just happened.

    Cut back to the interview studio; Jimmy Buzzard is sitting on the floor.

Buzzard I've fallen off my chair, Brian.

    Cut to a graveyard. The coffin, still moving of its own volition, enters the graveyard. A vicar walks up and motions gravediggers (who we cannot see) to get out of the grave. Out of the grave climb two gravediggers . . . then two more . . . then two more . . . yet another two . . . two miners . . . two uniformed men . . . a police dog with handler . . . and finally an Australian surfboarder. The coffin makes its way into the grave. Then a wonderful piece of animation by our amazing animator Terry Gilliam, wonderboy. Consisting of a very fast collage of extremely sexy stills of half-dressed and naked girls.

Incredibly torchy music, after eight seconds of which:

SUPERIMPOSED CAPTION: 'THE WORLD OF HISTORY'

SECOND CAPTION: 'SOCIAL LEGISLATION IN THE EIGHTEENTH CENTURY'

Cut to fantastically alluring boudoir: a plush four poster bed with silk drapes, silk sheets, a fur pillow etc. We look down on it from above. Stretched out on the bed is a girl (Carol) oozing with sex ... a real professional ... black net stockings, suspenders, bra and panties or what have you. She moves as if in the throes of orgasm as she mimes to a very masculine voice off.

SUPERIMPOSED CAPTION: 'A. J. P. TAYLOR'

Voice Over (JOHN) *(very masculine voice to which girl mimes)* Good evening. Tonight I want to examine the whole question of eighteenth-century social legislation – its relevance to the hierarchical structure of post-Renaissance society, and its impact on the future of parochial organization in an expanding agrarian economy. But first a bit of fun.

Cut to film of eight-second striptease.

Cut immediately back to the same set.

Voice Over To put England's social legislation in a European context is Professor Gert Van Der Whoops of the Rijksmuseum in the Hague.

Cut to another bed, equally seductive. A little bespectacled professor is lying on it being caressed and undressed by an amorous siren.

Professor (MICHAEL) *(German accent)* In Holland in the early part of the fifteenth century there was three things important to social legislation. One ... rise of merchant classes ... two, urbanization of craft guilds ... three, declining moral values in age of increasing social betterment. But first, a bit of fun ... *(grabs girl)*

A curtain and potted palms. Sound effects: angel choirs. A man in dinner jacket with angel's wings on is lowered from above. As he touches the ground the angel choirs fade out. He gets a crumpled piece of paper out of his pocket.

Man (TERRY J) And now Professor R. J. Canning.

He folds up the paper and puts it away. The angel choirs start again and he slowly rises up and out of frame.

Cut to Professor Canning in straight presentation-type set with BP screen behind him.

CAPTION: 'PROFESSOR R. J. CANNING AGAIN'

Canning (GRAHAM) The cat sat on the mat. And now the Battle of

Trafalgar . . . *(on the screen behind him a contemporary picture of the Battle of Trafalgar flashes up)* Tonight we examine popular views of this great battle. Was the Battle of Trafalgar fought in the Atlantic off southern Spain? Or was it fought on dry land near Cudworth in Yorkshire? Here is one man who thinks it was . . .

Cut to a man – a Gumby – with gum boots on, rolled up trousers, knotted handkerchief etc., looking very thick and standing in the middle of a field.

Canning *(voice over)* And here is his friend.

Camera pans lightly losing Gumby but revealing identically dressed thick man standing next to him. The camera pans back to original Gumby.

SUPERIMPOSED CAPTION: 'PROFESSOR R. J. GUMBY'

Canning *(voice over)* What makes you think the Battle of Trafalgar was fought near Cudworth?

There is a long pause.

Gumby (MICHAEL) Because . . . Drake . . . was . . . too . . . clever for . . . the German . . . fleet.

Canning *(voice over)* I beg your pardon?

Gumby . . . Oh I've forgotten what I said now.

Canning *(voice over)* Mr Gumby's remarkable views have sparked off a wave of controversy amongst his fellow historians.

Cut to identical Gumby figure in book lined study. He stands.

SUPERIMPOSED CAPTION: 'F. H. GUMBY. REGIUS PROFESSOR OF HISTORY AT HIS MOTHER'S'

Second Gumby (ERIC) Well I fink . . . we . . . should . . . reappraise . . . our concept of the . . . Battle of Trafalgar.

Cut to another Gumby, this time outside a university.

SUPERIMPOSED CAPTION: 'PROF. L. R. GUMBY'

Third Gumby (GRAHAM) Well . . . well . . . I agree with everything Mr Gumby says.

Cut to yet another Gumby. This time standing in a pig-sty with pigs.

SUPERIMPOSED CAPTION: 'PROF. ENID GUMBY'

Fourth Gumby (JOHN) Well, I think cement is more interesting than people think.

Original sexy girl in seductive boudoir as she mimes to masculine voice over.

SUPERIMPOSED CAPTION AS BEFORE: 'A. J. P. TAYLOR'

Voice Over One subject . . . four different views . . . *(brandishing egg-whisk)* twelve and six . . . in a plain wrapper.

Cut back to Canning.

Canning The stuff of history is indeed woven in the woof. Pearl Harbor. There are pages in history's book which are written on the grand scale. Events so momentous that they dwarf man and time alike. And such is the Battle of Pearl Harbor, re-enacted for us now by the women of Batley Townswomen's Guild.

Cut to a muddy corner of a field. Miss Rita Fairbanks stands talking straight to camera. Behind her lurk five more pepperpots.

Canning *(voice over)* Miss Rita Fairbanks – you organized this reconstruction of the Battle of Pearl Harbor – why?

Rita (ERIC) Well we've always been extremely interested in modern drama ... we were of course the first Townswomen's Guild to perform 'Camp On Blood Island', and last year we did our extremely popular re-enactment of 'Nazi War Atrocities'. So this year we thought we would like to do something in a lighter vein ...

Canning So you chose the Battle of Pearl Harbor?

Rita Yes, that's right, we did.

Canning Well I can see you're all ready to go. So I'll just wish you good luck in your latest venture.

Rita Thank you very much, young man.

She retreats and joins the other ladies who meanwhile separate into two opposing sides facing each other.

Canning *(reverential voice over)* Ladies and gentlemen, the World of History is proud to present the premiere of the Batley Townswomen's Guild's re-enactment of 'The Battle of Pearl Harbor'.

A whistle blows and the two sides set about each other with handbags etc., speeded up 50% just to give it a bit of edge.

Cut to Canning in studio:

Canning The Battle of Pearl Harbor. Incidentally, I'm sorry if I got a little bit shirty earlier on in the programme, when I kept getting interrupted by all these films and things that kept coming in, but I ...

Cut to vicar in a graveyard. He sprinkles dirt and gets mud thrown in his face. Vicar shoots a gun.

Cut to undertakers leaving graveyard. They get into a hearse. As they leave it and drive off we see the other side is painted with psychedelic flowers.

Cut to Canning:

Canning So I said if it happened again I'd get very angry and talk to Lord Hill and ...

Cut to 'It's' man.

Canning Tell Lord Hill.

CREDITS

Twelve

'It's' man.
Opening animation.
CAPTION: 'EPISODES 17–26'
CAPTION: 'THE NAKED ANT'
CAPTION: 'A SIGNALBOX SOMEWHERE NEAR HOVE'
Studio:

Voice Over I know you're down there.

Interior of a signalbox. A signalman (Terry J) stands by the signal levers. He is attacked by a bear. He wrestles it for 3.48 seconds.

CAPTION: 'BUT IN AN OFFICE OFF THE GOSWELL ROAD'

Two people seated opposite each other at a desk. Between them there is a large window. It appears that they are quite high up in a large office building. Every so often a body falls past the window. They are both working busily.

After a pause a body drops past the window. First man talks. Second man hasn't noticed.

First Man (ERIC) Hey, did you see that?

Second Man (JOHN) Uhm?

First Man Did you see somebody go past the window?

Second Man What?

First Man Somebody just went past the window. That way. *(indicates 'down')*

Second Man *(flatly)* Oh. Oh.

Second man returns to his work. First man looks for a little. As he starts to work again another body goes hurtling past the window.

First Man Another one.

Second Man Huh?

First Man Another one just went past downwards.

Second Man What?

First Man Two people have just fallen out of that window to their almost certain death.

Second Man Fine, fine. Fine.

First Man Look! Two people *(another falls)* three people have just fallen past that window.

Second Man Must be a board meeting.

First Man Oh yeah. *(another falls past)* Hey. That was Wilkins of finance.

Second Man Oh, no, that was Robertson.

First Man Wilkins.

Second Man Robertson.

First Man Wilkins.

Second Man Robertson.

> *Another falls.*

First Man *That* was Wilkins.

Second Man That was Wilkins. He was a good, good, er, golfer, Wilkins.

First Man Very good golfer. Very good golfer. Rotten at finance. It'll be Parkinson next.

Second Man Bet you it won't.

First Man How much.

Second Man What?

First Man How much do you bet it won't? Fiver?

Second Man All right.

First Man Done.

Second Man You're on.

First Man Fine. *(shakes; they look at the window)* Come on Parky.

Second Man Don't do it Parky.

First Man Come on Parky. Jump Parky. Jump.

Second Man Come on now be sensible Parky.

> *Cut to letter.*

Voice Over (GRAHAM) Dear Sir, I am writing to complain about that sketch about people falling out of a high building. I have worked all my life in such a building and have never once.

> *Cut to film of man falling out of window.*
> *Cut back to set. First man has hands in the air jubilantly.*

First Man Parkinson!

Second Man Johnson!

> ANIMATION *(possibly incorporating falling) which leads ingeniously into: A presenter at a desk. Urgent, current-affairs-type music.*

> SUPERIMPOSED CAPTION: 'SPECTRUM'

Presenter (MICHAEL) Good evening. Tonight 'Spectrum' looks at one of the major problems in the world today – that old vexed question of what is going on. Is there still time to confront it, let alone solve it, or is it too late? What are the figures, what are the facts, what do people mean when they talk about things? Alexander Hardacre of the Economic Affairs Bureau.

> *Cut to equally intense pundit in front of a graph with three different coloured columns with percentages at the top. He talks with great authority.*

Hardacre (GRAHAM) In this graph, this column represents 23% of the population. This column represents 28% of the population, and this column represents 43% of the population.

Cut back to presenter.

Presenter Telling figures indeed, but what do they mean to *you*, what do they mean to *me*, what do they mean to the average man in the street? With me now is Professor Tiddles of Leeds University . . .

Pull out to reveal bearded professor sitting next to presenter.

Presenter . . . Professor, you've spent many years researching into things, what do you think?

Professor (JOHN) I think it's too early to tell.

Cut to presenter, he talks even faster now.

Presenter 'Too early to tell' . . . too early to say . . . it means the same thing. The word 'say' is the same as the word 'tell'. They're not spelt the same, but they mean the same. It's an identical situation, we have with 'ship' and 'boat' *(holds up signs saying 'ship' and 'boat')*, but *not* the same as we have with 'bow' and 'bough' *(holds up signs)*, they're spelt differently, mean different things but *sound* the same. *(he holds up signs saying 'so there')* But the real question remains. What is the solution, if any, to this problem? What can we do? What am I saying? Why am I sitting in this chair? Why am I on this programme? And what am I going to say next? Here to answer this is a professional cricketer.

Cut to cricketer.

Cricketer (ERIC) I can say nothing at this point.

Cut back to presenter.

Presenter Well, you were wrong . . . Professor?

Pull out to reveal professor still next to him.

Professor Hello.

Cut to close-up of presenter.

Presenter Hello. So . . . where do we stand? Where do we stand? Where do we sit? Where do we come? Where do we go? What do we do? What do we say? What do we eat? What do we drink? What do we think? What do we do?

Mix to stock film of London–Brighton train journey in two minutes. After a few seconds the train goes into a tunnel. Blackness. Loud crash. Cut to signalbox as before.

Signalman *(calling out of window)* Sorry!

He goes back to wrestling with bear.
Cut to a small, tatty, little boarding house.

SUPERIMPOSED CAPTION: 'A SMALL BOARDING HOUSE IN MINEHEAD, SOMERSET'

Mr and Mrs Johnson, a typical holidaying bourgeois couple walk up to the front door and ring the bell. Inside the boarding house, the landlady goes up to the front door and opens it.

Landlady (TERRY J) Hello? Mr and Mrs Johnson isn't it?

Johnson (ERIC) That's right, yes.

Landlady Well come on in, excuse me not shaking hands, but I've just been putting a bit of lard on the cat's boil.

Johnson *(entering)* Very nice.

Landlady Well you must be tired, it's a long drive from Coventry isn't it?

Johnson Yes, well we usually reckon on five and a half hours, and it took us six hours and fifty-three minutes, with a twenty-five-minute wait at Frampton Cottrell to stretch our legs, only we had to wait half an hour to get on to the M5 near Droitwich.

Landlady Really?

Johnson Yes, then there was a three-mile queue just before Bridgwater on the A38, only normally we come round on the B3339 just before Bridgwater you see . . .

Landlady Really?

Johnson Yes, but this time we decided to risk it because they're always saying they're going to widen it there.

Landlady Are they?

Johnson Yes well just there by the intersection, where the A372 joins up, there's plenty of room to widen it there, there's only the grass verges. They could get another six feet . . . knock down that hospital . . . Then we took the coast road through Williton and got all the Taunton traffic on the A358 from Crowcombe and Stogumber . . .

Landlady Well you must be dying for a cup of tea.

Johnson Well, wouldn't say no, not if it's warm and wet.

Landlady Well come on in the lounge, I'm just about to serve afternoon tea.

Johnson *(following her into the lounge)* Very nice.

In the lounge are sitting another bourgeois couple Mr and Mrs Phillips.

Landlady Come on in Mr and Mrs Johnson, oh this is Mr and Mrs Phillips.

Phillips (TERRY G) Good afternoon.

Johnson Thank you.

Landlady It's their third year with us, we can't keep you away can we? Ha, ha, and over here is Mr Hilter.

Landlady leads Mr and Mrs Johnson over to a table at which Adolf Hitler is sitting poring over a map. He is in full Nazi uniform. Himmler and Von Ribbentrop are also sitting at the table with him, Himmler in Nazi uniform and Von Ribbentrop in evening dress, with an Iron Cross.

Hitler (JOHN) Ah good time . . . good afternoon.

Landlady Ooh planning a little excursion are we Mr Hilter?

Hitler Ja! Ja! We make a little ... *(to others)* Was ist rückweise bewegen?

Von Ribbentrop (GRAHAM) Hike.

Himmler (MICHAEL) Hiking.

Hitler We make a little hike for, for Bideford.

Johnson *(leaning over map)* Oh well you'll be wanting the A39 then ... no, no, you've got the wrong map there, this is Stalingrad, you want the Ilfracombe and Barnstaple section.

Hitler Ah Hein ... Reginald you have the wrong map here you silly old leg-before-wicket English person.

Himmler I'm sorry mein Führer. I did not ... *(Hitler slaps him)* Mein Dickie old chum.

Landlady Lucky Mr Johnson pointed that out, eh? You wouldn't have had much fun in Stalingrad would you ... *(they don't see the joke)* I said you wouldn't have had much fun in Stalingrad would you, ha, ha.

Hitler *(through clenched teeth)* Not much fun in Stalingrad, no.

Landlady Oh I'm sorry I didn't introduce you this is Ron ... Ron Vibbentrop.

Johnson Oh not Von Ribbentrop, eh? Ha, ha, ha.

Von Ribbentrop (GRAHAM) *(leaping two feet in fear, then realizing)* Nein! Nein! Nein!! Oh!! Ha, ha, ha. No different other chap. No I in Somerset am being born Von Ribbentrop is born in Gotterammerstrasse 46, Düsseldorf, West Eight. So they say!

Landlady And this is the quiet one, Mr Bimmler – Heimlich Bimmler.

Himmler How do you do there squire, also I am not Minehead lad but I in Peterborough, Lincolnshire house was given birth to, but stay in Peterborough Lincolnshire house all during war, owing to nasty running sores and was unable to go in the streets play football or go to Nürnberg. I am retired window cleaner and pacifist without doing war crimes, *(hurriedly corrects himself)* tch tch tch, and am very glad England win World Cup – Bobby Charlton, Martin Peters – and eating lots of chips and fisch and hole in the toads, and Dundee cakes on Piccadilly line. Don't you know old chap I was head of Gestapo for ten years. Five years! No, no, nein, I was not head of Gestapo at all ... I make joke.

Landlady Oooh Mr Bimmler, you do have us on. *(a telephone rings)* Oh excuse me I must just go and answer that. *(leaves the room)*

Johnson Er, how long are you down here for Mr Hilter? Just the fortnight?

Hitler *(shouting)* Why do you ask that? You a spy or something? *(drawing revolver)* Get over there against the wall Britischer pig, you're going to die.

Von Ribbentrop and Himmler grab Hitler and calm him.

Himmler Take it easy Dickie old chum.

Von Ribbentrop I'm sorry Mr Johnson, he's a bit on edge. He hasn't slept since 1945.

Hitler Shut your cake hole you Nazi.

Himmler Cool it Führer cat.

Von Ribbentrop Ha, ha, ha. *(laughing it off)* The fun we have.

Johnson Haven't I seen him on the television?

Von R. & Himmler Nicht. Nein. Nein, oh no.

Johnson Television Doctor?

Von Ribbentrop No!!! No!

The landlady enters.

Landlady Telephone Mr Hilter, it's that nice Mr McGoering from the Bell and Compasses. He says he's found a place where you can hire bombers by the hour.

Hitler If he opens his big mouth again . . . it's lampshade time!

Von Ribbentrop *(controlling Hitler and getting him towards the door)* Shut up. *(Hitler exits)* Hire bombers by the hour, ha ha, what a laugh he is, that Scottish person! Good old Norman. *(he exits)*

Landlady He's on the phone the whole time nowadays.

Johnson In business is he?

Himmler Soon baby.

Landlady Course it's his big day Thursday. Oh, they've been planning it for months.

Johnson What happens then?

Landlady Oh it's the North Minehead by-election. Mr Hilter's standing as a National Bocialist candidate. He's got wonderful plans for Minehead.

Johnson Like what?

Landlady Well for a start he wants to annex Poland.

Johnson Oh, North Minehead's Conservative isn't it?

Landlady Well, they get a lot of people at their rallies.

Johnson Rallies?

Landlady Well, their Bocialist meetings, down at the Axis Café in Rosedale Road.

Cut to a grotty Italian café. Sign above it reads 'Axis Café, Italian Food a Speciality'. A figure clearly belonging to Mussolini is nailing up a sign or poster which reads: 'Vote for Hitler'. He looks around and goes into the café furtively. At this moment past the café come Hitler, Von Ribbentrop and Himmler on bikes. Hitler at the front shouting German through a megaphone. Von Ribbentrop at the back with a large banner 'Hilter for a better Meinhead'. Himmler in the middle with an old gramophone playing 'Deutschland Uber Alles'.

Cut to Hitler ranting in German on a balcony with Himmler at his side. Beneath them is a Nazi flag.

Hitler I am not a racialist, but, und this is a big but, we in the National Bocialist Party believe das Überleben muss gestammen sein mit der schneaky Armstong-Jones. Historische Taunton ist Volkermeinig von Meinhead.

Himmler *(stepping forward)* Mr Hitler, *Hilter*, he says that historically Taunton is part of Minehead already.

Shot of a yokel looking disbelievingly at balcony. Von Ribbentrop appears behind.

Von Ribbentrop He's right, do you know that?

Meanwhile back on the balcony.

Hitler *(very excited)* Und Bridgwater ist die letzte Fühlung das wir haben in Somerset!

Over this we hear loud applause and 'Sieg Heils'. The yokel, who is not applauding, turns round rather surprised to see whence cometh the applause. He sees Von Ribbentrop operating a gramophone.

Cut to vox pops.

Interviewer (JOHN) *(voice over)* What do you think of Mr Hilter's policies?

Yokel (GRAHAM) I don't like the sound of these 'ere boncentration bamps.

Pepperpot (ERIC) Well I gave him my baby to kiss and he bit it on the head.

Stockbroker (JOHN) Well I think he'd do a lot of good for the Stock Exchange.

Pepperpot (MICHAEL) No . . . no . . .

Himmler *(thinly disguised as yokel)* Oh yes Britischer pals he is wunderbar . . . ful. So.

Pepperpot (TERRY J) I think he's right about the coons, but then I'm a bit mental.

Gumby (TERRY J) I think he's got beautiful legs.

Madd (GRAHAM) Well speaking as Conservative candidate I just drone on and on and on . . . never letting anyone else get a word in edgeways until I start foaming at the mouth and falling over backwards. *(he foams at the mouth and falls over backwards)*

Cut to 'Spectrum' studio: same presenter as before, sitting at desk.

Presenter (MICHAEL) Foam at the mouth and fall over backwards. Is he foaming at the mouth to fall over backwards or falling over backwards to foam at the mouth. Tonight 'Spectrum' examines the whole question of frothing and falling, coughing and calling, screaming and bawling, walling and stalling, galling and mauling, palling and hauling, trawling and squalling and zalling? Zalling? Is there a word zalling? If there is what does it mean . . . if there isn't what does it mean? Perhaps both. Maybe neither. What do I mean by the word mean? What do I mean by the word word, what do I mean by what do I mean, what do I mean by do, and what do I do by mean? What do I do by do by do and what do I mean by wasting your time like this? Goodnight.

Cut to police station.

Sergeant (JOHN) *(behind station counter into camera)* Goodnight.

Camera pulls back to show a man standing in front of the counter.

Man (TERRY J) Good evening, I wish to report a burglary.

Sergeant Speak up please, sir.

Man I wish to report a burglary.

Sergeant I can't hear you, sir.

Man *(bellowing)* I wish to report a burglary!!

Sergeant That's a little bit too loud. Can you say it just a little less loud than that?

Man *(a little louder than normal)* I wish to report a burglary.

Sergeant No . . . I'm still not getting anything . . . Er, could you try it in a higher register?

Man What do you mean in a higher register?

Sergeant What?

Man *(in a high-pitched voice)* I wish to report a burglary.

Sergeant Ah! That's it, hang on a moment. *(gets out pencil and paper)* Now a little bit louder.

Man *(louder and more high pitched)* I wish to report a burglary.

Sergeant Report a what?

Man *(by now a ridiculous high-pitched squeak)* Burglary!

Sergeant That's the exact frequency . . . now keep it there.

Another sergeant enters and goes round to back of counter.

Second Sergeant (GRAHAM) *(in high-pitched voice)* Hello, sarge!

Sergeant *(in very deep voice)* Evening Charlie.

The second sergeant is taking his coat off, and the first one begins to pack up his papers. The man carries on with his tale of woe, but still in a high-pitched shriek.

Man I was sitting at home with a friend of mine from Camber Sands, when we heard a noise in the bedroom. We went to investigate and found £5,000 stolen.

Sergeant Well, I'm afraid I'm going off duty now sir. Er, could you tell Sergeant Foster.

He leaves counter. Sergeant Foster comes forward with a helpful smile.

Man *(continues in high-pitched shriek)* I was sitting at home with a friend of mine.

Second Sergeant Excuse me sir, but, er, why the funny voice?

Man *(normal voice)* Oh, terribly sorry. I'd just got used to talking like that to the other sergeant.

Second Sergeant I'm terribly sorry . . . I can't hear you, sir, could you
try speaking in a lower register?

Man What! Oh *(in a very deep voice)* I wish to report the loss of £5,000.

Second Sergeant £5,000? That's serious, you'd better speak to the
detective inspector.

*At that moment, via the miracle of cueing, the detective inspector comes
out of his office.*

Inspector (ERIC) *(in very slow deep voice)* What's the trouble, sergeant?

Second Sergeant *(speaking at fantastic speed)* Well-this-gentleman-sir-has-
just-come-in-to-report-that-he-was-sitting-at-home-with-a-friend-
when-he-heard-a-noise-in-the-backroom-went-round-to-
investigate-and-found-that-£5,000-in-savings-had-been-stolen.

Inspector *(deep voice)* I see. *(turns to man and addresses him in normal
voice)* Where do you live sir?

Man *(normal voice)* 121, Halliwell Road, Dulwich, SE21.

*The detective inspector has been straining to hear but has failed. The
second sergeant comes in helpfully.*

Second Sergeant *(fast)* 121-Halliwell-Road-Dulwich-SE21.

Inspector *(squeak)* Another Halliwell Road job eh, sergeant?

First Sergeant *(fast)* Yes-I-can't-believe-it-I-thought-the-bloke-who'd-
done-that-was-put-inside-last-year.

Second Sergeant *(squeak)* Yes, in Parkhurst.

First Sergeant *(deep)* Well it must have been somebody else.

Inspector *(very deep)* Thank you, sergeant. *(normal voice to man)* We'll get
things moving right away, sir. *(he picks up phone and dials, at the
same time he shrieks in high voice to the first sergeant)* You take over
here, sergeant *(very deep voice to the second sergeant)* Alert all squad
cars in the area. *(ridiculous sing-song voice into phone)* Ha-allo
Dar-ling, I'm afra-ID I sh-A-ll BE L-ate H-O-me this evening.

*Meanwhile the second sergeant has a radio-controlled microphone and is
singing down it in fine operatic tenor.*

Second Sergeant *(singing)* Calling all squad cars in the area . . .

Cut to vox pops.

Lovely Girl *(in deep male voice, dubbed on)* I think that's in very bad taste.

Pig *(miaows)*

Giraffe *(barks)*

President Nixon *(superimposed sheep bleating)*

Upperclass Twit (JOHN) Some people do talk in the most extraordinary
way.

*Cut to Upperclass Twit of the Year sketch. The five competitors run onto
the pitch.*

Commentator (JOHN) Good afternoon and welcome to Hurlingham
Park. You join us just as the competitors are running out onto the

field on this lovely winter's afternoon here, with the going firm underfoot and very little sign of rain. Well it certainly looks as though we're in for a splendid afternoon's sport in this the 127th Upperclass Twit of the Year Show. Well the competitors will be off in a moment so let me just identify them for you. *(close-up of the competitors)* Vivian Smith-Smythe-Smith has an O-level in chemo-hygiene. Simon-Zinc-Trumpet-Harris, married to a very attractive table lamp. Nigel Incubator-Jones, his best friend is a tree, and in his spare time he's a stockbroker. Gervaise Brook-Hampster is in the Guards, and his father uses him as a wastepaper basket. And finally Oliver St John-Mollusc, Harrow and the Guards, thought by many to be this year's outstanding twit. Now they're moving up to the starting line, there's a jolly good crowd here today. Now they're under starter's orders . . . and they're off! *(starter fires gun; nobody moves)* Ah no, they're not. No they didn't realize they were supposed to start. Never mind, we'll soon sort that out, the judge is explaining it to them now. I think Nigel and Gervaise have got the idea. All set to go. *(starter fires gun; the twits move off erratically)* Oh, and they're off and it's a fast start this year. Oliver St John-Mollusc running a bit wide there and now they're coming into their first test, the straight line. *(the twits make their way erratically along five white lines)* They've got to walk along this straight line without falling over and Oliver's over at the back there, er, Simon's coming through quite fast on the outside, I think Simon and Nigel, both of them coming through very fast. There's Nigel there. No. Three, I'm sorry, and on the outside there's Gervaise coming through just out of shot and now, the position . . . *(the twits approach a line of matchboxes piled three high)* Simon and Vivian at the front coming to the matchbox jump . . . three layers of matchboxes to clear . . . and Simon's over and Vivian's over beautifully, oh and the jump of a lifetime – if only his father could understand. Here's Nigel . . . and now Gervaise is over he's, er, Nigel is over, and it's Gervaise, Gervaise is going to jump it, is it, no he's jumped the wrong way, there he goes, Nigel's over, beautifully. Now it's only Oliver. Oliver . . . and Gervaise . . . oh bad luck. And now it's Kicking the Beggar. *(the twits are kicking a beggar with a vending tray)* Simon's there and he's putting the boot in, and not terribly hard, but he's going down and Simon can move on. Now Vivian's there. Vivian is there and waiting for a chance. Here he comes, oh a piledriver, a real piledriver, and now Simon's on No. 1, Vivian 2, Nigel 3, Gervaise on 4 and Oliver bringing up the rear. Ah there's Oliver *(Oliver is still trying to jump the matchboxes)*, there's Oliver now, he's at the back. I think he's having a little trouble with his old brain injury, he's going to have a go, no, no, bad luck, he's up, he doesn't know when he's beaten, this boy, he doesn't know when he's winning either. He doesn't have any sort of sensory apparatus. Oh there's Gervaise *(still kicking the beggar)* and he's putting the boot in there and he's got the beggar down and the steward's giving him a little bit of advice, yes, he can move on now, he can move on to the Hunt Photograph. He's off, Gervaise is there and Oliver's still at the back having trouble with the matchboxes. *(the twits approach a table with two attractive girls and a photographer)* Now here's the Hunt Ball Photograph and the first here's Simon, he's going to enjoy a joke with Lady Arabella Plunkett. She hopes to go into films, and Vivian's through there and, er, Nigel's there enjoying a joke with Lady Sarah Pencil Farthing Vivian Streamroller Adams Pie Biscuit Aftershave Gore Stringbottom Smith. *(shot of twit in a sports car reversing into cut-out of old woman)* And there's, there's Simon now in the sports car, he's reversed into the old woman, he's caught her absolutely beautifully. Now he's going to accelerate forward there to wake up the neighbour. There's Vivian I think, no Vivian's lost his keys, no there's Vivian, he's got the old woman, slowly but surely right in the midriff, and here he is. Here he is to wake up the neighbour now. *(a man in bed in the middle of the pitch; twit slams car door repeatedly)* Simon right in the lead, comfortably in the lead, but he can't get this neighbour woken up. He's slamming away there as best he can. He's getting absolutely no reaction at all. There, he's woken him up and Simon's through. Here comes Vivian, Vivian to slam the door, and there we are back at the Hunt Ball, I think that's Gervaise there, that's Gervaise going through there, and here, here comes Oliver, brave Oliver. Is he going to make it to the table, no I don't think he is, yes he is, *(Oliver falls over the table)* he did it, ohh. And the crowd are rising to him there, and there I can see, who is that there, yes that's Nigel, Nigel has woken the neighbour – my God this is exciting. Nigel's got very excited and he's going through and here comes Gervaise. Gervaise, oh no this is, er, out in the front there is Simon who is supposed to insult the waiter and he's forgotten. *(Simon runs past a waiter standing with a tray)* And Oliver has run himself over, *(Oliver lying in front of car)* what a great twit! And now here comes Vivian, Vivian to insult the waiter, and he is heaping abuse on him, and he is humiliating him, there and he's gone into the lead. Simon's not with him, no Vivian's in front of him at the bar. *(the twits each have several goes at getting under a bar of wood five feet off the ground)* Simon's got to get under this bar and this is extremely difficult as it requires absolutely expert co-ordination between mind and body. No Vivian isn't there. Here we go again and Simon's fallen backwards. Here's Nigel, he's tripped, Nigel has tripped, and he's under and Simon fails again, er, here is Gervaise, and Simon is through by accident.

Here's Gervaise to be the last one over, there we are, here's Nigel right at the head of the field, *(the twits approach five rabbits staked out on the ground; they fire at them with shotguns)* and now he's going to shoot the rabbit, and these rabbits have been tied to the ground, and they're going to be a bit frisky, and this is only a one-day event. And they're blazing away there. They're not getting quite the results that they might, Gervaise is in there trying to bash it to death with the butt of his rifle, and I think Nigel's in there with his bare hands, but they're not getting the results that they might, but it is a little bit misty today and they must be shooting from a range of at least one foot. But they've had a couple of hits there I think, yes, they've had a couple of hits, and the whole field is up again and here they are. *(they approach a line of shop-window dummies each wearing only a bra)* They're coming up to the debs, Gervaise first, Vivian second, Simon third. And now they've got to take the bras off from the front, this is really difficult, this is really the most, the most difficult part of the entire competition, and they're having a bit of trouble in there I think, they're really trying now and the crowd is getting excited, and I think some of the twits are getting rather excited too. *(the twits are wreaking havoc on the dummies)* Vivian is there, Vivian is coming through, Simon's in second place, and, no there's Oliver, he's not necessarily out of it. There goes Nigel, no he's lost something, and Gervaise running through to this final obstacle. *(they approach a table with five revolvers laid out on it)* Now all they have to do here to win the title is to shoot themselves. Simon has a shot. Bad luck, he misses. Nigel misses. Now there's Gervaise, and Gervaise has shot himself – Gervaise is Upperclass Twit of the Year. There's Nigel, he's shot Simon by mistake, Simon is back up and there's Nigel, Nigel's shot himself. Nigel is third in this fine and most exciting Upperclass Twit of the Year Show I've ever seen. Nigel's clubbed himself into fourth place. *(three coffins on stand with medals)* And so the final result: The Upperclass Twit of the Year – Gervaise Brook-Hampster of Kensington and Weybridge; runner up – Vivian Smith-Smythe-Smith of Kensington; and third – Nigel Incubator-Jones of Henley. Well there'll certainly be some car door slamming in the streets of Kensington tonight.

Letter and voice over.

Voice Over (TERRY J) Dear Sir, how splendid it is to see the flower of British manhood wiping itself out with such pluck and tenacity. Britain need have no fear with leaders of this calibre. If only a few of the so-called working classes would destroy themselves so sportingly. Yours etc., Brigadier Mainwaring Smith Smith Smith etc. Deceased etc. PS etc. Come on other ranks, show your stuff.

ANIMATION:
Soldier Yes Sir, I'll do me best, sir! *(coughs)*
Voice *(off)* No, not good enough.
Soldier *(coughs again, his leg falls off)*
Voice No, still not good enough.
Soldier *(coughs again, he completely disintegrates)*
First Voice Yes, that's better.

> *A hand picks up the animated bits and we see Terry J. stuffing them into a pipe. He puts the pipe down and various strange beasties climb out of it. Cartoon link into still of beautiful country house. 'Hearts of Oak'-type music. The camera tracks into the house and mixes to: close-up of distinguished, noble father and gay, innocent beautiful daughter – a delicately beautiful English rose.*

Father (GRAHAM) Now I understand that you want to marry my daughter?

> *Pull out to reveal that he is addressing a ghastly thing: a grubby, smelly, brown mackintoshed shambles, unshaven with a continuous hacking cough, and an obscene leer. He sits on the sofa in this beautiful elegant lounge.*

Shabby (MICHAEL) *(sniffing and coughing)* That's right ... yeah ... yeah ...
Father Yes, you realize of course that Rosamund is still rather young?
Rosamund (CONNIE) Daddy you make me feel like a child. *(she gazes at Shabby fondly)*
Shabby *(lasciviously)* Oh yeah ... you know ... get 'em when they're young eh ... eh! OOOOH! Know what I mean eh, oooh! *(makes obscene gesture involving elbow)*
Father Well I'm sure you know what I mean, Mr ... er ... Mr ... er ... er?
Shabby Shabby ... Ken Shabby ...
Father Mr Shabby ... I just want to make sure that you'll be able to look after my daughter ...
Shabby Oh yeah, yeah. I'll be able to look after 'er all right sport, eh, know what I mean, eh emggh!
Father And, er, what job do you do?
Shabby I clean out public lavatories.
Father Is there promotion involved?
Shabby Oh yeah, yeah. *(produces handkerchief and clears throat horribly into it)* After five years they give me a brush ... eurggha eurgh ... I'm sorry squire, I've gobbed on your carpet ...
Father And, ah, where are you going to live?
Shabby Well round at my gran's ... she trains polecats, but most of them have suffocated so there should be a bit of spare room in the attic, eh. Know what I mean. Oooh!

Father And when do you expect to get married?

Shabby Oh, right away sport. Right away . . . you know . . . I haven't had it for weeks . . .

Father Well look I'll phone the bishop and see if we can get the Abbey . . .

Shabby Oh, diarrhoea. *(coughing fit)*

> *Cut to strange PHOTO CAPTION SEQUENCE (to be worked out with Terry 'the sap' Gilliam) (if he can find the time).*

Voice Over (JOHN) The story so far: Rosamund's father has become ensnared by Mr Shabby's extraordinary personal magnetism. Bob and Janet have eaten Mr Farquar's goldfish during an Oxfam lunch, and Mrs Elsmore's marriage is threatened by Doug's insistence that he is on a different level of consciousness. Louise's hernia has been confirmed, and Jim, Bob's brother, has run over the editor of the 'Lancet' on his way to see Jenny, a freelance Pagoda designer. On the other side of the continent Napoleon still broods over the smouldering remains of a city he had crossed half the earth to conquer . . .

> *Mix from photo captions to studio.*
>
> CAPTION: 'A CORNER OF A BED-SITTER'
>
> *A girl in bra and pants goes over to television and switches it on.*

Voice Over . . . whilst Mary, Roger's half-sister, settles down to watch television . . .

> *On the screen comes the start of a Party Political Broadcast.*
>
> CAPTION: 'A PARTY POLITICAL BROADCAST ON BEHALF OF THE WOOD PARTY'

Voice Over There now follows a Party Political Broadcast on behalf of the Wood Party.

> *Cut to a traditional grey-suited man at desk looking straight into camera.*
>
> SUPERIMPOSED CAPTION: 'THE RT. HON. LAMBERT WARBECK'

Minister (GRAHAM) Good evening. We in the Wood Party feel very strongly that the present weak drafting of the Local Government Bill leaves a lot to be desired, and we intend to fight.

> *He thumps on the desk and he falls through the floor. (Yes Mr Director you did read that right: he fell through the floor and added a fortune to the budget). As he falls he emits a long scream, fading away slowly. Another man comes on and looks down into the pit.*

Man (ERIC) Hello! Hellllllllllloooooooooo! *(to camera)* Er I, I'm afraid the minister's fallen through the Earth's crust. Er . . . excuse me a moment. *(goes and looks at pit)* Helloooo.

Minister *(unseen, a long way down)* Helloooooo.

Man Are you all right minister?

Minister I appear to have landed on this kind of ledge thing.

Man Shall we lower down one of the BBC ropes?

Minister If you'd be so kind.

Man What length of BBC rope will we be likely to need?

Minister I should use the longest BBC rope. That would be a good idea I would imagine.

Man Okey doke chief. Er, Tex get the longest BBC rope, and bring it here pronto.

Minister *(still a long way down)* In the meantime, since I am on all channels, perhaps I'd better carry on with this broadcast by shouting about our housing plans from down here as best I can. Could someone throw me down a script. *(man drops the script down and Tex appears with enormous coil of rope)* The script would appear to have landed on a different ledge somewhat out of my grasp, don't you know.

Man Er, well perhaps when the rope reaches you minister you could kind of swing over to the ledge and grab it.

Minister Good idea.

Cut to minister swinging on rope.

CAPTION: 'THE RT. HON. LAMBERT WARBECK'

Minister Well I'm going to carry on, if I can read the script.

He swings over to a ledge opposite with a script on it. As he gets near he peers and starts reading.

Minister Good evening. We in the Wood Party *(he swings away and then back)* feel very strongly about *(swings away and back)* the present weak drafting of the Local Government Bill and no, no – it's no good, it's not working . . . I think I'll have to try and make a grab for it. Ah. There we are. *(he swings over and grabs the script with one hand; he tries to turn to camera and continues)* Good evening. We in the Wood Party feel very strongly about the present *(he makes a vigorous gesture and in so doing lets go of rope and slips so that he is now hanging upside down)* agh, agh. Oh dear. Hello!

Man *(out of vision)* Hello.

Minister Look, look, I must look a bit of a chump hanging upside down like this.

Man *(out of vision)* Don't worry minister. *(cut to man looking off-camera)* I think love if we turn the picture upside down we should help the minister, then.

Cut to minister. The picture is now the other way up. The minister now appears to be the right way up.

SUPERIMPOSED NAME CAPTION *(upside down)*

Minister Oh good. Look, er, I'm sorry about this, but there seem to be a few gremlins about . . . I think I'd better start from the beginning.

Er, good evening, we in the Wood Party feel very strongly about, oh . . . *(he drops script)* Bloody heck. Oh, oh dear, er terribly sorry about this, about saying bloody heck on all channels, but, er . . .

Man *(out of vision)*   There's another script on the way down minister.

Minister   Oh good, good. Well . . . er . . . er . . . um . . . Good evening. Er . . . well . . . er . . . how are you? Er . . . Oh yes look, I don't want you to think of the Wood Party as a load of old men that like hanging around on ropes only I . . . er . . . oh . . . oh.

Meanwhile a man, the right way up, has been lowered down to the minister. As the picture is reversed, he appears to be moving straight up towards him. The minister sees him.

Minister   Ah. Thank you. *(taking script; the man on the rope starts to climb back up)* Good evening, we in the Wood Party feel very strongly about the present weak drafting . . . *(man falls past with a scream)* Look. I think we'd better call it a day.

Cut to two men at a desk in a discussion set.

First Robert (TERRY J)   Is this the furthest distance that a minister has fallen? Robert.

Cut to Robert.

Second Robert (ERIC)   Well surprisingly not. The Canadian Minister for External Affairs fell nearly seven miles during a Liberal Conference in Ottawa about six years ago, and then quite recently the Kenyan Minister for Agric. and Fish fell nearly twelve miles during a Nairobi debate in Parliament, although this hasn't been ratified yet.

First Robert   Er, how far did the Filipino cabinet fall last March?

Second Robert   Er, well they fell nearly thirty-nine miles but it's not really so remarkable as that was due to their combined weight, of course. Robert.

First Robert   Thank you, Robert. Well now what's your reaction to all this, Robert?

Cut to third Robert who is staring intently into camera. He is wearing a fright wig and has a left eyebrow four inches above his right one.

Third Robert (JOHN)   Well, well Robert the main thing is that it's terribly exciting. You see the minister is quite clearly lodged between rocks we know terribly little of. Terribly little. Of course the main thing is we're getting colour pictures of an extraordinarily high quality. The important thing is, the really exciting thing is the minister will *(as he gets more excited he starts to emit smoke)* be bringing back samples of the Earth's core which will give us a tremendous, really tremendous tremendous tremendous clue about the origins of the Earth and what God himself is made of. *(he bursts into fire and someone has to throw a bucket of water over him)* Oh, oh I needed that.

Cut back to first Robert.

First Robert Thank you Robert. Well that seems to be about all we have time for tonight. Unless anyone has anything else to say. Has anyone anything else to say?

Various 'noes' plus one 'bloody fairy' and more noes, from a very rapid montage of all the possible characters in this week's show saying 'no'. The last one we come to is the Spectrum presenter. He says more than no.

Presenter (MICHAEL) What do we mean by no, what do we mean by yes, what do we mean by no, no, no. Tonight Spectrum looks at the whole question of what is no.

The sixteen-ton weight falls on him. Cut to the 'It's' man running away.

CREDITS

Thirteen

Four undertakers carrying a coffin. The lid opens and the 'It's' man looks out.

It's Man It's . . .

Cut to large animated sign saying: 'Intermission'.

Voice Over (TERRY J) There will now be a short intermission.

After this seven seconds of (slightly) speeded up Mantovani. Two animated cars race in and crash.
Cut to animated opening credits.
Cut to the same sign saying: 'Intermission'

Voice Over There will now be a medium-sized intermission.

Same music, same speed, slightly longer. Short animation, then cut to restaurant vestibule. He and she are already there, entering. She is nattering. The waiter is waiting.

She (ERIC) Oo I don't like this. Ooh I don't like that. Oh I don't think much to all this. Oh fancy using that wallpaper. Fancy using mustard. Oo is that a proper one? Oo it's not real. Oh I don't think it's a proper restaurant unless they give you finger bowls. Oo I don't like him. I'm going to have a baby in a few years.

He (JOHN) Er, please excuse my wife. She may appear to be rather nasty but underneath she has a heart of formica. *(the waiter grimaces)* I'm sorry about that.

Waiter (TERRY J) That's all right sir, we get all sorts of lines in here. The head waiter will be along to abuse you in a few moments, and now if you'll excuse me I have to go and commit suicide.

He Oh I'm sorry.

Waiter It's all right. It's not because of anything serious.

He exits. Shot off-screen and scream.

She Quite frankly I'm against people who commit suicide, I don't like that sort of person at all. I'm plain people and I'm proud of it, my mother's the salt of the earth, and I don't take the pill 'cos it's nasty.

The head waiter comes in.

He Please excuse my wife, she may not be very beautiful, and she may have no money, and she may be a little talentless, boring and dull, but on the other hand . . . *(long pause)* . . . sorry I can't think of anything.

Head Waiter (MICHAEL) Fine. I'm the head waiter. This is a vegetarian restaurant only, we serve no animal flesh of any kind. We're not only proud of that, we're smug about it. So if you were to come in here asking me to rip open a small defenceless chicken, so you

could chew its skin and eat its intestines, then I'm afraid I'd have
to ask you to leave.

He No, no, no, no.

Head Waiter Likewise if you were to ask us to slice the sides of a cow
and serve it with small pieces of its liver . . . *(small tic developing,
getting carried away)* or indeed drain the life blood from a pig before
cutting off one of its legs . . . or carve the living giblets from a
sheep and serve them with the fresh brains, bowels, guts and
spleen of a small rabbit . . . WE WOULDN'T DO IT. *(reaction)*
Not for food anyway.

She Quite frankly I'm against people who give vent to their loquacity by
extraneous bombastic circumlocution. *(they both look at her; pause)*
Oh I don't like that.

He Sometimes Shirley I think you're almost human.

Head Waiter *(thinking)* Do you know I *still* wet my bed.

He Once I married someone who was beautiful, and young, and gay, and
free. Whatever happened to her?

She You divorced her and married me.

Head Waiter I met my second wife at a second-wife-swapping party.
Trust *me* to arrive late.

Enter headmaster.

Headmaster (GRAHAM) Always were late weren't you Thompson?

Head Waiter Hello Headmaster. What are you doing here?

Headmaster Fine, fine, fine, thank you. Fine, thank you. No more sherry
for me don't you know. Warner House beat Badger House for the
Second Cuppa, remarkable. We had to put most of the second form
to sleep. No padre. Bad business. They were beginning to play with
themselves. Still . . . You haven't seen my wife anywhere have you?

Head Waiter No.

Headmaster Oh thank God for that. *(exits)*

She Oh I don't like him. Do you know what I mean. *Do* you know what I
mean. I mean do you know what I mean. Do you know what I
mean. Do you know what I mean. I mean do you know what I
mean. All men are the same.

*Enter prologue, long white Greek robes, long white beard, holding a large
staff.*

Prologue Imagine not that these four walls contain the Mighty Owl of
Thebes. For, gentles all, beauty sits most closely to them it can
construe . . .

Head Waiter No it doesn't.

Prologue Sorry. *(he exits)*

Head Waiter Fine. Would you care for a glass of blood? Oh what a
giveaway.

She No, we'd like to see the menu please. I don't think it's a proper restaurant unless you have a proper menu, and anyway I might be pregnant.

He Perhaps you'd care for a drink?

She Ever since you've married me, Douglas, you've treated me like an albatross.

A waiter enters pushing a large serving dish with a semi-naked Hopkins sitting unconcernedly in it.

Hopkins (TERRY J) Evening.

He Good evening.

Hopkins I hope you're going to enjoy me this evening. I'm the special. Try me with some rice.

He I beg your pardon?

Hopkins A Hopkins au gratin à la chef.

He Ah, oh how do you . . . *(makes to shake hands)*

Hopkins *(skittishly)* Don't play with your food.

She *(examining him)* I don't like that. There's *dust* on here. I don't think it's a proper meal without a pudding. *My* husband's an architect.

Hopkins Oh, one word of warning, sir, a little tip. *(lowering voice)* Don't have any of the vicar over there. *(cut to vicar sitting thin and unhappy in a pot)* He's been here two weeks and nobody's touched him. 'Nuff said?

He Yes thank you.

Hopkins Well I must get on or I'll spoil. Janet – to the kitchen.

Waiter There's a dead bishop in the lobby, sir.

Head Waiter I don't know who keeps bringing them in here.

She Oh I don't like that. I think it's silly. It's not a proper sketch without a proper punchline. I mean I don't know much about anything, I'm stupid. I'm muggins. Nobody cares what I think. I'm always the one that has to do everything. Nobody cares about me. Well I'm going to have a lot of bloody babies and *they* can bloody well care about me. Makes you sick half this television. They never stop talking, *he'll* be the ruination of her, *rhythm method*!

Cut to animated sign saying 'Intermission'.

Voice Over (TERRY J) There will now be a whopping great intermission, during which small ice creams in very large boxes will be sold. Another way we can drive people away from the cinema is by showing you advertisements.

Intermission changes to adverts. Animated title: 'Pearls For Swine Presents'. Shots of various cars with young ladies posing on them.

Voice Over (ERIC) Do you like this? Or how about this? Or perhaps you prefer this latest model? Then why not come to us. We supply only the very best models. *(a card saying 'Soho Motors 2nd floor' on a board with advertisement cards for 'Rita' etc.; cut to a restaurant)* After the show why not visit the La Gondola Restaurant. Just two minutes from this performance. The manager Mr Luigi Vercotti will be pleased to welcome you and introduce you to a wide variety of famous Sicilian delicacies. *(as Vercotti poses for the camera policemen bundle his staff and several half-dressed girls through and out of the restaurant)* Here you can relax in comfort in friendly surroundings. Or if you wish, you may drink and dance till midnight. At the La Gondola Restaurant you can sample all the spicy pleasures of the Mediterranean. The head waiter will be pleased to show you his specialities. Or why not ask the cook for something really hot? *(the police remove a chef carrying an 8mm projector and film)* Yes, for an evening you will never forget – it's the La Gondola Restaurant, Chelsea, Parkhurst, Dartmoor and the Scrubs. *(the police remove Mr Vercotti)*

'Pearls for Swine' closing title.

Cut to corner of cinema. A man in an ice-cream girl's uniform is standing in a spotlight with an ice-cream tray with an albatross on it.

Man (JOHN) Albatross! Albatross! Albatross!

A person approaches him.

Person (TERRY J) Two choc-ices please.

Man I haven't got choc-ices. I only got the albatross. Albatross!

Person What flavour is it?

Man It's a bird, innit. It's a bloody sea bird . . . it's not any bloody flavour. Albatross!

Person Do you get wafers with it?

Man 'Course you don't get bloody wafers with it. Albatross!

Person How much is it?

Man Ninepence.

Person I'll have two please.

Man Gannet on a stick.

The camera zooms past back onto the screen. On screen appears another 'Intermission' sign.

Voice Over There will now be a very short . . .

The intermission sign explodes.

ANIMATED CAPTIONS:
'NOW SHOWING AT OTHER DANK CINEMAS'
'AT THE PORTNOY CINEMA PICCADILLY'
'WINNER OF THE GOLDEN PALM, TORREMOLINOS'
'RAINWEAR THROUGH THE AGES'
'COMING SOON'
'AT THE JODRELL CINEMA, COCKFOSTERS'

Voice Over (TERRY G) and CAPTION: 'The management regrets that it will not be showing a feature film this evening as it eats into the profits'

Cut to the Queen on horseback; first few bars of National Anthem.

Cut to person sitting in cinema seat clutching albatross.

Person Well that's quite enough of that. And now a policeman near Rottingdeans ... Albatross!

Cut to a policeman standing in a street. A man comes up to him.

Man (MICHAEL) Inspector, inspector.

Inspector (JOHN) Uh huh.

Man I'm terribly sorry but I was sitting on a park bench over there, took my coat off for a minute and then I found my wallet had been stolen and £15 taken from it.

Inspector Well did you er, did you see anyone take it, anyone hanging around or ...

Man No no, there was no one there at all. That's the trouble.

Inspector Well there's not very much we can do about that, sir.

Man Do you want to come back to my place?

Inspector ... Yeah all right.

Women's Institute applauding.
Cut to a man on a bench in casualty ward set.

Man (TERRY J) Albatross.

Doctor and sister enter and go up to him.

Doctor (ERIC) Mr Burtenshaw?

Man Me, Doctor?

Doctor No, *me* Doctor, *you* Mr Burtenshaw.

Man My wife, Doctor?

Doctor No. Your wife *patient, me* Doctor.

Sister (CAROL) Come this way please.

Man Me, Sister?

Doctor No. She Sister. Me Doctor. You Mr Burtenshaw.

Nurse enters.

Nurse (JOHN) Doctor Walters?

Doctor Me, Nurse. *(to sister)* You Mr Burtenshaw. *(to man)* She Sister. You Doctor. *(to nurse)*

Nurse No Doctor.

Doctor No Doctor. Call ambulance. Keep warm.

Sister Drink Doctor?

Doctor Drink Doctor. Eat Sister. Cook Mr Burtenshaw. Nurse me.

Nurse You, Doctor?

Doctor *Me* Doctor. You Mr Burtenshaw. She Nurse.

Man But my wife, Nurse.

Doctor Your wife not Nurse. She Nurse. Your wife patient. Be patient. She Nurse. Your wife. Me Doctor. Yew Tree. U-trecht. U-trillo, U Thant, Euphemism. Me Doctor. *(knight walks in quickly and hits him over the head with a chicken)* Albatross!

Women's Institute applaud.

Cut to film of Gumbys (vox pop).

Gumby (MICHAEL) I would like to meet someone of superior intelligence.

Second Gumby (TERRY J) I would like to hear the sound of two bricks being bashed together.

Gumby I would like to see John the Baptist's impersonation of Graham Hill.

Cut to historical impersonation sketch. Big zoom in to linkman. Glittery linkman set, showbizzy music and applause.

Voice Over (JOHN) Yes, it's Historical Impersonations. When you in the present can make those in the past stars of the future. And here is your host for tonight – Wally Wiggin.

CAPTION: 'HISTORICAL IMPERSONATIONS'

Fade applause and music.

Wiggin (MICHAEL) Hello, good evening and welcome to Historical Impersonations. And we kick off tonight with Cardinal Richelieu and his impersonation of Petula Clark.

Cut to Cardinal Richelieu, he mimes to the phrase from the record.

Richelieu (MICHAEL) 'Don't sleep in the subway darling and don't stand in the pouring rain'.

Vast applause.

Wiggin Cardinal Richelieu – sixteen stone of pure man. And now your favourite Roman Emperor Julius Caesar as Eddie Waring.

Cut to Caesar; cloud effects behind.

Caesar (ERIC) *(in Waring voice)* Tota gallia divisa est in tres partes Wigan, Hunslett and Hull Kingston Rovers.

Cut back to Wiggin.

Wiggin Well done indeed, Julius Caesar, a smile, a conquest and a dagger up your strap. Our next challenger comes all the way from the Crimea. It's the very lovely Florence Nightingale as Brian London.

Florence Nightingale (Graham) stands there with a lamp, simpering femininely. A boxing bell goes, slight pause, then she is hit on the side of the cheek with a boxing glove, and falls straight on her back.
Cut back to Wiggin.

Wiggin And now for our most ambitious attempt tonight – all the way from Moscow in the USS of R – Ivan the Terrible as a sales assistant in Freeman, Hardy and Willis.

In a shoe department. Three people are sitting in chairs, only the middle one is a dummy. Ivan the Terrible comes in and splits the man in the middle in half with an immense two-handed sword: the model splits in two.

Wiggin And now W. G. Grace as a music box.

ANIMATION: *Still picture of W. G. Grace. Slowly his head starts to revolve as a musical box plays Swiss-type music.*
Cut back to Wiggin.

Wiggin And now it's France's turn. One of their top statesmen, Napoleon as the R101 disaster.

Cut to a sky background. Napoleon comes into frame horizontally, moving along a wire very slowly. In each hand he has a small propeller. A sign hangs below his belly saying R101. Marseillaise plays. As he passes out of shot there is an explosion.

Wiggin And now it's request time.

Cut to Gumby.

Gumby (MICHAEL) I would like to see John the Baptist's impersonation of Graham Hill.

A head on a platter is pulled by a string across the floor. We hear brm, brm, brm, noises. The head of John the Baptist has a Graham Hill moustache, obviously stuck on.
Women's Institute applaud.

Wiggin And now a short intermission during which Marcel Marceau will impersonate a man walking against the wind.

Marcel Marceau (Graham) walks against the wind.

Wiggin And now Marcel will mime a man being struck about the head by a sixteen-ton weight.

Cut to him starting the mime. He doesn't get very far as a sixteen-ton weight is dropped on his head.
Cut to Wembley crowd cheering.
Cut to interviewer and two small boys.

Interviewer (JOHN) (*gently*) What's your name?
Eric (ERIC) Eric.
Interviewer Would you like to have a sixteen-ton weight dropped on top of you, Eric?
Eric Don't know.

Brief stock shot of theatre audience applauding.

Interviewer How about you?
Michael (MICHAEL) I want to have.
Interviewer What do you want to have?
Michael I want to have . . . I want to have Racquel Welch dropped on top of me.
Interviewer Dropped on top of you.
Michael Oh yes, not climbing.
Eric She's got a big bottom.

Applause stock shot.
Cut to interviewer and two city gents (on their knees).

Interviewer And what's your name?

Trevor (GRAHAM) Trevor Atkinson.

Interviewer And how old are you, Trevor?

Trevor I'm forty-two.

> *Applause stock shot.*

Interviewer *(to other city gent)* Are you a friend of Trevor's?

City Gent (MICHAEL) Yes, we're all colleagues from the Empire and General Insurance Company.

Interviewer And what do you do?

City Gent Well I deal mainly with mortgage protection policies, but I also do certain types of life assurance.

Interviewer Now if you and your pal had one big wish, Trevor, what would you like to see on television?

Trevor I'd like to see more fairy stories about the police.

> *Fairy godmother trips lightly into shot.*

Fairy (ERIC) And so you shall.

> *Cut to open country. A policeman cycles up and parks his bike. From the saddlebag he takes a burglar's outfit – striped jersey, cap, and trousers. He lays them out on the ground, and inflates them with a bicycle pump. The inflated burglar runs away in speeded-up motion. The policeman blows his whistle. Three more policemen appear out of nowhere. He points forward and the four of them move off (in pixilated motion) after the burglar. The burglar runs across moorland; the policemen follow him. Dick Barton theme music. The burglar lures the policemen into a large packing crate, slams the door on them and nails on it a label: 'Do not open until Christmas'. In the background a policeman with a fairy tutu appears suddenly out of thin air. He waves his wand at the burglar, who disappears. Cut to policeman, with wand, standing in a street.*

Policeman (MICHAEL) Yes, we in Special Crime Squad have been using wands for almost a year now. You find it's easy to make yourself invisible. You can defy time and space, and you can turn violent criminals into frogs. Something which you could never do with the old truncheons.

> *'Panorama' music and still photos of policemen in tutus.*
>
> CAPTION: 'PROBE AROUND'
>
> *Cut to interviewer at desk of 'Panorama' type set-up.*

Interviewer (JOHN) Yes, tonight 'Probe Around' takes a look at crime . . .

> *A shot rings out and he slumps forward. A second interviewer runs into shot from behind camera with smoking gun.*

Second Interviewer (ERIC) I'm sorry about that, but *I* always introduce this programme, not him. *(he pushes the first interviewer off his chair with his foot and takes his place)* Yes, tonight 'Probe Around' takes a look at Crime. Is it true that the police are using dachshunds to combat the crime wave? And can the head of the Vice Squad turn himself into an albatross whenever he wants to? Just what are the police up to?

Cut to close-up of a constable reading big book. He is very, very, very stupid.

Policeman (TERRY J) Oh, I'm up to page 39, where Peter Pan first manifests himself.

Cut back to interviewer.

Second Interviewer With me now is Inspector Harry H 'Snapper' Organs of 'H' Division.

Cut to another part of the 'Panorama' set. Detective Inspector Organs is sitting next to a Viking.

Organs (MICHAEL) Good evening.

Cut back to interviewer and hereafter cross cut between them.

Interviewer Er, Inspector, I believe you are encouraging magic in the Police Force?

Organs That is correct. *(as he speaks we notice he is sticking pins into a model of a burglar)* The criminal mind is a strange and contorted one. Good evening. The mind is subject to severe mental stresses. Good evening. Guilt fears abound, good evening. In the subconscious in this state, one of our lads, with a fair training in the black arts can scare the fertilizer out of them.

Interviewer Just how are the police combatting the increase with the use of the occult? Ex-King Zog of Albania reports . . . *(phone rings)* Well we seem to have lost ex-King Zog there, but who cares. Just what kinds of magic are the police introducing into their crime prevention techniques?

Cut to four chief constables huddled round an Ouija board. They have their fingers on a tumbler which moves swiftly from one letter to the next.

Policemen U-P Y-O-U-R-S.

Policeman (JOHN) Up yours? What a rude Ouija board!

Cut to more film: policeman with wand. By pointing the wand at illegally parked cars he makes them disappear. Another policeman on the pavement helping an old lady across road. He looks to see if the road is clear, waves his wand and she jumps across to other side.

Another street: a police siren is heard, then five policemen on broom sticks appear from round corner and disappear across frame.

Cut to police dancing round Stonehenge. A burglar is bound to a stone altar. Mix to picture of same thing in newspaper which is being read by a chief constable in his office.

Chief Constable (TERRY J) Now this is the kind of thing that gives the police a bad name, sergeant.

Pull out further to reveal police sergeant in long shimmering slim-fitting ladies evening gown, diamanté handbag and helmet.

Sergeant (GRAHAM) I know, sir.

Intercom buzzer goes on desk.

Chief Constable *(depressing knob)* Yes, Beryl?

Beryl *(male voice)* Attila the Hun to see you, sir.

Chief Constable Who?

Beryl Attila the Hun, sir.

Chief Constable Oh botherkins! Er, constable, go and see to him will you?

Sergeant What! In this dress?

Chief Constable Oh all right, I'll go.

Sergeant Oh, I have got a little green pinny I could wear . . .

Chief Constable No, no, no, I'll go. You stay here.

Sergeant Oh goody! I can get on with the ironing.

The chief constable walks through the door into the reception area of the police station. There is a policeman behind the counter and a little insignificant man is standing waiting.

Chief Constable *(to policeman)* Right where is he?

Beryl (JOHN) Over there, sir.

Chief Constable Right, er, all right sergeant leave this to me. Er, now then sir, you are Attila the Hun.

Attila the Hun (MICHAEL) That's right, yes. A. T. Hun. My parents were Mr and Mrs Norman Hun, but they had a little joke when I was born.

Chief Constable Yes well, Mr Hun . . .

Attila Oh! Call me 'The', for heaven's sake!

Chief Constable Oh well, The . . . what do you want to see us about?

Attila I've come to give myself up.

Chief Constable What for?

Attila Looting, pillaging and sacking a major city.

Chief Constable I beg your pardon?

Attila Looting, pillaging, sacking a major city, and I'd like nine thousand other charges to be taken into consideration, please.

Chief Constable I say, excuse me, Mr Hun. *(he takes his hat off, removes his moustache, puts it in the hat and puts the hat back on)* Have you any objection to taking a breath test?

Attila Oh, no. No, no, no, no.

Chief Constable Right, er, sergeant will you bring the Hunalyser, please?

The constable produces a breathalyser.

Beryl Here we are, sir.

Hands it to the chief constable.

Chief Constable Er, how's it work?

Beryl Well he breathes into it, sir, and the white crystals turn lime green. Then he is Attila the Hun, sir.

Chief Constable I see. Right. Would you mind breathing into this Mr Hun?

Attila Right. *(blows into bag)*

Chief Constable What if nothing happens, sergeant?

Beryl He's Alexander the Great!

Chief Constable Ha, ha! Caught you, Mr A. T. Great!

Attila *(who is now Alexander the Great)* Oh curses! Curses! I thought I was safe, disguised as Attila the Hun.

Chief Constable Oh perhaps so, but you made one fatal mistake . . . you see, this wasn't a Hunalyser . . . it was an Alexander the Greatalyser! Take him away, Beryl!

Cut to letter (as used for 'Xmas night with the stars' after pet shop. I'm sorry . . . as not used in 'Xmas night with the stars').

Voice Over (ERIC) Dear Sir, I object very strongly to that last scene, and to the next letter.

Cut to second letter.

Voice Over (MICHAEL) Dear Sir, I object to being objected to by the last letter, before my drift has become apparent. I spent many years in India during the last war and am now a part-time notice board in a prominent public school. Yours etc., Brigadier Zoe La Rue (deceased). PS Aghhh!

Cut to third letter.

Voice Over (JOHN) Dear Sir, When I was at school, I was beaten regularly every thirty minutes, and it never did me any harm – except for psychological maladjustment and blurred vision. Yours truly, Flight Lieutenant Ken Frankenstein (Mrs).

Animation link runs into a psychiatrist's consulting room. The psychiatrist at his desk. The door opens and a receptionist looks in.

Receptionist (CAROL) Dr Larch . . . there's a Mr Phelps to see you.

Psychiatrist (JOHN) Er, nurse!

Receptionist Yes?

Psychiatrist *(whispering)* Er, you don't think you should make it clear that I'm a psychiatrist?

Receptionist What?

Psychiatrist Well, I could be any type of doctor.

Receptionist Well I can't come in and say 'Psychiatrist Larch' or 'Dr Larch who is a psychiatrist'. Oh, anyway look, it's written on the door.

Psychiatrist *(still whispering)* That's outside.

Receptionist Well, I don't care, you'll just have to do it yourself. *(she leaves)*

Psychiatrist *(goes 'brr brr', then picks up phone)* Hello. Er, no, wrong number I'm afraid, this is a psychiatrist speaking. Next please. *(knock at the door)* Er, come in.

Phelps comes in dressed as Napoleon, with a parrot on his head, and a lead with nothing on it.

Phelps (TERRY J) Bow, wow, wow.

Psychiatrist Ah Mr Phelps. Come on in, take a seat. Now what seems to be the matter?

Phelps No, no, no. No. No.

Psychiatrist I'm sorry?

Phelps Oh can't you do better than that? I mean it's so predictable I've seen it a million times. Knock, knock, knock come in, ah Mr Phelps take a seat. I've seen it and seen it.

Psychiatrist Well look will you please sit down and do your first line.

Phelps No. No. I've had enough. I've had enough. *(he exits)*

Psychiatrist I can't even get it started.

Phelps *(off)* Albatross!

Psychiatrist Shut up! Oh it drives me mad.

Cut to a man in limbo: Mr Notlob.

Notlob (MICHAEL) A mad psychiatrist, that'd be new.

Cut back to the psychiatrist.

Psychiatrist Next please.

Knocking at door. Psychiatrist is about to call when he picks up a thesaurus and thumbs through it.

Psychiatrist Cross the threshold, arrive, ingress, gain admittance, infiltrate. *(Notlob enters in an ordinary suit)* Ah Mr Notlob, ah park your hips, on the sitting device.

Notlob *(to camera)* It is a mad psychiatrist.

Psychiatrist I'm not. I'm not. Come on in. Take a seat. What's, what's the matter?

Cut to Napoleon in limbo; he blows a raspberry.

Psychiatrist Now what's the matter?

Notlob Well I keep hearing guitars playing and people singing when there's no one around.

Psychiatrist Yes, well this is not at all uncommon. In certain mental states we find that auditory hallucinations occur which are of a most . . . *(he stops suddenly and listens; the sound of 'We're all going to the zoo tomorrow' is heard)* Is that 'We're all going to the zoo tomorrow'?

Notlob Yes. Yes.

Psychiatrist Is it always that?

Notlob No.

Psychiatrist Well that's something.

Notlob But it's mainly folk songs.

Psychiatrist *(concerned)* Oh my God.

Notlob Last night I had 'I'll never fall in love again' for six hours.

Psychiatrist Well look, I think I'd better have a second opinion on this. I want you to see a colleague of mine, a specialist in these sort of things, who has an office very much like this one as a matter of fact.

Jump cut of same office now occupied by a surgeon. Start on portrait which has moustache and beard and glasses being added by surgeon.

Surgeon (GRAHAM) Brr brr *(picks up phone)* No, no wrong number I'm a colleague of his, a surgeon, who specializes in these kind of things. Yes thank you very much. *(replaces phone)* Next please. *(knock at door)* Come in. *(Notlob enters; 'Going to the zoo' is faintly heard)* Ah come in, please take a seat. *(cut to terribly quick shot of Napoleon, then back)* My colleague who has a similar office has explained your case to me *(he is rising from seat)* Mr Notlob, as you know I am a leading Harley Street surgeon as seen on television. *(he puts needle down on ancient gramophone; Dr Kildare theme begins playing)* I'm afraid I'm going to have to operate. It's nothing to worry about although it is *extremely* dangerous. I shall be juggling with your life, I shall be playing ducks and drakes with your very existence, I shall be running me mits over the pith of your marrow. Yes! These hands, these fingers, these sophisticated organs of touch, these bunches of five, these maulers, these German bands that have pulled many a moribund unfortunate back from the very brink of Lazarus's box. No, it was Pandora's box wasn't it? Well anyway these mits have earned yours truly a lot of bread. So if you'll just step through here I'll slit you up a treat.

Notlob What?

Surgeon Mr Notlob, there's nothing wrong with you that an expensive operation can't prolong.

Cut to operating theatre. The conversation and the guitar can still be heard. Notlob is on the table. His head is real but the rest of the body is false. Table is covered with green cloth for reality. Surgeon is swabbing. 'Going to the zoo' is still audible.

Surgeon Right, I'm ready to make the incision. Knife please, sister *(takes knife)* What's that supposed to be. Give me a big one. *(takes big knife and strops it on steel sharpener)* . . . oh I do enjoy this. Right. *(he stabs the body and makes a slit four feet long)* Oh what a great slit. Now, gentlemen, I am going to open the slit.

He pulls it apart. The song gets louder. The head of a squatter pops out.

Squatter (ERIC) Too much man, groovy, great scene. Great light show, baby.

Surgeon What are you doing in there?

Squatter We're doing our own thing, man.

Surgeon Have you got Mr Notlob's permission to be in there?

Squatter We're squatters, baby.

Surgeon What? *(to nurse about Notlob)* Nurse, wake him up. *(she slaps his face)*

Squatter Don't get uptight, man. Join the scene and other phrases. Money isn't real.

Surgeon It is where I'm standing and it blows my mind, young lad. *(looks inside Notlob)* Good Lord! Is that a nude woman?

Squatter She's doing an article on us for 'Nova', man.

Girl (CAROL) *(her head also appearing through slit)* Hi everyone. Are you part of the scene?

Surgeon Are you rolling your own jelly babies in there?

Notlob *(waking up)* What's going on? Who are they?

Surgeon That's what we are trying to find out.

Notlob What are they doing in my stomach?

Surgeon We don't know. Are they paying you any rent?

Notlob Of course they're not paying me rent!

Squatter You're not furnished, you fascist.

Notlob Get them out!

Surgeon I can't.

Notlob Get them out.

Surgeon No I can't. Not, not without a court order.

Indian *(also appearing)* Shut up. You're keeping us awake.

> CAPTION: 'ONE COURT ORDER LATER'
> *Some policemen walk in.*

First Policeman (JOHN) *(into slit)* You are hereby ordered to vacate Mr Notlob forthwith. And or.

Squatter Push off, fuzz.

Policeman Right, that's it, we're going in. Release the vicious dogs. *(dives into slit)*

> ANIMATION:

Animated Character What a terrible way to end a series. Why couldn't it end with something like this? *(a short piece of confusing animation later)* Now there's an ending for you. Romance. Laughter.

> *Cut to film of 'It's' man being pursued by undertaker; roll credits over.*
> CAPTION: 'INTERMISSION'

Voice Over (JOHN) When this series returns it will be put out on Monday mornings as a test card and will be described by the 'Radio Times' as a history of Irish agriculture.

Fourteen

A man in evening dress, sitting in a cage at the zoo.

Man (JOHN) And now for something completely different.

Pan to show 'It's' man in next cage.

It's Man (MICHAEL) It's . . .

Animated titles.

Cut to studio: interviewer in chair.

SUPERIMPOSED CAPTION: 'FACE THE PRESS'

Interviewer (ERIC) Hello. Tonight on 'Face the Press' we're going to examine two different views of contemporary things. On my left is the Minister for Home Affairs *(cut to minister completely in drag and a moustache)* who is wearing a striking organza dress in pink tulle, with matching pearls and a diamanté collar necklace. *(soft fashion-parade music starts to play in background)* The shoes are in brushed pigskin with gold clasps, by Maxwell of Bond Street. The hair is by Roger, and the whole ensemble is crowned by a spectacular display of Christmas orchids. And on my right – putting the case against the Government – is a small patch of brown liquid . . . *(cut to patch of liquid on seat of chair)* which could be creosote or some extract used in industrial varnishing. *(cut back to interviewer)* Good evening. Minister, may I put the first question to you? In your plan, 'A Better Britain For Us', you claimed that you would build 88,000 million, billion houses a year in the Greater London area alone. In fact, you've built only three in the last fifteen years. Are you a bit disappointed with this result?

Minister (GRAHAM) No, no. I'd like to answer this question if I may in two ways. Firstly in my normal voice and then in a kind of silly high-pitched whine . . . You see housing is a problem really . . .

Cut back to the interviewer. The minister is heard droning on in the background. The soft fashion-parade music starts again.

Interviewer Well, while the minister is answering this question I'd just like to point out the minister's dress has been made entirely by hand from over three hundred pieces of Arabian shot silk *(at this point we can hear the minister's high-pitched whine beneath the fashion music)* especially created for the minister by Vargar's of Paris. The low slim-line has been cut off-the-shoulder to heighten the effect of the minister's fine bone structure. Well I think the minister is coming to the end of his answer now so let's go back over and join the discussion. Thank you very much minister. Today saw the appointment of a new head of . . .

Minister Don't I say any more?

Interviewer No fear! Today saw the appointment of a new head of Allied
Bomber Command – Air Chief Marshal Sir Vincent 'Kill the Japs'
Forster. He's in our Birmingham studio . . .

*Cut to close-up on what appears to be a monitor with Sir Vincent on it –
in outrageous drag, heavy lipstick, big bust etc. – Draped on a
chaise-longue. A small black boy is fanning him.*

Sir Vincent (JOHN) Hello Sailors! Listen, guess what. The Minister of
Aviation has made me head of the RAF Ola Pola.

*As he talks we zoom out quickly from the set to reveal it is not a monitor
in the studio but a TV set in a G-plan type sitting room. A housewife
(Mrs Pinnet) sits watching, wearing an apron and a scarf, and with her
hair in curlers. The doorbell sounds. She switches the TV off and answers
the door which opens straight into the living room. There in the street
stands a truly amazing figure of fun. A man in a bowler hat with an axe
sticking out of it, big red joke nose, illuminated bow tie that revolves, joke
broad shoulders, clown's check jacket, long johns with sock suspenders,
heavy army boots and leading a goat with a hat. Close-up.*

Man Hello. Mrs Rogers?

Mrs Pinnet (TERRY J) No. Ooh I must be in the wrong house.

*She shuts the door on him and we follow her as she crosses the room.
She climbs out of the window. Back yard of terraced house. She scrambles
over a quite high dividing wall into next door and starts to scramble into
next-door window.*

*Interior of a more cluttered working-class sitting-room. There is a TV
in there with Sir Vincent still camping it up.*

Sir Vincent So from now on we're going to do things my way. For a start
David Hockney is going to design the bombs. And I've seen the
plans . . .

The doorbell rings.

Mrs Pinnet That must be the new gas cooker.

She switches the TV off. Immediate thunderous epic music.

SUPERIMPOSED CAPTION: *(in stone lettering, as for Ben Hur)* 'NEW
COOKER SKETCH'

*Both caption and music switch off suddenly as she opens the door.
Outside the door are two gas men with a new cooker.*

First Gas Man (MICHAEL) Morning. Mrs G. Crump?

Mrs Pinnet No – Mrs G. Pinnet.

First Gas Man This is 46 Egernon Crescent?

Mrs Pinnet No – Road. Egernon Road.

First Gas Man *(looks at a bit of paper)* Road, yes, says here. Yeah. Right,
could I speak to Mrs G. Crump please?

Mrs Pinnet Oh there's nobody here of that name. It's Mrs G. Pinnet. 46
Egernon Road.

First Gas Man Well it says 'Crump' here. Don't it, Harry?

Second Gas Man (GRAHAM) Yeah – it's on the invoice.

First Gas Man Yeah, definitely Crump.

Mrs Pinnet Well there must have been a mistake, because the address is right, and that's definitely the cooker I ordered – a blue and white CookEasi.

First Gas Man Well you can't have this. This is Crump.

Mrs Pinnet Oh dear, what are we going to do?

First Gas Man Well I don't know. What we can do for you is take it back to the Depot, get a transfer slip from Crump to Pinnet, and put it on a special delivery.

Second Gas Man Yeah – that's best. We'll special it for you, we'll get it down there today and you'll get it back in ten weeks.

Mrs Pinnet Ten weeks! Blimey, can't you just leave this one?

First Gas Man What this? What leave it here? *(they seem thunderstruck)*

Mrs Pinnet Yes.

First Gas Man Well I dunno. I suppose we could.

Second Gas Man Oh, but she'd have to fill out a temporary despatch note.

First Gas Man Yeah we could leave it on a temporary despatch note.

Mrs Pinnet Well that's sorted out then. What a mess, isn't it.

First Gas Man I know, it's ridiculous really, but there you are. Glad we could be of such a help. Right, would you sign it down there please, Mrs Crump?

Mrs Pinnet Pinnet.

First Gas Man Pinnet. Listen, just for the books make it a bit easier, could you sign it Crump-Pinnet.

Mrs Pinnet Right. *(she signs)*

First Gas Man Right. Thank you very much, dear. The cooker's yours. Right. Thank you very much, dear. Right. *(they push it just inside the door and move off)* Sorry about the bother . . . but there you are . . . you know . . . cheerio!

Second Gas Man Cheerio, Mrs Crump!

Mrs Pinnet Heh, excuse me! Cooey! Er, can you put it in the kitchen?

First Gas Man *(coming back)* You what?

Mrs Pinnet Well I can't cook on it unless it's connected up.

First Gas Man Oh we didn't realize you had an installation invoice.

Second Gas Man An MI.

First Gas Man No, we can't touch it without an MI, you see.

Second Gas Man Or an R16.

Third Gas Man (JOHN) *(who is suddenly revealed behind the two of them)* If it's a special.

Second Gas Man Nah – it's not special . . . the special's back at the Depot.

First Gas Man No, the special's the same as installation invoice.

Third Gas Man So it's an R16.
Mrs Pinnet What's an installation invoice?
First Gas Man A pink form from Reading.
Mrs Pinnet Oh – we wondered what that was. Now these are the forms.
     (she produces a large wad of papers, sorts through and produces a pink form which she hands to them)
First Gas Man That's the one, love. Yeah, this should be all I need. Hang on. This is for Pinnet. Mrs G. Pinnet.
Mrs Pinnet That's right. I'm Mrs G. Pinnet.
First Gas Man Well we've got Crump-Pinnet on the invoice.
Mrs Pinnet Well shall I sign it Crump-Pinnet then?
First Gas Man No, no, no – not an MI – no.
Second Gas Man No – that's from Area Service at Reading.
Fourth Gas Man (ERIC) *(suddenly revealed)* No, Cheltenham isn't it?
Second Gas Man No, not this side of the street.
Mrs Pinnet Look I just want it connected up.
     Much doubtfulness.
Third Gas Man What about London Office?
First Gas Man Well they haven't got the machinery.
Second Gas Man Not now.
Fifth Gas Man (TERRY G) *(suddenly revealed)* What! The Hounslow Depot?
Fourth Gas Man No – they're still on standard pressure.
Sixth Gas Man *(suddenly revealed)* Same with Twickenham.
Mrs Pinnet But surely they can connect up a gas cooker?
First Gas Man Oh yeah, we could connect it up, love, but not unless it's an emergency.
Mrs Pinnet But this *is* an emergency.
First Gas Man No it's not. An emergency is 290 . . . 'where there is actual or apparent loss of combustible gaseous substances'.
Second Gas Man Yeah, it's like a leak.
     Seventh gas man is revealed.
Seventh Gas Man Yeah, or a 478.
Third Gas Man No – that's valve adjustment.
Mrs Pinnet But there can't be a leak unless you've connected it up.
First Gas Man No, quite. We'd have to turn it on.
Mrs Pinnet Well can't you turn it on *and* connect it up?
First Gas Man No. But what we can do, and this is between you and me, I shouldn't really be telling you this, we'll turn your gas on, make a hole in your pipe, you ring Hounslow emergency, they'll be around here in a couple of days.
Mrs Pinnet What, a house full of gas! I'll be dead by then!
First Gas Man Oh well, in that case you'd have the South East Area Manager round here like a shot.

Mrs Pinnet Really?

First Gas Man Ah yes. 'One or more persons overcome by fumes', you'd have Head Office, Holborn, round here.

Mrs Pinnet Really?

First Gas Man Yes. That's murder you see.

Second Gas Man Or suicide.

Fifth Gas Man No. That's S42.

Second Gas Man Oh.

> *Eighth gas man is revealed.*

Eighth Gas Man Still? I thought it was Hainault.

Fifth Gas Man No – Central area and Southall Marketing Division, they're both on the S42 now.

Mrs Pinnet And they'd be able to connect it up?

First Gas Man Oh – they'd do the lot for you, love.

Mrs Pinnet And they'd come round this afternoon?

First Gas Man ... Well what is it now ... 11.30 ... murder ... they'll be round here by two.

Mrs Pinnet Oh well that's wonderful.

First Gas Man Oh well, right love, if you'd like to lie down here.

Mrs Pinnet All right. *(she does so)*

First Gas Man Okay Harry.

Second Gas Man Okay. Gas on.

First Gas Man *(holding a gas pipe to her mouth)* Right, deep breaths love. Ring Head Office would you Norman ...

Fourth Gas Man Shall I go through maintenance?

Fifth Gas Man No, you'd better go through Deptford maintenance.

Sixth Gas Man Peckham's on a 207 ...

Voices ... that's Lewisham. What about Tottenham? No that would be a 5.4 ... what about Lewisham? It's central isn't it? Or Ruislip ...

> *The camera pans along line of gas men all turning to each other and muttering incomprehensible technicalities, the line stretches across to front door. Line continues outside in street and goes into animation sequences which eventually bring us through to close-up on a small ad, which is one of many on the door of a small newsagent's shop. A shabby man is running an evil eye down the adverts, puzzling, looking for something. He walks up to the counter. He has a reflex wink.*

Customer (ERIC) Good morning.

Shopkeeper (TERRY J) Good morning, sir. Can I help you?

Customer Help me? Yeah, I'll say you can help me.

Shopkeeper Yes, sir?

Customer I come about your advert – 'Small white pussy cat for sale. Excellent condition'.

Shopkeeper Ah. You wish to buy it?

The It's man (p 1)

Bicycle repair man (p 33)

Nudge nudge (p 40)

Red Indian in theatre (p 74)

The colonel (p 96)

A man with a tape recorder up his nose (p 109)

Dead parrot (p 104)

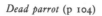

The lumberjack song (p 114)

The refreshment room at Bletchley (p 116)

The visitors (p 118)

The North Minehead by-election (p 149)

The Upperclass Twit of the Year (p 155)

Ken Shabby (p 159)

Restaurant (p 164)

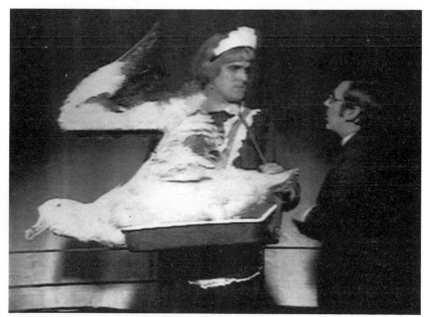

Albatross (p 168)

The Spanish Inquisition (p 193)

The Poet McTeagle (p 212)

'The Bishop' (p 225)

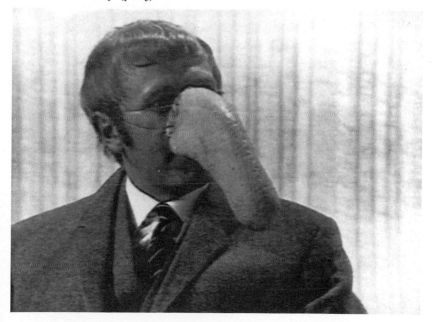

Raymond Luxury Yacht interview (p 259)

Appeal for sanity (p 282)

The Bruces (p 294)

Customer That's right. Just for the hour. Only I aint gonna pay more'n a fiver cos it aint worth it.

Shopkeeper Well it's come from a very good home – it's house trained.

Customer *(long think, goes to door, looks at ads again)* Chest of drawers? Chest. Drawers. I'd like some chest of drawers please.

Shopkeeper Yes, sir.

Customer Does it go?

Shopkeeper Er, it's over there in the corner. *(indicates a wooden chest of drawers)*

Customer Oh. *(goes to door, runs his finger down the list of adverts)* Pram for sale. Any offers. I'd like a bit of pram please.

Shopkeeper Ah yes, sir. That's in good condition.

Customer Oh good, I like them in good condition, eh? Eh?

Shopkeeper Yes, here it is you see. *(picks up pram)*

Customer *(looks, pauses, goes back to the door, runs finger again)* Babysitter. No, it's a babysitter. Babysitter?

Shopkeeper Babysitter.

Customer Babysitter – I don't want a babysitter. Be a blood donor – that's it. I'd like to give some blood please, argh! *(shopkeeper shakes head)* Oh spit. Which one is it? *(shopkeeper slips him a card from out of his pocket)* Blond prostitute will indulge in any sexual activity for four quid a week. What does that mean?

A city gent comes into shop. He has a silly walk and keeps doing little jumps and then three long paces without moving the top of his body. He buys a paper, then we follow him as he leaves shop.

City Gent (JOHN) 'Times' please.

Shopkeeper Oh yes sir, here you are.

City Gent Thank you.

Shopkeeper Cheers.

The city gent leaves the shop, from which we see a line of gas men stretching back up the road to Mrs Pinnet's house, and walks off in an indescribably silly manner. Cut to him proceeding along Whitehall, and into a building labelled 'Ministry of Silly Walks'. Inside the building he passes three other men, each walking in their own eccentric way. Cut to an office; a man is sitting waiting. The city gent enters eccentrically.

Minister Good morning. I'm sorry to have kept you waiting, but I'm afraid my walk has become rather sillier recently, and so it takes me rather longer to get to work. *(sits at desk)* Now then, what was it again?

Man (MICHAEL) Well sir, I have a silly walk and I'd like to obtain a Government grant to help me develop it.

Minister I see. May I see your silly walk?

Man Yes, certainly, yes.

He gets up and does a few steps, lifting the bottom part of his left leg sharply at every alternate pace. He stops.

Minister   That's it, is it?

Man   Yes, that's it, yes.

Minister   It's not *particularly* silly, is it? I mean, the right leg isn't silly at all and the left leg merely does a forward aerial half turn every alternate step.

Man   Yes, but I think that with Government backing I could make it very silly.

Minister *(rising)*   Mr Pudey, *(he walks about behind the desk in a very silly fashion)* the very real problem is one of money. I'm afraid that the Ministry of Silly Walks is no longer getting the kind of support it needs. You see there's Defence, Social Security, Health, Housing, Education, Silly Walks . . . they're all supposed to get the same. But last year, the Government spent less on the Ministry of Silly Walks than it did on National Defence! Now we get £348,000,000 a year, which is supposed to be spent on all our available products. *(he sits down)* Coffee?

Man   Yes please.

Minister *(pressing intercom)*   Now Mrs Two-Lumps, would you bring us in two coffees please?

Intercom Voice   Yes, Mr Teabag.

Minister   . . . Out of her mind. Now the Japanese have a man who can bend his leg back over his head and back again with every single step. While the Israelis . . . here's the coffee.

Enter secretary with tray with two cups on it. She has a particularly jerky silly walk which means that by the time she reaches the minister there is no coffee left in the cups. The minister has a quick look in the cups, and smiles understandingly.

Minister   Thank you – lovely. *(she exits still carrying tray and cups)* You're really interested in silly walks, aren't you?

Man   Oh rather. Yes.

Minister   Well take a look at this, then.

He produces a projector from beneath his desk already spooled up and plugged in. He flicks a switch and it beams onto the opposite wall. The film shows a sequence of six old-fashioned silly walkers. The film is old silent-movie type, scratchy, jerky and 8mm quality. All the participants wear 1900s type costume. One has huge shoes with soles a foot thick, one is a woman, one has very long 'Little Tich' shoes. Cut back to office. The minister hurls the projector away. Along with papers and everything else on his desk. He leans forward.

Minister   Now Mr Pudey. I'm not going to mince words with you. I'm going to offer you a Research Fellowship on the Anglo-French Silly Walk.

Man La Marche Futile?

 Cut to two Frenchmen, wearing striped jerseys and berets, standing in a field with a third man who is entirely covered by a sheet.

First Frenchman (JOHN) Bonjour ... et maintenant ... comme d'habitude, au sujet du Le Marché Commun. Et maintenant, je vous presente, encore une fois, mon ami, le pouf célèbre, Jean-Brian Zatapathique. *(he removes his moustache and sticks it onto the other Frenchman)*

Second Frenchman (MICHAEL) Merci, mon petit chou-chou Brian Trubshawe. Et maintenant avec les pieds à droite, et les pieds au gauche, et maintenant l'Anglais-Française Marche Futile, et voilà.

 They unveil the third man and walk off. He is facing to camera left and appears to be dressed as a city gent; then he turns about face and we see on his right half he is dressed au style français. He moves off into the distance in eccentric speeded-up motion.

Voice Over (ERIC) And now a choice of viewing on BBC Television. *(cut to BBC world symbol)* Just started on BBC 2 the semi-final of Episode 3 of 'Kierkegaard's Journals', starring Richard Chamberlain, Peggy Mount and Billy Bremner; and on BBC 1, 'Ethel the Frog'.

 Stirring music – 'This Week' type.

 SUPERIMPOSED CAPTION: 'ETHEL THE FROG'

 Cut to presenter at desk in usual grey suit and floral tie.

Presenter (JOHN) Good evening. On 'Ethel the Frog' tonight we look at violence. The violence of British Gangland. Last Tuesday a reign of terror was ended when the notorious Piranha brothers, Doug and Dinsdale, *(photo of same)* after one of the most extraordinary trials in British legal history, were sentenced to four hundred years imprisonment for crimes of violence. Tonight Ethel the Frog examines the rise to power of the Piranhas, the methods they used to subjugate rival gangs and their subsequent tracking down and capture by the brilliant Superintendent Harry 'Snapper' Organs of Q Division. *(photo of Eastend grotty house)* Doug and Dinsdale Piranha were born, on probation, in this house in Kipling Road, Southwark, the eldest sons in a family of sixteen. Their father *(photo (aged) of father)* Arthur Piranha, a scrap-metal dealer and TV quizmaster, was well known to the police, and a devout Catholic. In January 1928, he had married Kitty Malone, *(old wedding photo)* an up-and-coming Eastend boxer. Doug was born in February 1929 and Dinsdale two weeks later, and again a week after that. Their next door neighbour was Mrs April Simnel.

 Exterior in street: interviewer and Mrs Simnel. Line of gas men behind.

Mrs Simnel (MICHAEL) Kipling Road was a typical sort of Eastend street.

People were in and out of each other's houses with each other's property all day long. They were a cheery lot though.

Interviewer (ERIC) Was it a terribly violent area?

Mrs Simnel *(laughs deprecatingly)* Oh, ho . . . yes. Cheerful and violent. I remember, Doug was very keen on boxing, until he learned to walk, then he took up putting the boot in the groin. Oh he was very interested in that. His mother used to have such trouble getting him to come in for his tea. He'd be out there putting his little boot in, you know, bless him. You know kids were very different then. They didn't have their heads filled with all this Cartesian dualism.

Cut to school playground.

Voice Over (JOHN) At the age of fifteen Doug and Dinsdale started attending the Ernest Pythagoras Primary School in Clerkenwell.

Pan to show Anthony Viney and interviewer with stick mike.

Interviewer (TERRY J) Anthony Viney. You taught the Piranha brothers English. What do you remember most about them?

He fails to point stick mike at Viney (Graham) who answers. However, when the interviewer poses the next question he points stick mike to Viney as he does so. This continues, with the mike always pointing at the one who is not talking while Viney relates a fascinating tale complete with large riveting gestures.

Interviewer . . . Anthony Viney.

Cut to the presenter.

Presenter When the Piranhas left school they were called up but were · found by an Army Board to be too mentally unstable even for National Service. Denied the opportunity to use their talents in the service of their country, they began to operate what they called 'The Operation'. They would select a victim and then threaten to beat him up if he paid them the so-called protection money. Four months later they started another operation which they called 'The Other Operation'. In this racket they selected another victim and threatened *not* to beat him up if he *didn't* pay them. One month later they hit upon 'The Other Other Operation'. In this the victim was threatened that if he didn't pay them they would beat him up. This for the Piranha brothers was the turning point.

Cut to Superintendent Organs.

SUBTITLE: 'HARRY "SNAPPER" ORGANS'

Organs (TERRY J) Doug and Dinsdale Piranha now formed a gang which they called 'The Gang' and used terror to take over night clubs, billiard halls, gaming casinos and race tracks. When they tried to take over the MCC they were, for the only time in their lives, slit up a treat. As their empire spread, however, we in Q Division were keeping tabs on their every movement by reading the colour supplements.

Presenter A small-time operator who fell foul of Dinsdale Piranha was Vince Snetterton-Lewis.

Cut to Vince in a chair in a nasty flat.

Vince (GRAHAM) Well one day I was sitting at home threatening the kids, and I looked out of the hole in the wall and I saw this tank drive up and one of Dinsdale's boys gets out and he comes up, all nice and friendly like, and says Dinsdale wants to have a talk with me. So he chains me to the back of the tank and takes me for a scrape round to Dinsdale's. And Dinsdale's there in the conversation pit with Doug and Charles Paisley, the baby crusher, and a couple of film producers and a man they called 'Kierkegaard', who just sat there biting the heads off whippets, and Dinsdale said 'I hear you've been a naughty boy Clement' and he splits me nostrils open and saws me leg off and pulls me liver out, and I said my name's not Clement, and then he loses his temper, and nails my head to the floor.

Interviewer *(off-screen)* He nailed your head to the floor?

Vince At first, yeah.

Cut to presenter.

Presenter Another man who had his head nailed to the floor was Stig O'Tracey.

Cut to another younger more cheerful man on sofa.

Interviewer Stig, I've been told that Dinsdale Piranha nailed your head to the floor.

Stig (ERIC) No, no. Never, never. He was a smashing bloke. He used to give his mother flowers and that. He was like a brother to me.

Interviewer But the police have film of Dinsdale actually nailing your head to the floor.

Stig Oh yeah, well – he did that, yeah.

Interviewer Why?

Stig Well he had to, didn't he? I mean, be fair, there was nothing else he could do. I mean, I had transgressed the unwritten law.

Interviewer What had you done?

Stig Er . . . Well he never told me that. But he gave me his word that it was the case, and that's good enough for me with old Dinsy. I mean he didn't want to nail my head to the floor. I had to insist. He wanted to let me off. There's nothing Dinsdale wouldn't do for you.

Interviewer And you don't bear him any grudge?

Stig A grudge! Old Dinsy? He was a real darling.

Interviewer I understand he also nailed your wife's head to a coffee table. Isn't that right Mrs O' Tracey?

Camera pans to show woman with coffee table nailed to head.

Mrs O'Tracey (GRAHAM) Oh no. No. No.

Stig Yeah, well, he did do that. Yeah, yeah. He was a cruel man, but fair.

Cut back to Vince.

Interviewer Vince, after he nailed your head to the floor, did you ever see him again?

Vince Yeah . . . after that I used to go round to his flat every Sunday lunchtime to apologize, and we'd shake hands and then he'd nail my head to the floor.

Interviewer Every Sunday.

Vince Yeah, but he was very reasonable about it. I mean one Sunday when my parents were coming round for tea, I asked him if he'd mind very much not nailing my head to the floor that week, and he agreed and just screwed my pelvis to a cake stand.

Cut to man affixed to a coffee table and a standard lamp.

Man (TERRY J) He was the only friend I ever had.

Cut to block of concrete with a man upside down with his head buried in it.

Block I wouldn't hear a word against him.

Cut to a gravestone, which says: 'R.I.P. and Good Luck, Dinsdale'.

Voice Lovely fella.

Cut to presenter.

Presenter Clearly Dinsdale inspired tremendous loyalty and terror amongst his business associates, but what was he really like?

Cut to a bar.

Gloria (JOHN) I walked out with Dinsdale on many occasions and found him a most charming and erudite companion. He was wont to introduce one to many eminent persons, celebrated American singers, members of the aristocracy and other gangleaders.

Interviewer (ERIC) *(off-screen)* How had he met them?

Gloria Through his work for charity. He took a warm interest in Boys' Clubs, Sailors' Homes, Choristers' Associations, Scouting Jamborees and of course the Household Cavalry.

Interviewer Was there anything unusual about him?

Gloria I should say not. Dinsdale was a perfectly normal person in every way. Except in as much as he was convinced that he was being watched by a giant hedgehog whom he referred to as Spiny Norman.

Interviewer How big was Norman supposed to be?

Gloria Normally he was wont to be about twelve feet from nose to tail, but when Dinsdale was *very* depressed Norman could be anything up to eight hundred yards long. When Norman was about, Dinsdale would go very quiet and his nose would swell up and his teeth would start moving about and he'd become very violent and claim that he'd laid Stanley Baldwin. Dinsdale was a gentleman. And what's more he knew how to treat a female impersonator.

Cut to dark-suited loony in armchair.

SUPERIMPOSED CAPTION: 'A CRIMINOLOGIST'

Criminologist (GRAHAM) It's easy for us to judge Dinsdale Piranha too harshly. After all, he only did what most of us simply dream of doing ... *(tic ... controls himself)* I'm sorry. After all a murderer is only an extroverted suicide. Dinsdale was a loony, but he was a happy loony. Lucky bastard.

Cut to presenter.

Presenter Most of these strange tales concern Dinsdale, but what of Doug? One man who met him was Luigi Vercotti.

Cut to tatty office with desk and phone. Vercotti at desk.

Vercotti (MICHAEL) Well, I had been running a successful escort agency – high-class, no really, high-class girls ... we didn't have any of that. That was right out. And I decided. *(phone rings on desk)* Excuse me. *(he answers it)* Hello ... no, not now ... shtoom ... shtoom ... right ... yes we'll have the *watch* ready for you at midnight ... the watch ... the *Chinese watch* ... yes, right oh, bye-bye mother. *(he replaces receiver)* Anyway, I decided then to open a high-class night club for the gentry at Biggleswade with international cuisine, cooking, top-line acts, and not a cheap clip joint for picking up tarts, that was right out, I deny that completely, and one night Dinsdale walked in with a couple of big lads, one of whom was carrying a tactical nuclear missile. They said I'd bought one of their fruit machines and would I pay for it.

Interviewer (TERRY J) How much did they want?

Vercotti Three quarters of a million pounds. Then they went out.

Interviewer Why didn't you call for the police?

Vercotti Well, I'd noticed that the lad with the thermo-nuclear device was the Chief Constable for the area. Anyway a week later they came back, said that the cheque had bounced and that I had to see Doug.

Interviewer Doug?

Vercotti Doug. *(takes a drink)* I was terrified of him. Everyone was terrified of Doug. I've seen grown men pull their own heads off rather than see Doug. Even Dinsdale was frightened of Doug.

Interviewer What did he do?

Vercotti He used sarcasm. He knew all the tricks, dramatic irony, metaphor, bathos, puns, parody, litotes and satire.
Cut to map.

Presenter *(voice over)* By a combination of violence and sarcasm the Piranha brothers, by February 1966, controlled London and the South East. In February though, Dinsdale made a big mistake.
Cut back to bar and Gloria.

Gloria Latterly Dinsdale had become increasingly worried about Spiny Norman. He had come to the conclusion that Norman slept in an aeroplane hangar at Luton Airport.
Cut to presenter.

Presenter And so on February 22nd, 1966, at Luton Airport . . . *(stock film of H-bomb explosion)* Even the police began to sit up and take notice.
Cut to 'Snapper' Organs.

Organs The Piranhas realized they had gone too far and that the hunt was on. They went into hiding and I decided on a subtle approach, viz. some form of disguise, as the old helmet and boots were a bit of a give-away. Luckily my years with Bristol Rep stood me in good stead as I assumed a bewildering variety of disguises. I tracked them to Cardiff posing as the Reverend Smiler Egret. Hearing they'd gone back to London, I assumed the identity of a pork butcher, Brian Stoats. *(photo of Organs disguised as a butcher)* On my arrival in London I discovered they had returned to Cardiff. I followed as Gloucester from 'King Lear'. *(photo of Organs as Gloucester)* Acting on a hunch I spent several months in Buenos Aires as Blind Pew, returning through the Panama Canal as Ratty in 'Toad of Toad Hall'. *(photo of Ratty)* Back in Cardiff I relived my triumph as Sancho Panza *(photo)* in 'Man of La Mancha' which the 'Bristol Evening Post' described as 'a glittering performance of rare perception', although the 'Bath Chronicle' was less than enthusiastic. In fact it gave me a right panning. I quote:
Cut to press cutting, which reads:

Voice Over (ERIC) 'As for the performance of Superintendent Harry "Snapper" Organs as Sancho Panza, the audience were bemused by his high-pitched Welsh accent and intimidated by his abusive ad-libs.'
Cut to letterhead of newspaper – 'The Western Daily News'.

Organs *(off-screen)* 'The Western Daily News' said . . .

Voice Over (JOHN) 'Sancho Panza (Mr Organs) spoilt an otherwise impeccably choreographed rape scene by his unscheduled appearance and persistent cries of "What's all this then?".'

Cut to back-stage-type dressing-room, with make-up mirrors.

Policeman (GRAHAM) Never mind, Snapper, love, you can't win 'em all.

Organs True, constable. Could I have my eye-liner, please?

Second Policeman Telegram for you, love.

Organs Good-oh. Bet it's from Binkie.

Second Policeman Those flowers are for Sergeant Lauderdale – from the gentleman waiting outside.

Organs Oh good.

Knock, knock. Head comes round the door.

Head Thirty seconds, superintendent.

Organs Oh blimey, I'm on. Is me hat straight, constable?

Policeman Oh, it's fine.

Organs Right, here we go then, Hawkins.

Policeman Oh, merde, superintendent.

Organs Good luck, then.

Cut to exterior of police station. They come down the stairs and walk off along pavement. The city gent passes them, doing his silly walk. Cut to a little newspaper seller.

Newspaper Seller Read all about it. Piranha brothers escape.

Cut to a suburban street: it completely clears very fast. Freeze frame on empty street. An enormous hedgehog, higher than the houses comes into shot saying 'Dinsdale?'
Roll credits, behind which we see the enormous hedgehog appearing in various well-known London locations.

Hedgehog Dinsdale? Dinsdale? Dinsdale?

Cut to John in cage as in opening shot.

John Well, that's all for now and so until next week . . . *(roars)*
Pan to next cage to show skeleton of 'It's' Man. Fade out.

Fifteen

A field. A man with large mechanical wings, pulleys and gears contraption, running along trying to fly. Cut to him going faster. Cut to him going even faster. Cut to him even faster and suddenly he appears to take off, jumping off a dune or a hillock. Cut to him flying in slow motion so that it looks like he is gliding. He hits what seems to be a cliff. Camera twists round so that it is the right way up, showing that the flyer has fallen down a cliff onto a beach. It pans across from the wreck of the flyer. As it pans across the sand, various other would-be fliers can be seen, heads in the sand, legs kicking up in the air, amidst the broken debris of their planes. Camera continues to pan until it comes across an announcer in DJ sitting at his desk:

Announcer (JOHN) And now for something completely different. It's Man It's . . .

Animated titles. Music: Black Dyke Mills Band playing a slow dirge. Stock shot of mill town at the turn of the century – at night.

SUBTITLE: 'JARROW – NEW YEAR'S EVE 1911'
SUBTITLE: 'JARROW 1912'

Mix through to mill-owner's opulent sitting room at the turn of the century. Lady Mountback sits with her crochet. There is a knock on the door.

Lady Mountback (CAROL) Come in.

Enter Reg, cap in hand.

Reg (GRAHAM) Trouble at mill.

Lady Mountback Oh no. What sort of trouble?

Reg One on't cross beams gone owt askew on treddle.

Lady Mountback Pardon?

Red One on't cross beams gone owt askew on treddle.

Lady Mountback I don't understand what you're saying.

Reg *(slightly irritatedly and with exaggeratedly clear accent)* One of the cross beams has gone out askew on the treddle.

Lady Mountback But what on earth does that mean?

Reg *I* don't know. Mr Wentworth just told me to come in here and say there was trouble at the mill, that's all. I didn't expect a kind of Spanish Inquisition.

Jarring chord. The door flies open and Cardinal Ximinez of Spain enters flanked by two junior cardinals. Cardinal Biggles has goggles pushed over his forehead. Cardinal Fang is just Cardinal Fang.

Ximinez (MICHAEL) Nobody expects the Spanish Inquisition. Our chief weapon is surprise . . . surprise and fear . . . fear and surprise . . . our two weapons are fear and surprise . . . and ruthless efficiency.

Our *three* weapons are fear and surprise and ruthless efficiency and an almost fanatical devotion to the Pope . . . Our *four* . . . no . . . *amongst* our weapons . . . amongst our weaponry are such elements as fear, surprise . . . I'll come in again. *(exit and exeunt)*

Reg I didn't expect a kind of Spanish Inquisition.

Jarring chord. They burst in.

Ximinez Nobody expects the Spanish Inquisition. Amongst our weaponry are such diverse elements as fear, surprise, ruthless efficiency, and an almost fanatical devotion to the Pope, and nice red uniforms – oh, damn! *(to Biggles)* I-I can't say it, you'll have to say it.

Biggles What?

Ximinez You'll have to say the bit about 'our chief weapons are . . .'

Biggles I couldn't do that . . .

Ximinez bundles the cardinals outside.

Reg I didn't expect a kind of Spanish Inquisition.

They all enter.

Biggles Er . . . um . . . nobody . . .

Ximinez Expects.

Biggles Expects . . . Nobody expects the . . . er . . . um . . . Spanish um . . .

Ximinez Inquisition.

Biggles I know . . . I know. Nobody expects the Spanish Inquisition. In fact, those who do expect . . .

Ximinez Our chief weapons are . . .

Biggles Our chief weapons are . . . er . . . er . . .

Ximinez Surprise.

Biggles Surprise and . . .

Ximinez Stop! Stop there! Stop there. Whew! Our chief weapon is surprise, blah, blah, blah, blah. Cardinal, read the charges.

Fang You are hereby charged that you did on diverse dates commit heresy against the Holy Church. My old man said follow the . . .

Ximinez That's enough! *(to Lady Mountback)* Now, how do you plead?

Lady Mountback We're innocent.

Ximinez Ha! Ha! Ha!

SUPERIMPOSED CAPTION: 'DIABOLICAL LAUGHTER'

Ximinez We'll soon change your mind about that!

SUPERIMPOSED CAPTION: 'DIABOLICAL ACTING'

Ximinez Fear, surprise and a most ruthless . . . *(controls himself with a supreme effort)* ooooh! Now cardinal, the rack!

Biggles produces a plastic-coated modern washing-up rack. Ximinez looks at it and clenches his teeth in an effort not to lose control. He hums heavily to cover his anger.

You . . . right! Tie her down. *(Fang and Biggles make a pathetic attempt to tie her on to the rack)* Right, how do you plead?

Lady Mountback   Innocent.

Ximinez   Ha! Right! Cardinal, give the rack . . . oh dear . . . give the rack a turn.

Cardinal Biggles stands there awkwardly and shrugs.

Biggles   I . . .

Ximinez   *(gritting his teeth)* I *know*. I know you can't. I didn't want to say anything, I just wanted to try and ignore your crass mistake.

Biggles   I . . .

Ximinez   It makes it all seem so stupid.

Biggles   Shall I, um . . . ?

Ximinez   Oh, go on, just pretend for God's sake.

Biggles turns an imaginary handle on the side of the rack. The doorbell rings. Reg detaches himself from scene and answers it. Outside there is a dapper BBC man with a suit and a beard, slightly arty.

BBC Man (JOHN)   Ah, hello, you don't know me, but I'm from the BBC. We were wondering if you'd come and answer the door in a sketch over there, in that sort of direction . . . You wouldn't have to do anything – just open the door and that's it.

Reg   Oh, well all right, yes.

BBC Man   Jolly good. Come this way.

Cut to film of them coming out of the front door of the house and walking to BBC van. Conversation is heard throughout (slightly faintly).

BBC Man   Yes, we're on film at the moment you see.

Reg   It's a link, is it?

BBC Man   Yes that's right, that sort of thing, yes, a link. It's all a bit zany – you know a bit madcap funster . . . frankly I don't fully understand it myself, the kids seem to like it. I much prefer Des O'Connor . . . Rolf Harris . . . Tom Jones, you know . . .

They get into the van. It drives off. They pass an AA sign saying 'To the Sketch'. Panning shot of them, in which we see them conversing and hear . . .

Reg   You do a lot of this sort of thing, do you?

BBC Man   Quite a lot yes, quite a lot. I'm mainly in comedy. I'd like to be in Programming Planning actually, but unfortunately I've got a degree.

They arrive outside a suburban house, where the novelty salesman, Mr Johnson, is already waiting outside the front door. BBC man points and gives Reg direction. Reg goes to the door saying: 'Excuse me' and goes in, closing the front door. The novelty man rings bell. Reg opens the door.

Johnson (ERIC)   Joke, sir? Guaranteed amusing. As used by the crowned heads of Europe. Has brought tears to the eyes of Royalty.

'Denmark has never laughed so much' – 'The Stage'. Nice little novelty number – 'a naughty Humphrey' – breaks the ice at parties. Put it on the table. Press the button. It vomits. Absolutely guaranteed. With refills. 'Black soap' – leave it in the bathroom, they wash their hands, real fungus grows on the fingers. Can't get it off for hours. Guaranteed to break the ice at parties. Frighten the elderly – real snakes. Comedy hernia kit. Plastic flesh wounds – just keep your friends in stitches. Guaranteed to break the ice at parties. Hours of fun with 'honeymoon delight' – empty it into their beds – real skunk juice. They won't forget *their* wedding night. Sticks to the skin, absolutely waterproof, guaranteed to break the ice at parties. Amuse your friends – CS gas canisters – smells, tastes and acts just like the real thing – can blind, maim or kill. Or for drinks, why not buy a 'wicked willy' with a life-size winkle – serves warm beer. Makes real cocktails. Hours of amusement. Or get the new Pooh-Pooh machine. Embarrass your guests – completely authentic sound. Or why not try a new 'naughty nightie' – put it on and it melts – just watch their faces. Guaranteed to break the ice at naughty parties. Go on, go on.

Reg What?

Johnson Do the punchline.

Reg What punchline?

Johnson The punchline for this bit.

Reg I don't know it. They didn't say anything about a punchline.

Johnson Oh! Oh well in that case I'll be saying goodbye then, sir . . . Goodbye then, sir.

He turns and walks away. Reg looks around desperately. And then runs out of the door. He runs to BBC van as Johnson walks out of picture. Cut to cabin of BBC van with the BBC man sitting there.

Reg What's the punchline?

BBC Man Punchline? I don't think there's a punchline scheduled, is there? Where are we? A week 39.4 . . . no, it's Friday, isn't it – 39.7. Oh . . . here we are. Oh! *(laughs)* Ha, ha, ha, very good. Ha, ha, ha, very good. What a good punchline. Pity we missed that. Still, never mind, we can always do it again. Make a series out of it. Now if you'll just sign there, I'll put this through to our contracts department and you should be hearing from them in a year or two.

Reg Can you give me a lift back?

BBC Man Ah – can do. But won't. We were wondering if we could possibly borrow your head for a piece of animation.

Reg What?

BBC Man Oh jolly good. Thanks very much. You will get expenses.

BBC staff set on Reg and saw his head off.

ANIMATION: *Reg's head starts off by being thrown into picture. Animation leads to an oak panelled, Civil Service committee room. A politician is addressing three officials.*

Politician (JOHN) Gentlemen, our MP saw the PM this AM and the PM wants more LSD from the PIB by tomorrow AM or PM at the latest. I told the PM's PPS that AM was NBG so tomorrow PM it is for the PM it is nem. con. Give us a fag or I'll go spare. Now – the fiscal deficit with regard to the monetary balance, the current financial year excluding invisible exports, but adjusted of course for seasonal variations and the incremental statistics of the fiscal and revenue arrangements for the forthcoming annual budgetary period terminating in April.

First Official (GRAHAM) I think he's talking about taxation.

Politician Bravo, Madge. Well done. Taxation is indeed the very nub of my gist. Gentlemen, we have to find something new to tax.

Second Official (ERIC) I understood that.

Third Official (TERRY J) If I might put my head on the chopping block so you can kick it around a bit, sir . . .

Politician Yes?

Third Official Well most things we do for pleasure nowadays are taxed, except one.

Politician What do you mean?

Third Official Well, er, smoking's been taxed, drinking's been taxed but not . . . thingy.

Politician Good Lord, you're not suggesting we should tax . . . thingy?

First Official Poo poo's?

Third Official No.

First Official Thank God for that. Excuse me for a moment. *(leaves)*

Third Official No, no, no – thingy.

Second Official Number ones?

Third Official No, thingy.

Politician Thingy!

Second Official Ah, thingy. Well it'll certainly make chartered accountancy a much more interesting job.

Cut to vox pops.

Gumby (JOHN) *(standing in water)* I would put a tax on all people who stand in water . . . *(looks round him)* . . . Oh!

Man In Bowler Hat (TERRY J) To boost the British economy I'd tax all foreigners living abroad.

Man In Suit (ERIC) I would tax the nude in my bed. No – not tax. What is the word? Oh – welcome.

It's Man (MICHAEL) I would tax Racquel Welch. I've a feeling she'd tax me.

Business Man (JOHN) Bring back hanging and go into rope.

Second Business Man (MICHAEL) I would cut off the more disreputable parts of the body and use the space for playing fields.

Man In Cap (MICHAEL) I would tax holiday snaps.

Freeze frame. Cut to snapshot of same still which is being held by a dear old lady. Pull out to reveal she is sitting with a large photo album on her knees, lovingly extracting photos from the piles on top of the album and passing them to her friend sitting on the same settee. Her friend is a young lady, who tears up the photos as they are handed to her. The dear old lady is in a world of her own and does not notice.

Dear Old Lady (MARJORIE WILDE) This is Uncle Ted in front of the house. *(she hands over the photo and the young lady tears it up)* This is Uncle Ted at the back of the house. *(she hands over the photo and the young lady tears it up)* And this is Uncle Ted at the side of the house. *(she hands over the photo and the young lady tears it up)* This is Uncle Ted, back again at the front of the house, but you can see the side of the house. *(she hands over the photo and the young lady tears it up)* And this is Uncle Ted even nearer the side of the house, but you can still see the front. *(she hands over the photo and the young lady tears it up)* This is the back of the house, with Uncle Ted coming round the side to the front. *(she hands over the photo and the young lady tears it up)* And this is the Spanish Inquisition hiding behind the coal shed.

Friend takes it with the first sign of real interest.

Young Lady (CAROL) Oh! I didn't expect the Spanish Inquisition.

Jarring chord. The door flies open and Ximinez, Biggles and Fang enter.

Ximinez Nobody expects the Spanish Inquisition!

Cut to film: moving over Breugel drawing of tortures; epic film music.

Voice Over (JOHN) and CAPTION: 'IN THE EARLY YEARS OF THE SIXTEENTH CENTURY, TO COMBAT THE RISING TIDE OF RELIGIOUS UNORTHODOXY, THE POPE GAVE CARDINAL XIMINEZ OF SPAIN LEAVE TO MOVE WITHOUT LET OR HINDRANCE THROUGHOUT THE LAND, IN A REIGN OF VIOLENCE, TERROR AND TORTURE THAT MAKES A SMASHING FILM. THIS WAS THE SPANISH INQUISITION . . .'

Torchlit dungeon. We hear clanging footsteps. Shadows on the Grille. The footsteps stop and keys jangle. The great door creaks open and Ximinez walks in and looks round approvingly. Fang and Biggles enter behind pushing in the dear old lady. They chain her to the wall.

Ximinez Now, old woman! You are accused of heresy on three counts. Heresy by thought, heresy by word, heresy by deed, and heresy by action. *Four* counts. Do you confess?

Dear Old Lady I don't understand what I'm accused of.

Ximinez   Ha! Then we shall *make* you understand ... Biggles! Fetch ... the cushions!

Jarring chord. Biggles holds out two ordinary modern household cushions.

Biggles   Here you are, lord.

Ximinez   Now, old lady, you have one last chance. Confess the heinous sin of heresy, reject the works of the ungodly – *two* last chances. And you shall be free ... *three* last chances. You have three last chances, the nature of which I have divulged in my previous utterance.

Dear Old Lady   I don't know what you're talking about.

Ximinez   Right! If that's the way you want it – Cardinal! Poke her with the soft cushions! *(Biggles carries out this rather pathetic torture)* Confess! Confess! Confess!

Biggles   It doesn't seem to be hurting her, my lord.

Ximinez   Have you got all the stuffing up one end?

Biggles   Yes, lord.

Ximinez   *(angrily hurling away the cushions)* Hm! She's made of harder stuff! Cardinal Fang – fetch ... the comfy chair!

Another loud jarring chord. Zoom in on Fang's horrified face.

Fang   The comfy chair?

Fang pushes in comfy chair – a really plush one.

Ximinez   Yes. So you think you are strong because you can survive the soft cushions. Well, we shall see. Biggles, put her in the comfy chair. *(Biggles roughly pushes her into the comfy chair)* Now. You will stay in the comfy chair until lunchtime, with only a cup of coffee at eleven ... *(to Biggles)* Is that really all it is?

Fang   Why, yes lord.

Ximinez   I see. I suppose we make it worse by shouting a lot do we? Confess, woman! Confess! Confess! *Confess! Confess!*

Biggles   I confess!

Ximinez   Not you!

Animation Voice   I confess.

Ximinez   Who was that?

ANIMATION: *'I confess'*

Voice Over   Now for the very first time on the silver screen comes the film from two books which once shocked a generation. From Emily Brontë's 'Wuthering Heights' and from the 'International Guide to Semaphore Code'. Twentieth Century Vole presents 'The Semaphore Version of Wuthering Heights'.

CAPTION: 'THE SEMAPHORE VERSION OF WUTHERING HEIGHTS'

Film: appropriate film music throughout. Heathcliffe (Terry J) in close-up profile, his hair is blowing in the wind, he looks intense. Cut to close-up Catherine (Carol) also in profile, with hair streaming in wind. As if they are looking into each other's eyes. Pull out to reveal, on very long zoom, that they are each on the top of separate small hills, in rolling countryside. Heathcliffe produces two semaphore flags from behind him, and waves them.

SUBTITLE: 'OH! CATHERINE'

Pan across to Catherine who also produces two flags and waves.

SUBTITLE: 'OH! HEATHCLIFFE'

Heathcliffe waves flags again.

SUBTITLE: 'OH! OH! CATHERINE'

With each cut they are further and further away from each other. Catherine waves flags again.

SUBTITLE: 'OH! OH! HEATHCLIFFE'

Cut to her husband at front door of early Victorian manor house, looking stern. He waves two flags.

SUBTITLE: 'CATHERINE!'

Cut back to Catherine on hilltop.

SUBTITLE: 'HARK! I HEAR MY HUSBAND'

Cut to husband with two enormous flags.

SUBTITLE: 'CATHERINE!'

Cut to interior of the early Victorian manor house. Close-up of a cradle. Suddenly two little semaphore flags pop up from inside the cradle and wave.

SUBTITLE: 'WAAAAAGH! WAAAAAAGH!'

Pull back to reveal a nurse who walks over to cradle and waves flag briefly.

SUBTITLE: 'SSSH!'

The nurse points across the room. Cut to shot of old man asleep in chair with head slumped forward on his chest. He has two flags which he waves.

SUBTITLE: 'ZZZ . . . ZZZ . . .'

Cut to front door again. Exterior. Husband is waiting. Catherine comes up the path towards him. As she approaches he flags.

SUBTITLE: 'YOU'VE BEEN SEEING HEATHCLIFFE'

Catherine waves frantically.

SUBTITLE: 'YES! YES! I'VE BEEN SEEING HEATHCLIFFE, AND WHY NOT? HE'S THE ONLY MAN I EVER LOVED. HE'S FINE. HE'S STRONG. HE'S ALL THE THINGS YOU'LL NEVER BE, AND WHAT'S MORE . . .'

CAPTION: 'MONDAY FOR 7 DAYS'

Stock film of a Roman chariot race.

Voice Over (MICHAEL) From the pulsating pages of history, from the dark and furious days of Imperial Rome we bring you a story that shattered the world! A tale so gripping that they said it could not be filmed. A unique event in cinema history! Julius Caesar on an Aldis lamp!

SUPERIMPOSED CAPTION: 'JULIUS CAESAR ON AN ALDIS LAMP'

Close-up of Caesar walking in Roman street. Soothsayer pushes his way up to him wild eyed and produces Aldis lamp and starts flashing:

SUBTITLE: 'BEWARE THE IDES OF MARCH'

Some steps at the foot of a statue. Caesar is stabbed. As he falls he brings out a really big Aldis lamp and flashes to the assassins around him.

SUBTITLE: 'ET TU BRUTE'

A Western street. Two cowboys facing each other with morse buzzers.

Voice Over From the makers of 'Gunfight at the OK Corral in Morse Code'.

SUPERIMPOSED CAPTION: 'GUNFIGHT AT THE OK CORRAL IN MORSE CODE'

They buzz a bit.

SUBTITLE: 'AAAAHHH!'

Cut to a Red Indian making smoke signals.

Voice Over And the smoke-signal version of 'Gentlemen Prefer Blondes'!

SUPERIMPOSED CAPTION: 'AND THE SMOKE-SIGNAL VERSION OF GENTLEMEN PREFER BLONDES'

Cut to a courtroom: Usual set up with a judge, clerk of the court and defence counsel sitting in the well of the court. The defendant is in the witness box.

SUPERIMPOSED CAPTION: 'CENTRAL CRIMINAL COURT'

Judge (GRAHAM) Ladies and gentlemen of the jury, have you reached a verdict?

Foreman (MICHAEL) We have m'lud.

Judge And how do you find the defendant? *(the foreman puts his hand out with two fingers extended)* Two words. *(the foreman nods and holds up one finger)* First word. *(the foreman mimes taking a piece of string and tying it in knot)* Rope? String?

The foreman shakes his head and points to the knot.

Counsel (JOHN) Point?

Clerk (ERIC) Belt?

Judge Tie?

The foreman nods and points to the knot.

Counsel Cravat? Silk square?

Clerk Knot?

The foreman nods enthusiastically.

All Knot!

The foreman gives a thumbs up and points to his second finger.

Judge Second word. *(foreman indicates two syllables)* Two syllables. *(the foreman points to his first finger)* First syllable. *(the foreman starts to mime a fish while pointing at his throat)* Bird?

Clerk Swimmer?

Judge Breast stroke.

Counsel Brian Phelps.

Judge No, no, no, he was a diver.

Clerk Esther Williams then.

Judge No, no, don't be silly. How can you find someone 'Not Esther Williams'.

Counsel Fish. *(the foreman nods and points at throat)* Fish wheeze. Fish wheeze?

Judge Fish breathe.

Counsel Fish breathe, throat.

Judge Fish breathe, throat? GILL! *(the foreman gives a thumbs up and the court applauds excitedly)* Not gill. *(the foreman mimes the second syllable)* Second syllable. Not gill.

Foreman mimes drinking a cup of tea.

Counsel Drink.

Clerk Sip? Imbibe?

The foreman points to the mimed cup itself.

Judge Not gill . . . cup? Not gillcup! *(the foreman looks disappointed)* You have been found not gillcup of the charges made against you and may leave this court a free man. Right. My turn. *(the defendant leaves)*

The judge holds up four fingers.

Counsel Four words.

The judge mimes shouting for the first word.

Foreman First word shout?

Counsel Bellow?

Clerk Call?

All Call!

The judge gives a thumbs up and indicates that the second word is very small.

Counsel Second word is very small.

Foreman A?

Counsel An?

Clerk Up?

Foreman The?

> *The judge gives a thumbs up.*

All The!

Clerk Call the, third word.

> *The judge points to his neck.*

Counsel Gill?

Member of Jury Fish?

Clerk Adam's apple. *(the judge shakes his head)* Neck. *(the judge mimes 'sounds like')* Sounds like neck?

Second Counsel Next.

Foreman Call the . . . next!

> *The judge gives a thumbs up and indicates that the fourth word is three syllables. First syllable: he mimes deafness.*

Clerk Fourth word, three syllables. First syllable . . . ear?

Counsel Hear. Can't hear.

Clerk Deaf!!! Call the next def-.

> *The judge leaps onto the desk and points at his own bottom.*

Counsel Bottom.

Clerk Seat? Trouser? Cheek?

Foreman End! Call the next defend-.

> *The judge leaps down, disappears under the desk and appears with an enormous model of an ant about four feet long.*

Whole Court Ant!

Clerk Call the next defendant! *(the court applauds the judge who bows and sits; the whole mood changes)* Call the next defendant. The Honourable Mr Justice Kilbraken. *(a very elderly judge in full robes comes into the dock)* If I may charge you m'lud, you are charged m'lud that on the fourteenth day of June 1970, at the Central Criminal Court, you did commit acts likely to cause a breach of the peace. How plead you m'lud, guilty or not guilty?

Judge Kilbraken (TERRY J) Not guilty. Case not proven. Court adjourned.

> *He hits the dock. Everyone gets up and starts walking out talking to each other.*

Judge No, no, no, no, no, no, no. *(they all stop, go back and sit down again)* No, you're in the dock, m'lud.

Judge Kilbraken I'm a judge, m'lud.

Judge So am I, m'lud, so watch it.

Judge Kilbraken Hah! Call this a court.

All Call this a court. Call this a court. Call this a court.

Judge Shut up. Right now get on with the spiel.

Counsel M'lud, and my other lud, the prosecution will endeavour to show m'lud, that m'lud – ah, not *you* m'lud, that m'lud, m'lud, while passing sentence at the Central Criminal Court blotted his copy book. Call exhibit Q.

Judge Q?

Counsel Sorry did I say Q? I meant A. Sorry, call exhibit A.

Clerk Call exhibit A.

Two court ushers carry in a thing with a sheet over it. They pull off the sheet to reveal a very sexy girl in a provocative pose.

Counsel Exhibit A m'lud, Miss Rita Thang, an artist's model, Swedish accordian teacher and cane-chair sales lady, was found guilty under the Rude Behaviour Act in the accused's court. The accused, m'lud, sentenced her 'to be taken from this place and brought round to his place'.

Other Counsel Objection, m'lud.

Judge Kilbraken Objection sustained.

Judge You shut up! Objection overruled.

Counsel The accused then commented on Miss Thang's bodily structure, made several not-at-all legal remarks on the subject of fun and then placed his robes over his head and began to emit low moans.

Judge Have you anything to say in your defence?

Judge Kilbraken I haven't had any for weeks.

Judge Oh no? What about that little number you've got tucked away in Belsize Park?

Judge Kilbraken Oh, I never!

Judge Oh no. Ho! Ho! Ho!

Judge Kilbraken All right then what about 8a Woodford Square?

Judge You say anything about that and I'll do you for treason.

Counsel M'lud if we could continue . . .

Judge Kilbraken He's got a Chinese bit there.

Judge No, that's contempt of court.

Judge Kilbraken It was only a joke.

Judge Contempt of court. However, I'm not going to punish you, because we're so short of judges at the moment, what with all of them emigrating to South Africa. I'm going tomorrow; I've got my ticket. Get out there and get some decent sentencing done. Ooh, England makes you sick. Best I can manage here is life imprisonment. It's hardly worth coming in in the morning. Now, South Africa? You've got your cat of nine tails, you've got four death sentences a week, you've got cheap drinks, slave labour and a booming stock market. I'm off, I tell you. Yes, I'm up to here with probation and bleeding psychiatric reports. That's it, I'm off. That's it. Right. Well I'm going to have one final fling before I leave, so I sentence you to be burnt at the stake.

Judge Kilbraken Blimey! I didn't expect the Spanish Inquisition.

Court reacts expectantly. Cut to suburban house. The three members of the Spanish Inquisition suddenly belt out of the door and down the path. Dick Barton music. Cut to them leaping onto a bus.

Ximinez Two, er, three to the Old Bailey please.

Credits start superimposed.

Biggles Look they've started the credits.

Ximinez Hurry. Hurry. Hurry.

Biggles Come on hurry. Hurry!

We see shots of them coming through London.

Ximinez There's the lighting credit, only five left. *(more shots of the bus going through London; the credits reach the producer)* Hell, it's the producer – quick!

They leap off the bus into the Old Bailey. Cut to court room. They burst in.

Ximinez Nobody expects the Spanish . . . *('The End' appears)* Oh bugger!

Sixteen

Wide shot of enormous high block of flats. The camera seems to be searching. Suddenly it zooms in on one window. It is a bedroom . . . a busty girl is looking out of the window. She stretches languorously and mouths.

Girl (CAROL) *(dubbed on very badly)* My, isn't it hot in here.

She starts to undress. She gets down to bra and panties, unhitches her bra and is about to slip it off her shoulders exposing her heavy bosoms when . . . the announcer rises up in front of the window on window cleaner's hoist.

Announcer (JOHN) And now for something completely different.

Cut to an orchard or a woodland clearing, in which are a group of stuffed animals; a lion, a tiger, a cow, an elk, a leopard, two small ferrets and an owl on an overhanging branch. Sound of birdsong. The elk explodes.

Cut back to John still in front of the window. We can just see Carol behind him in bedroom casting her panties to one side – that is we just see her arm.

Announcer And now for something more completely different . . .

Cut to 'It's' man.

It's Man It's . . .

Animated titles.

Cut back to the same group of animals minus the elk. Birdsong etc. The elk's remains are smouldering. The owl explodes. Pan away from the woodland clearing to an open field in which at a distance a bishop in full mitre and robes is pacing up and down holding a script. Mr Chigger in a suit approaches the bishop and we zoom in to hear their conversation.

Bishop (MICHAEL) 'Oh Mr Belpit your legs are so swollen' . . . *swollen* . . . 'Oh Mr Belpit – oh Mr Belpit your legs are so swollen'. *(tries a different voice)* 'Oh Mr Belpit . . .'

Mr Chigger (TERRY J) Excuse me, excuse me. I saw your advertisement for flying lessons and I'd like to make an application.

Bishop Nothing to do with me. I'm not in this show.

Mr Chigger Oh I see. D'you . . . d'you . . . do you know about the flying lessons?

Bishop Nothing to do with me. I'm not in this show. This is show five – I'm not in until show eight.

Mr Chigger Oh I see.

Bishop I'm just learning my lines, you know. 'Oh Mr Belpit, your legs . . .'

Mr Chigger Bit awkward, I'm a bit stuck.

Bishop Yes, well. Try over there.

Bishop points to a secretary some yards away sitting at a desk typing. She wears glasses and is very typically a secretary.

Mr Chigger Oh yes, thanks. Thanks a lot.

Bishop 'Oh Mr Belpit' – not at all – 'your legs are so swollen'. *(he continues rehearsing as Mr Chigger moves over to the secretary)*

Mr Chigger Excuse me, I saw your advertisement for flying lessons and I'd like to make an application.

Secretary (CAROL) Appointment?

Mr Chigger Yes, yes.

Secretary Certainly. Would you come this way, please.

She gets up, clutching a file and trips off in a typical efficient secretary's walk. Mr Chigger follows. Cut to a river. She goes straight in without looking to right or left, as if she does this routine as a matter of course. Mr Chigger follows. Halfway across the river they pass a couple of business executives hurrying in the opposite direction.

Secretary Morning, Mr Jones, Mr Barnes.

Cut to a forest. They come past towards camera, passing a tea trolley on the way with a tea lady and a couple of men round it.

Secretary Morning Mrs Wills.

Mrs Wills (MICHAEL) Morning, luv.

Arty shot. Skyline of a short sharp hill, as in Bergman's 'Seventh Seal'. They come in frame right and up and over, passing two men and exchanging 'good mornings'. Cut to seashore. Tripping along, they pass another executive.

Executive Take this to Marketing, would you.

They disappear into a cave. We hear footsteps and a heavy door opening.

Secretary's Voice Just follow me.

Mr Chigger's Voice Oh thank you.

Cut to a shopping street. Camera pans in close-up across road surface.

Secretary's Voice Oh, be careful.

Mr Chigger's Voice Yes, nearly tripped.

Secretary's Voice Be there soon.

Mr Chigger's Voice Good. It's a long way, isn't it?

Secretary's Voice Oh, get hold of that – watch it.

Voice Morning.

Secretary's Voice Morning. Upstairs. Be careful, it's very steep. Almost there.

Camera reaches a GPO tent in middle of road.

Voice Morning.

Secretary Morning. *(they emerge from the tent)* Will you come this way, please. *(cut to interior office, another identical secretary at the desk)* In here, please.

Mr Chigger Thank you. *(he enters and first secretary trips off; he approaches the second secretary)* Hello, I saw your advertisement for flying lessons and I'd like to make an appointment.

Second Secretary Well, Mr Anemone's on the phone at the moment, but I'm sure he won't mind if you go on in. Through here.

Mr Chigger Thank you.

> *He goes through door. Mr Anemone is suspended by a wire about nine feet off the ground. He is on the telephone.*

Mr Anemone (GRAHAM) Ah, won't be a moment. Make yourself at home. *(into phone)* No, no, well look, you can ask Mr Maudling but I'm sure he'll never agree. Not for fifty shillings . . . no . . . no. Bye-bye Gordon. Bye-bye. Oh dear. Bye-bye. *(he throws receiver at telephone but misses)* Missed. Now Mr er . . .

Mr Chigger Chigger.

Mr Anemone Mr Chigger. So, you want to learn to fly.

Mr Chigger Yes.

Mr Anemone Right, well, up on the table, arms out, fingers together, knees bent . . .

Mr Chigger No, no, no.

Mr Anemone *(very loudly)* Up on the table! *(Mr Chigger gets on the table)* Arms out, fingers together, knees bent, now, head well forward. Now, flap your arms. Go on, flap, faster . . . faster . . . faster . . . faster, faster, faster, faster – now jump! *(Mr Chigger jumps and lands on the floor)* Rotten. Rotten. You're no bloody use at all. You're an utter bloody wash-out. You make me sick, you weed!

Mr Chigger Now look here . . .

Mr Anemone All right, all right. I'll give you one more chance, get on the table . . .

Mr Chigger Look, I came here to learn how to fly an aeroplane.

Mr Anemone A what?

Mr Chigger I came here to learn how to fly an aeroplane.

Mr Anemone *(sarcastically)* Oh, 'an aeroplane'. Oh, I say, we are grand, aren't we? *(imitation posh accent)* 'Oh, oh, no more buttered scones for me, mater. I'm off to play the grand piano'. 'Pardon me while I fly my aeroplane.' Now get on the table!

Mr Chigger Look. No one in the history of the world has ever been able to fly like that.

Mr Anemone Oh, I suppose mater told you that while you were out riding. Well, if people can't fly what am I doing up here?

Mr Chigger You're on a wire.

Mr Anemone Oh, a wire. I'm on a wire, am I?

Mr Chigger Of course you're on a bloody wire.

Mr Anemone I am *not* on a wire. I am flying.

Mr Chigger You're on a wire.

Mr Anemone I am flying.

Mr Chigger You're on a wire.

Mr Anemone I'll show you whether I'm on a wire or not. Give me the 'oop.

Mr Chigger What?

Mr Anemone Oh, I don't suppose we know what an 'oop is. I suppose pater thought they were a bit common, except on the bleedin' croquet lawn.

Mr Chigger Oh, a *hoop*.

Mr Anemone 'Oh an *h*oop.' *(taking hoop)* Thank you, your bleeding Highness. Now. Look. *(he waves hoop over head and feet)*

Mr Chigger Go on, right the way along.

Mr Anemone All right, all right, all right. *(he moves hoop all the way along himself allowing the wire to pass through obvious gap in hoop's circumference)* Now, where's the bleeding wire, then?

Mr Chigger That hoop's got a hole in.

Mr Anemone Oh Eton and Madgalene. The *h*oop has an *h*ole in. Of course it's got a hole in, it wouldn't be a hoop otherwise, would it, mush!

Mr Chigger No, there's a gap in the middle, there.

Mr Anemone Oh, a gahp. A gahp in one's hhhhhoop. Pardon me, but I'm orf to play the grahnd piano.

Mr Chigger Look, I can see you're on a wire – look, there it is.

Mr Anemone Look, I told you, you bastard, I'm not on a wire.

Mr Chigger You are. There is.

Mr Anemone There isn't.

Mr Chigger Is.

Mr Anemone Isn't!

Mr Chigger Is!

Mr Anemone Isn't!

Mr Chigger Is!

Mr Anemone Isn't!

Mr Chigger Is!

Mr Anemone Isn't!!

Mr Chigger Is!!!

Voice Over (JOHN) Anyway, this rather pointless bickering went on for some time until . . .

CAPTION: 'TWO YEARS LATER'

Interior cockpit of airliner. Mr Chigger (pilot) and a second pilot sitting at controls.

Pilot Gosh, I am glad I'm a fully qualified airline pilot.

Cut to BALPA spokesman sitting at a desk. He is in Captain's uniform and has a name plate in front of him on the desk saying 'BALPA Spokesman'.

BALPA Man (ERIC) The British Airline Pilots Association would like to point out that it takes a chap six years to become a fully qualified airline pilot, and not two.

CAPTION: 'FOUR YEARS LATER THAN THE LAST CAPTION'

Interior cockpit. For three seconds. Then cut back to BALPA spokesman.

BALPA Man Thank you. I didn't want to seem a bit of an old fusspot just now you know, but it's just as easy to get these things right as they are easily found in the BALPA handbook. Oh, one other thing, in the Sherlock Holmes last week Tommy Cooper told a joke about a charter flight, omitting to point out that one must be a member of any organization that charters a plane for at least six months beforehand, before being able to take advantage of it. Did rather spoil the joke for me, I'm afraid. *(phone rings)* Yes, ah yes – yes. *(puts phone down)* My wife just reminded me that on a recent 'High Chapparal' Kathy Kirby was singing glibly about 'Fly me to the Stars' when of course there are no scheduled flights of this kind, or even chartered, available to the general public at the present moment, although of course, when they are BALPA will be in the vanguard. Or the Trident. Little joke for the chaps up at BALPA House. And one other small point. Why is it that these new lurex dancing tights go baggy at the knees after only a couple of evenings' fun. Bring back the old canvas ones I say. It is incredible, isn't it, that in these days when man can walk on the moon and work out the most complicated hire purchase agreements, I still get these terrible headaches. Well . . . I seem to have wandered a bit, but still, no harm done. Jolly good luck.

Back in the cockpit of the airliner. The two pilots sit there. Atmospheric noise of a big airliner in flight. Suddenly there is a banging on the door at the back of the cockpit.

Zanie (GRAHAM) *(off-screen)* Are you going to be in there all day? *(the two pilots exchange a puzzled look, then shrug and go back to flying; suddenly another series of bangs on door)* Other people want to go you know! *(they exchange another look; pause; a heavier bang on the door)* The door's jammed, if you ask me. *(a crash as he attempts to force it; another crash and the door flies open; Mr Zanie enters)* Ah. *(suddenly realizing where he is)* Oh my God. Oh, I'm terribly sorry. I thought this was the bally toilet.

Second Pilot (JOHN) This is the control cabin.

Zanie Oh I know. I'm a flying man, you know . . . oh yes . . . Bally stupid mistake . . .

A pause. Zanie remains standing at the back of cockpit. The pilots go on as if he is not there.

Second Pilot Cloud's heavy . . . What's the reading?

Pilot 4.8 . . . Steady.

Zanie If they had all those dials in the toilet . . . there wouldn't be room for anything else, would there. *(another nervous laugh; not the slightest reaction from the pilots)*

Pilot *(into intercom)* Hello, Geneva this is Roger Five-O . . . What is your cloud reading? Hello, Geneva . . .

Zanie I wouldn't fancy flying one of those sitting on the toilet . . . I mean it'd take the glamour out of being a pilot, wouldn't it, ha ha, flying around the world sitting on a toilet.

Radio Voice Geneva here. 4.9 . . . Heavy . . . Over.

Pilot Serious?

Second Pilot No, not if it keeps at that level, no.

Zanie Mind you, if you did fly it from the toilet it would leave a lot more space up here, wouldn't it. *(finally he realizes his attempt at small talk is not working)* Well, I'd better get back to the cabin, then. Sorry about the silly intrusion. Bally stupid. *(he pushes lever down on the door which opens directly out of the plane)* Door's jammed. *(he gives it a shoulder charge and flies straight out of the plane)* Aaaaaaaaaaaarrrrrrrrrrrrghhhhhh!

Plane noise overhead. Continue scream. Outside of a gent's lavatory, there is a big pile of straw. Pause, then Zanie drops onto the straw. He looks up at gent's sign.

Zanie Bally piece of luck . . .

He brushes himself down and goes into gents. Cut back to cockpit. A hostess enters from the passenger cabin.

Second Pilot Oh hello. Everything all right at the back?

Hostess (CAROL) Yes, they're as quiet as dormice.

Second Pilot Dormice?

Door opens and a man in a neat suit enters. From beneath his jacket he produces a revolver with silencer attachment. He points it at the pilots.

Gunman (MICHAEL) All right, don't anybody move . . . except to control the aeroplane . . . you can move a little to do that.

Hostess Can I move?

Gunman Yes, yes, yes. You can move a little bit. Yes. Sorry, I didn't mean to be so dogmatic when I came in. Obviously you can all move a little within reason. There are certain involuntary muscular movements which no amount of self-control can prevent. And obviously any assertion of authority on my part, I've got to take that into account.

The ensuing conversation is perfectly calm and friendly.

Second Pilot Right. I mean one couldn't for example, stop one's insides from moving.

Gunman No, no. Good point, good point.

Second Pilot And the very fact that the plane is continuously vibrating means that we're all moving to a certain extent.

Gunman And we're all moving our lips, aren't we?

Pilots Yes, yes.

Second Pilot Absolutely.

Gunman No, the gist of my meaning was that sudden ... er ...

Hostess Exaggerated movements ...

Gunman Exaggerated *violent* movements ... are ... are out.

Second Pilot Well, that's the great thing about these modern airliners. I mean, I can keep this plane flying with only the smallest movement and Pancho here doesn't have to move at all.

Gunman Oh, that's marvellous.

Hostess *(joining in the general spirit of bonhomie)* And I don't really need to move either ... unless I get an itch or something ...

They all laugh.

Gunman Well that's wonderful ... 60% success, eh? *(they laugh again)* Anyway, bearing all that in mind, will you fly the plane to Luton, please?

Second Pilot Well, this is a scheduled flight to Cuba.

Gunman I know, I know, that's rather why I came in here with that point about nobody moving.

Pilot Within reason.

Gunman Within reason – yes. I ... er ... er ... you know, I want you to fly this plane to Luton ... please.

Second Pilot Right, well I'd better turn the plane round then. Stand by emergency systems.

Gunman Look I don't want to cause any trouble.

Second Pilot No, no, we'll manage, we'll manage.

Gunman I mean, *near* Luton will do, you know. Harpenden, do you go near Harpenden?

Pilot It's on the flight path.

Gunman Okay, well, drop me off there. I'll get a bus to Luton. It's only twenty-five minutes.

Hostess You can be in Luton by lunchtime.

Gunman Oh, well that's smashing.

First Pilot Hang on! There's no airport at Harpenden.

Gunman Oh well, look, forget it. Forget it. I'll come to Cuba, and get a flight back to Luton from there.

Second Pilot Well, we could lend you a parachute.

Gunman No, no, no, no, no. I wouldn't dream of it ... wouldn't dream of it ... dirtying a nice, clean parachute.

Pilot I know – I know. There's a bale of hay outside Basingstoke. We could throw you out.

Gunman Well, if it's all right.

All Sure, yeah.

Gunman Not any trouble?

Pilots None at all.

Gunman That's marvellous. Thank you very much. Sorry to come barging in.

Hostess Bye-bye.

Gunman Thank you. Bye.

Pilots Bye.

They open the door and throw him out.

Gunman *(as he falls)* Thank you!

Cut to haystack in a field (not the same bale of hay that was landed on before). Aeroplane noise overhead. The gunman suddenly falls into the haystack. He gets up, brushes himself down, hops over a fence, and reaches a road. He puts his hand out and a bus stops. It has 'Straight to Luton' written on it. He gets in. Conductor is just about to take his fare, when an evil-looking man with a gun jumps up and points gun at conductor.

Man (JOHN) Take this bus to Cuba.

Bus moving away from camera. The destination board changes to 'Straight to Cuba'. The bus does a speeded up u-turn, and goes out of frame. Camera pans away revealing a rather rocky highland landscape. As camera pans across country we hear inspiring Scottish music.

Voice Over (JOHN) From these glens and scars, the sound of the coot and the moorhen is seldom absent. Nature sits in stern mastery over these rocks and crags. The rush of the mountain stream, the bleat of the sheep, and the broad, clear Highland skies, reflected in tarn and loch . . . *(at this moment we pick up a highland gentleman in kilt and tam o'shanter clutching a knobkerry in one hand and a letter in the other)* . . . form a breathtaking backdrop against which Ewan McTeagle writes such poems as 'Lend us a quid till the end of the week'.

Cut to crofter's cottage. McTeagle sits at the window writing. We zoom in very slowly on him as he writes.

Voice Over But it was with more simple, homespun verses that McTeagle's unique style first flowered.

McTeagle (TERRY J) *(voice over)* If you could see your way to lending me sixpence. I could at least buy a newspaper. That's not much to ask anyone.

Voice Over One woman who remembers McTeagle as a young friend – Lassie O'Shea.

Cut to Lassie O'Shea – a young sweet innocent Scots girl – she is valiantly trying to fend off the sexual advances of the sound man. Two other members of the crew pull him out of shot.

Lassie (ERIC) Mr McTeagle wrote me two poems, between the months of January and April 1969 . . .

Interviewer Could you read us one?

Lassie Och, I dinna like to . . . they were kinda personal . . . but I will.
(she has immediately a piece of paper in her hand from which she reads) 'To Ma Own beloved Lassie. A poem on her 17th Birthday. Lend us a couple of bob till Thursday. I'm absolutely skint. But I'm expecting a postal order and I can pay you back as soon as it comes. Love Ewan.'
There is a pause. She looks up.

Sound Man *(voice over)* Beautiful.

Another pause. The soundman leaps on her and pulls her to the ground. Cut to abstract trendy arts poetry programme set. Intense critic sits on enormous inflatable see-through pouffe.

CAPTION: 'ST JOHN LIMBO – POETRY EXPERT'

Limbo (JOHN) *(intensely)* Since then, McTeagle has developed and widened his literary scope. Three years ago he concerned himself with quite small sums – quick bits of ready cash: sixpences, shillings, but more recently he has turned his extraordinary literary perception to much larger sums – fifteen shillings, £4.12.6d . . . even nine guineas . . . But there is still nothing to match the huge sweep . . . the majestic power of what is surely his greatest work: 'Can I have fifty pounds to mend the shed?'.

Pan across studio to a stark poetry-reading set. A single light falls on an Ian McKellan figure in black leotard standing gazing dramatically into space. Camera crabs across studio until it is right underneath him. He speaks the lines with great intensity.

Ian (ERIC) Can I have £50 to mend the shed?
I'm right on my uppers.
I can pay you back
When this postal order comes from Australia.
Honestly.
Hope the bladder trouble's getting better.
Love, Ewan.

Cut to remote Scottish landscape, craggy and windtorn and desolate. In stark chiaroscuro against the sky we see McTeagle standing beside a lonely pillar box, writing postcards. The sun setting behind him.

Limbo *(voice over)* There seems to be no end to McTeagle's poetic invention. 'My new cheque book hasn't arrived' was followed up by the brilliantly allegorical 'What's twenty quid to the bloody Midland Bank?' and more recently his prizewinning poem to the Arts Council: 'Can you lend me one thousand quid?'
Cut to David Mercer figure in his study at a desk.

CAPTION: 'A VERY GOOD PLAYWRIGHT'

David (MICHAEL) I think what McTeagle's pottery . . . er . . . poetry is doing is *rejecting* all the traditional clichés of modern pottery. No longer do we have to be content with Keats's 'Seasons of mists and mellow fruitfulness', Wordsworth's 'I wandered lonely as a cloud' and Milton's 'Can you lend us two bob till Tuesday' . . .

Cut to long shot of McTeagle walking through countryside.

McTeagle *(voice over)* Oh gie to me a shillin' for some fags and I'll pay yer back on Thursday, but if you wait till Saturday I'm expecting a divvy from the Harpenden Building Society . . . *(continues muttering indistinctly)*

He walks out of shot past a glen containing several stuffed animals, one of which explodes. A highland spokesman stands up into shot.

SUPERIMPOSED CAPTION: 'A HIGHLAND SPOKESMAN'

Highlander (JOHN) As a Highlander I would like to complain about some inaccuracies in the preceding film about the poet Ewan McTeagle. Although his name was quite clearly given as McTeagle, he was throughout wearing the Cameron tartan. Also I would like to point out that the BALPA spokesman who complained about aeronautical inaccuracies was himself wearing a captain's hat, whereas he only had lieutenant's stripes on the sleeves of his jacket. Also, in the Inverness pantomime last Christmas, the part of Puss in Boots was played by a native of New Guinea with a plate in her lip, so that every time Dick Whittington gave her a French kiss, he got the back of his throat scraped.

A doctor's head appears out from under the kilt.

Doctor (MICHAEL) Look, would you mind going away, I'm trying to examine this man. *(he goes back under the kilt; a slight pause; he re-emerges)* It's – er – it's all right – I *am* a doctor. Actually, I'm a gynaecologist . . . but this is my lunchhour.

ANIMATION:

Animation Voice I've a nasty feeling I *am* somebody's lunchhour.

Animation leads to a living room. Doorbell rings. Lady opens the door, a milkman stands there.

Milkman (ERIC) Pat-a-cake, pat-a-cake baker's man. Good morning, madam, I'm a psychiatrist.

Lady (GRAHAM) You look like a milkman to me.

Milkman Good. *(ticks form on his clipboard)* I am in fact *dressed* as a milkman . . . you spotted that – well done.

Lady Go away.

Milkman Now then, madam. I'm going to show you three numbers, and

I want you to tell me if you see any similarity between them. *(holds up a card saying '3' three times)*

Lady They're all number three.

Milkman No. Try again.

Lady They're *all* number three?

Milkman No. They're *all* number three. *(he ticks his board again)* Right. Now. I'm going to say a word, and I want you to say the first thing that comes into your head. How many pints do you want?

Lady *(narrowing her eyes, suspecting a trap)* Er, three?

Milkman Yogurt?

Lady Er . . . no.

Milkman Cream?

Lady No.

Milkman Eggs?

Lady No.

Milkman *(does some adding up and whistling)* Right. Well, you're quite clearly suffering from a repressive libido complex, probably the product of an unhappy childhood, coupled with acute insecurity in adolescence, which has resulted in an attenuation of the libido complex.

Lady You *are* a bloody milkman.

Milkman Don't you shout at me, madam, don't come that tone. Now then, I must ask you to accompany me down to the dairy and do some aptitude tests.

Lady I've got better things to do than come down to the dairy!

Milkman Mrs Ratbag, if you don't mind me saying so, you are badly in need of an expensive course of psychiatric treatment. Now I'm not going to say a trip to our dairy will cure you, but it will give hundreds of lower-paid workers a good laugh.

Lady All right . . . but how am I going to get home?

Milkman I'll run you there and back on my psychiatrist's float.

Lady All right.

The milkman and lady walk down her garden path. As they go out of the garden gate there is a cat on the garden wall.

CAPTION and arrow: 'A CAT'

The cat explodes. The milkman motions her towards the milk float with a large signboard which reads: 'Psychiatrist's Dairy Ltd'. Just as they are getting in, she points to all the files in the back in milk crates.

Lady What are those?

Milkman They're case histories. *(drives off; the van's speaker announces: 'Psychiatrists! Psychiatrists!' The doctor from the Scots sketch hails him)* Yes, sir?

Doctor (MICHAEL) Ah, good morning. I'm afraid our regular psychiatrist hasn't come round this morning . . . and I've got an ego block which is in turn making my wife over-assertive and getting us both into a state of depressive neurosis.

Milkman Oh, I see, sir. Who's your regular, sir?

Doctor Jersey Cream Psychiatrists.

Milkman Oh yes, I know them. *(puts down crate and gets out note pad)* Right, well, er, what's your job, then?

Doctor I'm a doctor.

Milkman ... Didn't I see you just now under a Scotsman?

Doctor Yes, but I *am* a doctor. Actually, I'm a gynaecologist but that was my lunchhour.

Milkman *(taking a card out of crate and showing it to the doctor)* What does *this* remind you of?

Doctor Two pints of cream.

Milkman Right ... well I should definitely say you're suffering from a severe personality disorder, sir, sublimating itself in a lactic obsession which could get worse depending on how much money you've got.

Doctor Yes, yes, I see. And a pot of yogurt, please.

Cut to a psychiatrist called Dr Cream in his office.

Dr Cream (TERRY J) I would like to take this opportunity of complaining about the way in which these shows are continually portraying psychiatrists who make pat diagnoses of patients' problems without first obtaining their full medical history.

Cut back to milkman with doctor.

Milkman *(handing over yogurt)* Mind you, that's just a pat diagnosis made without first obtaining your full medical history.

Cut to man at desk.

Man (JOHN) I feel the time has come to complain about people who make rash complaints without first making sure that those complaints are justified.

Cut to Dr Cream.

Dr Cream Are you referring to me?

Cut back to man.

Man Not necessarily, however, I would like to point out that the BALPA spokesman was wearing the British Psychiatric Association Dinner Dance Club cuff-links.

Cut to Dr Cream.

Dr Cream Oh yes, I noticed that too.

Cut to BALPA man.

BALPA Man (ERIC) These are not British Psychiatric Association Dinner Dance Club cuff-links.

Cut to man.

Man Sorry.

Cut to BALPA man.

BALPA Man They are in fact British Sugar Corporation Gilbert-and-Sullivan Society cuff-links. It is in fact a sort of in-joke with us lads here at BALPA. I think the last speaker should have checked his facts before making his *own* rash complaint.

Cut to Dr Cream.

Dr Cream Yes, that'll teach him.

Cut to BALPA man.

BALPA Man However, I would just like to add a complaint about shows that have too many complaints in them as they get very tedious for the average viewer.

Cut to another man.

Another man (MICHAEL) I'd like to complain about people who hold things up by complaining about people complaining. It's about time something was done about it. *(the sixteen-ton weight falls on him)*

Cut to a street with milkman and lady riding on milk float. It comes to a halt. They get out, milkman hails a milkmaid with yoke and two pails.

Milkman Nurse! Would you take Mrs P̄im to see Dr Cream, please.

Milkmaid (CAROL) Certainly, doctor. Walk this way, please.

Lady Oh, if I could walk that way I . . .

Milkman and Milkmaid Sssssh!

The milkmaid leads Mrs Pim into a building, and into a psychiatrist's office. Dr Cream is in a chair.

Milkmaid Mrs Pim to see you, Dr Cream.

Dr Cream Ah yes. I just want another five minutes with Audrey. Could you show Mrs Pim into the waiting room, please.

Milkmaid Yes, doctor.

As milkmaid and Mrs Pim leave the room we see that there is a cow on the couch.

Dr Cream Right, Audrey. When did you first start thinking you were a cow?

Milkmaid and Mrs Pim emerge from building through a herd of cows and we then have a montage of shots of them walking through countryside as in opening sequence of flying lesson sketch at beginning of show. They pass the tea trolley woman, the bishop learning his script . . .

Bishop *(Australian accent)* 'Jeez, Mr Belpit your legs is all swollen' . . .

. . . the secretary at her desk, past a stuffed animal which explodes, then past the tea lady again, and then past the bishop again and then past the secretary again, still going in the same direction.

Bishop *(Scots accent)* Oi! Mr Belpit – your great legs is all swollen! *(then again with Japanese accent)*

Cut to montage of photographs of sections of brain, a man with an egg on his head, a man looking through microscope, diagrams of brain, music over this and:

CAPTION: 'IT'S THE MIND – A WEEKLY MAGAZINE OF THINGS PSYCHIATRIC'

Cut to a man sitting at usual desk. He is Mr Boniface.

Boniface (MICHAEL) Good evening. Tonight on 'It's the Mind', we examine the phenomenon of déjà vu. That strange feeling we sometimes get that we've lived through something before, that what is happening now has already happened. Tonight on 'It's the Mind' we examine the phenomenon of déjà vu, that strange feeling we sometimes get that we've . . . *(looks puzzled for a moment)* Anyway, tonight on 'It's the Mind' we examine the phenomenon of déjà vu, that strange . . .

Cut to opening title sequence with montage of psychiatric photos and the two captions and music over. Cut back to Mr Boniface at desk, shaken.

CAPTION: 'IT'S THE MIND'

Boniface Good evening. Tonight on 'It's the Mind' we examine the phenomenon of déjà vu, that strange feeling we someti . . . mes get . . . that . . . we've lived through something . . .

Cut to opening titles again. Back then to Boniface, now very shaken.

CAPTION: 'IT'S THE MIND'

Boniface Good . . . good evening. Tonight on 'It's the Mind' we examine the phenomenon of dddddddddddéjà vvvvvvvu, that extraordinary feeling . . . quite extraordinary . . . *(he tails off, goes quiet, the phone rings, he picks it up)* No, fine thanks, fine. *(he rings off; a man comes in on the right and hands him glass of water and leaves)* Oh, thank you. That strange feeling we sometimes get that we've lived through something before. *(phone rings again; he picks it up)* No, fine thank you. Fine. *(he rings off; a man comes in from right and hands him a glass of water; he jumps)* . . . Thank you. That strange feeling . . . *(phone rings; he answers)* No. Fine, thank you. Fine, *(rings off; a man enters and gives him glass of water)* thank you. *(he screams with fear)* Look, something's happening to me. I – I – um, I think I'd better go and see someone. Goodnight.

Phone rings again. He leaps from desk and runs out of shot. He runs out of building into street and chases after passing milk float and leaps aboard.

Milkman Oi, haven't I seen you somewhere before?

Boniface No, doctor, no. Something very funny's happening to me.

CAPTION: 'IT'S THE MIND – A WEEKLY MAGAZINE OF THINGS PSYCHIATRIC'

Cut to montage of photographs again with captions and music. Cut to Boniface at desk. Boniface screams and runs out of shot. Cut to same piece of film as just previously, when he chases float, leaps on and the milkman says:

Milkman Oi, haven't I seen you somewhere before?

Boniface No, doctor, no. Something very funny's happening to me.

The milk float goes past in the background with the milkman and Boniface on it. We see the float go along the country lane past the clearing, past the bishop . . .

Bishop *(camp)* 'Oh, Mr Belpit, your legs are so swollen'.

. . . and the secretary at her desk, past a sign saying 'to the zoo' where explosions are heard, and stops outside Dr Cream's building . . . Boniface runs into building and enters Dr Cream's office.

Dr Cream Ah, come in. Now what seems to be the matter?

Boniface I have this terrible feeling of déjà vu.

Repeat same clip from Boniface entering.

Dr Cream Ah, come in. Now what seems to be the matter?

Boniface I have this terrible feeling of déjà vu . . .

Repeat clip again.

SUPERIMPOSED CREDITS

Dr Cream Ah, come in. Now what seems to be the matter?

Boniface I have this terrible feeling of déjà vu . . .

Clip starts to repeat again as the programme ends.

Seventeen

Opens with animated item (the Butterfly). The announcer at a desk with propellors rises into view.

Announcer (JOHN) And now for something completely different.

It's Man (MICHAEL) It's . . .

Animated titles.

Announcer and CAPTION: 'THE BBC WOULD LIKE TO APOLOGIZE FOR THE NEXT ANNOUNCEMENT'

Cut to a group of Gumbys, all with rolled-up trousers and knotted handkerchiefs on their heads, attempting to shout in unison and failing miserably.

Gumbys Hello, and welcome to the show. Without more ado, the first item is a sketch about architects, called The Architects Sketch . . . The Architects Sketch . . . The Architects Sketch . . . *(as the sketch fails to start they point up at a nearby building)* Up there! . . . Up there! . . . Up there! . . .

The camera pans to a window in the building. Cut to the office inside, where a board meeting is taking place. The Chairman is Mr Tid.

Mr Tid (GRAHAM) Gentlemen, we have two basic suggestions for the design of this . . . *(he is distracted by the two gumbys still shouting)* . . . Gentlemen we have two basic suggestions for the design of this . . . *(shouts out of window at the gumbys)* Shut up! Gentlemen, we have two basic suggestions . . . *(but the gumbys are still shouting 'Architects Sketch'; he throws a bucket of water over them; they subside, damply)* Gentlemen, we have two basic suggestions for the design of this residential block, and I thought it best that the architects themselves came in to explain the advantages of both designs. *(knock at door)* That must be the first architect now. *(Mr Wiggin comes in)* Ah, yes – it's Mr Wiggin of Ironside and Malone.

Wiggin walks to the table on which his model stands.

Mr Wiggin (JOHN) Good morning, gentlemen. This is a twelve-storey block combining classical neo-Georgian features with all the advantages of modern design. The tenants arrive in the entrance hall here, are carried along the corridor on a conveyor belt in extreme comfort and past murals depicting Mediterranean scenes, towards the rotating knives. The last twenty feet of the corridor are heavily soundproofed. The blood pours down these chutes and the mangled flesh slurps into these . . .

First City Gent (MICHAEL) Excuse me . . .

Mr Wiggin Hm?

First City Gent Did you say knives?

Mr Wiggin Rotating knives, yes.

Second City Gent (TERRY J) Are you proposing to slaughter our tenants?

Mr Wiggin Does that not fit in with your plans?

First City Gent No, it does not. We wanted a simple block of flats.

Mr Wiggin Oh, I see. I hadn't correctly divined your attitude towards
your tenants. You see I mainly design slaughter houses. Yes, pity.
Mind you this is a real beaut. I mean, none of your blood caked on
the walls and flesh flying out of the windows, inconveniencing
passers-by with this one. I mean, my life has been building up to
this.

Second City Gent Yes, and well done. But we did want a block of flats.

Mr Wiggin Well, may I ask you to reconsider? I mean, you wouldn't
regret it. Think of the tourist trade.

First City Gent No, no, it's just that we wanted a block of flats, not an
abattoir.

Mr Wiggin Yes, well, of course, that's just the sort of blinkered philistine
pig ignorance I've come to expect from you non-creative garbage.
You sit there on your loathsome, spotty behinds squeezing
blackheads, not caring a tinker's cuss about the struggling artist.
(*shouting*) You excrement! You lousy hypocritical whining toadies
with your lousy colour TV sets and your Tony Jacklin golf clubs
and your bleeding masonic handshakes! You wouldn't let me join,
would you, you blackballing bastards! Well I wouldn't become a
freemason now if you went down on your lousy, stinking, purulent
knees and begged me.

Second City Gent Well, we're sorry you feel like that but we, er, did
want a block of flats. Nice though the abattoir is.

Mr Wiggin Oh (*blows raspberry*) the abattoir, that's not important. But if
one of you could put in a word for me I'd love to be a freemason.
Freemasonry opens doors. I mean, I was . . . I was a bit on edge
just now, but if I was a mason I'd just sit at the back and not get in
anyone's way.

First City Gent Thank you.

Mr Wiggin I've got a second-hand apron.

Second City Gent Thank you.

Mr Wiggin (*going to door but stopping*) I nearly got in at Hendon.

First City Gent Thank you.

Mr Wiggin leaves and the familiar figure of Mr Tid comes forward.

Mr Tid I'm sorry about that, gentlemen. The second architect is a Mr
Leavey of Wymis and Dibble.

Mr Leavey comes in and goes to his model.

Mr Leavey (ERIC) Good morning, gentlemen. This is a scale model of
the block. There are twenty-eight storeys, with two hundred and
eighty modern apartments. There are three main lifts and two

service lifts. Access would be from Dibbingley Road. *(the model falls over and he quickly puts it upright)* The structure is built on a central pillar system *(the model falls over again)* with *(he puts model upright and holds onto it)* cantilevered floors in pre-stressed steel and concrete. The dividing walls on each floor section are fixed with recessed magnalium flanged grooves. *(the model partly collapses, the bottom ten floors giving way)* By avoiding wood and timber derivatives and all other flammables, *(the model is smoking and flames are seen)* we have almost totally removed the risk of . . .

SUPERIMPOSED CAPTION: 'SATIRE'

Mr Leavey Quite frankly I think the central pillar system may need strengthening a bit.

Second City Gent Isn't that going to put the cost up?

Mr Leavey It might.

Second City Gent Well, I don't know whether I'd worry about strengthening *that* much. After all they're not meant to be luxury flats.

First City Gent I quite agree. I mean, providing the tenants are of light build and relatively sedentary and er, given a spot of good weather, I think we're on to a winner here.

Mr Leavey Oh, thank you.

The model explodes.

Second City Gent Quite agree. Quite agree.

Mr Leavey Thank you very much. Thank you. *(he shakes hands with them in an extraordinary way)*

Mr Wiggin *(at door)* It opens doors. I'm telling you.

Voice Over (ERIC) Let's have a look at that handshake again in slow motion.

CAPTION: 'BBC TV ACTION REPLAY'

They do the handshake again, only slowly.

Voice Over What other ways are there of recognizing a mason?

Shot from camera concealed in a car so we get reactions of passers-by. A busy city street – i.e. Threadneedle Street. In amongst the throng four city gents are leaping along with their trousers round their ankles. They are wearing bowler hats and pinstripes. Another city street or another part of the same street. Two city gents, with trousers rolled up to the knee, approach each other and go into the most extraordinary handshake which involves rolling on the floor etc.

Voice Over (JOHN) Having once identified a mason immediate steps must be taken to isolate him from the general public. Having accomplished that it is now possible to cure him of these unfortunate masonic tendencies through the use of behavioural psychotherapy. *(we see a cartoon city gent locked into a cell)* In this treatment the patient is rewarded for the correct response and punished for the wrong one. Let us begin. Would you like to give up being a mason? Think carefully. Think. Think.

Cartoon City Gent No.

A large hammer attacks the city gent.

Voice Over No? That's wrong! Wrong! Wrong! Wrong! No! No! No! Bad! Bad.

CAPTION: 'AN APOLOGY'

Announcer (JOHN) The BBC would like to apologize for the following announcement.

Pull out from the caption to reveal that it is not a caption after all but a huge twenty-foot-square poster on a hoarding at the side of the road. After we pull out we hear the shuffling of many feet and grunting. A group of Gumbys shuffle into extreme left edge of frame. They do not move any further into the picture. After a bit of humming and harring:

Gumbys Oh! And the next item is a sketch about insurance called 'Insurance Sketch'. 'Insurance Sketch'. 'Insurance Sketch' . . .

Cut to Mr Devious's insurance office. Devious and a man are sitting there.

Devious (MICHAEL) What do you want?

SUPERIMPOSED CAPTION: 'STRAIGHT MAN'

Man (GRAHAM) Well I've come about your special fully comprehensive motor insurance policy offer . . .

Devious What was that?

Man Fully comprehensive motor insurance for one-and-eightpence.

Devious Oh, oh, yes . . . yeah well, unfortunately, guv, that offer's no longer valid. You see, it turned out not to be economically viable, so we now have a totally new offer . . .

Man What's that?

Devious A nude lady.

Man A nude lady?

Devious Yes. You get a nude lady with a fully comprehensive motor insurance. If you just want third party she has to keep her bra on, and if it's just theft . . .

Man No, no, I don't really want that, Mr er . . . Mr . . .

Devious Devious.

Man Mr Devious. I just want to know what it would cost me to have a fully comprehensive insurance on a 1970 Aston Martin.

Devious Aston Martin?

Man Yes.

Devious (*quickly*) Five hundred quid.

Man Five hundred quid?

Devious Forty quid.

Man Forty quid?

Devious Forty quid and a nude lady.

Man No, no, I'm not interested in a nude lady.

Devious Dirty books?

Man No, no, look, I'm not interested in any of that. *(superimposed 'STRAIGHT MAN' caption again)* I just want to know what it would cost me to have a fully comprehensive insurance on a 1970 Aston Martin. Can you please quote me your price.

Cut to outside the door of the office. A vicar stands there.

Vicar (ERIC) Knock knock.

Cut to inside office.

Devious Who's there?

Cut to outside.

Vicar The Reverend . . .

Cut to inside.

Devious The Reverend who?

Vicar The Reverend Morrison.

    CAPTION: 'ANOTHER STRAIGHT MAN'

Cut to inside.

Devious Oh, come in.

The vicar enters.

Devious Now then, vic. What's the trouble?

Vicar Well, it's about this letter you sent me.

Man Excuse me, do I have any more lines?

Devious I don't know, mush, I'll have a look in the script . . . *(he gets script out of drawer)* Where are we? Show 8. Are you 'man'?

Man Yeah.

Devious No . . . no, you've finished.

Man Well, I'll be off then. *(he leaves)*

Devious *(reading script)* 'The vicar sits'.

The vicar sits.

Vicar It's about this letter you sent me regarding my insurance claim.

Devious Oh, yeah, yeah – well, you see, it's just that we're not . . . as yet . . . *totally* satisfied with the grounds of your claim.

Vicar But it says something about filling my mouth in with cement.

Devious Oh well, that's just insurance jargon, you know.

Vicar But my car was hit by a lorry while standing in the garage and you refuse to pay my claim.

Devious *(rising and crossing to a filing cabinet)* Oh well, Reverend Morrison . . . in your policy . . . in your policy . . . *(he opens the drawer of the filing cabinet and takes out a shabby old sports jacket; he feels in the pocket and pulls out a crumpled dog-eared piece of paper then puts the* *coat back and shuts the filing cabinet)* ... here we are. It states quite clearly that no claim you make will be paid.

Vicar Oh dear.

Devious You see, you unfortunately plumped for our 'Neverpay' policy, which, you know, if you never claim is very worthwhile ... but you had to claim, and, well, there it is.

Vicar Oh dear, oh dear.

Devious Still, never mind – could be worse. How's the nude lady?

Vicar Oh, she's fine. *(he begins to sob)*

Devious Look ... Rev ... I hate to see a man cry, so shove off out the office, there's a good chap.

The vicar goes out sobbing. Cut to outside. Vicar collects a nude lady sitting in a supermarket shopping trolley ... and wheels her disconsolately away. Cut back to inside of office. Close-up on Devious. He gets out some files and starts writing. Suddenly a bishop's crook slams down on the desk in front of Devious. He looks up – his eyes register terror. Cut to reverse angle shot from below. The bishop in full mitre and robes.

Bishop (TERRY J) OK, Devious ... Don't move!

Devious The bishop!

Animated crime-series-type titles, with suitable music:

'C. OF E. FILMS'

'IN ASSOCIATION WITH THE SUNDAY SCHOOLS BOARD'

'PRESENT'

'THE BISHOP'

'STARRING THE REVEREND E. P. NESBITT'

'AND INTRODUCING F. B. GRIMSBY URQHART-WRIGHT AS THE VOICE OF GOD'

'SPECIAL EFFECTS BY THE MODERATOR OF THE CHURCH OF SCOTLAND'

'DIRECTED BY PREBENDARY "CHOPPER" HARRIS'

Exterior beautiful English church. Birds singing, a hymn being sung. Suddenly sound of a high-powered car roaring towards the church. Screech of tyres as a huge open-top American car screeches to a halt outside the church. The bishop leaps out. Behind him (as throughout the film) are his four henchmen ... vicars with dark glasses. They wear clerical suits and dog collars. They leap out of their car and race up the drive towards the church. As they do so the hymn is heard to come to an end. Sound of people sitting down.

Cut to interior of church. Vicar climbing up into pulpit. Cut back to exterior. The bishop and his vicars racing through the doors. Interior of church. Shot of vicar in pulpit.

Vicar (GRAHAM) I take as my text for today ...

Cut to bishop and vicars at doorway.

Bishop The text, vic! Don't say the text!

Cut back to vicar.

Vicar Leviticus 3–14 . . .

The pulpit explodes. Vicar disappears in smoke, flying up into the air. Cut to close-up of the bishop. Behind him there is smoke and people rushing about. Sound of people scrambling over pews in panic etc.

Bishop We was too late. The Reverend Grundy bit the ceiling.

The end of the bishop's crook suddenly starts flashing. He lifts the flashing end off and it stops. Using it like a telephone receiver, he speaks into the staff.

Bishop Hello? . . . What? . . . We'll be right over!

Still of another church exterior. Crash zoom in on door. Cut to interior. A baptism party round the font. An innocent vicar is just testing the water. Pan across to the parents – a couple of shifty crooks – and two godmothers, obviously all-in wrestlers in drag (cauliflower ears etc.). As the vicar takes the baby it starts to tick loudly.

Vicar (JOHN) And it is for this reason that the Christian Church lays upon you, the godparents, the obligation of seeing this child is brought up in the Christian faith. Therefore, I name this child . . .

Cut to door of church. The bishop and vicars rush in.

Bishop Don't say the kid's name, vic!

Cut back to vicar.

Vicar Francesco Luigi . . .

Explosion. Cut to close-up of bishop. Smoke and panic as before.

Bishop We was too late . . . The Rev. Neuk saw the light.

Whip pan to interior of yet another church. A wedding. Bride and groom standing in front of a vicar. Cut to door of church. The bishop and vicars burst in.

Bishop The ring, vic! Don't touch the ring! Hey vic!

Cut to vicar taking the ring out of the bible. The ring is attached to a piece of string. A sixteen-ton weight falls on top of them with a mighty crunch – the camera shakes as it hits the floor.
Cut to two bell ringers. One pulls his rope, and the other rises off the floor, hanged by the neck. The bishop arrives, just too late.
Cut to another vicar at graveside.

Vicar (GRAHAM) . . . dust to dust, ashes to ashes.

He sprinkles dust on the grave. A huge prop cannon rises up out of the grave until its mighty barrel (twelve inches wide) is pointing right in the vicar's face. He does not notice. Sound of car screeching to a halt. We pan away from grave to reveal the bishop leaping out of the car. Sound of an almighty blast from the cannon. The bishop gets back into the car immediately and turns it round.

> *Cut to a street. Outside a cigarette shop the four clerics lounge against a wall. The bishop walks out rolling his own. Suddenly he stops.*
> *Close-up. He looks up as he hears a faint cry. Camera swings round and up – enormous zoom to high window in huge, drab city office block, where a vicar is looking out.*

Vicar (ERIC) Help ... help ... help ... help ... help ... help ...

> *Cut back to the bishop breaking into a run, throwing his cigarette into the gutter. Peter Gunn music. Hand-held shots of the bishop and the four vicars running through crowded streets. He reaches the office block, rushes in. Interior: a stair well. Right at the bottom we see the bishop and the vicars. Close-up hand-held shot of bishop running up stairs. Shadows running up the stair well. The bishop arrives on the top landing. Door of office. The bishop tries the door. It won't open. One vicar goes rigid. The other three take hold of him and use him as a battering ram and go straight through the balsa wood door first time.*

Bishop OK, Devious, don't move!
Devious The bishop!

> *'The Bishop' titles again.*
> *Cut to interior of cinema. A couple holding hands. Bishop film titles start up again exactly as before. After a couple of seconds of titles we cut to an old couple sitting in the back row of the cinema facing camera. The sound of the bishop's titles continues. The light from the projector is streaming out above their heads.*

Mr Potter (MICHAEL) This is where we came in.
Mrs Potter (GRAHAM) Yes.

> *Cut immediately to the front of the cinema. A working-class lounge is arranged on the pavement. There are no walls, just the furnishings: settee, two armchairs, sideboard, table, standard lamp, a tiled fireplace with ornaments on it. There is also a free-standing inside door. Mr and Mrs Potter come out of the cinema and go straight to their chairs and sit down. Passers-by have to skirt the living-room furniture.*

Mrs Potter *(settling into her chair)* Oh, it's nice to be home.
Mr Potter *(looking round)* Builders haven't been then.
Mrs Potter No.

> *A trendy interviewer with hand mike comes into shot.*

Interviewer (ERIC) These two old people are typical of the housing problem facing Britain's aged.
Mrs Potter Here! Don't you start doing a documentary on us, young man.
Interviewer Oh please ...
Mrs Potter No, you leave us alone!
Interviewer Oh, just a little one about the appalling conditions under which you live.
Mrs Potter No! Get out of our house! Go on!

Interviewer turns, motions to his cameraman and soundman and they all trail off miserably.

Cameraman   Oh all right. Come on, George, pick it up.

Mrs Potter   Why don't you do a documentary about the drug problem round in Walton Street?

Cut to the camera crew. They stop, turn and mutter 'a drug problem!' and they dash off.

Mrs Potter   Oh, I'll go and have a bath.

She goes to the free-standing door and opens it. Beyond it we see the furnishings of a bathroom. In the bath is Alfred Lord Tennyson, fully clad. As she opens the door we hear him reciting:

Tennyson   The splendour falls on castle walls
And snowy summits old in story . . .

She slams the door.

Mrs Potter   'Ere, there's Alfred Lord Tennyson in the bathroom.

Mr Potter   Well, at least the poet's been installed, then.

Cut to an officious-looking man in Gas Board type uniform and peaked cap.

CAPTION: 'SALES MANAGER EAST MIDLANDS POET BOARD'

Sales Manager (JOHN)   Yes, a poet is essential for complete home comfort, and all-year round reliability at low cost. We in the East Midlands Poet Board hope to have a poet in every home by the end of next year.

ANIMATION: *an advertisement.*

Voices *(singing)*   Poets are both clean and warm
And most are far above the norm
Whether here or on the roam
Have a poet in every home.

Cut to middle-class hall. The front doorbell rings. Housewife opens door to Gas Board type inspector with bicycle clips, rubber mac and cap and notebook. In the background we can hear muffled Wordsworth.

Voice (ERIC)   I wandered lonely as a cloud
That floats on high . . .

Inspector (MICHAEL)   Morning, madam, I've come to read your poet.

She (TERRY J)   Oh yes, he's in the cupboard under the stairs.

Inspector   What is it, a Swinburne? Shelley?

She   No, it's a Wordsworth.

Inspector   Oh, bloody daffodils.

He opens the door of the cupboard under the stairs. Inside is Wordsworth crouching and reciting.

Wordsworth (ERIC)   A host of golden daffodils

Beside the lake, beneath the trees
Fluttering and dancing in the breeze
All this while the inspector is shining his torch over him and noting things on his clip board.

Wordsworth Continuous as the stars that shine
And twinkle in the Milky Way
They stretch in . . .
The inspector shuts the door in the middle of this and we hear Wordsworth reciting on, though muffled, throughout the remainder of the sketch.

Inspector Right. Thank you, madam.
He makes as if to go, but she seems anxious to detain him and bars his way.

She Oh, not at all. Thank *you* . . . It's a nice day, isn't it?

Inspector Yes, yes, the weather situation is generally favourable. There's a ridge of high pressure centred over Ireland which is moving steadily eastward bringing cloudy weather to parts of the West Country, Wales and areas west of the Pennines. On tomorrow's chart . . . *(he reaches up and pulls down a big weather chart from the wall)* the picture is much the same. With this occluded front bringing drier, warmer weather. Temperatures about average for the time of year. That's three degrees centigrade, forty-four degrees fahrenheit, so don't forget to wrap up well. That's all from me. Goodnight.
Cut to BBC world symbol.

Continuity Voice (ERIC) Now on BBC television a choice of viewing. On BBC 2 – a discussion on censorship between Derek Hart, The Bishop of Woolwich and a nude man. And on BBC 1 – me telling you this. And now . . .
Sound of TV set being switched off. The picture reduces to a spot and we pull out to see that it was actually on a TV set which has just been switched off by the housewife. She and the gas man are now sitting in her living room. He is perched awkwardly on the edge of the sofa. He holds a cup of tea with a cherry on a stick in it.

She We don't want that, do we. Do you really want that cherry in your tea? Do you like doing this job?

Inspector Well, it's a living, isn't it?

She I mean, don't you get bored reading people's poets all day?

Inspector Well, you know, sometimes . . . yeah. Anyway, I think I'd better be going.
As he gets up she comes quickly to his side.

She *(seductively)* You've got a nice torch, haven't you?

Inspector *(looking at it rather baffled)* Er, yeah, yeah, it er . . . it er . . . it goes on and off.
He demonstrates.

She *(drawing closer and becoming breathy)* How many volts is it?

Inspector Er ... um ... well, I'll have a look at the batteries. *(he starts unscrewing the end)*

She Oh yes, yes.

Inspector It's four and a half volts.

She *(rubbing up against him)* Mmmm. That's wonderful. Do you want another look at the poet?

Inspector No, no, I must be off, really.

She I've got Thomas Hardy in the bedroom. I'd like you to look at him.

Inspector Ah well, I can't touch him. He's a novelist.

She Oh, he keeps mumbling all night.

Inspector Oh well, novelists do, you see.

She *(dragging him onto the sofa)* Oh forget him! What's your name, deary?

Inspector Harness.

She No, no! Your first name, silly!

Inspector Wombat.

She Oh, Wombat. Wombat Harness! Take me to the place where eternity knows no bounds, where the garden of love encloses us round. Oh Harness!

Inspector All right, I'll have a quick look at yer Thomas Hardy.

> *Cut to studio discussion.*
> CAPTION: 'DEREK HART'

Derek (JOHN) Nude man, what did you make of that?

Nude Man (GRAHAM) Well, don't you see, that was exactly the kind of explicit sexual reference I'm objecting to. It's titillation for the sake of it. A deliberate attempt at cheap sensationalism. I don't care what the so-called avant-garde, left-wing, intellectual namby-pambies say ... It is *filth*!

Derek Bishop.

> *Cut to crook hitting desk in Devious's office.*

Bishop Okay, don't anybody move!

> *Titles for 'The Bishop' start and then stop abruptly.*
> CAPTION: 'AN APOLOGY'

Voice Over (ERIC) The BBC would like to apologize for the constant repetition in this show.

> DIFFERENT CAPTION READING: 'AN APOLOGY'

Voice Over The BBC would like to apologize for the constant repetition in this show.

> ANIMATION: *the 'five frog curse'.*
> *Cut to the five Gumbys standing in a tight group.*

Gumbys Thank you. And now a sketch about a chemist called The Chemist Sketch.

A number of men and women are sitting around in an area by the counter where there is a large sign saying 'Dispensing Department'. A cheerful chemist appears at the counter.

Chemist (JOHN) Right. I've got some of your prescriptions here. Er, who's got the pox? *(nobody reacts)* . . . Come on, who's got the pox . . . come on . . . *(a man timidly puts his hand up)* . . . there you go. *(throws bottle to the man with his hand up)* Who's got a boil on the bum . . . boil on the botty. *(throws bottle to the only man standing up)* Who's got the chest rash? *(a woman with a large bosom puts up hand)* Have to get a bigger bottle. Who's got wind? *(throws bottle to a man sitting on his own)* Catch.

CAPTION: 'THE CHEMIST SKETCH – AN APOLOGY'

Voice Over (ERIC) The BBC would like to apologize for the poor quality of the writing in that sketch. It is not BBC policy to get easy laughs with words like bum, knickers, botty or wee-wees. *(laughs off camera)* Ssssh!

Cut to a man standing by a screen with a clicker.

BBC Man (MICHAEL) These are the words that are not to be used again on this programme.

He clicks the clicker. On screen appear the following slides:

B*M
B*TTY
P*X
KN*CKERS
W**-W**
SEMPRINI

A girl comes into shot.

Girl Semprini!?
BBC Man *(pointing)* Out!!

Cut back to the chemist's shop. The chemist appears again.

Chemist Right, who's got a boil on his Semprini, then?

A policeman appears and bundles him off.
Cut to another chemist's shop with a different chemist standing at the counter.

SUPERIMPOSED CAPTION: 'A LESS NAUGHTY CHEMIST'S'

A man walks in.

Man (ERIC) Good morning.
Chemist (TERRY J) Good morning, sir.
Man Good morning. I'd like some aftershave, please.
Chemist Ah, certainly. Walk this way, please.
Man If I could walk that way I wouldn't need aftershave.

The policeman runs into the shop and hauls the man off. Cut to shop again.

CAPTION: 'A NOT AT ALL NAUGHTY CHEMIST'S'

Another chemist is standing with a large sign reading 'A Not At All Naughty Chemist'. Pull back to reveal sign above stock reads 'Not At All Naughty Chemists Ltd'. A man enters.

Man (ERIC)   Good morning.

Chemist (MICHAEL) *(puts down sign)*   Good morning, sir. Can I help you?

Man   Yes. I'd like some aftershave.

Chemist   Ah. A toilet requisite-t-t-t-t-t . . . ! Would you like to try this, sir. It's our very very latest, it's called Sea Mist.

Man *(sniffs it)*   I *quite* like it.

Chemist   How about something a little more musky? This one's called Mimmo.

Man   Not really, no. Have you anything a little more fishier?

Chemist   Fishier?

Man   Fishier.

Chemist   Fish, fish, fish. A fishy requisite-t-t-t-t-t . . .

Man   Like halibut or sea bass.

Chemist   Or bream?

Man   Yes.

Chemist   No, we haven't got any of that . . . ah, I've got mackerel . . . or cod . . . or hake . . .

Man   You haven't got anything a little more halibutish?

Chemist   Er . . . parrot? What's that doing there? Or skate with just a hint of prawn? Or crab, tiger and almonds, very unusual.

Man   I really had my heart set on halibut.

Chemist   Well, sir, we had a fishy consignment in this morning, so I could nip down to the basement and see if I can come up trumps on this particular requisite-t-t-t-t-t. So it was halibut . . . or . . . ?

Man   Sea bass.

Chemist   Sea bass. Won't be a moment.

The man waits for a few seconds, starts becoming uncomfortable, looks at watch, hums.

Man *(to camera)*   Sorry about this . . . pom pom pom . . . Normally we try to avoid these little . . . pauses . . . longeurs . . . only dramatically he's gone down to the basement, you see. 'Course, there isn't really a basement but he just goes off and we pretend . . . Actually what happens is he goes off there, off camera, and just waits there so it *looks* as though he's gone down . . . to the basement. Actually I think he's rather overdoing it. Ah!

Long shot of the chemist with carton waiting off camera. Floor manager cues him and he walks to counter.

Chemist   Well, sorry, sir. *(out of breath)* Lot of steps. *(man winks at camera)*

Well, I'm afraid it didn't come in this morning, sir. But we have got some down at our Kensington branch. I'll just nip down there and get it for you.

Man How long will that be?

Chemist Twenty minutes.

Man Twenty minutes!

As he stands getting embarrassed, a girl hastily dressed as an assistant approaches him and hands him a message on a long stick.

Man Oh . . . I wonder what other people use for aftershave lotion?

Cut to vox pops film.

Gumby (MICHAEL) I use a body rub called Halitosis to make my breath seem sweet.

Second Gumby (JOHN) I use an aftershave called Semprini.

He is hauled off by policeman.

Chemist *(hurrying past)* I'm sorry, sorry – can't stop now, I've got to get to Kensington.

Cardinal Ximinez (MICHAEL) I use two kinds of aftershave lotions – Frankincense, Myrrh – *three* kinds of aftershave lotions, Frankincense, Myrrh, Sandalwood – *four* kinds of aftershave lotion. Frankincense, . . .

Man (GRAHAM) I have a cold shower every morning just before I go mad, and then I go mad, 1. Mad, 2. Mad, 3. Mad, 4 . . .

Shabby (MICHAEL) I use Rancid Polecat number two. It keeps my skin nice and scaly.

Chemist *(hurrying past)* Sorry again. Can't stop – got to get back.

Cut back to chemist's where the man is at a clock on wall pushing minute hand round twenty minutes. He looks at the camera guiltily and returns to right side of counter. The chemist enters.

Chemist Well I'm afraid they don't have any at our Kensington branch. But we have some down at the depot.

Man Where's that?

Chemist Aberdeen.

Man Aberdeen?!

Chemist It's all right. Wait here . . . I've got a car.

Man No, no, no. I'll take the other, the crab, tiger and . . .

Chemist Almond requisite . . . t . . . t . . . ?

Man I'll take it.

The chemist turns his back. A shoplifter enters. He is two men inside a large mac. He has false arms behind his back à la Duke of Edinburgh. The man watches him. He strolls to the counter and then two arms come out of coat and grab things from counter taking them inside the coat. Then these two arms are joined by a third arm which is black. All these arms steal stuff. The man taps the chemist and points at shoplifter.

> *Chemist watches and then blows whistle. They wait for a tick. Then the policeman runs into the shop.*

Policeman (GRAHAM) Right. Right! RIGHT! Now then! Now then! Your turn.

Chemist Aren't you going to say 'What's all this then?'?

Policeman Oh! Right, what's all this, then?

Chemist This man has been shoplifting, officer.

Policeman Oh, he has? Yus?

Chemist Yes.

Policeman Are you trying to tell me my job?

Chemist No, but he's been shoplifting.

Policeman Look! I must warn you that anything you may say will be ignored and furthermore, given half a chance I'll put my fist through your teeth. F'tang. F'tang.

Man But officer, this man here . . .

Policeman I've had enough of you. You're under arrest.

> *He makes noises of plane flying and firing.*

Chemist Officer, it wasn't him. *(indicates shoplifter)* He's the shoplifter.

Shoplifter (TERRY G) No I'm not.

Shoplifter's Mate *(sticking his head out of mac)* He's not . . . I'm a witness.

Policeman *(to chemist)* One more peep out of you and I'll do you for heresy.

Chemist Heresy. Blimey. I didn't expect the Spanish Inquisition.

Policeman Shut up! F'tang. F'tang. Oh, that's nice. *(he takes an object off the counter and pockets it)* Right. I'm taking you along to the station.

Man What for?

Policeman I'm charging you with illegal possession of whatever we happen to have down there. Right. *(makes plane noise again)* Lunar module calling Buzz Aldrin. Come in. Raindrops keep falling on my head . . . but that doesn't mean that my . . .

> CAPTION: 'AN APOLOGY'

Voice Over (JOHN) The BBC would like to apologize to the police about the character of Police Constable Pan Am. He was not meant to represent the average police officer. Similarly, the reference to Buzz Aldrin, the astronaut, was the product of a disordered mind and should not be construed as having any other significance.

> *Photo of Buzz Aldrin.*

> SUPERIMPOSED CAPTION: 'THE BUZZ ALDRIN SHOW STARRING BUZZ ALDRIN WITH . . . (CREDITS)'

> *Cut to Gumbys as at start of show.*

Gumbys And now for something completely different. *(jump cut to female Gumbys; then back to original shot)* Oh that was fun. And now . . . CAPTION: 'THE END'

Gumbys The end. The end! The end! The end!

Eighteen

BBC world symbol.

Voice Over (MICHAEL) Monty Python's Flying Circus tonight comes to you live from the Grillomat Snack Bar, Paignton.

Interior of a nasty snack bar. Customers around, preferably real people. Linkman sitting at one of the plastic tables.

Linkman (JOHN) Hello to you live from the Grillomat Snack Bar, Paignton. And so, without any more ado, let's have the titles.

It's Man Voice It's . . .

Animated titles.
Back to the snack bar.

Linkman *(with rather forced bonhomie)* Well, those were the titles. And now for the first item this evening on the Menu – ha ha – the team have chosen as a little hors d'oeuvres an item – and I think we can be sure it won't be an ordinary item – in fact the team told me just before the show that anything could happen, and probably would – so let's have . . . the item.

Cut to the word 'Blackmail' in letters four feet high, picked out in light bulbs which flash on and off. Big showbiz music crashes in. Camera pulls back to reveal glittery showbiz set. A presenter in a glittery showbiz jacket sits behind a glittery desk, with a telephone on it.

Presenter (MICHAEL) Hello, good evening, and welcome to 'Blackmail'! And to start tonight's programme, we go north to Preston in Lancashire, and Mrs Betty Teal!

Cut to a slightly blurred black and white photo of a housewife with her face blotted out by a black oblong.

Presenter's Voice Hello, Mrs Teal!

Cut back to presenter. He picks up a letter and reads it.

Presenter Now this is for £15 and it's to stop us revealing the name of your lover in Bolton.

SUPERIMPOSED CAPTION: '£15' *(which flashes on and off quickly)*

Presenter So Mrs Teal . . . if you send us £15 by return of post, please, and your husband Trevor, and your lovely children, Diane, Janice and Juliet need never know the name of your lover in Bolton.

Cut to a nude man (except for a collar and tie) at organ. He plays a few stirring chords. Cut back to presenter.

Presenter *(as he speaks he holds up the various items)* And now . . . a letter . . . a hotel registration book . . . and a series of photographs . . . which could add up to divorce, premature retirement, and possible criminal proceedings for a company director in Bromsgrove. He's a

freemason, and a prospective Tory MP ... that's Mr S. of
Bromsgrove ... £3,000 ...

SUPERIMPOSED CAPTION: '£3,000' *(which flashes on and off)*

Presenter ... to stop us revealing your name, the name of the three
other people involved, the youth organization to which they belong,
and the shop where you bought the equipment.

*Cut back to nude man at organ with chords again. Cut to still of two
pairs of naked feet and lower legs. Organ music over this. Cut back to
presenter.*

Presenter We'll be showing you more of that photograph later in the
programme ... unless we hear from Charles or Michael. And now
it's time for our 'Stop the Film' spot!

SUPERIMPOSED FLASHING CAPTION: 'STOP THE FILM'

Presenter The rules are very simple. We have taken a film which
contains compromising scenes and unpleasant details, which could
wreck a man's career. But the victim may phone me at any point
and stop the film. But remember, the money increases as the film
goes on. So the longer you leave it ... the more you have to pay.
So now, with the clock at £300 this week 'Stop the Film' visited
Thames Ditton ...

*The following film is shot in murky 8mm. As the film progresses we have
a £ sign with numerals in one corner which increase. Shot of a
residential street in Thames Ditton (sic). Another section of a street with
a figure in a Robin Hood hat and raincoat – in the distance on the far
side of the road, so we can't really make him out. Cut to slightly closer
shot of him about to cross the road. Cut to suburban house. The man is
standing at the door pressing the bell and looking round rather furtively.
Again shot from some distance and over a hedge. Cut back to the studio.
The presenter looking at a monitor and then at the phone. Back to the
film: a woman opens the door. She wears a dressing gown over lingerie.
A shaky zoom in to reveal her clothing. Wide shot of house with door
shut. Jump cut to shot obviously taken from a window in the house.
Shaky zoom in on window. We can see in the window ... both the man
and woman enter the bedroom. He goes out of shot, taking his coat off.
Cut back to the studio.*

Presenter He's being very brave here ...

*Cut back to the film: even closer perhaps of window. A series of short
jump cuts. She is undressing. She throws off her dressing gown. A jump
and she's taking off her negligee. Underneath she wears black corsets. She
produces a whip and seems to be beckoning to the man. Phone rings. Cut
back to the studio. The presenter picks up the phone.*

Presenter Hello, sir, hello, yes. No sir, no, I'm sure you didn't. No, it's
all right, sir, we don't morally censure, we just want the money ...

Yes, and here's the address to send it to:

Voice Over (TERRY J) and CAPTION: 'BLACKMAIL
BEHIND THE HOT WATER PIPES
THIRD WASHROOM ALONG
VICTORIA STATION'

Presenter Not at all, sir . . . thank *you. (he puts the phone down)*

Cut to a hallway in which a middle-aged man in dinner dress is putting down the telephone rather furtively. He leaves the booth and goes through a door into a large room where a banquet is in progress. There are tables on three sides of a square and he joins the head table which faces as it were downstage. He sits beside other middle-aged and rather elderly men all of whom are the city of London ex-public school type. As he sits, the toastmaster standing behind speaks.

Man (TERRY J) Sorry chaps, it was my mother.

Toastmaster (ERIC) Gentlemen, pray silence for the President of the Royal Society for Putting Things on Top of Other Things.

There is much upperclass applause and banging on the table as Sir William rises to his feet.

Sir William (GRAHAM) I thank you, gentlemen. The year has been a good one for the Society *(hear, hear).* This year our members have put more things on top of other things than ever before. But, I should warn you, this is no time for complacency. No, there are still many things, and I cannot emphasize this too strongly, *not* on top of other things. I myself, on my way here this evening, saw a thing that was not on top of another thing in any way. *(shame!)* Shame indeed but we must not allow ourselves to become too despondent. For, we must never forget that if there was not one thing that was not on top of another thing our society would be nothing more than a meaningless body of men that had gathered together for no good purpose. But we flourish. This year our Australasian members and the various organizations affiliated to our Australasian branches put no fewer than twenty-two things on top of other things. *(applause)* Well done all of you. But there is one cloud on the horizon. In this last year our Staffordshire branch has not succeeded in putting one thing on top of another *(shame!).* Therefore I call upon our Staffordshire delegate to explain this weird behaviour.

As Sir William sits a meek man rises at one of the side tables.

Mr Cutler (JOHN) Er, Cutler, Staffordshire. Um . . . well, Mr Chairman, it's just that most of the members in Staffordshire feel . . . the whole thing's a bit silly.

Cries of outrage. Chairman leaps to feet.

Sir William Silly! SILLY!!!! *(he pauses and thinks)* Silly! I suppose it is, a bit. What have we been doing wasting our lives with all this nonsense *(hear, hear)*. Right, okay, meeting adjourned for ever.

He gets right up and walks away from the table to approving noises and applause. He walks to a door at the side of the studio set and goes through it. Exterior shot: a door opens and Sir William appears out of it into the fresh air. He suddenly halts.

Sir William Good Lord. I'm on film. How did that happen?

He turns round and disappears into the building again. He reappears through door, crosses set and goes out through another door. Exterior: he appears from the door into the fresh air and then stops.

Sir William It's film again. What's going on?

He turns and disappears through the door again. Cut to him inside the building. He crosses to a window and looks out, then turns and says . . .

Sir William Gentlemen! I have bad news. This room is surrounded by film.

Members What! What!

Several members run to window and look out. Cut to film of them looking out of window. Cut to studio: the members run to a door and open it. Cut to film: of them appearing at the door hesitating and then closing door. Cut to studio: with increasing panic they run to the second door. Cut to film: they appear, hesitate, and go back inside. Cut to studio: they run to Sir William in the centre of the room.

A Member We're trapped!

Sir William Don't panic, we'll get out of this.

A Member How?

Sir William We'll tunnel our way out.

Barnes (MICHAEL) Good thinking, sir. I'll get the horse.

Sir William Okay Captain, you detail three men, start digging and load them up with cutlery, and then we'll have a rota, we'll have two hours digging, two hours vaulting and then two hours sleeping, okay?

Barnes and others carry a vaulting horse into shot. The members start vaulting over it. Two Gestapo officers walk by.

Mr Cutler All right, Medwin, let's see you get over that horse. Pick your feet up, Medwin. Come on, boy!

First German Officer (IAN DAVIDSON) Ze stupid English. Zey are prisoners and all they do is the sport.

Second German Officer (TERRY G) One thing worries me, Fritz.

First German Officer Ja?

Second German Officer Where's the traditional cheeky and lovable Cockney sergeant?

Sergeant (TERRY J) *(donning tin helmet)* Cheer up, Fritz, it may never happen. *(sings)* Maybe it's because I'm a Londoner . . .

Second German Officer Good. Everything seems to be in order.

> *The Gestapo officers leave. Mr Cutler runs up to Sir William.*

Mr Cutler Colonel! I've just found another exit, sir.

Sir William Okay, quickly, run this way.

Everyone If we could run that way ... *(he stops them with a finger gesture)* sorry.

> ANIMATION: *A bleak landscape. A large foot with a Victorian lady on top of it comes hopping past. A door in a building opens and the society members (real people, superimposed) run out, along the cartoon, and disappear, falling into nothingness. Cut to section of an oesophagus. The members (now animated cut-outs) fall down it into a stomach where they are joined by various large vegetables. Pull back to show that this is a cutaway view of an Edwardian gentleman. He belches.*

Animation Voice Oh, I'm terribly sorry, excuse me.

> *He moves through a door marked 'gents'. We hear a lavatory flushing. Cut to café: linkman at table as before.*

Linkman (JOHN) Ah, hello. Well they certainly seem to be in a tight spot, and *I* spot ... our next item – so let's get straight on with the fun and go over to the next item – or dish! Ha, ha!

> *Cut to a simple set with two chairs in it. Close up of Mr Praline.*

Praline (JOHN) Hello. 'Ow are you? I'm fine. Welcome to a new half-hour chat show in which me, viz the man what's talking to you now, and Brooky – to wit my flat mate – and nothing else, I'd like to emphasize that – discuss current affairs issues of burning import.

> *Pull back to show Brooky.*

Brooky (ERIC) Have you heard the one about the three nuns in the nudist colony?

Praline Shut up. Tonight, the population explosion.

Brooky Apparently there were these three nuns ...

Praline Shut up. Come the year 1991, given the present rate of increase in the world's population, the Chinese will be three deep. Another thing ...

> *Floor manager comes in.*

Floor Manager (TERRY J) Sorry, loves, sorry, the show is too long this week and this scene's been cut.

Praline Lord Hill's at the bottom of this.

Floor Manager But if you can find a piano stool you can appear later on in the show on film.

Brooky 'Ow much?

Floor Manager Oh, about ten bob each.

Praline I wouldn't wipe me nose on it.

Brooky 'Ave you 'eard the one about these three nuns ...

Praline   Sh. I can hear something. 'Ang about, we may still get in this show as a link.

Praline kneels and puts his ear to the floor. In the bottom section of the shot we see beneath the floor an animation of the unfortunate members of the Society for Putting Things on Top of Other Things being flushed along a pipe.

Brooky   That's clever. How do they do that?

Praline   Colour separation, you cotton head.

ANIMATION: *various adventures of the Society members.*
Cut back to linkman. There is a loud argument going on in the café behind him.

Linkman   Well, they seem to be in another tight spot . . . *(to the argument)* Could you . . . could you, could you keep it down a little, please. Thank you so much. Could you keep it down, please . . . Thank you. *(to camera)* Well and now we move on to our, to our main course. Prawn salad . . . Prawn salad?

Oak-panelled door with notice on it saying 'Prawn Salad Ltd'. The butler pushes it open and shows man into living room. The room is fairly large, containing at one end opposite the door a big window, making the room look quite high up – although it should be stately rather than modern. In the middle of the room's back wall there is a large ornate mirror, over a mantelpiece filled with objects. To the right of this wall there is a large bookshelf filled with books, and in front of it there is a drinks trolley.

Butler (GRAHAM)   Well, if you'll just wait in here, sir, I'm sure Mr Thompson won't keep you waiting long.

Man (ERIC)   Fine. Thanks very much.

He picks up a magazine. The mirror behind him without warning falls off the wall and smashes to the ground. The butler returns, and looks at the man enquiringly.

Man   The mirror fell off the wall.

Butler   Sir?

Man   The mirror fell off . . . off the wall . . . it fell.

Butler   *(polite but disbelieving)* I see. You'd better wait here. I'll get a cloth.

The butler just closes the door behind him and the bookcase detaches itself from the wall and comes sweeping down, bringing with it the drinks trolley. The butler opens the door.

Man   Ah, it . . . it came off the wall.

Butler   Yes, sir?

Man   It just came right off the wall.

Butler   Really, sir.

Man   Yes, I . . . I didn't touch it.

Butler (*politely ironic*) Of course not. It just fell off the wall.
Man Yes. It just fell off the wall.
Butler Don't move. I'll get help.

    He goes.

Man Yes – er, fell off the wall.

    A maid enters.

Maid (CAROL) Oh my God, what a mess. 'Ere, did you do this?
Man No, no. I didn't do all this. It . . . it did it all.
Maid Oh? Well . . . 'ere, hold this. I'll get started.

    She hands him a dagger.

Man Oh, it's jolly nice. What is it?
Maid It's a Brazilian dagger. Ooops.

    She trips, falls lethally on to the dagger he is holding. She collapses at his feet. There is blood on the dagger and his hand. He is looking down at her, when he becomes aware of a man in a green baize apron at the door, who is looking at him in horror.

Man Er, she just fell on . . . on to the dagger.
Green (TERRY J) (*soothingly*) Yes, of course she did, sir.
Man Yes, just gave me the dagger and tripped, and went, 'Oops'.

    Green starts backing round the room away from him, but humouring him.

Green Yes sir, I understand.
Man I mean, I didn't er . . .
Green Oh no, no, of course not, sir, I understand.
Man I mean she . . . she just, er . . .
Green Fell?
Man Fell.
Green (*backs off too far and falls backwards through the window*) Arrghh!
Man (*to window*) I'm terribly sorry.

    A policeman and the butler appear at the door.

Butler That's him.
Policeman (MICHAEL) Right, sir.
Man Hello, officer. There seems to have been an accident. Well, several accidents actually.
Policeman That's right, sir. Would you come this way, please. (*goes towards him*) Ahh! (*clutches chest*) It's me . . . me heart, sir. (*collapses*)
Butler You swine. I'll get you for that.

    He is about to move forward when a large portion of the ceiling collapses on him. He goes down, too.

Man Er, I won't wait. I'll phone.

    He moves off through door. Large crashing sounds. He comes downstairs into a stretch of hall leading to an outside door. As he comes suits of armour collapse, bookcase glass smashes, a grandfather clock tips over and smashes, pictures fall off walls. All this quite quickly in sequence as he passes in horror. He gets to the main door. We see his relief. He closes the main door behind him, slamming it: it's a country-house-type entrance. Cut to stock film of country house being blown up. Cut back to man looking in horror, with dust and rubble swirling around. He is holding the remains of the door.

Man Sorry.

Pull wide. He is in a patch of rubble. The Society for Putting Things on Top of Other Things members walk by in their evening dress.

Members I think we're really out this time. Yes. Jolly good. Now where's the school hall. I think it's over there. Come on. Sorry. Jolly good.

They go past the bishop in the field.

Bishop (MICHAEL) *(singing)* Oh, Mr Belpit. Your legs are so swollen.

Sir William Excuse me, is that the school hall?

Bishop Um, I'm sorry, I don't know. I'm not in this one – I'm in next week's, I think.

Sir William Oh, come on.

Bishop Oh, Mr Belpit! . . .

They come to a school hall. A sign says 'Seven Brides for Seven Brothers, presented by the staff and pupils of the Dibley School for Boys'.

Sir William Oh, here we are. *(they go in)*

Cut to linkman in cafeteria.

Linkman Ah well, they seem to have linked that themselves, so there's no need for me to interrupt at all. So, ah, back to the school hall.

A school hall with a stage. Mr Praline and Brooky enter. Praline sits at piano and plays something very badly; Brooky turns the pages for him. Music ends. Unseen schoolmaster announcer:

Schoolmaster 'Seven Brides for Seven Brothers'. *(slight applause)*

The curtain parts. Enter headmaster in mortar board and gown.

Headmaster (GRAHAM) 'Tis time the seven Smith brothers had brides. Fetch me Smith Major.

Enter Smith Major in short pants.

First Smith (TERRY J) Sir.

Headmaster 'Tis time you and your six brothers were married.

First Smith Thank you, Headmaster.

Headmaster Fetch me your six brothers, that the seven brothers may be together.

Smith Major rings handbell. Three boys enter and stand next to him.

Boys Behold, the seven brothers.

Headmaster Right, I'll see Watson, Wilkins, and Spratt in my study afterwards.

First Smith *(has to be prompted, then declaims badly)* But where shall we find seven brides for seven brothers?

Second Smith (TERRY G.) The Sabine School for Girls.

Third Smith (ERIC) Yes, and it's the Annual Dance.

Headmaster Fetch hither the seven brides for seven brothers.

> *Enter two schoolgirls.*

Two Girls Behold the seven brides.

Headmaster Fetch hither the padre that the seven brides may marry the seven brothers. *(nothing happens)* Fetch hither the master on duty that the seven brides may marry the seven brothers.

Padre (MICHAEL) *(entering)* Sorry, I'm late, Headmaster – I've been wrestling with Plato.

Headmaster What you do in your own time, Padre, is written on the wall in the vestry.

Padre Right, do you four boys take these two girls to be your seven brides?

Boys Yes, sir.

Padre Right, go and do your prep.

> *The curtain comes across quickly.*
> *Animation sketch links us to a butcher's shop. Harmless looking city gent enters.*

Gent (MICHAEL) Good morning, I'd care to purchase a chicken, please.

Butcher (ERIC) Don't come here with that posh talk you nasty, stuck-up twit.

Gent I beg your pardon?

Butcher A chicken, sir. Certainly.

Gent Thank you. And how much does that work out to per pound, my good fellow?

Butcher Per pound, you slimy trollope, what kind of a ponce are you?

Gent I'm sorry?

Butcher 4/6 a pound, sir, nice and ready for roasting.

Gent I see, and I'd care to purchase some stuffing in addition, please.

Butcher Use your own, you great poovy po-nagger!

Gent What?

Butcher Ah, certainly sir, some stuffing.

Gent Oh, thank you.

Butcher 'Oh, thank you' says the great queen like a la-di-dah poofta.

Gent I beg your pardon?

Butcher That's all right, sir, call again.

Gent Excuse me.

Butcher What is it now, you great pillock?

Gent Well, I can't help noticing that you insult me and then you're polite to me alternately.

Butcher I'm terribly sorry to hear that, sir.

Gent That's all right. It doesn't really matter.

Butcher Tough titty if it did, you nasty spotted prancer.

Cut to the Grillomat in Paignton. The announcer is just handing back a cup and saucer to a waitress.

Linkman Sorry, I asked for tea. *(she takes it grudgingly)* Thank you very much. *(to camera)* Well we've had the dessert and then, and so the first item, the *last* item on our menu of fun is the coffee. *(waitress hands him back his cup)* Now I did ask for tea.

Waitress (GRAHAM) But you just said coffee.

Linkman No, no, that was just my announcement, just a metaphor.

She shrugs and begins to move off. At the table just behind him we hear her complaining noisily in the background.

Linkman We come . . . look would you mind keeping it down, please . . . we come as – as I said just now, to the coffee.

Waitress Here, he said it again!

Linkman Shut up!

Film of a boxer (John) in training, running along a country road. All this is shot in 'Man Alive' style: plenty of hand-held documentary work. Sound of boxer's feet on the leaves and heavy breathing.

Voice Over (MICHAEL) This is Ken Clean-air Systems, the great white hope of the British boxing world. After three fights – and only two convictions – his manager believes that Ken is ready to face the giant American, Satellite Five.

Cut to manager being driven in Rolls.

SUPERIMPOSED CAPTION: 'MR ENGLEBERT HUMPERDINCK – MANAGER'

Manager (GRAHAM) The great thing about Ken is that he's almost totally stupid.

Cut back to Ken jogging, the early morning sun filtering through the trees.

Voice Over Every morning, he jogs the forty-seven miles from his two-bedroomed, eight-bathroom, six-up-two-down, three-to-go-house in Reigate, to the Government's Pesticide Research Centre at Shoreham. Nobody knows why.

Cut to Ken's wife (a young married with her head in a scarf and curlers), hanging out the washing in a council estate.

CAPTION: 'MRS CLEAN-AIR SYSTEMS'

Mrs CAS (ERIC) Basically Ken is a very gentle, home-loving person. I remember when one of his stick insects had a knee infection. He stayed up all night rubbing it with germoline and banging its head on the table.

Cut to Ken's mother – an old lady in a wheelchair. Hand-held big close-up against the sky.

CAPTION: 'MRS NELLIE AIR-VENT, MOTHER'

Mother (TERRY J) Oh he was such a pretty baby, always so kind and gentle. He was really considerate to his mother, and not at all the kind of person you'd expect to pulverize their opponent into a bloody mass of flesh and raw bone, spitting teeth and fragments of gum into a ring which had become one man's hell and Ken's glory.

The wheelchair moves away and we see that it is on top of a car. Cut to exterior of a semi-detached house. Night.

Voice Over Every morning at his little three-room semi near Reading Ken gets up at three o'clock *(light goes on)* and goes back to bed again because it's far too early.

Light goes out. Close-up alarm clock at 7.05. General shot of room, Ken coming out of bathroom pulling his track-suit on.

Voice Over At seven o'clock Ken gets up, he has a quick shower, a rub-down, gets into his track-suit, and goes back to bed again. *(shot of trainer running)* At 7.50 every morning Ken's trainer runs the 13,000 miles from his two-room lean-to in Bangkok and gets him up.

General shot of room to show his trainer standing over the sleeping Ken. He holds a large mallet and a steel peg.

Trainer (MICHAEL) I used to wake Ken up with a crowbar on the back of the head. But I recently found that this was too far from his brain and I wasn't getting through to him anymore. So I now wake him up with a steel peg driven into his skull with a mallet.

Cut to the empty kitchen, shot from ground level. The camera pans across to show plate of food under an upright chair, and then pans across the room to the kitchen cupboard; Mrs Clean-Air Systems at the sink.

Voice Over For breakfast every day, Ken places a plate of liver and bacon under his chair, and locks himself in the cupboard.

Cut to gym. Manager standing beside ropes of the ring. Again a hand-held 'Man Alive' type interview, with camera noise and all.

Manager Well, he's having a lot of mental difficulties with his breakfasts, but this is temperament, caused by a small particle of brain in his skull, and once we've removed that he'll be perfectly all right.

Close-up alarm clock. Hands at 8.30.

Voice Over At 8.30 the real training begins. *(General shot of room. Ken asleep in bed)* Ken goes back to bed and his trainer gets him up. *(The door bursts open but we don't stay to see what happens. We cut immediately to outside of the house. His trainer pushes Ken out. Trainer goes back into the house (obviously to Ken's wife). Cut to Ken jogging* *through town. Hand held. Ken finds his way blocked by a parked car. He stops and looks very puzzled, then instead of going round it turns and runs back the way he has come.)* At 10.30 every morning Ken arrives at what he thinks is the gym. Sometimes it's a sweetshop, sometimes it's a private house. Today it's a hospital.

Ken turns into the gates or doors of a hospital. There is a slight pause, and a white-coated doctor arrives at the door and points right up the street.

Doctor   Um, straight down there. Straight down there.

Ken follows his finger and looks very hard in that direction. When he is satisfied that Ken has understood where he is pointing, the doctor retires back inside. Ken turns and watches him as he does this, then turns and sets off in the opposite direction. Cut to a shot of a roadside diner.

Voice Over   For lunch Ken crouches down in the road and rubs gravel into his hair. *(Pan down to roadside to reveal Ken just finishing rubbing gravel into his hair; he stands up and hops over a railing to a riverside where a bed stands)* But lunch doesn't take long. Ken's soon up on his feet and back to bed. *(Ken hops into the bed)* And his trainer has to run the 49,000 miles from his two-bedroom, six-living-room tree-house in Kyoto to wake him up. *(Trainer runs into shot, pauses by bedside and turns to camera. He has large plumber's bag.)*

Trainer   Hello. When Ken is in a really deep sleep like this one, the only way to wake him up is to saw his head off.

Cut to stock close-up of punchbag and glove smashing into it. Continual hitting and impact-bang-bang-bang-bang throughout.

Voice Over   What is he like in the ring, this human dynamo, this eighteen-stone bantamweight battering-ram? We asked his sparring partner and one-time childhood sweetheart, Maureen Spencer.

Cut to medium close-up of Maureen, very busty in boxing gear and sparring helmet.

Maureen (CAROL)   Well, I think that if Ken keeps his right up, gets in with the left jab and takes the fight to his man – well, he should go for a cut eye in the third and put Wilcox on the canvas by six.

She goes back to sparring and we see it is she who is hitting the punchbag. Remaining on her we hear the voice over.

Voice Over   Ken's opponent in Tuesday's fight is Petula Wilcox, the Birmingham girl who was a shorthand typist before turning pro in 1968. *(Cut to typical teenage girl's bedsit. Pin-ups of popstars on the walls. Teddy bears on the bed and gonks. Petula Wilcox is sitting up on the bed knitting.)* She's keen on knitting and likes Cliff Richard records. How does she rate her chances against Ken?

Petula (CONNIE)   Well, I'm a southpaw and I think this will confuse him, particularly with his brain problem.

Cut to the ring. Floodlight. The night of the big fight. Murmur of a huge crowd. Excitement, cigar smoke rising in front of the camera. Bustle of activity all round. In medium close-up the master of ceremonies walks out into the middle of the ring, and takes the microphone.

Master of Ceremonies My lords, ladies and gedderbong . . . On my right, from the town of Reigate in the county of Kent, the heavyweight . . . *(unintelligible)* Mr Ken Clean-Air Systems! . . . *(applause, cut to Ken's corner; Ken raises his arms above his head)* and on my left! Miss Petula Wilcox.

SUPERIMPOSE CAPTION: ROUND I

For the first time we see Connie as Petula dance out into the middle of the ring, frail and lovely in a white muslin dress, with a bow in her hair and boxing gloves. The referee brings them together, cautions them and then they separate. The bell goes. As speeded-up as we can manage and with the same stupendous sound effects as for all-in cricket, Ken belts the hell out of Petula. While this goes on, we hear a few voice overs.

Colonel Type (JOHN) I think boxin's a splendid sport – teaches you self-defence.

Critic (TERRY J) Obviously boxing must have its limits, but providing they're both perfectly fit I can see nothing wrong with one healthy man beating the living daylights out of a little schoolgirl.

Voice It's quick and it's fun.

Boxing match is still in full swing as we cut away to the Grillomatic snack bar. A dim light; the announcer has gone. There is only a waitress setting chairs on the tables, and cleaning. She looks up as the camera comes on her.

Waitress Oh, no, he's gone. But he left a message. Jack! Where's that note that fellow left?

Jack (ERIC) Oh, here you are.

Waitress It says sorry, had to catch the last bus. Am on the 49b to Babbacombe.

Cut to the top of an open-top bus driving along.

Linkman Oh, er, there you are. Hello. You got the note, jolly good. Well, um, that's all the items that we have for you this week and er, what a jolly nice lot of items too, eh? Um . . . well, the same team will be back with you again next week with another menu full of items. Um . . . I don't know if I shall be introducing the show next week as I understand my bits in this show have not been received quite as well as they might *(start to roll credits over this)* but er, never mind, the damage is done – no use crying over spilt milk. *(miserably)* I've had my chance and I've muffed it. Anyway, there we are. I'm not really awfully good with words. You see, I'm more of a visual performer. I have a very funny – though I say so myself

– very funny funny walk. I wish I'd been in that show. I'd have done rather well. But anyway, there we are – the show's over. And ... we'll all be – *they'll* all be back with you again next week ... *(starting to cry)* Sorry. I do beg your pardon. I don't like these ... displays of emotion ... I wish it would say the end.

It says 'The End'.

Nineteen

Quiz show set-up. Two contestants either side, compère in the middle. On the back wall in large letters it says 'It's a living'. Music plays brightly. Track quickly into compère, losing contestants, as he starts his quick spiel.
CAPTION: 'IT'S A LIVING'

Compère (ERIC) Hello, good evening, and welcome to 'It's A Living'. The rules are very simple: each week we get a large fee; at the end of that week we get another large fee; if there's been no interruption at the end of the year we get a repeat fee which can be added on for tax purposes to the previous year or the following year if there's no new series. Every contestant, in addition to getting a large fee is entitled to three drinks at the BBC or if the show is over, seven drinks − unless he is an MP, in which case he can have seven drinks before the show, or a bishop only three drinks in toto. The winners will receive an additional fee, a prize which they can flog back and a special fee for a guest appearance on 'Late Night Line Up'. Well, those are the rules, that's the game, we'll be back again same time next week. Till then. Bye-bye.
Cut to BBC world symbol.

Voice Over (MICHAEL) Well, it's five past nine and nearly time for six past nine. On BBC 2 now it'll shortly be six and a half minutes past nine. Later on this evening it'll be ten o'clock and at 10.30 we'll be joining BBC 2 in time for 10.33, and don't forget tomorrow when it'll be 9.20. Those of you who missed 8.45 on Friday will be able to see it again this Friday at a quarter to nine. Now here is a time check. It's six and a half minutes to the big green thing.

Second Voice Over (TERRY J) You're a loony.

First Voice Over I get so bored. I get so bloody bored.

ANIMATION: *for a minute or two strange things happen on animation until suddenly we find ourselves into the animated title sequence.*
Cut to the announcer in a silly location, sitting at his desk as usual.

Announcer (JOHN) You probably noticed that I didn't say 'and now for something completely different' just now. This is simply because I am unable to appear in the show this week. *(looks closely at script, puzzled)* Sorry to interrupt you.
Cut to a man holding his mouth open to show the camera his teeth.

Man (TERRY J) I'm terribly sorry to interrupt but my tooth's hurting, just around here.

Voice Get off.

Man Oh, sorry.

Cut to pompous moustached stockbroker type.

Nabarro (GRAHAM) I'm not sorry to interrupt – I'll interrupt anything if it gets people looking in my direction – like at my old school where, by a coincidence, the annual prize giving is going on at this very moment.

There is a ripple effect, and a muted trumpet plays a corny segue sequence. We mix through to the trumpeter at a school prize giving. On the stage of the school hall there is a long table behind which are sitting several distinguished people. A bishop in a grey suit and purple stock and dog collar gets up.

Bishop (MICHAEL) My Lord Mayor, Lady Mayoress, it gives me very great pleasure to return to my old school, to present the prizes in this centenary year. This school takes very justifiable pride in its fine record of . . . aaaaagh!

Hands pull him down behind the table. Fighting, punching, struggle, grunts etc. No reaction at all from the distinguished guests. The bishop's head reappears for a moment.

Bishop . . . scholarship and sporting achievement in all . . . aaaagh!

He disappears again. More noises. Up comes another bishop dressed identically.

Second Bishop (ERIC) I'm, I'm afraid there's been a mistake. The man who has been speaking to you is an impostor. He is not in fact the Bishop of East Anglia, but a man wanted by the police. *I* am the Bishop of East Anglia and anyone who doesn't believe me can look me up in the book. Now then, the first prize is this beautiful silver cup, which has been won by me. *(he puts the silver cup into a sack)* Next we come to the Fairfax Atkinson Trophy for outstanding achievement in the field of Applied Mathematics. Well, there was no-one this year who reached the required standard so it goes in my sack. And by an old rule of the school all the other silver trophies also go in my sack . . . aaagh!

He is dragged down by an unseen hand. More sounds of fighting, noisier than before even. A Chinaman in Mao jacket and cap appears.

Chinaman (GRAHAM) Velly solly for hold-up . . . no ploblem now . . . me are Bishop of East Anglia, now plesent plizes . . . Eyes down for first plize . . . The Fyffe-Chulmleigh Spoon for Latin Elegaics . . . goes to . . . People's Republic of China! Aaaagh!

The Chinaman is dragged down beneath the table as were the others. Again sound of struggle, thumps etc. A plainclothes policeman stands up.

Detective (TERRY J) Good evening, everybody. My name's Bradshaw – Inspector Elizabeth Bradshaw, of the Special Branch Speech Day Squad, but I'd like you to think of me as the Bishop of East

Anglia, and I'd like to present the first prize, the Grimwade Gynn Trophy to . . .

A shot. He leaps backwards. Sound of machine guns and exploding shells. Two men in army uniform (could they be soldiers?) with camouflage sticking out of tin helmets rush up to the table and exchange fire. They have a huge bazooka which they fire from time to time.

Soldier (JOHN) *(appearing from beneath the table, shouting above the din of the battle)* Lord Mayor, Lady Mayoress, ladies, gentlemen and boys. Please do not panic. Please keep your heads right down now, and at the back please keep your heads right down. Do not panic, don't look round – this building is surrounded. There is nothing to worry about. I am the Bishop of East Anglia. Now the first prize is the Granville Cup for French Unseen Translation . . . *(explosion and smoke, debris over the stage)* and it goes to Forbes Minor . . . Forbes Minor . . . right, give him covering fire . . . *(explosion)* Come on Forbes. Come on boy. Come and get it. Keep down. *(a wretched schoolboy appears on the stage keeping his head down)* Well done . . . *(he manages to get the cup but as he stands to shake hands he is shot)* Oh . . . bad luck! The next prize . . .

Mix through to a picture on a TV monitor and pull out from monitor to reveal a studio set as for a late-night discussion programme.

Interviewer (GRAHAM) Mr L. F. Dibley's latest film 'if'. *(he turns to Dibley)* Mr Dibley, some people have drawn comparisons between your film, 'if', which ends with a gun battle at a public school, and Mr Lindsay Anderson's film, 'if', which ends with a gun battle at a public school.

Dibley (TERRY J) Oh yes, well, I mean, there were some people who said my film '2001 – A Space Odyssey', was similar to Stanley Kubrick's. I mean, that's the sort of petty critical niggling that's dogged my career. It makes me sick. I mean, as soon as I'd made 'Midnight Cowboy' with the vicar as Ratso Rizzo, John Schlesinger rushes out his version, and gets it premiered while mine's still at the chemist's.

Interviewer Well, we have with us tonight one of your films, 'Rear Window', which was to become such a success for Alfred Hitchcock a few weeks later. Now this is a silent film, so perhaps you could talk us through it . . .

Cut to a dim, shaky 8mm shot of a window. It is open. After a few seconds a man appears and looks out. He then performs over-exaggerated horror and points, looking at camera. Then he disappears and then he reappears.

Dibley Yes, well, let's see now . . . there's the rear window. There's the man looking out of the window. He sees the murder. The murderer's come into the room to kill him, but he's outwitted him and he's all right. The End. I mean, Alfred Hitchcock, who's supposed to be so bloody wonderful, padded that out to one and a half hours ... lost all the tension ... just because he had bloody Grace Kelly he made £3 million more than I did. Mind you, at least she can act a bit, I could have done with her in 'Finian's Rainbow' ... The man from the off-licence was terrible ... a real failure that was – ten seconds of solid boredom.

Cut to shaky titles: Mr Dibley's 'Finian's Rainbow starring the man from the off-licence'. Cut to the man from the off-licence standing by a tennis-court. He wears a dress and appears to be trying to say something – he has forgotten his words. He does an unconvincing little dance.

CAPTION: 'THE END'

Dibley Bloody terrible.

Interviewer Mr L. F. Dibley's 'Finian's Rainbow'. And now over to me. *(close-up of interviewer)* Exclusively on the programme today we have the Foreign Secretary, who has just returned from the bitter fighting in the Gulf of Amman. He's going to tell us about canoeing.

On the bank of a river seen from the other side. There is a canoe on the bank. A man in a pinstripe suit stands beside it.

SUPERIMPOSED CAPTION: 'THE FOREIGN SECRETARY'

He gives a little cough and gets in. Two Arabs run in from either side of frame, lift up the canoe and throw it and the Foreign Secretary into the water. Cut back to the interviewer.

Interviewer That gives you just some idea of what's going on out there. Today saw the long-awaited publication of the Portman Committee's Report on Industrial Reorganization ...

CAPTION: 'SOMETHING SILLY'S GOING TO HAPPEN'

Interviewer It's taken five years to prepare and it's bound to have an enormous impact on the future of industrial relations in this country. In the studio tonight Lord Portman, Chairman of the Committee, Sir Charles Avery, Employers' Reorganization Council, and Ray Millichope, leader of the Allied Technicians' Union. And they're going to make a human pyramid.

Three men in shorts run on to accompaniment of tinkly music and form a pyramid. As they complete it we cut to film of Vatican crowds and dub on enormous ovation.

Interviewer Bra ... vo. Now the President of the Board of Trade ...

Cut back to the same river bank shot from across the river. The President of the Board of Trade in pinstripes is standing beside a hamper. He smiles and gets in, and lowers the lid. Once again two Arabs run in from either side and throw it in. All these sequences are speeded up.

Interviewer Now here's the Vice-Chairman of ICI.

Cut back to same river bank. A head looking out of the hamper. It disappears as two Arabs run in and toss it in.

Interviewer Well, so much for politics and the problems of Britain's industrial reorganization. Now we turn to the lighter subject of sport, and Reg Harris, the former world cycling sprint champion, talks to us about the psychological problems of big race preparation. *(Reg and his bike are thrown in the river by the Arabs)* And now the world of song – Anne Zeigler and Webster Booth. *(two hampers thrown in river by four Arabs)* Well, all good things must come to an end, and that's all for this week. But to close our programme, Dame Irene Stoat, who celebrates her eighty-fifth birthday this month, reads one of her most famous poems.

Cut to the river bank. An old lady is standing beside it, but this time on the bank of the river nearest the camera. On the other bank we see the Arabs run into shot, realize they've been foiled and leap up and down in anger.

Dame Irene (MICHAEL) Who shall declare this good, that ill
When good and ill so intertwine
But to fulfil the vast design
Of an omniscient will.
When seeming again but turns to loss
When earthly treasure proves but dross
And what seems lost but turns again
To high eternal gain.

The Arabs run out of vision. Suddenly, from right beside the camera, with a bloodcurdling scream a Samurai warrior with drawn sword leaps upon her and hurls her backwards into the water. The warrior then strikes up a fierce heroic pose for the camera.

SUPERIMPOSED CAPTION: 'NEWHAVEN–LE HAVRE. GETAWAY TO THE CONTINENT'

Cut to a smart dinner party. There are two couples in evening dress at the table. Candles burning on the polished wood, a fire burning in the grate. Muted music and sophisticated lighting.

Hostess (RITA) We had the most marvellous holiday. It was absolutely fantastic.

Host (MICHAEL) Absolutely wonderful.

Hostess Michael, you tell them about it.

Host No, darling, you tell them.

Hostess You do it so much better.

The doorbell rings.

Host Excuse me a moment.

The host goes and answers the door of the flat, which opens straight into the dining room. Standing at the door is a large grubby man carrying a tin bath on his shoulder. There are flies buzzing around him. He walks straight in.

Man (JOHN) Dung, sir.

Host What?

Man We've got your dung.

Host What dung?

Man Your dung. Three hundredweight of heavy droppings. Where do you want it? *(he looks round for a likely place)*

Host I didn't order any dung.

Man Yes you did, sir. You ordered it through the Book of the Month Club.

Host Book of the Month Club?

Man That's right, sir. You get 'Gone with the Wind', 'Les Misérables' by Victor Hugo, 'The French Lieutenant's Woman' and with every third book you get dung.

Host I didn't know that when I signed the form.

Man Well, no, no. It wasn't on the form – they found it wasn't good for business. Anyway, we've got three hundredweight of dung in the van. Where do you want it?

Host Well, I don't think we do. We've no garden.

Man Well, it'll all fit in here – it's top-class excrement.

Host You can't put it in here, we've having a dinner party!

Man 'Salright. I'll put it on the telly.

He brings it into the dining room. The guests ignore him.

Host Darling . . . there's a man here with our Book of the Month Club dung.

Hostess We've no room, dear.

Man Well, how many rooms have you got, then?

Host Well, there's only this room, the bedroom, a spare room.

Man Oh well, I'll tell you what, move everything into the main bedroom, then you can use the spare room as a dung room.

The doorbell goes and there standing at the door which hasn't been closed is a gas board official with a dead Indian over his shoulders.

Host Yes.

Gas Man (GRAHAM) Dead Indian.

Host What?

Gas Man Have you recently bought a new cooker, sir?

Host Yes.

Gas Man Ah well, this is your free dead Indian, as advertised . . .

Host I didn't see that in the adverts . . .

Gas Man No, it's in the very small print, you see, sir, so as not to affect the sales.

Host We've no room.

Man That's all right – you can put the dead Indian in the spare room on top of the dung.

Dead Indian Me . . . heap dizzy.

Host He's not dead!

Gas Man Oh well, that's probably a faulty cooker.

> *The phone rings. The wife goes to answer it.*

Man Have you, er . . . you read and enjoyed 'The French Lieutenant's Woman', then?

Host No.

Man No . . . still, it's worth it for the dung, isn't it?

Hostess Darling, it's the Milk Marketing Board. For every two cartons of single cream we get the M4 motorway.

> *Cut to man and wife standing bewildered in the middle of a motorway. Beside them is a steaming pile of dung, and a dead Indian. They look round in amazement. A police car roars up to them and two policemen leap out.*

Policeman (ERIC) Are you Mr and Mrs P. Forbes of 7, the Studios, Elstree?

Man Yes.

Policeman Right, well, get in the car. We've won you in a police raffle.

> *Speeded up, they are bundled into the car. Cut to inspector.*

Inspector (TERRY J) Yes! This couple is just one of the prizes in this year's Police Raffle. Other prizes include two years for breaking and entering, a crate of search warrants, a 'What's all this then?' T-shirt and a weekend for two with a skinhead of your own choice.

> CAPTION: 'STOP PRESS'

Voice Over (MICHAEL) And that's not all! Three fabulous new prizes have just been added, a four-month supply of interesting undergarments *(picture)*, a fully motorized pig *(picture c/o Mr Gilliam)*, and a hand-painted scene of Arabian splendour, complete with silly walk.

> *Animation sketch leading to a booth in a quite expensive looking coffee shop, Italian style. Nigel is sitting there. Timmy Williams comes in. He has just the faintest passing resemblance to David Frost.*

Timmy (ERIC) Nigel! Wonderful to see you, super, super, super. Am I a teeny bit late?

Nigel (TERRY J) A bit, an hour.

Timmy Oh, super! Only Snowdon's been re-touching my profile and we can't upset the lovely Snowdon, can we?

Nigel Gosh, no.

> *A man passes.*

Timmy *(gets up and clasps his hands)* . . . David Bloggs . . . the one and only . . . super to see you. Who are you working for? Come and work for me, I'll call you tomorrow. *(sits down)* It's really lovely to have this little chat with you.

Nigel Well, I . . .

Timmy It is so nice to have this little talk about things. I heard a teeny rumourlette that you were married.

Nigel Well, not quite, no. My wife's just died, actually.

Timmy Oh dear. *(sees another man passing)* Brian! *(extends his arm)* We must get together again soon. See you. Bye. *(to Nigel)* Well, perhaps we could do a tribute to her on the show.

Nigel Well, no. I . . .

Timmy I'll get Peter, William, Arthur, Alex, Joan, Ted, Scott, Wilf, John and Ray to fix it up. It is *so* nice having this little chat.

Nigel Well, actually Timmy, I'm glad to get you on your own . . .

A reporter comes up to the table.

Timmy You don't mind if Peter just sits in, do you?

Nigel Well, actually . . .

Timmy Only he's doing an article on me for the 'Mail'. He's such a lovely person.

Reporter (GRAHAM) Hello.

Timmy Peter, this is one of the nicest people in the world, Nigel Watt. *(Peter scribbles it down)* W-A-double T. That's right, yes.

Nigel Well, actually, Timmy, the thing is, it's a bit private.

A writer comes to the table.

Timmy Oh, you don't mind if Peter just sits in, do you? Only Peter's writing a book on me. Peter, you know Tony from the 'Mail', don't you?

Peter (JOHN) Yes, we met in the Turkish bath yesterday.

Timmy Super, super. Did it come up well in the writing yesterday?

Peter Great, great, great.

Timmy You took out the tummy references? *(makes fatness signs)*

Peter Yes, I did.

Timmy Super, super, super. Just to fill you in, this is Nigel Watt and we are having a little heart-to-heart. H-E-A-R-T. Smashing. Do go on, Nigel.

They both start writing.

Nigel Well, well, the thing is, Timmy, um er . . .

Timmy is smiling and posing. Nigel stops and looks. There is a photographer, hovering.

Timmy Do carry on, it's the 'TV Times', only they syndicate these photographs to America. Would you mind if we just er . . . *(grabs him by the hand and poses hearty friendship photo)* Super, super. One over here, I think, Bob. A little smile, please, smashing, smashing. Feel free, Bob, to circulate, won't you. Do go on, this is most interesting.

Nigel Well, the thing is, Timmy, I'm a bit embarrassed.

Waiter (MICHAEL) *(coming to table)* Oh, Mr Williams, it's so nice to see you. Will you sign this for my little daughter, please?

Timmy Hello, Mario. Super, wonderful. *(signs)* Just two lovely coffees, please.

Director comes in.

Director Sorry, sorry, Timmy. Can we just go from where Mario comes in, we're getting bad sound, OK?

Timmy It's German television. Isn't it exciting, Nigel? They're doing a prize-winning documentary on me.

We see a film camera and the whole crew gathered round.

Clapper Boy 'The Wonderful Mr Williams', scene 239, take 2.

Director Action!

Timmy *(taking the cue, switches)* Mario, how super to see you. How are the lovely family? Please give your little daughter this. *(hands him a five pound note)* Thank you. And just two lovely coffees, please.

Mario Yes, sir.

Timmy *(to Nigel)* Such a lovely waiter. Now, go on please, this is *most* interesting.

Nigel Well . . . er . . . as I was saying, Timmy, my wife's gone . . . gone. *(close-up on him)* I've got three children and I'm at my wits' end. No job, no insurance, no money at all. I'm absolutely flat broke, I just don't know where to turn. I . . . I'm absolutely at the end of my tether. You're my only chance. Can you help me, please, Timmy?

He looks up, Timmy isn't there. Timmy comes bounding back.

Timmy Sorry, I was on the phone to America. It's been super having this lovely little chat. We must do this again more often. Er . . . will you get the coffees? I'm afraid I must dash, I'm an hour late for the Israeli Embassy. *(there is a shot; Nigel slumps over the table, gun in his hand)* Er . . . did you get that shot all right, sound?

Sound Man *(off)* Yes, fine.

Timmy It . . . it wasn't a bit too wicked, was it? I mean, it wasn't too cruel?

Tony and Peter No, no, no. It was great.

Timmy No, super . . . well, cr . . . I think it shows I'm human, don't you?

Tony and Peter Yes, great.

Timmy Super, super. Well, the charabanc's here. Go on, everybody. Bye. *(he waves)*

They all troop off after him. Theme music starts to come up, we pull back and see the camera set-up. Credits start to roll:

Voice Over (JOHN) 'Timmy Williams' Coffee Time' was brought to you live from Woppi's in Holborn.

Credits continue to roll:

THEME SCRIPT BY *(enormous letters)* TIMMY WILLIAMS

ENTIRELY WRITTEN BY *(enormous letters)* TIMMY WILLIAMS

ADDITIONAL MATERIAL BY: *(these go straight through very fast)*
PETER WRAY
LEN ASHLEY
GEOFFREY INGERSOLL
GEORGE HERBERT
HARRY LOWALL
RALPH EMERSON
HATTY STARR
FRANK PICKSLEY
JOHN STAMFORD
SHELLEY BUNHEUR
MALCOLM KERR
JAMES BEACH
ALAN BAILEY
BRIAN FELDMAN
STIRLING HARTLEY
ADRIAN BEAMISH
GUY WARING
MARK TOMKINS
SIDNEY SMITH
RICHARD HOVEY
EDMUND GOSSE
JONATHAN ASHMORE
BILL WRIGHT
ARTHUR FULLER
RICHARD SAVAGE
MICHAEL WHITEMORE
BUDGE RYAN
CEDRIC HAZLETT
TERRY JONES
MICHAEL PALIN
JOHN GAYNOR
GEORGE COLEMAN
SAMUEL SPURGEON
THOMAS MASSINGER
STEPHEN DAVIS
WALTER CHAPMAN
REGINALD MARWOOD
DAVID GOSCHEN
PETER SCHULMAN
DENNIS FRANKEL
DAVID ROBINSON
PAUL RAYMOND
JOHN WILLDER
JOHNNY LYNN

JOE SHAW
SIMON SMITH
MONTY PYTHON
MICHAEL LAPIN
SYDNEY LOTTERBY
IAN MATHERSON
HUMPHREY BARCLAY
BURT ANCASTER
KIRK OUGLAS
KEN SMITH
GEOFFREY HUGHES
BRIAN FITZJONES
MICHAEL GOWERS
JOHN PENNYCATE
PETER BAKER
NEIL SHAND

Fade out. Fade in on ordinary interview set. Interviewer sitting with man with large semitic polystyrene nose.

Interviewer (MICHAEL) Good evening. I have with me in the studio tonight one of Britain's leading skin specialists – Raymond Luxury Yacht.

Raymond (GRAHAM) That's not my name.

Interviewer I'm sorry – Raymond Luxury *Yach-t*.

Raymond No, no, no – it's spelt Raymond Luxury Yach-t, but it's pronounced 'Throatwobbler Mangrove'.

Interviewer You're a very silly man and I'm not going to interview you.

Raymond Ah, anti-semitism!

Interviewer Not at all. It's not even a proper nose. *(takes it off)* It's polystyrene.

Raymond Give me my nose back.

Interviewer You can collect it at reception. Now go away.

Raymond I want to be on the television.

Interviewer Well you can't.

Animation sketch. Then cut to a large sign saying 'Registry Office', 'Marriages' etc. A man is talking to the registrar.

Man (TERRY J) Er, excuse me, I want to get married.

Registrar (ERIC) I'm afraid I'm already married, sir.

Man Er, no, no. I just want to get married.

Registrar I could get a divorce, I suppose, but it'll be a bit of a wrench.

Man Er, no, no. That wouldn't be necessary because . . .

Registrar You see, would you come to my place or should I have to come to yours, because I've just got a big mortgage.

Man No, no, I want to get married *here*.

Registrar Oh dear. I had my heart set on a church wedding.

Man Look, I just want *you* to marry *me* . . . to . . .

Registrar I want to marry you too sir, but it's not as simple as that. You sure you want to get married?

Man Yes. I want to get married very quickly.

Registrar Suits me, sir. Suits me.

Man I don't want to marry you!

Registrar There is such a thing as breach of promise, sir.

Man Look, I just want you to act as registrar and *marry* me.

Registrar I *will* marry you sir, but please make up your mind. Please *don't* trifle with my affections.

Man I'm sorry, but . . .

Registrar That's all right, sir. I forgive you. Lovers' tiff. But you're not the first person to ask me today. I've turned down several people already.

Man Look, I'm already engaged.

Registrar *(agreeing and thinking)* Yes, and I'm already married. Still we'll get round it.

Second Man (MICHAEL) *(entering)* Good morning. I want to get married.

Registrar I'm afraid I'm already marrying this gentleman, sir.

Second Man Well, can I get married *after* him?

Registrar Well, divorce isn't as quick as that, sir. Still, if you're keen.

Third Man (GRAHAM) *(entering)* I want to get married, please.

Registrar Heavens, it's my lucky day, isn't it. All right, but you'll have to wait until I've married these two, sir.

Third Man What, those two getting married . . . Nigel! What are you doing marrying him?

Registrar He's marrying me first, sir.

Third Man He's engaged to me.

Fourth Man (JOHN) *(big and butch)* Come on, Henry.

Registrar Blimey, the wife.

Second Man Will *you* marry me?

Fourth Man I'm already married.

Cut to a photo of all five of them standing happily outside a house.

Voice Over (TERRY J) Well, things turned out all right in the end, but you mustn't ask how 'cos it's naughty. They're all married and living quite well in a council estate near Dulwich.

ANIMATION: *'The Spot'*

CAPTION: 'ELECTION NIGHT SPECIAL'

Cut to linkman sitting at desk.

Linkman (JOHN) *(very excited)* Hello and welcome to 'Election Night Special'. There's great excitement here as we should be getting the first result through any minute now. We don't know where it'll be from . . . it might be from Leicester or from Luton. The polling's been quite heavy in both areas ... oh, wait a moment ... I'm just getting ... I'm just getting a loud buzzing noise in my left ear. Excuse me a moment. *(he bangs ear and knocks a large bee out)* Uuggh! *(cheering from crowd)* Anyway, let's go straight over to James Gilbert at Leicester.

Shot of returning officer in front of a group consisting half of grey-suited, half of silly-dressed candidates and agents. The silly ones are in extraordinary hats, false noses etc.

Voice Over (MICHAEL) Well, it's a straight fight here at Leicester ... On the left of the Returning Officer *(camera shows grey-suited man)* you can see Arthur Smith, the Sensible candidate and his agent, *(camera pans to silly people)* and on the other side is the silly candidate Jethro Walrustitty with his agent and his wife.

Officer (TERRY J) Here is the result for Leicester. Arthur J. Smith ...

Voice Over Sensible Party.

Officer 30,162 ... Jethro Q. Walrustitty ...

Voice Over Silly Party.

Officer 30,612 ... Jethro Q. Walrustitty ...

Cheering from the crowd. Cut back to the studio.

Linkman *(even more excited)* Well, there's the first result and the Silly Party have held Leicester. What do you make of that, Norman?

Cut to Norman. He is very excited.

Norman (MICHAEL) Well, this is largely as I predicted except that the Silly Party won. I think this is mainly due to the number of votes cast. Gerald?

Cut to Gerald standing by 'swingometer' – a pivoted pointer on a wall chart.

Gerald (ERIC) Well, there's a swing here to the Silly Party ... but how big a swing I'm not going to tell you.

Cut to George also standing by a swingometer.

George (TERRY J) Well, if I may ... I think the interesting thing here is the big swing to the Silly Party and of course the very large swing back to the Sensible Party ... and a tendency to wobble up and down in the middle because the screw's loose.

Cut to Alphonse.

Alphonse (GRAHAM) No, I'm afraid I can't think of anything.

Cut to Eric.

Eric (TERRY G) I can't add anything to that. Colin?

Cut to Colin.

Colin (IAN DAVIDSON) Can I just butt in at this point and say this is in fact the very first time I've ever appeared on television.

Cut to linkman.

Linkman No, no, we haven't time, because we're going straight over to Luton.

Cut to Luton Town Hall. There are sensible, silly and slightly silly candidates.

Voice Over (MICHAEL) Here at Luton, it's a three-cornered fight between Alan Jones – Sensible Party, in the middle, Tarquin Fin-tim-lin-bin-whin-bim-lim-bus-stop-F'tang-F'tang-Olé-Biscuitbarrel – Silly Party, and Kevin Phillips-Bong, the Slightly Silly candidate.

Officer (ERIC) Alan Jones . . .

Voice Over On the left, Sensible Party.

Officer 9,112 . . . Kevin Phillips-Bong . . .

Voice Over On the right, Slightly Silly.

Officer Nought . . . Tarquin Fin-tim-lin-bin-whin-bim-lin-bus-stop-F'tang-F'tang-Olé-Biscuitbarrel . . .

Voice Over Silly.

Officer 12,441.

Voice Over And so the Silly Party has taken Luton.

Quick cut to linkman.

Linkman A gain for the Silly Party at Luton. The first gain of the election, Norman?

Cut to each speaker in close-up throughout the scene.

Norman Well, this is a highly significant result. Luton, normally a very sensible constituency with a high proportion of people who aren't a bit silly, has gone completely ga-ga.

Linkman Do we have the swing at Luton?

Gerald Well, I've worked out the swing, but it's a secret.

Linkman Er, well, ah, there . . . there *isn't* the swing, how about the swong?

Norman Well, I've got the swong here in this box and it's looking fine. I can see through the breathing holes that it's eating up peanuts at a rate of knots.

Linkman And how about the swang?

Alphonse Well, it's 29% up over six hundred feet but it's a little bit soft around the edges about . . .

Linkman What do you make of the nylon dot cardigan and plastic mule rest?

Voice (*off*) There's no such thing.

Linkman Thank you, Spike.

Norman Can I just come in here and say that the swong has choked itself to death.

George Well, the election's really beginning to hot up now.

Eric I can't add anything to that.

Colin Can I just add at this point this is in fact the second time I've ever appeared on television?

Linkman I'm sorry, Sasha, we're just about to get another result.

A large number of candidates in Harpenden Town Hall.

Voice Over (TERRY J) Hello, from Harpenden. This is a key seat because in addition to the official Silly candidate there is an independent Very Silly candidate *(in large cube of polystyrene with only his legs sticking out)* who may split the silly vote.

Officer (JOHN) Mr Elsie Zzzzzzzzzzzz. *(obvious man in drag with enormous joke breasts)*

Voice Over Silly.

Officer 26,317 . . . James Walker . . .

Voice Over Sensible.

Officer 26,318.

Voice Over That was close.

Officer Malcolm Peter Brian Telescope Adrian Umbrella Stand Jasper Wednesday *(pops mouth twice)* Stoatgobbler John Raw Vegetable *(sound effect of horse whinnying)* Arthur Norman Michael *(blows squeaker)* Featherstone Smith *(blows whistle)* Northgot Edwards Harris *(fires pistol, which goes 'whoop')* Mason *(chuff-chuff-chuff)* Frampton Jones Fruitbat Gilbert *(sings)* We'll Keep a Welcome In The *(three shots, stops singing)* Williams If I Could Walk That Way Jenkin *(squeaker)* Tiger-draws Pratt Thompson *(sings)* 'Raindrops Keep Falling On My Head' Darcy Carter *(horn)* Pussycat 'Don't Sleep In The Subway' Barton Mannering *(hoot, 'whoop')* Smith.

Voice Over Very Silly.

Officer Two.

Voice Over Well, there you have it. A Sensible gain here at Driffield.

Back to the studio.

Linkman Norman.

Norman Well, I've just heard from Luton that my auntie's ill er, possibly, possibly gastro-enteritis – Gerald.

Gerald Er, well, if this were repeated over the whole country it'd probably be very messy. Colin.

Colin Can I just butt in and say here that it's probably the last time I shall ever appear on television.

Linkman No, I'm afraid you can't, we haven't got time. Just to bring you up to date with a few results, er, that you may have missed. Engelbert Humperdinck has taken Barrow-in-Furness, that's a gain from Ann Haydon-Jones and her husband Pip. Arthur Negus has held Bristols. That's not a result, that's a bit of gossip. Er . . . Mary Whitehouse has just taken umbrage. Could be a bit of trouble there. And apparently Wales is not swinging at all. No surprise there. And . . . Monty Python has held the credits.

Roll credits. Lots of activity behind from the experts.

SUPERIMPOSED FLASHING CAPTION: 'NO CHANGE'

Twenty

Stock film of fast moving Huns thundering around on horseback.

Voice Over (JOHN) In the fifth century, as the once-mighty Roman Empire crumbled, the soft underbelly of Western Europe lay invitingly exposed to the barbarian hordes to the East. Alaric the Visigoth, Gaiseric the Vandal and Theodoris the Ostrogoth in turn swept westward in a reign of terror. But none surpassed in power and cruelty the mighty Attila the Hun.

Voice Over (MICHAEL) Ladies and gentlemen, it's the 'The Attila the Hun Show'.

Cut to film. Music plays: 'The Debbie Reynolds Show' theme – 'With a little love, just a little love'. We see Attila the Hun running towards Mrs Attila the Hun in slow motion, laughing and smiling.

CAPTION: 'THE ATTILA THE HUN SHOW'

Attila and his wife frolic and fall over in slow motion for a bit (copying Debbie Reynolds credits as closely as possible).

CAPTIONS: 'STARRING ATTILA THE HUN'
'AND KAY SLUDGE AS MRS ATTILA THE HUN'
'WITH TY GUDRUN AND NIK CON AS JENNY AND ROBIN ATTILA THE HUN'
'MUSIC BY THE HUNLETS'

Cut to stock film of fast-moving Huns on horseback.

Voice Over (JOHN) In the second quarter of the fifth century, the Huns became a byword for merciless savagery. Their Khan was the mighty warrior Attila. With his devastating armies he swept across Central Europe.

Cut to American-living-room-type set. Doorbell rings. Attila the Hun enters the door.

Attila (JOHN) Oh darling, I'm home.

Mrs Attila (CAROL) Hello darling. Had a busy day at the office?

Attila Not at all bad. *(playing to camera)* Another merciless sweep across Central Europe.

Canned laughter.

Mrs Attila I won't say I'm glad to see you, but boy, am I glad to see you.

Enormous canned laughter and applause. Enter two kids.

Jenny (GRAHAM) Hi, daddy.

Robin (MICHAEL) Hi, daddy.

Attila Hi, Jenny, hi, Robby. *(brief canned applause)* Hey, I've got a present for you two kids in that bag. *(they pull out a severed head)* I want you kids to get a-head.

Enormous shriek of canned laughter and applause. Enter one of us blacked up like Rochester, holding a tray of drinks.

Uncle Tom (ERIC) Heah you are, Mr Hun!

Masses of dubbed applause.

Attila Hi, Uncle Tom.

Uncle Tom There's a whole horde of them marauding Visigoths to see y'all.

Cut to more stock film of these Huns rushing about on their horses. Superimposed image of announcer at his desk.

Announcer (JOHN) And now for something completely different. **It's Man** It's . . .

Massive canned applause.
Animated credit titles.
At the end of these titles cut to a country road. After three seconds a motorbike appears in the distance and speeds towards the camera. We see that a wild-looking nun is riding it.

Voice Over (JOHN) Yes, it's Attila the Nun.

Attila the Nun flashes past the camera. There is a loud sound of the bike crashing off camera.

Voice Over (MICHAEL) A simple country girl who took a vow of eternal brutality.

Attila the Nun on a hospital bed, struggling wildly with two doctors and a nurse who are trying to hold her down. She looks really fearsome. Another doctor enters and summons the nurse away.

Doctor (GRAHAM) Nurse!

The camera tracks away and comes up on another bed in which is sitting a beautiful girl revealing more than a patient normally would and endowed with Carol's . . . undoubted attributes. Screens are placed around her. The doctor and nurse come in through the screens.

Doctor Hello, Miss Norris. How are you?

Miss Norris (CAROL) Not too bad, thank you, doctor.

Doctor Yes, well I think I'd better examine you.

Cut to a line of half a dozen shabby men in filthy macs down to the floor and caps, who shuffle in through the screens and stand at the foot of the bed leering.

Miss Norris What are they doing here?

Doctor It's all right, they're students. Um . . . light please, nurse. *(a single red spotlight falls down on the girl; cut back to the men leering)* Oh . . . and . . . er . . . music, too. *(nurse presses a switch beside bed; stripper music; very loud; cut to line of men getting very excited – hands deep in pockets)* Breathe in . . . out . . . in . . . out . . .

After about five seconds the music reaches a climax and ends. The men in macs all applaud.

Cut to reverse angle to show that we are no longer in a hospital but in a seedy strip club. The curtains have just swished shut.

Compère (ERIC)   Thank you, thank you. Charles Crompton, the Stripping Doctor. And next, gentlemen and ladies, here at the Peephole Club for the very first time – a very big welcome please for the Secretary of State for Commonwealth Affairs.

Curtains open. The compère leaves the stage. A man in city gent's outfit walks into the spotlight.

Minister (TERRY J)   Good evening. Tonight I'd like to restate our position on agricultural subsidies, *(soft breathy jazzy music creeps in behind his words and he starts to strip as he talks)* and their effect on our Commonwealth relationships. Now although we believe, theoretically, in ending guaranteed farm prices, we also believe in the need for a corresponding import levy to maintain consumer prices at a realistic level. But this would have the effect of consolidating our gains of the previous fiscal year, prior to the entry. But I pledge that should we join the Common Market – even maintaining the present position on subsidies – we will never jeopardize, we will never compromise our unique relationship with the Commonwealth countries. A prices structure related to any import charges will be systematically adjusted to the particular requirements of our Commonwealth partners *(he has now removed all his clothes apart from a tassel on each nipple and one on the front of some skin-tight briefs; he starts to revolve the tassels on his nipples)* – so that together we will maintain a positive, and mutually beneficial alliance in world trade *(he turns revealing a tassle on each buttock which he also revolves)* and for world peace. Thank you and goodnight.

He removes the last tassle from his G-string with a flourish. Blackout and curtains quickly close. Compère bounces back on stage.

Compère   Wasn't he marvellous? The Secretary of State for Commonwealth Affairs! And now gentlemen and ladies, a very big welcome please for the Minister of Pensions and Social Security!

Burst of Turkish music and curtains swish back as another bowler-hatted pinstriped minister enters doing a Turkish dance.

Cut to still of Houses of Parliament. Slow track in. Music changes to impressive patriotic music.

Voice Over (GRAHAM)   Yes, today in Britain there is a new wave of interest in politics and politicians.

Cut to vox pops outside Houses of Parliament.

CAPTION: 'A GROUPIE'

First Girl (ERIC) Well, we're just in it for the lobbying, you know. We just love lobbying.

Second Girl (GRAHAM) And the debates – you know a good debate . . . is just . . . fabulous.

Third Girl (MICHAEL) Well, I've been going with ministers for five years now and, you know . . . I think they're wonderful.

Fourth Girl (TERRY J) Oh yes, I like civil servants.

Third Girl Oh yes, they're nice.

Fifth Girl (JOHN) I like the Speaker.

Fourth Girl Oh yes.

Second Girl I like Black Rod.

Voice Over What do their parents think?

> *Cut to suburban house. Mr Concrete standing in front of door of outside loo.*

Mr Concrete (TERRY J) Well she's broken our hearts, the little bastard. She's been nothing but trouble and if she comes round here again I'll kick her teeth in.

> *He turns and goes in. Cut to interior: the Concrete's sitting room. Mrs Concrete is sitting on the sofa, knitting. Mr Concrete enters.*

Mrs Concrete (MICHAEL) Have you been talking to television again, dear?

Mr Concrete Yes, I bloody told 'em.

Mrs Concrete What about?

Mr Concrete I dunno.

Mrs Concrete Was it Reginald Bosanquet?

Mr Concrete No, no, no.

Mrs Concrete Did he have his head all bandaged?

Mr Concrete No, it wasn't like that. They had lots of lights and cameras and tape recorders and all that sort of thing.

Mrs Concrete Oh, that'll be Ray Baxter and the boys and girls from 'Tomorrow's World'. Oh, I prefer Reginald Bosanquet, there's not so many of them. *(the doorbell rings)* Oh – that'll be the ratcatcher. *(she lets the ratcatcher in)*

Ratcatcher (GRAHAM) Hello – Mr and Mrs Concrete?

Both Yes.

Ratcatcher Well, well, well, well, well, well, well, well, well, well, well, how very nice. Allow me to introduce myself. I am Leslie Ames, the Chairman of the Test Selection Committee, and I'm very pleased to be able to tell you that your flat has been chosen as the venue for the third test against the West Indies.

Mrs Concrete Really?

Ratcatcher No, it was just a little joke. Actually, I am the Council Ratcatcher.

Mrs Concrete Oh yes, we've been expecting you.

Ratcatcher Oh, I gather you've got a little rodental problem.

Mrs Concrete Oh, blimey. You'd think he was awake all the night, scrabbling down by the wainscotting.

Ratcatching Um, that's an interesting word, isn't it?

Mrs Concrete What?

Ratcatcher Wainscotting . . . Wainscotting . . . Wainscotting . . . sounds like a little Dorset village, doesn't it? Wainscotting.

Cut to the village of Wains Cotting. A woman rushes out of a house.

Woman We've been mentioned on telly!

Cut back to Concretes' house.

Ratcatcher Now, where is it worst?

Mrs Concrete Well, down here. You can usually hear them.

Indicates base of wall, which has a label on it saying 'Wainscotting'.

Ratcatcher Ssssh!

Voice Over Baa . . . baa . . . baa . . . baa . . . baa . . . baa . . .

Ratcatcher No, that's sheep you've got there.

Voice Over Baa . . . baa.

Ratcatcher No, that's definitely sheep. A bit of a puzzle, really.

Mrs Concrete Is it?

Ratcatcher Yeah, well, I mean it's (a) not going to respond to a nice piece of cheese and (b) it isn't going to fit into a trap.

Mrs Concrete Oh – what are you going to do?

Ratcatcher Well, we'll have to look for the hole.

We follow them as they look along the wainscotting.

Mrs Concrete Oh yeah. There's one here.

She indicates a small black mousehole.

Ratcatcher No, no, that's mice.

He reaches in and pulls out a line of mice strung out on a piece of elastic. Then he lets go so they shoot in again. The ratcatcher moves on. He moves a chair, behind which there is a three-foot-high black hole.

Ratcatcher Ah, this is what we're after.

The baaings get louder. At this point six cricketers enter the room.

Cricketer (JOHN) Excuse me, is the third test in here?

Mr Concrete No – that was a joke – a joke!

Cricketer Oh blimey. *(exeunt)*

Ratcatcher Right. Well, I'm going in the wainscotting.

Cut to 'Wains Cotting' woman, who rushes out again.

Woman They said it again.

Back to the sitting room.

Ratcatcher I'm going to lay down some sheep poison.

He disappears into the hole. We hear:

Voice Over Baa, baa, baa.

A gunshot. The ratcatcher reappears clutching his arm.

Ratcatcher Aagh. Ooh! It's got a gun!

Mrs Concrete Blimey.

Ratcatcher Now, normally a sheep is a placid, timid creature, but you've got a killer.

Poster: 'Wanted For Armed Robbery – Basil' with a picture of a sheep. Exciting crime-type music. Mix through to newspaper headlines: 'Farmers Ambushed in Pen', 'Merino Ram in Wages Grab'. Eerie science fiction music; mix through to a laboratory. A scientist looking through microscope and his busty attractive assistant.

Professor (ERIC) It's an entirely new strain of sheep, a killer sheep that can not only hold a rifle but is also a first-class shot

Assistant But where are they coming from, professor?

Professor That I don't know. I just don't know. I really just don't know. I'm afraid I really just don't know. I'm afraid even I really just don't know. I have to tell you I'm afraid even I really just don't know. I'm afraid I have to tell you . . . *(she hands him a glass of water which she had been busy getting as soon as he started into this speech)* . . . thank you . . . *(resuming normal breezy voice)* . . . I don't know. Our only clue is this portion of wolf's clothing which the killer sheep . . .

Cut to Viking.

Viking (TERRY G) . . . was wearing . . .

Cut back to sketch.

Professor . . . in yesterday's raid on Selfridges.

Assistant I'll carry out tests on it straight away, professor.

She opens a door to another lab; but it is full of cricketers.

Cricketer (JOHN) Hello, is the third test in here, please?

She slams the door on them.

Assistant Professor, there are some cricketers in the laboratory.

Professor This may be even more serious than even I had at first been imagining. What a strange . . . strange line. There's no time to waste. Get me the Chief Commissioner of Police.

Assistant Yes, sir!

She opens a cupboard and slides out the Chief Commissioner of Police on a sort of slab. He grins and waves cheerily. 'This is Your Life' music and applause.

Professor No, no, on the phone.

Assistant Oh . . . *(she pushes him back in)*

Professor Look of fear! *(he is staring transfixed at something in the doorway)* Another strange line. Look out, Miss Garter Oil!

Assistant Professor! What is it? What have you seen?

Professor Look – there, in the doorway.

Cut to doorway: through it is animation of a huge sheep with an eye patch.

Assistant Urghhh! Arthur X! Leader of the Pennine Gang!

ANIMATION: *perhaps even mixed with stock film – as the fevered mind of Gilliam takes it – sheep armed to the teeth, sheep executing dangerous raids, Basil Cassidy and the Sundance Sheep, sheep with machine gun coming out of its arse etc.*
At the end of the animation, cut to studio. A narrator sitting in what could be a news set at a desk.

Narrator (MICHAEL) But soon the killer sheep began to infect other animals with its startling intelligence. Pussy cats began to arrange mortgages, cocker spaniels began to design supermarkets ...
Cut back to the animation again: a parrot.

Parrot And parrots started to announce television programmes. It's 8 o'clock and time for the News.
Cut back to the same narrator at desk.

Narrator Good evening. Here is the News for parrots. No parrots were involved in an accident on the M1 today, when a lorry carrying high octane fuel was in collision with a bollard ... that is a *bollard* and not a *parrot*. A spokesman for parrots said he was glad no parrots were involved. The Minister of Technology *(photo of minister with parrot on his shoulder)* today met the three Russian leaders *(cut to photograph of Brezhnev, Podgorny and Kosygin all in a group and each with a parrot on his shoulder)* to discuss a £4 million airliner deal ... *(cut back to narrator)* None of them went in the cage, or swung on the little wooden trapeze, or ate any of the nice millet seed yum, yum. That's the end of the news. Now our programmes for parrots continue with part three of 'A Tale of Two Cities' specially adapted for parrots by Joey Boy. The story so far ... Dr Manette is in England after eighteen years *(as he speaks French Revolution type music creeps in under his words)* in the Bastille. *(cut through to a Cruikshank engraving of London).* His daughter Lucy awaits her lover Charles Darnay, whom we have just learnt is in fact the nephew of the Marquis de St Evremond, whose cruelty had placed Manette in the Bastille. Darnay arrives to find Lucy tending her aged father ...

SUPERIMPOSED CAPTION: 'LONDON 1793'
Music reaches a climax and we mix slowly through to an eighteenth-century living room. Lucy is nursing her father. Some low music continues over. Suddenly the door bursts open and Charles Darnay enters.

Darnay (GRAHAM) *(in parrot voice)* 'Allo, 'allo.

Lucy (CAROL) 'Allo, 'allo, 'allo.
Old Man (TERRY J) 'Allo, 'allo, 'allo.
Darnay Who's a pretty boy, then?
Lucy 'Allo, 'allo, 'allo.

> *And more of the same.*
> *Cut back to the narrator.*

Narrator And while that's going on, here is the news for gibbons. No gibbons were involved today in an accident on the M1 . . .

> *The narrator's voice fades.*

Voice Over (TERRY J) And while that's going on, here from Westminster is a Parliamentary report for humans.

> *Man sitting at a desk; the set behind him says 'Today in Parliament'.*

Cyril (ERIC) In the debate a spokesman accused the Government of being silly and doing not at all good things. The member accepted this in a spirit of healthy criticism, but denied that he'd ever been naughty with a choirboy. Angry shouts of 'what about the watermelon, then?' were ordered by the Speaker to be stricken from the record and put into a brown paper bag in the lavvy. Any further interruptions would be cut off and distributed amongst the poor. For the Government a Front Bench Spokesman said the agricultural tariff *would* have to be raised, and he fancied a bit. Furthermore, he argued, this would give a large boost to farmers, and a lot of fun to him, his friend and Miss Moist of Knightsbridge. From the back benches there were opposition shouts of 'postcards for sale' and a healthy cry of 'who likes a sailor, then?' from the Minister without Portfolio. Replying, the Shadow Minister said, he could no longer deny the rumours but he and the dachshund were very happy; and, in any case, he argued, rhubarb was cheap and what was the harm in a sauna bath.

> *Cut to original narrator.*

CAPTION: '7 HOURS LATER'

Narrator . . . were not involved. The Minister of Technology *(cut to photograph of minister with a wombat on his shoulder)* met the three Russian leaders today *(Russian leaders again all with wombats on their shoulders)* to discuss a £4 million airliner deal. None of them were indigenous to Australia, carried their babies in pouches or ate any of those yummy eucalyptus leaves. Yum, yum. That's the news for wombats, and now Attila the Bun!

> ANIMATION: *a vicious rampaging bun.*

Voice Over (JOHN) Well that's all for Attila the Bun, and now – idiots!

> *A village idiot in smock and straw hat, red cheeks, straw in mouth, sitting on a wall, making funny noises and rolling his eyes.*

Voice Over (ERIC) Arthur Figgis is an idiot. A village idiot. Tonight we look at the idiot in society.

Cut to close-up of Figgis talking to camera. Very big close-up losing the top and bottom of his head.

Figgis (JOHN) *(educated voice)* Well I feel very keenly that the idiot *is* a part of the old village system, and as such has a vital role to play in a modern rural society, because you see ... *(suddenly switches to rural accent)* ooh ar ooh ar before the crops go gey are in the medley crun and the birds slides nightly on the oor ar ... *(vicar passes and gives him sixpence)* Ooh ar thankee, Vicar ... *(educated voice)* There is this very real need in society for someone whom almost anyone can look down on and ridicule. And this is the role that ... ooh ar naggy gamly rangle tandle oogly noogle ooblie oog ... *(passing lady gives him sixpence)* Thank you, Mrs Thompson ... this is the role that I and members of my family have fulfilled in this village for the past four hundred years ... Good morning, Mr Jenkins, ICI have increased their half-yearly dividend, I see.

We see Mr Jenkins pass, he is also an idiot, identically dressed.

Mr Jenkins (MICHAEL) Yes, splendid.

Figgis That's Mr Jenkins – he's another idiot. And so you see the idiot does provide a vital psycho-social service for this community. Oh, excuse me, a coach party has just arrived. I shall have to fall off the wall, I'm afraid.

He falls backwards off the wall. Cut to Figgis in idiot's costume coming out of a suburban house. He walks on to the lawn on which are several pieces of gym equipment. He runs head-on into horse (speeded up) and falls over, concussed.

Voice Over (ERIC) Arthur takes idiotting seriously. He is up at six o'clock every morning working on special training equipment designed to keep him silly. And of course he takes great pride in his appearance.

Figgis, dressed in nice clean smock, jumps into a pond. He immediately scrambles up, pulls out a mirror and pats mud on his face critically, as if making-up.

Voice Over Like the doctor, the blacksmith, the carpenter, Mr Figgis is an important figure in this village and – like them – he uses the local bank.

Village square. A bank. Figgis is walking towards it. People giggling and pointing. He goes into a silly routine. Figgis enters the bank. Cut to bank manager standing outside bank.

CAPTION: 'M. BRANDO – BANK MANAGER'

Bank Manager (GRAHAM) Yes, we have quite a number of idiots banking here.

Voice Over (MICHAEL) What kind of money is there in idiotting?

Manager Well nowadays a really blithering idiot can make anything up to ten thousand pounds a year – if he's the head of some big industrial combine. But of course, the more old-fashioned idiot still refuses to take money.

We see Figgis handing over a cheque to cashier; cashier pushes across a pile of moss, pebbles, bits of wood and acorns.

Manager *(voice over)* He takes bits of string, wood, dead budgerigars, sparrows, anything, but it does make the cashier's job very difficult; but of course they're fools to themselves because the rate of interest over ten years on a piece of moss or a dead vole is almost negligible.

A clerk appears at door of bank.

Clerk (TERRY J) Mr Brando.

Manager Yes?

Clerk Hollywood on the phone.

Manager I'll take it in the office.

Cut to a woodland glade.

Voice Over (ERIC) But Mr Figgis is no ordinary idiot. He is a lecturer in idiocy at the University of East Anglia. Here he is taking a class of third-year students.

Half a dozen loonies led by Figgis come dancing through the glade singing tunelessly. They are wearing long University scarves.

Voice Over After three years of study these apprentice idiots receive a diploma of idiocy, a handful of mud and a kick on the head.

A vice-chancellor stands in a University setting with some young idiots in front of him. They wear idiot gear with BA hoods. One walks forward to him, he gets a diploma, a faceful of mud and stoops to receive his kick on the head. Cut to happy parents smiling proudly.

Voice Over But some of the older idiots resent the graduate idiot.

Old Idiot (ERIC) I'm a completely self-taught idiot. I mean, ooh arh, ooh arhh, ooh arhh, . . . nobody does that anymore. Anybody who did that round here would be laughed off the street. No, nowadays people want something wittier.

Wife empties breakfast over him. Cut to idiot falling repeatedly off a wall.

Voice Over Kevin O'Nassis works largely with walls.

Kevin (JOHN) *(voice over)* You've got to know what you're doing. I mean, some people think I'm mad. The villagers say I'm mad, the tourists say I'm mad, well I *am* mad, but I'm *naturally* mad. I don't use any chemicals.

Voice Over But what of the idiot's private life? How about his relationship with women?

Idiot in bed. Pull back to reveal he shares it with two very young, thin, nude girls.

Idiot (JOHN) Well I may be an idiot but I'm no fool.

Voice Over But the village idiot's dirty smock and wall-falling are a far cry from the modern world of the urban idiot. *(stock film of city gents in their own clothes pouring out of trains)* What kinds of backgrounds do these city idiots come from?

Vox pops film of city gents. Subtitles explain their exaggerated accents.

First City Idiot (JOHN) Eton, Sandhurst and the Guards, ha, ha, ha, ha.

Second City Idiot (MICHAEL) I can't remember but I've got it written down somewhere.

Third City Idiot (GRAHAM) Daddy's a banker. He needed a wastepaper basket.

Fourth City Idiot (TERRY J) Father was Home Secretary and mother won the Derby.

Cut to a commentator with mike in close-up. Pull back in his speech, to discover he is standing in front of the main gate at Lords cricket ground.

Interviewer (GRAHAM) The headquarters of these urban idiots is here in St John's Wood. Inside they can enjoy the company of other idiots and watch special performances of ritual idiotting.

Cut to quick wide-shot of cricket match being played at Lords. Cut to five terribly old idiots watching.

First Idiot (MICHAEL) Well left.

Second Idiot (GRAHAM) Well played.

Third Idiot (ERIC) Well well.

Fourth Idiot (JOHN) Well bred.

Fifth Idiot (TERRY J) *(dies)* Ah!

Another very quick wide-shot of Lords. There is nothing at all happening and we can't distinguish anyone. Cut to three TV commentators in modern box, with sliding window open. They are surrounded by bottles.

Jim (JOHN) Good afternoon and welcome to Lords on the second day of the first test. So far today we've had five hours batting from England and already they're nought for nought. Cowdrey is not out nought. Naughton is not in. Knott is in and is nought for not out. Naughton of Northants got a nasty knock on the nut in the nets last night but it's nothing of note. Next in is Nat Newton of Notts. Not Nutting – Nutting's at nine, er, Nutting knocked neatie nighty knock knock . . . *(another commentator nudges him)* . . . anyway England have played extremely well for nothing, not a sausage, in reply to Iceland's first innings total of 722 for 2 declared, scored yesterday disappointingly fast in only twenty-one overs with lots of wild slogging and boundaries and all sorts of rubbishy things. But

the main thing is that England have made an absolutely
outstanding start so far, Peter?

Peter (GRAHAM) Splendid. Just listen to those thighs. And now it's the
North East's turn with the Samba. Brian.

Brian (ERIC) *(he has an enormous nose)* Rather. *(opens book)* I'm reminded
of the story of Gubby Allen in '32 . . .

Jim Oh, shut up or we'll close the bar. And now Bo Wildeburg is running
up to bowl to Cowdrey, he runs up, he bowls to Cowdrey . . .

*Cut to fast bowler. He bowls the ball but the batsman makes no move
whatsoever. The ball passes the off stump.*

Jim . . . and no shot at all. Extremely well not played there.

Peter Yes, beautifully not done anything about.

Brian A superb shot of no kind whatsoever. I well remember Plum
Warner leaving a very similar ball alone in 1732.

Jim Oh shut up, long nose.

Peter falls off his chair.

And now it's Bo Wildeburg running in again to bowl to Cowdrey,
he runs in. *(bowler bowls as before; ball goes by as before)* He bowls to
Cowdrey – and no shot at all, a superb display of inertia there . . .
And that's the end of the over, and drinks.

Peter Gin and tonic please.

Jim No, no the *players* are having drinks. And now, what's happening? I
think Cowdrey's being taken off.

*Two men in white coats, à la furniture removers, so maybe they're brown
coats, are carrying the batsman off. Two men pass them with a green
Chesterfield sofa making for the wicket.*

Yes, Cowdrey is being carried off. Well I never. Now who's in
next, it should be number three, Natt Newton of Notts . . . get
your hand off my thigh, West . . . no I don't think it is . . . I think
it's er, it's the sofa . . . no it's the Chesterfield! The green
Chesterfield is coming in at number three to take guard now.

Brian I well remember a similar divan being brought on at Headingley in
9 BC against the darkies.

Jim Oh, shut up, elephant snout. And now the green Chesterfield has
taken guard and Iceland are putting on their spin dryer to bowl.

*Furniture fielding. The whole pitch is laid out with bits of furniture in
correct positions. Three chairs in the slips; easy chair keeping wicket; bidet
at mid; TV set at cover; bookcase at mid off; roll-top writing desk at
square; radiator at mid wicket etc. The spin dryer moves forward and
bowls a real ball with its snozzle to a table, which is at the batting end
with cricket pads on. It hits the table on the pad. Appeal.*

Jim The spin dryer moves back to his mark, it runs out to the wicket,
bowls to the table . . . a little bit short but it's coming in a bit there

and it's hit him on the pad ... and the table is out, leg before wicket. That is England nought for one.

Different Voice Over (MICHAEL) And now we leave Lords and go over to Epsom for the three o'clock.

Cut to a race course. Furniture comes into shot racing the last fifty yards to the finishing post.

Commentator (ERIC) Well here at Epsom we take up the running with fifty yards of this mile and a half race to go and it's the wash basin in the lead from WC Pedestal. Tucked in nicely there is the sofa going very well with Joanna Southcott's box making a good run from hat stand on the rails, and the standard lamp is failing fast but it's wash basin definitely taking up the running now being strongly pressed by ... At the post it's the wash basin from WC then sofa, hat stand, standard lamp and lastly Joanna Southcott's box.

Cut to three bishops shouting from actual studio audience.

Bishops Open the box! Open the box! Open the box! Open the box! Open the box!

A simple 'Take Your Pick' style set with a Michael Miles grinning type monster standing at centre of it.

Michael Miles (JOHN) And could we have the next contender, please? *(a pepperpot walks out into the set towards Michael Miles)* Ha ha ha ... Good evening, madam, and your name is?

Woman (TERRY J) Yes, yes.

Michael Miles And what's your name?

Woman I go to church regularly.

Michael Miles Jolly good, I see, and which prize do you have particular eyes on this evening?

Woman I'd like the blow on the head.

Michael Miles The blow on the head.

Woman Just there.

Michael Miles Jolly good. Well your first question for the blow on the head this evening is: what great opponent of Cartesian dualism resists the reduction of psychological phenomena to physical states?

Woman I don't know that!

Michael Miles Well, have a guess.

Woman Henri Bergson.

Michael Miles Is the correct answer!

Woman Ooh, that was lucky. I never even heard of him.

Michael Miles Jolly good.

Woman I don't like darkies.

Michael Miles Ha ha ha. Who does! And now your second question for the blow on the head is: what is the main food that penguins eat?

Woman Pork luncheon meat.

Michael Miles No.

Woman Spam?

Michael Miles No, no, no. What do penguins eat? Penguins.

Woman Penguins?

Michael Miles Yes.

Woman I hate penguins.

Michael Miles No, no, no.

Woman They eat themselves.

Michael Miles No, no, what do *penguins* eat?

Woman Horses! . . . Armchairs!

Michael Miles No, no, no. What do penguins eat?

Woman Oh, penguins.

Michael Miles Penguins.

Woman Cannelloni.

Michael Miles No.

Woman Lasagna, moussaka, lobster thermidor, escalopes de veau à
l'estragon avec endives gratinéed with cheese.

Michael Miles No, no, no, no. I'll give you a clue. *(mimes a fish
swimming)*

Woman Ah! Brian Close.

Michael Miles No. no.

Woman Brian Inglis, Brian Johnson, Bryan Forbes.

Michael Miles No, no!

Woman Nanette Newman.

Michael Miles No. What swims in the sea and gets caught in nets?

Woman Henri Bergson.

Michael Miles No.

Woman Goats. Underwater goats with snorkels and flippers.

Michael Miles No, no.

Woman A buffalo with an aqualung.

Michael Miles No, no.

Woman Reginald Maudling.

Michael Miles Yes, that's near enough. I'll give you that. Right, now,
Mrs Scum, you have won your prize, do you still want the blow on
the head?

Woman Yes, yes.

Michael Miles I'll offer you a poke in the eye.

Woman No! I want a blow on the head.

Michael Miles A punch in the throat.

Woman No.

Michael Miles All right then, a kick in the kneecap.

Woman No.

Michael Miles Mrs Scum, I'm offering you a boot in the teeth and a
dagger up the strap.

Woman Er . . .

Voices Blow on the head! Take the blow on the head!

Woman No, no. I'll take the blow on the head.

Michael Miles Very well then, Mrs Scum, you have won tonight's star prize, the blow on the head.

> *He strikes her on head with an enormous mallet and she falls unconscious. A sexily dressed girl in the background (Graham) strikes a small gong. The three bishops rush in and jump on her. Cut to sign:*

LICENCE FEES FROM 1ST JANUARY 1969

COLOUR TV AND RADIO £11-0-0

TV AND RADIO £6-0-0

RADIO ONLY £1-5-0

Roll credits over.

CAPTION: THE END

Twenty-one

BBC 1 World symbol.

Voice Over (ERIC) Here is a preview of some of the programmes you'll be able to see coming shortly on BBC Television. To kick off with there's variety . . . *(still picture of Peter West and Brian Johnston)* Peter West and Brian Johnston star in 'Rain Stopped Play', a whacky new comedy series about the gay exploits of two television cricket commentators *(photo of E. W. Swanton)* with E. W. Swanton as Aggie the kooky Scots maid. For those of you who don't like variety, there's variety, with Brian Close at the Talk of the Town. *(Brian Close in cricket whites on a stage)* And of course there'll be sport. The Classics series *(engraving of London and caption: 'The Classics')* return to BBC 2 with twenty-six episodes of John Galsworthy's 'Snooker My Way' *(composite photo of Nyree Dawn Porter holding a snooker cue)* with Nyree Dawn Porter repeating her triumph as Joe Davis. And of course there'll be sport. Comedy is not forgotten *(Caption: 'Comedy')* with Jim Laker *(photo of Laker)* in 'Thirteen Weeks of Off-spin Bowling'. Jim plays the zany bachelor bowler in a new series of 'Owzat', with Anneley Brummond-Haye on Mr Softee *(photo of same)* as his wife. And of course there'll be sport. 'Panorama' will be returning, introduced *('Panorama' caption with photo of Tony Jacklin)* as usual by Tony Jacklin, and Lulu *(photo of Lulu)* will be tackling the Old Man of Hoy *(photo of same)*. And for those of you who prefer drama – there's sport. On 'Show of the Week' Kenneth Wostenholme sings. *(still of him, superimposed over Flick Colby Dancers, Pans People, ono)* And for those of you who don't like television there's David Coleman. *(picture of him smiling)* And of course there'll be sport. But now for something completely different – sport.

'Grandstand' signature tune starts and then abruptly cuts into the usual animated credit titles.

ANIMATION: *a sketch about an archaeological find leads to:*

CAPTION: 'ARCHAEOLOGY TODAY'

Interview set for archaeology programme. Chairman and two guests sit in chairs in front of a blow-up of an old cracked pot.

Interviewer (MICHAEL) Hello. On 'Archaeology Today' tonight I have with me Professor Lucien Kastner of Oslo University.

Kastner (TERRY J) Good evening.

Interviewer How tall are you, professor?

Kastner . . . I beg your pardon?

Interviewer How tall are you?

Kastner I'm about five foot ten.

Interviewer ... and an expert in Egyptian tomb paintings. Sir Robert ... *(turning to Kastner)* are you really five foot ten?

Kastner Yes.

Interviewer Funny, you look much shorter than that to me. Are you slumped forward in your chair at all?

Kastner No, er I ...

Interviewer Extraordinary. Sir Robert Eversley, who's just returned from the excavations in El Ara, and you must be well over six foot. Isn't that right, Sir Robert?

Sir Robert (JOHN) *(puzzled)* Yes.

Interviewer In fact, I think you're six foot five aren't you?

Sir Robert Yes.

Applause from off. Sir Robert looks up in amazement.

Interviewer Oh, that's marvellous. I mean you're a totally different kind of specimen to Professor Kastner. Straight in your seat, erect, firm ...

Sir Robert Yes. I thought we were here to discuss archaeology.

Interviewer Yes, yes, of course we are, yes, absolutely, you're absolutely right! That's positive thinking for you. *(to Kastner)* You wouldn't have said a thing like that, would you? You five-foot-ten weed. *(he turns his back very ostentatiously on Kastner)* Sir Robert Eversley, (who's very interesting) what have you discovered in the excavations at El Ara?

Sir Robert *(picking up a beautiful ancient vase)* Well basically we have found a complex of tombs ...

Interviewer Very good speaking voice.

Sir Robert ... which present dramatic evidence of Polynesian influence in Egypt in the third dynasty which is quite remarkable.

Interviewer How tall were the Polynesians?

Kastner They were ...

Interviewer Sh!

Sir Robert Well, they were rather small, seafaring ...

Interviewer Short men, were they ... eh? All squat and bent up?

Sir Robert Well, I really don't know about that ...

Interviewer Who were the tall people?

Sir Robert I'm afraid I don't know.

Interviewer Who's that very tall tribe in Africa?

Sir Robert Well, this is hardly archaeology.

Interviewer The Watutsi! That's it – the Watutsi! Oh, that's the tribe, some of them were eight foot tall. Can you imagine that. Eight foot of Watutsi. Not one on another's shoulders, oh no – eight foot of solid Watutsi. That's what I call tall.

Sir Robert Yes, but it's nothing to do with archaeology.

Interviewer *(knocking Sir Robert's vase to the floor)* Oh to hell with archaeology!

Kastner Can I please speak! I came all the way from Oslo to do this programme! I'm a professor of archaeology. I'm an expert in ancient civilizations. All right, I'm only five foot ten. All right my posture is bad, all right I slump in my chair. But I've had more women than either of you two! I've had half bloody Norway, that's what I've had! So you can keep your Robert Eversley! And you can keep your bloody Watutsi! I'd rather have my little body . . . my little five-foot-ten-inch body . . . *(he breaks down sobbing)*

Sir Robert Bloody fool. Look what you've done to him.

Interviewer Don't bloody fool me.

Sir Robert I'll do what I like, because I'm six foot five and I eat punks like you for breakfast.

Sir Robert floors the interviewer with an almighty punch. Interviewer looks up rubbing his jaw.

Interviewer I'll get you for that, Eversley! I'll get you if I have to travel to the four corners of the earth!

Crash of music. Music goes into theme and film titles as for a Western.

CAPTION: 'FLAMING STAR – THE STORY OF ONE MAN'S SEARCH FOR VENGEANCE IN THE RAW AND VIOLENT WORLD OF INTERNATIONAL ARCHAEOLOGY'

Cut to stock film of the pyramids (circa 1920).

SUPERIMPOSED CAPTION: 'EGYPT – 1920'

An archaeological dig in a flat sandy landscape. All the characters are in twenties' clothes. Pan across the complex of passages and trenches.

Danielle (CAROL) *(voice over)* The dig was going well that year. We had discovered some Hittite baking dishes from the fifth dynasty, and Sir Robert was happier than I had ever seen him.

Camera comes to rest on Sir Robert Eversley digging away. We close in on him as he sings to Hammond organ accompaniment.

Sir Robert Today I hear the robin sing
Today the thrush is on the wing
Today who knows what life will bring
Today . . .

He stops and picks up an object, blows the dust off it and looks at it wondrously.

Sir Robert Why, a Sumerian drinking vessel of the fourth dynasty. *(sings)* Today!!!! *(speaks)* Catalogue this pot, Danielle, it's fourth dynasty.

Danielle Oh, is it . . . ?

Sir Robert Yes, it's . . . Sumerian.

Danielle Oh, how wonderful! Oh, I am so happy for you.

Sir Robert I'm happy too, now at last we know there was a Sumerian

influence here in Abu Simnel in the early pre-dynastic period, two thousand years before the reign of Tutankhamun. *(he breaks into song again)*
(singing) Today I hear the robin sing
Today the thrush is on the wing
(Danielle joins in)
Today who knows what life will bring.

They are just about to embrace, when there is a jarring chord and long crash. The interviewer, in the clothes he wore before, is standing on the edge of the dig.

Interviewer All right Eversley, get up out of that trench.

Sir Robert Don't forget . . . I'm six foot five.

Interviewer That doesn't worry me . . . Kastner!

He snaps his fingers. From behind him Professor Kastner appears, fawningly.

Kastner Here Lord.

Interviewer Up!

He snaps his fingers and Kastner leaps onto his shoulders.

Sir Robert Eleven foot three!

Kastner I'm so tall! I am so tall!

Sir Robert Danielle!

Danielle leaps on his shoulders.

Interviewer Eleven foot six – damn you! Abdul!

A servant appears on Kastner's shoulders.

Sir Robert Fifteen foot four! Mustapha!

A servant appears on Danielle's shoulders.

Interviewer Nineteen foot three . . . damn you!

The six of them charge each other. They fight in amongst the trestle tables with rare pots on them breaking and smashing them. When the fight ends everyone lies dead in a pile of broken pottery. The interviewer crawls up to camera and produces a microphone from his pocket. He is covered in blood and in his final death throes.

Interviewer And there we end this edition of 'Archaeology Today'. Next week, the Silbury Dig by Cole Porter with Pearl Bailey and Arthur Negus. *(he dies)*

Voice Over (MICHAEL) And now an appeal for sanity from the Reverend Arthur Belling.

Cut to studio. A vicar sitting facing camera. He has an axe in his head.

Reverend Belling (GRAHAM) You know, there are many people in the country today who, through no fault of their own, are sane. Some of them were born sane. Some of them became sane later in their lives. It is up to people like you and me who are out of our tiny little minds to try and help these people overcome their sanity. You can start in small ways with ping-pong ball eyes and a funny voice and then you can paint half of your body red and the other half green and then you can jump up and down in a bowl of treacle going 'squawk, squawk, squawk . . .' And then you can go 'Neurhhh! Neurhh!' and then you can roll around on the floor going 'pting pting pting' . . . *(he rolls around on the floor)*

Voice Over The Reverend Arthur Belling is Vicar of St Loony Up The Cream Bun and Jam. And now an appeal on behalf of the National Trust.

CAPTION: 'AN APPEAL ON BEHALF OF THE NATIONAL TRUSS'
Cut to a smartly dressed woman.

Woman (ERIC) Good evening. My name is Leapy Lee. No, sorry. That's the name of me favourite singer. My name is Mrs Fred Stolle. No, no, Mrs Fred Stolle is the wife of me favourite tennis player. My name is Bananas. No, no, that's me favourite fruit. I'm Mrs Nice-evening-out-at-the-pictures-then-perhaps-a-dance-at-a-club-and-back-to-his-place-for-a-quick-cup-of-coffee-and-little-bit-of – no! No, sorry, that's me favourite way of spending a night out. Perhaps I *am* Leapy Lee? Yes! I must be Leapy Lee! Hello fans! Leapy Lee here! *(sings)* Little arrows that will . . . *(phone rings, she answers)* Hello? . . . Evidently I'm *not* Leapy Lee. I thought I probably wouldn't be. Thank you, I'll tell them. *(puts phone down)* Hello. Hello, Denis Compton here. No no . . . I should have written it down. Now where's that number? *(as she looks in her bag she talks to herself)* I'm Mao Tse Tung . . . I'm P. P. Arnold . . . I'm Margaret Thatcher . . . I'm Sir Gerald Nabarro . . . *(she dials)* Hello? Sir Len Hutton here. Could you tell me, please . . . oh, am I? Oh, thank you. *(puts phone down)* Good evening. I'm Mrs What-number-are-you-dialling-please?

A boxer (Terry G) rushes in and fells her with one blow. After Women's Institute applauding cut to: a man coming through a door with a neat little bride in a bridal dress. The man walks up to the registrar who is sitting at his desk with a sign saying 'Registrar of Marriages'.

Man (ERIC) Good morning.
Registrar (TERRY J) Good morning.
Man Are you the registrar?
Registrar I have that function.
Man I was here on Saturday, getting married to a blond girl, and I'd like to change please. I'd like to have this one instead please.
Registrar What do you mean?
Man Er, well, the other one wasn't any good, so I'd like to swap it for this one, please. Er, I have paid. I paid on Saturday. Here's the ticket. *(gives him the marriage licence.)*

Registrar Ah, ah, no. That was when you were married.

Man Er, yes. That was when I was married to the wrong one. I didn't like the colour. This is the one I want to have, so if you could just change the forms round I can take this one back with me now.

Registrar I can't do that.

Man Look, make it simpler, I'll pay again.

Registrar No, you can't *do* that.

Man Look, all I want you to do is change the wife, say the words, blah, blah, blah, back to my place, no questions asked.

Registrar I'm sorry sir, but we're not allowed to change.

Man You can at Harrods.

Registrar You can't.

Man You can. I changed my record player and there wasn't a grumble.

Registrar It's different.

Man And I changed my pet snake, and I changed my Robin Day tie.

Registrar Well, you can't change a bloody wife!

Man Oh, all right! Well, can I borrow one for the weekend.

Registrar No!

Man Oh, blimey, I only wanted a jolly good . . .

A whistle blows. A referee runs on, takes his book out and proceeds to take the name of the man in the registry office, amidst protests.

Referee (JOHN) All right, break it up. What's your number, then? All right. Name?

Man Cook.

Cut to the two in the next sketch waiting. Cut back to referee, who finishes booking the man and blows his whistle. The show continues. Cut to the two waiting. On the sound of the whistle they start acting.

Doctor (MICHAEL) Next please. Name?

Watson (GRAHAM) Er, Watson.

Doctor *(writing it down)* Mr Watson.

Watson Ah, no, Doctor.

Doctor Ah, Mr Doctor.

Watson No, not Mr, Doctor.

Doctor Oh, *Doctor* Doctor.

Watson No, Doctor *Watson*.

Doctor Oh, Doctor *Watson* Doctor.

Watson Oh, just call me darling.

Doctor Hello, Mr Darling.

Watson No, Doctor.

Doctor Hello Doctor Darling.

Sound of whistle; instant cut to:

CAPTION: 'THAT SKETCH HAS BEEN ABANDONED'

Animation sketch leads us into a cocktail party in Dulwich. Quiet party-type music. Constant chatter.

Host (GRAHAM) Ah, John. Allow me to introduce my next-door
    neighbour. John Stokes, this is A Snivelling Little Rat-Faced Git.
    Ah!

Git (TERRY J) Hello, I noticed a slight look of anxiety cross your face for a
    moment just then, but you needn't worry – I'm used to it. That's
    the trouble of having a surname like Git.

John (MICHAEL) Oh . . . yes, yes.

Git We did think once of having it changed by deed-poll, you know – to
    Watson or something like that. But A Snivelling Little Rat-Faced
    Watson's just as bad eh?

John Yes, yes, I suppose so.

    Mrs Git approaches.

Git Oh, that's my wife. Darling! Come and meet Mr . . . what was it?

John Stokes – John Stokes.

Git Oh yes. John Stokes, this is my wife, Dreary Fat Boring Old.

John Oh, er, how do you do.

Mrs Git (JOHN) How do *you* do.

    Mrs Stokes appears.

Mrs Stokes (CAROL) Darling, there you are!

John Yes, yes, here I am, yes.

Git Oh, is this your wife?

John Yes, yes, yes, this is the wife. Yes. Um darling, these, these are the
    Gits.

Mrs Stokes *(slightly shocked)* What?

John The Gits.

Git Oh, heaven's sakes we are being formal. Does it have to be
    surnames?

John Oh, no, no. Not at all. No. Um, no, this . . . this . . . this is my wife
    Norah, er, Norah Jane, Norah Jane Stokes. This is Snivelling
    Little Rat-Faced Git. And this is his wife Dreary Fat Boring Old
    Git.

Git I was just telling your husband what an awful bore it is having a
    surname like Git.

Mrs Stokes *(understanding at last)* Oh! Oh well, it's not that bad.

Git Oh, you've no idea how the kids get taunted. Why, only last week
    Dirty Lying Little Two-Faced came running home from school,
    sobbing his eyes out, and our youngest, Ghastly Spotty Horrible
    Vicious Little is just at the age when taunts like 'she's a git' really
    hurt. Yes.

    Mrs Git gobs colourfully into her handbag.

John Do . . . do you live round here?

Git Yes, we live up the road, number 49 – you can't miss it. We've just
    had the outside painted with warm pus.

John *(with increasing embarrassment)* Oh.

Git Yes. It's very nice actually. It goes nicely with the vomit and catarrh we've got smeared all over the front door.

Mrs Stokes I think we ought to be going. We have two children to collect.

Git Oh, well, bring them round for tea tomorrow.

Mrs Stokes Well . . .

Git It's Ghastly Spotty Cross-Eyed's birthday and she's having a disembowelling party for a few friends. The Nauseas will be there, and Doug and Janice Mucus, and the Rectums from Swanage.

Voice Over (MICHAEL) and CAPTION: 'AND NOW A NICE VERSION OF THAT SAME SKETCH'

Cut to exactly the same set-up as before.

Host John! Allow me to introduce our next-door neighbour. John, this is Mr Watson.

Watson Hello. I noticed a slight look of anxiety cross your face just then but you needn't worry.

Cut to nun.

Nun (CAROL) I preferred the dirty version.

She is knocked out by the boxer.
Cut to Women's Institute applause film.
Big close-up Hank Spim (face only). He is obviously walking along, the camera is following him hand held.

Hank (GRAHAM) Well, I've been a hunter all my life. I love animals. That's why I like to kill 'em. I wouldn't kill an animal I didn't like. Goodday Roy.

Pull back to reveal he is walking with his brother in fairly rough country location. They pull a small trailer with 'high explosives' written in large letters on the side. The trailer has bombs in it. Hank takes a bazooka from the trailer.

Voice Over (JOHN) Hank and Roy Spim are tough, fearless backwoodsmen who have chosen to live in a violent, unrelenting world of nature's creatures, where only the fittest survive. Today they are off to hunt mosquitoes.

Big close-up Roy Spim. He is obviously searching for something.

Roy (ERIC) *(voice over)* The mosquito's a clever little bastard. You can track him for days and days until you really get to know him like a friend. He knows you're there, and you know he's there. It's a game of wits. You hate him, then you respect him, then you kill him.

Cut to Hank Spim who stands peering toward the horizon. Suddenly he points.

Voice Over Suddenly Hank spots the mosquito they're after.

Dramatic music. Crash zoom along Hank's eyeline to as big a close-up as we can get of a patch in a perfectly ordinary field. Cut back to Hank and Roy starting to crawl towards some bushes.

Voice Over Now more than ever, they must rely on the skills they have learnt from a lifetime's hunting. *(tense music, as they worm their way forward)* Hank gauges the wind. *(shot of Hank doing complicated wind gauging biz.)* Roy examines the mosquito's spoor. *(shot of Roy examining the ground intently)* Then . . . *(Roy fires a bazooka. Hank fires off a machine gun; a series of almighty explosions in the small patch of field; the gunfire stops and the smoke begins to clear)* It's a success. The mosquito now is dead. *(Hank and Roy approach the scorched and blackened patch in the field)* But Roy must make sure. *(Roy points machine gun at head of mosquito and fires off another few rounds)*

Roy There's nothing more dangerous than a wounded mosquito.

Narrator But the hunt is not over. With well practised skill Hank skins the mosquito. *(Hank produces an enormous curved knife and begins to start skinning the tiny mosquito)* The wings of a fully grown male mosquito can in fact fetch anything up to point eight of a penny on the open market. *(shot of them walking, carrying weapons)* The long day is over and it's back to base camp for a night's rest. *(inside villa; Hank is cleaning bazooka)* Here, surrounded by their trophies Roy and Hank prepare for a much tougher ordeal – a moth hunt.

Hank Well, I follow the moth in the helicopter to lure it away from the flowers, and then Roy comes along in the Lockheed Starfighter and attacks it with air-to-air missiles.

Roy A lot of people have asked us why we don't use fly spray. Well, where's the sport in that?

Shot of them driving in Land Rover heavily loaded with weapons.

Narrator *(voice over)* For Roy, sport is everything. Ever since he lost his left arm battling with an ant, Roy has risked his life in the pursuit of tiny creatures. *(a peaceful river bank; Roy and Hank are fishing)* But it's not all work and for relaxation they like nothing more than a day's fishing. *(Hank presses a button and there is a tremendous explosion in the water)* Wherever there is a challenge, Hank and Roy Spim will be there ready to carry on this primordial struggle between man and inoffensive, tiny insects.

Pull out to reveal the brothers standing on a tank. Heroic music reaches a climax.

Apropos of nothing cut to oak-panelled robing chamber in the Old Bailey. Two Judges in full wigs and red robes enter.

First Judge (ERIC) *(very camp)* Oh, I've had such a morning in the High Court. I could stamp my little feet the way those QC's carry on.

Second Judge (MICHAEL) *(just as camp)* Don't I know it, love.

First Judge Objection here, objection there! And that nice policeman giving his evidence so well – beautiful speaking voice ... well after a bit all I could do was bang my little gavel.

Second Judge You what, love?

First Judge I banged me gavel. I did me 'silence in court' bit. Ooh! If looks could kill that prosecuting counsel would be in for thirty years. How did your summing up go?

Second Judge Well, I was quite pleased actually. I was trying to do my butch voice, you know, 'what the jury must understand', and they loved it, you know. I could see that foreman eyeing me.

First Judge Really?

Second Judge Yes, cheeky devil.

First Judge Was he that tall man with that very big ... ?

Second Judge No, just a minute – I must finish you know. Anyway, I finished up with 'the actions of these vicious men is a violent stain on the community and the full penalty of the law is scarcely sufficient to deal with their ghastly crimes', and I waggled my wig! Just ever so slightly, but it was a stunning effect.

First Judge Oh, I bet it was ... like that super time I wore that striped robe in the Magistrates Court.

Second Judge Oh, aye.

Fade out. Fade into a bench in a public park, garden or square. A pepperpot is sitting on the bench. Another pepperpot comes by pushing a shopping trolley.

First Pepperpot (ERIC) Hello, Mrs Thing.

Second Pepperpot (GRAHAM) Hello, Mrs Entity.

First Pepperpot How are you then?

Second Pepperpot Oh, I have had a morning.

First Pepperpot Busy?

Second Pepperpot Busy – huh! I got up at five o'clock, I made myself a cup of tea, I looked out of the window. Well, by then I was so worn out I had to come and have a sit-down. I've been here for seven hours.

First Pepperpot You must be exhausted.

Second Pepperpot Mm. Oh, have you been shopping?

First Pepperpot No, I've been shopping.

Second Pepperpot Funny.

First Pepperpot I'm worn out. I've been shopping for six hours.

Second Pepperpot What have you bought, then?

First Pepperpot Nothing. Nothing at all. A complete waste of time.

Second Pepperpot Wicked, isn't it?

First Pepperpot Wicked. It'll be worse when we join the Common Market.

Second Pepperpot That nice Mr Heath would never allow that.

First Pepperpot It's funny he never married.

Second Pepperpot He's a bachelor.

First Pepperpot Oooh! That would explain it. Oh dear me, this chatting away wears me out.

Second Pepperpot Yes. I bet Mrs Reginald Maudling doesn't have to put up with all this drudgery, getting up at five in the morning, making a cup of tea, looking out of the window, chatting away.

First Pepperpot No! It'd all be done for her.

Second Pepperpot Yes, she'd have the whole day free for playing snooker.

First Pepperpot She probably wouldn't go through all the drudgery of playing snooker, day in, day out.

Second Pepperpot No, it would all be done for her. She wouldn't even have to lift the cue.

First Pepperpot She probably doesn't even know where the billiard room is.

Second Pepperpot No, still, it's not as bad as the old days. Mrs Stanley Baldwin used to have to get up at five o'clock in the morning and go out and catch partridges with her bare hands.

First Pepperpot Yes ... and Mrs William Pitt the Elder used to have to get up at three o'clock and go burrowing for truffles with the bridge of her nose.

Second Pepperpot Mrs Beethoven used to have to get up at midnight to spur on the mynah bird.

First Pepperpot Lazy creatures, mynah birds ...

Second Pepperpot Yes. When Beethoven went deaf the mynah bird just used to mime.

The picture begins to wobble as in 'flashback'; appropriate dreamy music effect.

First Pepperpot *(looking at camera)* Ooh! What's happening?

Second Pepperpot It's all right. It's only a flashback.

Cut to Beethoven's living room. A model mynah bird is opening and shutting its beak. Beethoven is sitting at the piano.

Beethoven (JOHN) You don't fool me, you stupid mynah bird. I'm not deaf yet.

Mynah Just you wait ... ha, ha, ha, ha, ha! *(Beethoven pulls a revolver and shoots the bird which falls to the ground)* Oh! Bugger ...

Beethoven Shut up!

Mynah Right in the wing.

Beethoven Shut your beak. Gott in Himmel ... I never get any peace here.

He plays the first few notes of the fifth symphony, trying vainly to get the last note. Mrs Beethoven enters.

Mrs Beethoven (GRAHAM) Ludwig!

Beethoven What?

Mrs Beethoven Have you seen the sugar bowl?

Beethoven No, I haven't seen the bloody sugar bowl.

Mrs Beethoven You know ... the *sugar* bowl.

Beethoven Sod the sugar bowl ... I'm trying to finish this stinking tune! It's driving me spare ... so shut up! *(she leaves; he goes into opening bars of 'Washington Post March')* No, no, no, no, no.

Mrs Beethoven comes back in.

Mrs Beethoven Ludwig, have you seen the jam spoon?

Beethoven Stuff the jam spoon!

Mrs Beethoven It was in the sugar bowl.

Beethoven Look, get out you old rat-bag. Buzz off and shut up.

Mrs Beethoven I don't know what you see in that piano. *(she goes)*

Beethoven Leave me alone!! ... *(gets the first eight notes right at last)* ... Ha! ha! ha! I've done it, I've done it!

Mrs Beethoven comes in again.

Mrs Beethoven Do you want peanut butter or sandwich spread for your tea?

Beethoven What!!!!

Mrs Beethoven PEANUT BUTTER ...

Beethoven I've forgotten it. *(plays a few wrong notes)* I had it! I had it!

Mrs Beethoven Do you want peanut butter or sandwich spread?

Beethoven I don't care!!

Mrs Beethoven Ooooh! I don't know. *(she goes out)*

Beethoven I *had* it. I *had* it you old bag. *(at the same moment as he gets it right again, the door flies open and Mrs Beethoven charges in with a very loud hoover)* Mein lieber Gott!! What are you doing? *(a terrible clanking and banging comes from the wall)* What's that! What's that!

Mrs Beethoven *(still hoovering loudly)* It's the plumber!

A jarring ring of the doorbell adds to the din.

Beethoven Gott in Himmel, I'm going out.

Mrs Beethoven Well, if you're going out don't forget we've got the Mendelssohns coming for tea so don't forget to order some pikelets.

Beethoven Pikelets, pikelets. Shakespeare never had this trouble.

Shakespeare washing up at a sink (present day).

Shakespeare (ERIC) You wanna bet? Incidentally, it's da-da-da-dum, da-da-da-dum.

Cut back to Beethoven.

Beethoven You're right! Oh, incidentally, why not call him Hamlet?

Cut back to Shakespeare.

Shakespeare Hamlet! I like, *much* better than David. *(he shouts through open window next to sink)* Michelangelo! You *can* use David. I won't sue.

Cut to Michelangelo's studio. Michelangelo is in middle of feeding and looking after at least six screaming little babies. His statue of David is in the foreground.

Michelangelo (TERRY J) Thanks, but I've had a better idea.

Camera pans down to show engraved on plinth beneath statue the words 'Michelangelo's fifth symphony'.

Wife *(off-screen)* Michelangelo!

Michelangelo Yes, dear!

Wife I've had another son.

Michelangelo Oh, my life.

Cut to Mozart. He is scrubbing the floor.

CAPTION: 'W. A. MOZART'

Mozart (MICHAEL) *(Jewish accent)* Composer? Huh! I wouldn't wish it on my son. He's a sensitive boy, already. I'd rather he was a sewage attendant or a ratcatcher.

Cut to street with old-fashioned shops. Exterior. Camera tracks in to a shopfront with a large sign outside: 'Rodent Exterminating Boutique – Colin "Chopper" Mozart (Son Of Composer) Ratcatcher To The Nobility And Ordinary People, Too – Ici On Parle Portugaise'. At the door of shop stands Colin Mozart. A kid runs up to him bearing a long cleft stick. Mozart takes the note from the cleavage and reads it.

Colin Mozart (MICHAEL) Aha! Rats at 42a Kartoffelnstrasse. Hey Mitzi! I gotta go to Potato Street.

Mitzi *(off-screen)* Put your galoshes on.

Mozart leaps on to a bike carrying two shrimp-nets, and rides off.

SUPERIMPOSED CAPTION: 'MUNICH 1821'

Colin Mozart *(shouting)* Depressed by rats? Do mice get you down? Then why not visit Colin Mozart's Rodent Extermination Boutique. Rats extirpated, mice punished, voles torn apart by Colin Mozart, Munich's leading furry animal liquidator.

Colin Mozart cycles up to Beethoven's house. Outside is a noticeboard saying:

MR AND MRS EMMANUEL KANT
FRAU MITZI HANDGEPÄCKAUFBEWAHRUNG
MR DICKIE WAGNER
K. TYNAN (NO RELATION)
MR AND MRS J. W. VON GOETHE AND DOG
HERR E. W. SWANTON
MR AND MRS P. ANKA
MR AND MRS LUDWIG VAN BEETHOVEN (1770–1827) ACCEPT NO
SUBSTITUTE

CAPTION: '13.4 SECONDS LATER'

Beethoven's front door is opened by Mrs Beethoven.

Mrs Beethoven   Yes?

Colin Mozart   Colin Mozart.

Mrs Beethoven   Oh, thank goodness you've come. We're having a terrible time with them bleeding rats. I think they live in his stupid piano already.

They go into the house. We hear the first two bars of Beethoven's Fifth counterpointed by loud squeaking.

Beethoven's Voice   Get out the bloody piano you stupid furry bucktoothed gits! Get out! Gott in Himmel. Get your stinking tail out of my face.

Mrs Beethoven opens the door and we see for the first time a strange sight. Rats are flying across the room (thrown from out of vision) others scuttle across floor (pulled by strings) others up wall. One sits on Beethoven's head. The squeaking is deafening. Beethoven plays on relentlessly. Mozart and Mrs Beethoven run into room and start trying to catch the rats with the shrimp-nets.

CAPTION: '13.4 MINUTES LATER'

Colin Mozart is sitting on the piano. He rakes the rat-infested room with machine-gun fire.

Beethoven   Shut up!

The picture starts to wobble and mixes back to the two pepperpots.

Second Pepperpot   So anyway, Beethoven was rather glad when he went deaf.

Mix to Beethoven pushing the keys of the keyboard which is all that remains of his piano. He listens vainly. The mynah bird opens and shuts its beak. In the corner an old horn gramophone plays. We hear Jimmy Durante singing the end of 'I'm the guy that found the lost chord'. Cut back to judges' robing room.

First Judge   Well, I was ever so glad they abolished hanging, you know, because that black cap just didn't suit me.

Second Judge   Yes. Do you remember the Glasgow treason trial?

First Judge   Oh yes, I wore a body stocking all through it.

Second Judge   No, hen, with the party afterwards.

First Judge   Oh, that's right. You were walking out with that very butch Clerk of the Court.

Second Judge   That's right. Ooh, he made me want to turn Queen's evidence.

Superimposed credits. Theme tune heard quietly as judges continue.

First Judge   Oh, me too. One summing up and I'm anybody's.

Second Judge   Anyway, Bailie Anderson.

First Judge   Ooh, her?

Second Judge   Yes. She's so strict. She was on at me for giving dolly sentences, you know, specially in that arson case.

First Judge What was the verdict?

Second Judge They preferred the brown wig.

First Judge Mm. I love the Scottish Assizes. I know what they mean by a really well-hung jury.

Second Judge Ooh! Get back in the witness box, you're too sharp to live!

First Judge I'll smack your little botty!

Second Judge Ooh! and again.

First Judge Have you tried that new body rub JP's use?

Second Judge I had a magistrate in Bradford yesterday.

First Judge Funnily enough I felt like one in a lunchtime recess today. *(credits end)* But the ones I really like are those voice over announcers on the BBC after the programmes are over.

Second Judge Oh, aye, of course, they're as bent as safety pins.

First Judge I know, but they've got beautiful speaking voices, haven't they? 'And now a choice of viewing on BBC Television.'

Second Judge 'Here are tonight's football results.'

First and Second Judges Mmm.

　　　Fade out.

Twenty-two

The camera tracks past five gorgeous lovelies in bikinis, all in send-up provocative pin-up poses. The sixth in the pan is the announcer at his desk also posing in a bikini (with bikini top).

John And now for something completely different.

Cut to 'It's' man, also in bikini.

It's Man It's . . .

Cut to credit titles as normal, except that the last shot is the little chicken man who drags across a banner reading 'How to recognize different parts of the body'.

Voice Over (JOHN) How to recognize different parts of the body.

Hold long enough to read this new title before the foot comes down, stays in shot long enough for voice over to say:

Voice Over Number one. The foot.

A little arrow points to the foot simultaneously. Cut to picture of Venus de Milo (top half). Superimposed little white arrow pointing to shoulder.

Voice Over Number two. The shoulder.

Cut to picture of a foot cut off at the ankle. Cigarettes are parked in the top. Superimposed arrow.

Voice Over And number three. The other foot.

Cut to profile picture of strange person (provided by Terry Gilliam). Superimposed arrow pointing to bridge of nose.

Voice Over Number four. The bridge of the nose.

Cut to picture, full length, of man wearing polka-dotted Bermuda shorts. Arrow superimposed points to shorts.

Voice Over Number five. The naughty bits.

Cut to picture of crooked elbow. Superimposed arrow pointing just above the elbow.

Voice Over Number six. Just above the elbow.

Cut to closer picture of different person in identical Bermuda shorts. Superimposed arrow pointing to top of groin.

Voice Over Number seven. Two inches to the right of a very naughty bit indeed.

Cut to close-up of a real knee. Arrow superimposed pointing to knee.

Voice Over Number eight. The kneecap.

Pull back to reveal the knee belongs to First Bruce, an Australian in full Australian outback gear. We briefly hear a record of 'Waltzing Matilda'. He is sitting in a very hot, slightly dusty room with low wicker chairs, a table in the middle, big centre fan, and old fridge.

Second Bruce (GRAHAM) Goodday, Bruce.

First Bruce (ERIC) Oh, hello, Bruce.

Third Bruce (MICHAEL) How are yer, Bruce?

First Bruce Bit crook, Bruce.

Second Bruce Where's Bruce?

First Bruce He's not here, Bruce.

Third Bruce Blimey s'hot in here, Bruce.

First Bruce S'hot enough to boil a monkey's bum.

Second Bruce That's a strange expression, Bruce.

First Bruce Well Bruce, I heard the prime minister use it. S'hot enough
to boil a monkey's bum in 'ere your Majesty, he said, and she
smiled quietly to herself.

Third Bruce She's a good Sheila, Bruce and not at all stuck up.

Second Bruce Ah, here comes the Bossfella now – how are you, Bruce?

Enter Fourth Bruce with the English person, Michael.

Fourth Bruce (JOHN) Goodday Bruce, Hello Bruce, how are you, Bruce?
Gentlemen, I'd like to introduce a chap from pommie land . . .
who'll be joining us this year here in the Philosophy Department of
the University of Woolamaloo.

All Goodday.

Fourth Bruce Michael Baldwin – this is Bruce. Michael Baldwin – this
is Bruce. Michael Baldwin – this is Bruce.

First Bruce Is your name not Bruce, then?

Michael (TERRY J) No, it's Michael.

Second Bruce That's going to cause a little confusion.

Third Bruce Yeah. Mind if we call you Bruce, just to keep it clear?

Fourth Bruce Well, gentlemen I think we'd better start the meeting.
Before we start though, I'll ask the padre for a prayer.

*First Bruce snaps a plastic dog-collar round his neck. They all lower their
heads.*

First Bruce O Lord we beseech thee, have mercy on our faculty, Amen.

All Amen.

Fourth Bruce Crack the tubes, right. *(Third Bruce starts opening beer cans)*
Er, Bruce, I now call upon you to welcome Mr Baldwin to the
Philosophy Department.

Second Bruce I'd like to welcome the pommy bastard to God's own
earth and I'd like to remind him that we don't like stuck-up
sticky-beaks here.

All Hear, hear. Well spoken, Bruce.

Fourth Bruce Now, Bruce teaches classical philosophy, Bruce teaches
Hegelian philosophy, and Bruce here teaches logical positivism and
is also in charge of the sheepdip.

Third Bruce What does new Bruce teach?

Fourth Bruce New Bruce will be teaching political science – Machiavelli,

Bentham, Locke, Hobbes, Sutcliffe, Bradman, Lindwall, Miller, Hassett, and Benaud.

Second Bruce These are cricketers, Bruce.

Fourth Bruce Oh, spit.

Third Bruce Howls of derisive laughter, Bruce.

Fourth Bruce In addition, as he's going to be teaching politics I've told him he's welcome to teach any of the great socialist thinkers, provided he makes it clear that they were *wrong*.

They all stand up.

All Australia, Australia, Australia, Australia, we love you. Amen.

They sit down.

Fourth Bruce Any questions?

Second Bruce New Bruce – are you a pooftah?

Fourth Bruce Are you a pooftah?

Michael No.

Fourth Bruce No right, well gentlemen, I'll just remind you of the faculty rules. Rule one – no pooftahs. Rule two – no member of the faculty is to maltreat the Abbos in any way whatsoever, if there's anyone watching. Rule three – no pooftahs. Rule four – I don't want to catch anyone not drinking in their room after lights out. Rule five – no pooftahs. Rule six – there is *no* rule six. Rule seven – no pooftahs. That concludes the reading of the rules, Bruce.

First Bruce This here's the wattle – the emblem of our land. You can stick it in a bottle or you can hold it in yer hand.

All Amen.

Fourth Bruce Gentlemen, at six o'clock I want every man-Bruce of you in the Sydney Harbour Bridge room to take a glass of sherry with the flying philosopher, Bruce, and I call upon you, padre, to close the meeting with a prayer.

First Bruce Oh Lord, we beseech thee etc. etc. etc., Amen.

All Amen.

First Bruce Right, let's get some Sheilas.

An Aborigine servant bursts in with an enormous tray full of enormous steaks.

Fourth Bruce OK.

Second Bruce Ah, elevenses.

Third Bruce This should tide us over 'til lunchtime.

Second Bruce Reckon so, Bruce.

First Bruce Sydney Nolan! What's that! *(points)*

Cut to dramatic close-up of Fourth Bruce's ear. Hold close-up. The superimposed arrow pointing to the ear.

Voice Over (JOHN) Number nine. The ear.

Cut to picture of big toe. Superimposed arrow.

Voice Over Number ten. The big toe.

Cut to picture of another man in Bermuda shorts. Superimposed arrow pointing at shorts.

Voice Over Number eleven. More naughty bits.

Cut to full length shot of lady in Bermuda shorts and Bermuda bra. Superimposed arrow on each side of her body. One points to the bra, one to the Bermuda shorts.

Voice Over Number twelve. The naughty bits of a lady.

Cut to picture of a horse wearing Bermuda shorts. Superimposed arrow.

Voice Over Number thirteen. The naughty bits of a horse.

Cut to picture of an ant. In the very corner of a blank area. It is very tiny. Superimposed enormous arrow.

Voice Over Number fourteen. The naughty bits of an ant.

Cut to picture of Reginald Maudling with Bermuda shorts, put on by Terry Gilliam, over his dark suit. Superimposed arrow pointing to shorts.

Voice Over Number fifteen. The naughty bits of Reginald Maudling.

Cut to close-up of false hand sticking out of a sleeve. Superimposed arrow.

Voice Over Number sixteen. The hand.

Pull back to reveal that the hand appears to belong to a standard interviewer in two shot. Chair set up with standard interviewee. The interviewer suddenly pulls the hand off, revealing that he has a hook. He throws the hand away and starts the interview.

Interviewer (MICHAEL) Good evening. I have with me in the studio tonight Mr Norman St John Polevaulter, who for the past few years has been contradicting people ... Mr Polevaulter, why do you contradict people?

Polevaulter (TERRY J) I don't.

Interviewer You told me that you did.

Polevaulter I most certainly did not.

Interviewer Oh, I see. I'll start again.

Polevaulter No you won't.

Interviewer Shh. Mr Polevaulter I understand you don't contradict people.

Polevaulter Yes I do.

Interviewer When *didn't* you start contradicting people?

Polevaulter Well I did, in 1952.

Interviewer 1952?

Polevaulter 1947.

Interviewer Twenty-three years ago.

Polevaulter No.

Cut to announcer at desk in a farmyard. He is fondly holding a small pig.

Announcer (JOHN) And so on and so on and so on. And now . . .

> *Cut to picture of the Pope. Slight pause, so we think it might be something to do with the Pope. An arrow suddenly comes in above him pointing down at his head.*

Voice Over Number seventeen. The top of the head.

> *Cut to picture of an indeterminate bit of flesh with a feather sticking out. Superimposed arrow pointing to feather.*

Voice Over Number eighteen . . . the feather, rare.

> *Cut to profile of Raymond Luxury Yacht from next sketch who has an enormous false polystyrene nose. Superimposed arrow pointing at nose.*

Voice Over Number nineteen. The nose.

> *A man sitting behind a desk in a Harley Street consulting room. Close-up of the name plate on desk in front of him. Although the camera does not reveal this for a moment, this name plate, about two inches high, continues all along the desk, off the side of it at the same height and halfway round the room. We start to track along this name plate on which is written: 'Professor Sir Adrian Furrows F.R.S., F.R.C.S., F.R.C.P., M.D.M.S. (Oxon), M.A., Ph.D., M.Sc. (Cantab), Ph.D. (Syd), F.R.G.S., F.R.C.O.G., F.F.A.R.C.S., M.S. (Birm), M.S. (Liv), M.S. (Guadalahara), M.S. (Karach), M.S. (Edin), B.A. (Chic), B.Litt. (Phil), D.Litt (Phil), D.Litt (Arthur and Lucy), D.Litt (Ottawa), D.Litt (All other places in Canada except Medicine Hat), B.Sc.9 Brussels, Liège, Antwerp, Asse, (and Cromer)'. There is a knock on the door.*

Specialist (JOHN) Come in.

> *The door opens and Raymond Luxury Yacht enters. He cannot walk straight to the desk as his passage is barred by the strip of wood carrying the degrees, but he discovers the special hinged part of it that opens like a door. Mr Luxury Yacht has his enormous polystyrene nose. It is a foot long.*

Specialist Ah! Mr Luxury Yacht. Do sit down, please.

Mr Luxury Yacht (GRAHAM) Ah, no, no. My name is *spelt* 'Luxury Yacht' but it's pronounced Throatwobbler Mangrove.

Specialist Well, do sit down then Mr Throatwobbler Mangrove.

Mr Luxury Yacht Thank you.

Specialist Now, what seems to be the trouble?

Mr Luxury Yacht Um, I'd like you to perform some plastic surgery on me.

Specialist I see. And which particular feature of your anatomy is causing you distress?

Mr Luxury Yacht Well, well for a long time now, in fact, even when I was a child . . . I . . . you know, whenever I left home to . . . catch a bus, or . . . to catch a train . . . and even my tennis has suffered actually . . .

Specialist Yes. To be absolutely blunt you're worried about your enormous hooter.

Mr Luxury Yacht No!

Specialist No?

Mr Luxury Yacht Yes.

Specialist Yes, and you want me to hack a bit off.

Mr Luxury Yacht Please.

Specialist Fine. It is a startler, isn't it. Er, do you mind if I . . . er.

Mr Luxury Yacht What?

Specialist Oh, no nothing, then, well, I'll just examine your nose. *(he does so; as he examines it the nose comes off in his hand)* Mr Luxury Yacht, this nose of yours is false. It's made of polystyrene and your own hooter's a beaut. No pruning necessary.

Mr Luxury Yacht I'd still like the operation.

Specialist Well, you've had the operation, you strange person.

Mr Luxury Yacht Please do an operation.

Specialist Well, all right, all right, but only . . . if you'll come on a camping holiday with me.

Mr Luxury Yacht He asked me! He asked me!

> *Cut to lyrical film of Luxury Yacht and specialist, frolicking in countryside in slow motion.*
> *Cut to interviewer (the one with the hook) at desk.*

Interviewer Next week we'll be showing you how to pick up an architect, how to pull a prime minister, and how to have fun with a wholesale poulterer. But now the men of the Derbyshire Light Infantry entertain us with a precision display of bad temper.

Voice Over Attention!

> *Eight soldiers in two ranks of four. They halt, and start to chant with precision.*

Soldiers My goodness me, I am in a bad temper today all right, two, three, damn, damn, two, three, I am vexed and ratty. *(shake fists)* Two, three, and hopping mad. *(stamp feet)*

> *Cut to interviewer.*

Interviewer And next the men of the Second Armoured Division regale us with their famous close order swanning about.

> *Cut to sergeant with eight soldiers.*

Sergeant Squad. Camp it . . . up!

Soldiers *(mincing in unison)* Oooh get her! Whoops! I've got your number ducky. You couldn't afford me, dear. Two three. I'd scratch your eyes out. Don't come the brigadier bit with us, dear, we all know where you've been, you military fairy. Whoops, don't look now girls the major's just minced in with that dolly colour sergeant, two, three, ooh-ho!

Cut to interviewer.

Interviewer And finally . . .

ANIMATION: *dancing generals, then the story of the killer cars.*
Cut to air terminal. Pan along official air-terminal-type signs saying BEA, TWA, Air India, BOAC, the Verrifast Plaine Company Ltd. Pan down to reveal a checking-in desk. A man with porter's cap comes in, carrying two bags. He is followed by Mr and Mrs Irrelevant. He puts their cases down, hangs around and gets a tip. He goes behind the counter, takes off his porter's hat, puts on an airline-pilot-type cap, and puts on a moustache. There is a vicar standing next to him with an eye patch.

Man (ERIC) Morning sir, can I help you?

Mr Irrelevant (GRAHAM) Er, yes, we've booked on your flight for America.

Man Oh, we don't fly to America . . . *(vicar nudges him)* Oh, the American flight . . . Er, on the plane . . . oh yes, oh we do that, all right. Safe as houses, no need to panic.

Mrs Irrelevant (CAROL) Is it really 37/6d?

Man Thirty bob. I'm robbing myself.

Mr Irrelevant Thirty bob!

Man Twenty-five. Two quid the pair of yer. Er, that's without insurance.

Mr Irrelevant Well, how much is it *with* insurance?

Man Hundred and two quid. That's including the flight.

Mr Irrelevant Do we really need insurance?

Man No. *(vicar nudges him)* Yes, essential.

Mr Irrelevant Well, we'll have it with insurance please.

Man Right – do you want it with the body and one relative flown back, or you can have both bodies flown back and no relatives, or four relatives, no bodies, and the ashes sent by parcel post.

Mr Irrelevant How long will it take?

Man Er, let me put it this way – no idea.

Vicar (MICHAEL) Six hours.

Mr Irrelevant Six?

Man Five, ten for the pair of you.

Mrs Irrelevant Oh, is it a jet?

Man Well, no . . . It's not so much of a jet, it's more your, er, Triumph Herald engine with wings.

Mr Irrelevant When are you taking off?

Man 3300 hours.

Mr Irrelevant What?

Man 2600 hours for the pair of you.

Mrs Irrelevant What?

Man Have the injections, you won't care.

Mr Irrelevant What injections?

Man Barley sugar injections. Calm you down. They're compulsory – Board of Trade. Promise. *(he holds up his crossed fingers)*

Mrs Irrelevant Oh, I don't like the sound of injections.

Man *(making a ringing sound)* Brrp, brrp. *(picks up phone)* Hello, yes right. *(puts phone down)* You've got to make your mind up straight away if you're coming or not.

Mr and Mrs Irrelevant Yes.

Man Right, you can't change your mind. I'll ring the departure lounge. *(picks up phone)* Hello? Two more on their way, Mrs Turpin.

Cut to Mrs Turpin sitting in a suburban lounge. A big sign saying 'Intercontinental Arrivals', in airport writing, hangs from the ceiling. Mr and Mrs Irrelevant arrive and sit down.

Mrs Turpin (TERRY J) Now, the duty-free trolley is over there . . . there's some lovely drop scones and there's duty-free broccoli and there's fresh eccles cakes. You're allowed two hundred each on the plane. *(she picks up teacup and speaks into it)* The Verrifast Plane Company announce the departure of flight one to over the hills and far away. Will passengers for flight one, please assemble at gate one. Passengers are advised that there is still plenty of time to buy eccles cakes.

Man and vicar enter carrying a large wing.

Man Nearly ready.

They take the wing through. Hammering is heard.

Mrs Turpin *(speaking into cup)* All passengers please get ready for their barley sugar injections.

Japanese pilot comes in.

Kamikaze Today we all take vow. Today we smash the enemy fleet . . . we smash, smash.

Man and vicar grab him and take him back.

Mrs Turpin That's Mr Kamikaze, the pilot, he's very nice really, but make sure he stays clear of battleships.

Cut to stock film of battleships, steaming on the seas. Stirring music plays over.

Voice Over (JOHN) There have been many stirring tales told of the sea and also some fairly uninteresting ones only marginally connected with it, like this one. Sorry, this isn't a very good announcement. Sorry.

Cut from sea to announcer by his desk at the seaside.

Announcer (JOHN) And here is the result of the 'Where to put Edward Heath's statue' Competition. The winner was a Mr Ivy North who wins ten guineas and a visit to the Sailors Quarters.

Cut to quick clip of the Battle of Pearl Harbor from show eleven, first series. Beginning with Eric's blowing the whistle and the two sides rushing at each other. Cut back to announcer.

Announcer That was last year's re-enactment of the Battle of Pearl Harbor performed by the Batley Townswomen's Guild. It was written, directed and produced by Mrs Rita Fairbanks.

Cut to Rita Fairbanks on the beach.

Rita (ERIC) Hello again.

Voice Over (MICHAEL) And what are your ladies going to do for us this year?

Rita Well, this year we decided to re-enact something with a more modern flavour. We had considered a version of Michael Stewart's speech on Nigeria and there were several votes on the Committee for a staging of Herr Willi Brandt's visit to East Germany, but we've settled instead for a dramatization of the first heart transplant. Incidentally my sister Madge will be playing the plucky little springbok pioneer Christian Barnard.

Voice Over Well off we go, then with the Batley Townswomen's Guild re-enactment of the first heart transplant.

Mrs Fairbanks blows her whistle. The two groups of ladies rush at each other. They end up in the sea, rolling about splashing, and thumping each other with handbags.

Announcer *(his desk now surrounded by sea)* The first heart transplant. But this is not the only open-air production here that has used the sea. Theatrical managers in this area have not been slow to appreciate the sea's tremendous dramatic value. And somewhere, out in this bay, is the first underwater production of 'Measure for Measure'.

Expanse of sea water, nothing else at all. Dubbed over this is muffled, watery Shakespearian blank verse. We zoom in. Two Shakespearian actors (Michael and Terry J) leap up. They take a deep breath and go under again. The dialogue carries on muffled. Pull out to see a rowing boat. Three Shakespearian characters are sitting there waiting for their cue. One of the two characters leaps up and shouts:

Character (TERRY J) Servant ho!

He then goes underwater again. The servant in the boat steps into the water and goes under. Cut to announcer, now up to his waist in sea.

Announcer The underwater version of 'Measure for Measure', and further out to sea 'Hello Dolly' is also doing good business.

We see a buoy, on the top of which is a stiff piece of card which reads 'Hello Dolly, Tonight 7.30'. There is a muffled watery snatch of Hello Dolly. Swing round to a patch of open sea.

Announcer . . . and over there on the oyster beds Formula 2 car racing. *(underwater noises of Formula 2 cars)*

ANIMATION: *a racing car moves over a naked lady, going past a sign saying 'Pit Stop'. Close up of armpits. Superimposed little white arrow.*

Voice Over Number twenty. The armpits.

Cut to picture of a person. Superimposed white arrow on the neck.

Voice Over Number twenty-one. The bottom two-thirds of the nape of the neck.

Cut to radio.

Voice Over Number twenty-two. The nipple.

Arrow indicates the tuning dial. Pull back. Two women are listening to the set. The announcer continues from the radio set.

Announcer's Voice ... and that concludes the week's episode of 'How to Recognize Different Parts of the Body', adapted for radio by Ann Haydon-Jones and her husband, Pip. And now, we present the first episode of a new radio drama series, 'The Death of Mary Queen of Scots'. Part one, the beginning.

Theme music: 'Coronation Scot' as used in 'Paul Temple' for years.

Man's Voice You are Mary Queen of Scots?
Woman's Voice I am.

There now follows a series of noises indicating that Mary is getting the shit knocked out of her. Thumps, bangs, slaps, pneumatic drilling, sawing, flogging, shooting, all interlarded with Mary's screams. The two women listen calmly. After a few seconds: fade as the signature tune 'Coronation Scot' is brought up loudly to denote ending of episode.

Radio Announcer Episode two of 'The Death of Mary Queen of Scots' can be heard on Radio 4 almost immediately.

One of the women goes to the set and switches it over. As she goes back to her seat from the radio we hear the theme music again, fading out as sounds of violence and screaming start again and continue unabated in vigour.

Man's Voice I think she's dead.
Woman's Voice No I'm not.

After a time, sounds of violence and screaming start again rapidly fading under the tune of 'Coronation Scot'.

Announcer's Voice That was episode two of 'The Death of Mary Queen of Scots', adapted for the radio by Bernard Hollowood and Brian London. And now, Radio 4 will explode. *(the radio explodes)*

First Pepperpot (GRAHAM) We'll have to watch the telly then.
Second Pepperpot (JOHN) Yes.

The pepperpots swivel round to look at the TV set in the corner of the room.

First Pepperpot Well, what's on the television then?
Second Pepperpot Looks like a penguin.

On the TV set there is indeed a penguin. It sits contentedly looking at them in a stuffed sort of way. There is nothing on the screen.

First Pepperpot No, no, no, I didn't mean what's on the television set, I meant what programme?

Second Pepperpot Oh.

The second pepperpot goes to the TV, switches it on and returns to her chair. The set takes a long time to warm up and produce a picture. During this pause the following conversation takes place.

Second Pepperpot It's funny that penguin being there innit? What's it doing there?

First Pepperpot Standing.

Second Pepperpot I can see that.

First Pepperpot If it lays an egg, it will fall down the back of the television set.

Second Pepperpot We'll have to watch that. Unless it's a male.

First Pepperpot Ooh, I never thought of that.

Second Pepperpot Yes, looks fairly butch.

First Pepperpot Perhaps it comes from next door.

Second Pepperpot Penguins don't come from next door, they come from the Antarctic.

First Pepperpot Burma.

Second Pepperpot Why did you say Burma?

First Pepperpot I panicked.

Second Pepperpot Oh. Perhaps it's from the zoo.

First Pepperpot Which zoo?

Second Pepperpot How should I know which zoo? I'm not Dr Bloody Bronowski.

First Pepperpot How does Dr Bronowski know which zoo it came from?

Second Pepperpot He knows everything.

First Pepperpot Oh, I wouldn't like that, it would take the mystery out of life. Anyway, if it came from the zoo it would have 'property of the zoo' stamped on it.

Second Pepperpot No, it wouldn't. They don't stamp animals 'property of the zoo'. You couldn't stamp a huge lion.

First Pepperpot They stamp them when they're small.

Second Pepperpot What happens when they moult?

First Pepperpot Lions don't moult.

Second Pepperpot No, but penguins do. There, I've run rings round you logically.

First Pepperpot Oh, intercourse the penguin.

On the TV screen there now appears an announcer.

TV Announcer (TERRY J) It's just gone 8 o'clock and time for the penguin on top of your television set to explode.

The penguin on top of the set now explodes.

First Pepperpot How did he know that was going to happen?
TV Announcer It was an inspired guess. And now . . .

Cut to picture of a shin. Superimposed arrow.

Voice Over (JOHN) Number twenty-three. The shin.

Cut to Reginald Maudling. Superimposed arrow.

Voice Over Number twenty-four. Reginald Maudling's shin.

Cut to Gilliam-type open-head picture, with arrow superimposed.

Voice Over Number twenty-five. The brain.

Cut to picture of Margaret Thatcher. Arrow points to her knee.

Voice Over Number twenty-six. Margaret Thatcher's brain.

Cut to a fairly wide still picture of cricket match in progress. Batsman, bowler, ring of fielders all have on polka-dotted Bermuda shorts. Little arrows point to each pair of Bermuda shorts.

Voice Over Number twenty-seven. More naughty bits.

Cut to picture of the cabinet at a table. Arrows point down below the table to their naughty bits.

Voice Over Number twenty-eight. The naughty bits of the cabinet.

Cut to studio shot of the next set. Interior of country house. Superimposed arrow.

Voice Over Number twenty-nine. The interior of a country house.

Cut to room, with doctor, mother, and son.

Doctor (JOHN) That's not a part of the body.
Mother (CAROL) No, it's a link though.
Son (GRAHAM) I didn't think it was very good.
Doctor No, it's the end of the series, they must be running out of ideas.

Inspector Muffin the Mule bursts through the door.

Muffin (MICHAEL) All right, don't anybody move, there's been a murder.
Mother A murder?
Muffin No . . . no . . . not a murder . . . no what's like a murder only begins with B?
Son Birmingham.
Muffin No . . . no . . . no . . . no . . . no . . .
Doctor Burnley?
Muffin Burnley – that's right! Burnley in Lancashire. There's been a Burnley.
Son Burglary.
Muffin Burglary. Yes, good man. Burglary – that's it, of course. There's been a burglary.
Doctor Where?
Muffin In the back, just below the rib.
Doctor No – that's murder.
Muffin Oh . . . er no . . . in the band . . . In the bat . . . Barclays bat.

Son Barclays Bank?

Muffin Yes. Nasty business – got away with £23,000.

Son Any clues?

Muffin Any what?

Son Any evidence as to who did it?

Muffin *(sarcastically)* Any clues, eh? Oh, we don't half talk posh, don't we? I suppose you say 'ehnvelope' and 'larngerie' and 'sarndwiches on the settee'! Well this is a murder investigation, young man, and murder is a very serious business.

Doctor I thought you said it was a burglary.

Muffin Burglary is almost as serious a business as murder. Some burglaries are *more* serious than murder. A burglary in which someone gets stabbled *is* murder! So don't come these petty distinctions with me. You're as bad as a judge. Right, now! The first thing to do in the event of a breach of the peace of any kind, is to ... go ... *(pause)* and ... oh, sorry, sorry, I was miles away.

Doctor Ring the police?

Muffin Ring the police. Yes, that's a good idea. Get them over here fast ... no, on second thoughts, get them over here slowly, so they don't drop anything.

Mother Shall I make us all a cup of tea?

Muffin Make what you like, Boskovitch – it won't help you in court.

Mother I *beg* your pardon?

Muffin I'm sorry, sorry. That's the trouble with being on two cases at once. I keep thinking I've got Boskovitch cornered and in fact I'm investigating a Burnley.

Son Burglary.

Muffin Burglary! Yes – good man.

> *Sound of police siren and sound of cars drawing up outside.*

Doctor Who's Boskovitch?

Muffin Hah! Boskovitch is a Russian scientist who is passing information to the Russians.

Son Classified information?

Muffin Oh, there he goes again! 'Classified information'! Oh, sitting on the 'settee' with our 'scones' and our 'classified information'!

> *The door opens and a plainclothes detective plus ten PCs (the Fred Tomlinson Singers) enter.*

Muffin Ah! Hello, Duckie.

Duckie (TERRY J) Hello, sir. How are you?

Muffin I'm fine thanks. How are you?

Duckie Well, sir, I'm a little bit moody today, sir.

Muffin Why's that, Duckie?

Duckie Because ...

> *Rhythm combo starts up out of vision and Detective Duckie sings.*

SUPERIMPOSED CAPTION: 'SGT DUCKIE'S SONG'

Duckie I'm a little bit sad and lonely
Now my baby's gone away . . .
I'm feeling kinda blue
Don't know just what to do
I feel a little sad today.

Chorus of PCs He's a little bit sad and lonely
Now his baby's gone away
He's feeling kinda blue
He don't know just what to do
He's not feeling so good today.

Duckie *(solo)* When I smile
The sun comes flooding in
But when I'm sad
It goes behind the clouds again.

Chorus He's a little bit sad and lonely
Now his baby's gone away
He's feeling kinda *(they stop abruptly and say:)*
etcetera, etcetera. *(applause)*

Muffin A lovely song, Duckie.

Eurovision girl comes in.

Girl (ERIC) And that's the final entry. La dernière entrée. Das final entry. And now, guten abend. Das scores. The scores. Les scores. Dei scores. Oh! Scores. Ha! Scores! *(cut to scoreboard in Chinese)* Yes, Monaco is the winner – hah! Monaco is the linner – oh yes, man, Monaco's won de big prize, bwana . . . and now, here is Chief Inspector Jean-Paul Zatapathique with the winning song once again.

The accompaniment starts as the singers hum the intro. Cut to flashy Eurovision set. Zatapathique steps onto podium.

Voice Over (MICHAEL) *(hushed tone)* And so, Inspector Zatapathique, the forensic expert from the Monaco Murder Squad sings his song 'Bing Tiddle Tiddle Bong'.

Zatapathique (GRAHAM) *(spoken)* Quoi? Quoi? Tout le monde, quoi? . . . mais, le monde . . . d'habitude . . . mais . . . je pense . . .

Zatapathique and Singers Bing tiddle tiddle bang
Bing tiddle tiddle bing
Bing tiddle tiddle tiddle tiddle
Bing tiddle tiddle tiddle BONG!

Credits over.
Zatapathique finishes and bends over exhausted. An arrow indicates his rear.

Voice Over Number thirty-one. The end.

CAPTION: 'THE END'

Twenty-three

Exterior large rubbish dump. Hand-held camera tracks to girl in simple white dress with red hair fourteen foot long, who is sitting on a chair holding a cabbage in her hands. After a time Stig, in white jeans, shirt and scarf enters shot and stands around uneasily.

Stig (TERRY J) Bonjour.
> SUBTITLE: 'GOOD MORNING'

Girl (CAROL) Bonjour.
> SUBTITLE: 'GOOD MORNING'
> *Pause. Stig looks uneasy, glancing at camera.*

Stig Il fait beau ce matin.
> SUBTITLE: 'IT'S A NICE DAY'

Girl Oui, oui.
> SUBTITLE: 'YES, YES'

Stig D'accord . . .
> SUBTITLE: 'HEAR HEAR'

Stig Venez-vous ici souvent?
> SUBTITLE: 'DO YOU COME HERE OFTEN?'

Girl Oui.
> SUBTITLE: 'YES'

Stig Ah. Bon. Bon.
> SUBTITLE: 'GOOD, GOOD'
> *Pause.*

Stig Je vois que vous avez un chou.
> SUBTITLE: 'I SEE THAT YOU HAVE A CABBAGE'

Girl Oui.
> SUBTITLE: 'YES'
> *Stig starts to laugh falsely and then the girl joins in. It is a miserable attempt to capture joy and togetherness. The girl stops laughing before Stig does.*

Stig Certainement il fait beau ce matin.
> SUBTITLE: 'IT CERTAINLY IS A LOVELY DAY ALL RIGHT'
> *Stig wanders out of shot but is very obviously pushed back into the picture.*

Stig Je suis revolutionnaire.
> SUBTITLE: 'I AM A REVOLUTIONARY'

Girl Oh.

Stig Qu'est-ce que vous avez dit?

SUBTITLE: 'WHAT DID YOU SAY?'

Girl J'ai dit 'oh'.

SUBTITLE: 'I SAID "OH" '

Stig Ah. Très interessant.

SUBTITLE: 'AH. VERY INTERESTING'

Cut to pimply youth in studio.

Phil (ERIC) Brian Distel and Brianette Zatapathique there in an
improvised scene from Jean Kenneth Longueur's new movie 'Le
Fromage Grand'. Brian and Brianette symbolize the breakdown in
communication in our modern society in this exciting new film and
Longueur is saying to us, his audience, 'go on, protest, do
something about it, assault the manager, demand your money
back'. Later on in the film, in a brilliantly conceived montage,
Longueur mercilessly exposes the violence underlying our society
when Brian and Brianette again meet on yet another rubbish
dump.

*Different part of same dump, but not very different. Girl is still on chair
but this time with a cos lettuce. Then Stig enters shot.*

Stig Bonjour encore.

SUBTITLE: 'HELLO AGAIN'

Girl Bonjour.

SUBTITLE: 'GOOD MORNING'

Stig Je vois que aujourd'jui vous avez une co-laitue.

SUBTITLE: 'I SEE YOU'VE GOT A WEBB'S WONDER TODAY'

Girl Oui.
Stig Bon.

SUBTITLE: 'GOOD'

Intercut quick shot from war film: machine-gunner in plane.

Stig Il fait beau encore.

SUBTITLE: 'IT'S A LOVELY DAY AGAIN'

Shot of Paris riots and clubbing.

Girl Oui.

SUBTITLE: 'YES'

Stig Bon.

SUBTITLE: 'GOOD'

Shot of Michael being struck on head with a club by John.

Stig Vous pouvez dire ça encore.

SUBTITLE: 'IT CERTAINLY IS. A LOVELY DAY ALL RIGHT'

*Shot of collapsing building, then a man at a piano (Graham); the lid
slams on his hands.*

Stig Certainement il fait beau ce matin.

> SUBTITLE: 'IT CERTAINLY IS A LOVELY DAY ALL RIGHT'
> *Shot of aeroplanes bombing. Shot of chef receiving arrow in chest.
> Shot of girl kicking tall man on shin. Shot of rockets being fired from
> plane.*

Girl Oui.

> SUBTITLE: 'YES'
> *Shot of hydrogen bomb.*

Stig Il fait beau hier. Ha ha ha.

> SUBTITLE: 'IT WAS LOVELY YESTERDAY. HA HA HA'
> *Shot of ack ack gun. Shot of man receiving a punch in the head from a
> boxing glove. Shot of nun kicking a policeman in the crutch.*

Girl Ha ha.

> SUBTITLE: 'HA HA. HA HA. HA HA.'
> *Shot of Spitfire. Shot of Korean soldiers; then man being beheaded.*

Stig Quel surprise de vous voir encore.

> SUBTITLE: 'WHAT A SURPRISE TO SEE YOU AGAIN'
> *Shot of Paris riots. Shot of man having his foot stamped on. Shot of
> blazing building. Shot of man being poked in the eye with an umbrella.
> Shot of battleship firing broadside. Shot of man in underpants having a
> bucket of water thrown over him. Shot of soccer violence. Shot of man
> being knifed by a Greek Orthodox priest.*

Girl Je t'aime.

> SUBTITLE: 'I LOVE YOU'

Stig Je t'aime.

> SUBTITLE: 'I LOVE YOU'
> *They smile at each other happily for a moment. Then they hear
> something ticking. They listen carefully for a moment and then both start
> to look fearfully at the cos lettuce. After a moment of terror the cos lettuce
> explodes, in slow motion, blowing them apart. As tatters and pieces of cos
> lettuce float through the air in slow motion, the camera pans down to
> some autumn leaves. Freeze frame.*
> SUPERIMPOSED CAPTION: 'FIN'
> *Cut back to Phil.*

Phil Pretty strong meat there from Longueur who is saying, of course,
that ultimately materialism, in this case the Webb's Wonder
lettuce, must destroy us all. That was for O. Simon, K. Simon,
P. Simon and R. Sparrow of Leicester. Later on, we're going to
take a look at John Wayne's latest movie, 'Buckets of Blood
Pouring Out of People's Heads' but now we look ahead. On
Tuesday Chris Conger took a BBC film unit to the location where

20th Century Vole are shooting their latest epic 'Scott of the Antarctic'.

Chris Conger standing with back to pier and a few holidaymakers behind him.

Conger (GRAHAM) Sea, sand and sunshine make Paignton the queen of the English Riviera. But for the next six months this sleepy Devonshire resort will be transformed into the blizzard-swept wastes of the South Pole. For today shooting starts on the epic 'Scott of the Antarctic', produced by Gerry Schlick. *(walks over to Schlick)*

Schlick (ERIC) *(American)* Hello.

Conger Gerry, you chose Paignton as the location for Scott.

Schlick Right, right.

Conger Isn't it a bit of a drawback that there's no snow here?

Schlick Well, we have 28,000 cubic feet of Wintrex, which is a new white foam rubber which actually on screen looks more like snow than snow ...

Cut to shot of people nailing and sticking white foam rubber over things. It looks terrible. Others are painting the sand with white paint.

Schlick ... and 1,600 cubic US furlongs of white paint, with a special snow finish.

Conger And I believe Kirk Vilb is playing the title role.

Schlick That is correct. We were very thrilled and honoured when Kirk agreed to play the part of Lieutenant Scott *(cut to Kirk Vilb who is wearing furs open at the chest; he is having a chest wig stuck on and icing sugar squeezed on to his nose and eyebrows)* because a star of his magnitude can pick and choose, but he read the title and just flipped. *(cut back to Gerry Schlick and Chris Conger)* And directing we have a very fine young British director, James McRettin, who's been collaborating on the screenplay, of course Jimmy ...

McRettin rushes into foreground. He is in no way like J. McGrath.

McRettin (JOHN) Oh, there you are. Hello. Hello. No problem. Have a drink. Have a drink. Great. Hello. Marvellous. Marvellous. Hello. Rewrite. Oh this is really great. I mean, it's really saying something, don't you think?

Conger Have you started shooting yet?

McRettin Yes, yes. Great. Perfect. No, no, we haven't started yet. No. But great – great.

Conger What is the first scene that you shoot this morning?

McRettin Great. Terrific. Oh it's great. No problem. We'll sort it out on the floor. Sort it out on the floor. No problem. This film is basically pro-humanity and anti-bad things and it rips aside the hypocritical façade of our society's gin and tonic and leaves a lot of sacred cows rolling around in agony, have a drink, have a drink.

Conger But which *scene* are we shooting first, Jimmy?

McRettin Yes, great. Oh, marvellous. *(calls)* Which scene are we shooting first? What? *(to Conger)* it's scene one. Scene one. It's in the middle of the movie. Well, it is now. I rewrote it. *(calls)* I thought we cut that? Didn't we cut that?

Schlick No, we didn't.

McRettin We didn't. Oh great. That's even better. I'll put it back in. Rewrite. *(calling)* Scene one's back in everyone. Scene one's back in. Great. Great. *(to Conger)* This is the scene – outside the tent – it's all bloody marvellous. It makes you want to throw up.

Cut to Schlick and Conger on the beach.

Schlick Now in this scene Lieutenant Scott returns to camp in the early morning after walking the huskies to have brunch with the rest of his team. *(cut to shot of tent with Bowers, who is black, and Oates, sitting outside)* Oates, played by your very own lovely Terence Lemming, who is an English cockney officer seconded to the US Navy, and Bowers played by Seymour Fortescue, the Olympic pole vaulter.

Film: Scott comes up to them. He has two large boxes strapped to his feet to make him look tall.

Oates (TERRY J) Hi, Lieutenant.

Scott (MICHAEL) Hi, Oatesy. Sure is a beautiful day already.

McRettin *(rushing in)* Great, great.

Scott What? What are you saying?

McRettin I was just saying great, great. Cue Evans.

Sexy girl with long blond hair comes into shot with short pink fur coat. She walks up to Scott who towers four feet above her as she is walking in a trench.

Schlick And this is Vanilla Hoare as Miss Evans.

Conger Miss Evans?

Schlick Right.

Miss Evans is now beneath Scott at knee height.

Scott Good morning, Miss Evans.

Evans (CAROL) Oh, I've forgotten my line.

McRettin What's her line? What's her line?

Girl runs in with script.

Girl It's 'Good morning, Captain Scott'.

Evans Oh, yeah. 'Good morning, Captain Sc' . . . oh, I'm just not happy with that line. Could I just say 'Hi Scottie'?

McRettin Great. Great. Rewrite. Cue.

Girl Hi Scarrie! Oh, sorry. Hi Stocky! Oh – I'm sorry again. Oh, Jim. I'm just unhappy with this line. Hey, can I do it all sort of kooky, like this? *(goes berserk waving hands)* Hi Scottie!

McRettin Great! We'll shoot it.

Scott Are you sure that's right?

McRettin Oh, it's great.

> *Gerry Schlick walks into the shot.*

Schlick Jim.

McRettin Jim! Jim! Oh, me!

Schlick Jim, I feel we may be running into some problems here in the area of height.

McRettin Great! Where are they?

Schlick Where are who?

McRettin I don't know. I was getting confused.

Schlick Jim, I feel here, that Scott may be too tall in the area of height with reference to Vanilla who is too near the ground in the area of being too short at this time.

McRettin Great . . . Oh, I know. I'm going to dig a pit for Scott and put a box in Vanilla's trench.

Scott Say, why don't I take the boxes off and Vanilla get up out of the trench.

McRettin It wouldn't work . . . It's even better! Great. Rewrite!

Evans What was that?

McRettin Oh, it's easy. I've worked it out. Scott takes his boxes off and you don't stand in the trench.

Evans I say my lines *out* of the trench?

McRettin Even better. Great.

Evans But I've never acted out of a trench. I might fall over. It's dangerous.

McRettin Oh well, could you just try it?

Evans Look, you crumb bum, I'm a star. Star, star, star. I don't get a million dollars to act *out* of a trench. I played Miss St John the Baptist in a trench, *(she walks along in the trench and we see that she has two boxes strapped to her feet)* and I played Miss Napoleon Bonaparte in a trench, and I played Miss Alexander Fleming in a furrow so if you want this scene played out of a trench, well you just get yourself a goddamn stuntman. *(walks off)* I played Miss Galileo in a groove and I played Mrs Jesus Christ in a geological syncline, so don't . . .

McRettin Great. Great everyone. Lunch now. Lunch. It's all in the can. Good morning's work.

Schlick But you haven't done a shot.

McRettin Just keeping morale up. *(tries to take a drink from his viewfinder)*

> *The same: afternoon.*

Schlick Now this afternoon we're going to shoot the scene where Scott gets off the boat on to the ice floe and he sees the lion and he fights it and kills it and the blood goes pssssssssshhh in slow motion.

Conger But there aren't any lions in the Antarctic.

Schlick What?

Conger There aren't any lions in the Antarctic.

Schlick You're right. There are no lions in the Antarctic. That's ridiculous; whoever heard of a lion in the Antarctic. Right. Lose the lion.

McRettin Got to keep the lion. It's great!

Schlick Lose the lion.

McRettin Great. We're losing the lion. Rewrite. Lose the lion everyone. That's fantastic.

Scott What's this about our losing the lion?

Schlick Well, Kirk, we thought perhaps we might lose the fight with the lion a little bit, Kirk, angel.

Scott (loudly) Why?

Schlick Well, Kirkie, doll, there are no lions in the Antarctic, baby.

Scott (shouts) I get to fight the lion.

Schlick It'd be silly.

Scott Listen, I gotta fight the lion. That's what that guy Scott's all about. I know. I've studied him already.

Schlick But why couldn't you fight a penguin?

McRettin Great! (falls over)

Scott Fight a rotten penguin?

Schlick It needn't be a little penguin. It can be the biggest penguin you've ever seen. An electric penguin, twenty feet high, with long green tentacles that sting people, and you can stab it in the wings and the blood can go spurting pssssshhhh in slow motion.

Scott The lion is in the contract.

Schlick He fights the lion.

McRettin Even better. Great. Have a drink. Lose the penguin. Stand by to shoot. (falls over)

Schlick Where do they have lions?

Conger Africa.

Schlick That's it. Scott's in Africa. As many lions as we need.

McRettin Great!

Schlick He's looking for a pole no one else knows about. That ties in with the sand. Right. Paint the sand yellow again. Okay, let's get this show on the road. 'Scott of the Sahara.'

    Cut instantly to sky.

    CAPTION: 'SCOTT OF THE SAHARA'

Voice Over (MICHAEL) Booming out of the pages of history comes a story of three men and one woman whose courage shocked a generation.

Blinding sun. Pan down to Paignton beach. Scott, Evans, Oates and Bowers wearing furs crossing sand on snow shoes. With sledge pulled by motley selection of mongrel dogs, badly disguised as huskies.

Voice Over From the same team that brought you . . . *(the names come out superimposed)* 'Lawrence of Glamorgan' . . . 'Bridge Over the River Trent' . . . 'The Mad Woman of Biggleswade' . . . and 'Krakatoa, East of Leamington' . . . comes the story of three people and a woman united by fate who set out in search of the fabled Pole of the Sahara and found . . . themselves. See . . . Lieutenant Scott's death struggle with a crazed desert lion.

The four are walking along. Suddenly they stop, stare, and react in horror. Scott steps to the front to defend the others. Intercut, non-matching stock shot of lion running out of jungle and leaping at camera. Scott waits poised and is then struck by completely rigid stuffed lion. Montage of shots of him wrestling, firstly with the stuffed lion, then with an actor in a tatty lion suit. The lion picks up a chair, fends Scott off, smashes it over his head. Finally Scott kicks the lion on the shin. The lion leaps around on one leg and picks up a knife. Scott points, the lion looks, Scott kicks the knife out of the lion's paw. He advances on the lion, and socks him on the jaw. The lion collapses in slow motion. After a pause, phoney blood spurts out.

Voice Over See Ensign Oates' frank adult death struggle with the spine-chilling giant electric penguin . . .

Oates looks up in horror, a shadow crosses him. Reverse shot of model penguin (quite small, about a foot) which lights up and looks electric. The penguin is close to the camera in the foreground and appears huge. Oates looks around desperately then starts to undress. Shot of penguin throwing tentacle. Half-nude Oates struggles with it. Intercut a lot of phoney reverses. Oates by now clad only in posing briefs sees a stone. He picks up the stone, then camera zooms into above-navel shot; he removes his briefs, puts the stone in the briefs, twirls it like a sling, and releases stone. The penguin is hit on beak, and falls over backwards.

Voice Over . . . See Miss Evans pursued by the man-eating roll-top writing desk.

Miss Evans is running along screaming. Shot of desk chasing her (phoney desk with man inside). The roll top goes up and down, emitting roars, and displaying fearsome white teeth inside. As Evans runs, her clothing gets torn on each of the three cactuses. These are well spaced apart so that there is a lot of trouble to get near them. When she is practically nude, she runs out of shot revealing the announcer.

Announcer (JOHN) And now for something completely different.
It's Man (MICHAEL) It's . . .

Animated titles.

ANIMATION: *dancing teeth. Then animation of a letter being resealed and posted – all backwards – ending in a real post office.*

A post office worker removes the stamp from the letter and hands it to man.

Post Office Worker Five pence please.

The man walks out backwards, passing Mr Praline as he enters. He looks at the man, puzzled, and then goes up to first of two grilles which has a sign saying 'stamps and licences'.

Praline (JOHN) Excuse me, I would like to buy a fish licence, please. *(the man behind counter points to next grille; to camera)* The man's sign must be wrong. I have in the past noticed a marked discrepancy between these post office signs and the activities carried on beneath. But soft, let us see how Dame Fortune smiles upon my next postal adventure! *(he goes to next grille)* Hello, I would like to buy a fish licence, please.

Man (MICHAEL) A what?

Praline A licence for my pet fish, Eric.

Man How did you know my name was Eric?

Praline No, no, no. My *fish's* name is Eric. Eric the fish. 'E's an 'alibut.

Man A what?

Praline He is an halibut.

Man You've got a pet halibut?

Praline Yes, I chose him out of thousands. I didn't like the others. They were all too flat.

Man You're a loony.

Praline I am not a loony! Why should I be tarred with the epithet 'loony' merely because I have a pet halibut? I've heard tell that Sir Gerald Nabarro has a pet prawn called Simon, and you wouldn't call Sir Gerald a loony would you? Furthermore, Dawn Palethorpe, the lady show jumper had a clam called Sir Stafford after the late Chancellor. Alan Bullock has two pikes, both called Norman, and the late, great Marcel Proust had an 'addock. If you're calling the author of 'A La Recherche du Temps Perdu' a loony I shall have to ask you to step outside.

Man All right, all right, all right. You want a licence?

Praline Yes.

Man For a fish?

Praline Yes.

Man You *are* a loony.

Praline Look! It's a bleedin' pet, isn't it. I've got a licence for my pet dog, Eric, and I've got a licence for my pet cat, Eric.

Man You don't need a licence for a cat.

Praline You bleeding well do, and I've got one. Ho, ho, you're not catching me out there.

Man There is no such thing as a bloody cat licence.

Praline Yes there is.

Man No there isn't.

Praline Is!

Man Isn't!

Praline Is.

Man Isn't.

Praline Is.

Man Isn't.

Praline Is.

Man Isn't.

Praline Is.

Man Isn't.

Praline Is.

Man Isn't.

Praline What's that then?

Man That is a dog licence with the word 'dog' crossed out and the word 'cat' written in in crayon.

Praline The man didn't have the proper form.

Man What man?

Praline The man from the cat detector van.

Man Loony detector van you mean.

Praline It's people like you what causes unrest.

Man All right, what cat detector van?

Praline The cat detector van from the Ministry of Housinge.

Man Housinge???

Praline Yes, it was spelt that way on the van. I'm very observant. I've never seen so many aerials in my life. The man told me their equipment could pin-point a purr at four hundred yards . . . and Eric being such a happy cat was a piece of cake.

Man How much did this cost?

Praline Sixty quid, and eight guineas for the fruit bat.

Man What fruit bat?

Praline Eric the fruit bat.

Man Are all your pets called Eric?

Praline There's nothing so odd about that. Kemal Ataturk had an entire menagerie, all called Abdul.

Man No he didn't.

Praline *(takes book from pocket)* He did, he did, he did, he did and did. There you are. 'Kemal Ataturk, the Man' by E. W. Swanton with a foreword by Paul Anka, page 91, please.

Man *(referring to page 91)* I owe you an apology, sir.

Praline Spoken like a gentleman. Now are you going to give me this fish licence?

Man I promise you there is no such thing. You don't need one.

Praline Then I would like a statement to that effect signed by the Lord Mayor.

Fanfare of trumpets. Mayor gorgeously dressed with dignitaries enters flanked by trumpeters.

Man You're in luck.

In long shot now. The Mayor, who is nine foot high, and dignitaries approach a startled Praline. Organ music below a reverent voice over:

Voice Over (JOHN) And now, there is the Mayor. Surely the third tallest mayor in Derby's history. And there are the Aldermen magnificently resplendent in their Aldermanic hose and just look at the power in those thighs. The New Zealanders are going to find it pretty tough going in the set pieces in the second half . . . So Dawn Palethorpe with one clear round on Sir Gerald . . . and now the Mayor has reached the Great Customer Mr Eric Praline. *(the mayor takes a piece of paper from the post office man)* And now the Mayoral human being takes the Mayoral Pen in the Mayoral hand and watched by the Lady Mayoress, who of course scored that magnificent try in the first half, signs the fishy exemption *(the mayor signs it and hands it to Praline)* and the Great Customer, Mr Eric Praline, who is understandably awed by the magnificence and even the absurdity of this great occasion here at Cardiff Arms Park, *(Praline looks very confused)* has finally gone spare and there is the going sparal look on the front of his head. And now the Aldermen are finishing their oranges and leaving the post office for the start of the second half.

They all exit out of door, eating oranges, and Praline looks after them. Cut to a rugby field. Crowd roaring as the aldermen, mayor, mayoress, town clerk, Dawn Palethorpe (on a horse) and the borough surveyor run onto the pitch and take up their positions.

Commentator (JOHN) And here come the Derby Council XV following the All Blacks out on to the pitch. There, in the centre of the picture you can see Dawn Palethorpe on Sir Gerald – one of the fastest wingers we must have seen in England this season. On the left hand side of the picture the Lord Mayor has been running such wonderful possession for Derby Council in the lines out and it's the All Blacks to kick off. Wilson to kick off. Oh, I can see there the Chairman of the By-ways and Highways Committee who's obviously recovered from that very nasty blow he got in that loose ball in the first half. *(opposite them the All Blacks kick off)* And Wilson kicks off and it's the Town Clerk's taken the ball beautifully there, the All Blacks are up on it very fast and the whistle has gone. I'm not quite sure what happened there, I couldn't see, but there's a scrum-down. I think it's an All Blacks' ball. They were upon them very fast. Obviously they're going to try very hard in this half to wipe out this five-point deficit. Derby Council eight points to three up and Derby Council have got the ball against the head. There is the Borough Surveyor, the scrum-half is out of the . . . er, the Chairman of the Highway and By-way Committee who's kicked for touch. The line out – and it's into the line out and the Mayor has got the ball again. To the Borough Surveyor who's left out the Medical Officer of Health. Straight along the line to the Lady Mayoress and the Lady Mayoress has got to go through. Number two has missed her – he's taken to the full back – only the full back to beat and she has scored! The Lady Mayoress has scored, it's eleven points to three.

CAPTION: 'NEW ZEALAND 3 DERBY COUNCIL 11'

Cut to linkman and Cliff Morgan.

Linkman (MICHAEL) Cliff, this must have been a very disappointing result for the All Blacks.

Cliff (GRAHAM) *(Welsh)* Well, they've had very bad luck on the tour so far. They missed four very easy kicks against the Exeter Amateur Operatic Society, which must have cost them the match and then of course there was that crippling defeat at the hands of the Derry and Toms Soft Toy Department, so I don't think they can be really fancying their chances against the London Pooves on Saturday.

Linkman And what about China?

Cliff Well, whether Mao Tse Tung is alive or not, Lin Piao has a stranglehold on central committee which Lin Shao Chi can't break, so it remains to be seen whether Chou En Lai can really get his finger out and get going in the second half.

Linkman Well, thank you Cliff. Tonight's other outstanding match was the semi-final between the Bournemouth Gynaecologists and the Watford Long John Silver Impersonators. We bring you edited highlights of the match.

Rapid montage of goals scored by competent gynaecologists wearing surgical gowns and caps, against totally incompetent and immobile LJSI team who simply stand round going 'aaah! Jim lad' as the goals rain in. The ball is kicked off-screen. Sudden cut to studio. A presenter is standing in front of curtain; he catches the ball thrown from off. He smiles.

Presenter (MICHAEL) Well, that's about it for tonight ladies and gentlemen, but remember if you've enjoyed watching the show just half as much as we've enjoyed doing it, then we've enjoyed it twice as much as you. Ha, ha, ha.

The sixteen-ton weight falls on him. Cut to montage of scenes of destruction, buildings falling down, bombs etc. Roll credits over.

Appendix

Transmission details

Episode number as in this volume	Series/ number	Transmission date	Number as recorded	Recording date
First series				
One	1/1	5-10-69	2	7-9-69
Two	1/2	12-10-69	1	30-8-69
Three	1/3	19-10-69	3	14-8-69
Four	1/4	26-10-69	4	21-9-69
Five	1/5	16-11-69	5	3-10-69
Six	1/6	23-11-69	7	5-11-69
Seven	1/7	30-11-69	6	10-10-69
Eight	1/8	7-12-69	8	25-11-69
Nine	1/9	14-12-69	10	7-12-69
Ten	1/10	21-12-69	9	30-11-69
Eleven	1/11	28-12-69	11	14-12-69
Twelve	1/12	4-1-70	12	21-12-69
Thirteen	1/13	11-1-70	13	4-1-70
Second series				
Fourteen	2/1	15-9-70	4	9-7-70
Fifteen	2/2	22-9-70	3	2-7-70
Sixteen	2/3	29-9-70	5	16-7-70
Seventeen	2/4	20-10-70	9	18-9-70
Eighteen	2/5	27-10-70	7	10-9-70
Nineteen	2/6	3-11-70	8	10-9-70
Twenty	2/7	10-11-70	11	2-10-70
Twenty-one	2/8	17-11-70	12	9-10-70
Twenty-two	2/9	24-11-70	10	25-9-70
Twenty-three	2/10	1-12-70	2	2-7-70

Index